Risk & Rigor

A Lawyer's Guide to Decision Trees for Assessing Cases and Advising Clients

About the Author

Marjorie Corman Aaron is a Professor of Practice and Director of the Center for Practice at the University of Cincinnati College of Law where she teaches negotiation, client counseling, mediation, trial practice, and decision analysis. Professor Aaron has designed and taught workshops on these topics for law firms, law departments, federal court judges, magistrates, and mediator panelists, and other organizations in the U.S. and internationally. She is an active mediator, arbitrator, and dispute resolution consultant, and has used decision tree analysis in her practice for more than thirty years.

Professor Aaron was formerly Executive Director of the Program on Negotiation at Harvard Law School, and a Vice President and mediator at Endispute, Inc. (now JAMS). A graduate of Princeton University and Harvard Law School, she first practiced as a litigator in Massachusetts at Goodwin Proctor and as an assistant district attorney.

Professor Aaron is also the author of *Client Science: Advice for Lawyers on Counseling Clients Through Bad News and Other Legal Realities* (Oxford University Press, 2012) and has published many articles, chapters, and simulations, and videos in her field.

Published by DRI Press, an imprint of the
Dispute Resolution Institute at Mitchell Hamline School of Law

Dispute Resolution Institute
Mitchell Hamline School of Law
875 Summit Ave, St Paul, MN 55015
Tel. (651) 695-7676

Printed in the United States of America.
Library of Congress Control Number: 2019932219
ISBN: 978-0-9827946-7-8

Mitchell Hamline School of Law in Saint Paul, Minnesota has been education lawyers for more than 100 years yet remains committed to innovation to respond to the changing legal market. Featuring more enrollment options than any law school in the country, Mitchell Hamline is committed to accessibility and offers a curriculum rich in advocacy and problem solving. The law school's Dispute Resolution Institute, consistently ranked in the top five dispute resolution programs by *U.S. News & World Report*, offers more than 30 alternative dispue resolution courses each year in a wide variety of domestic and international programs, including certificate programs in arbitration law and practice, problem solving, and conflict resolution, and is the home of DRI Press. For more information on other DRI Press publications, visit http://open.mitchellhamline.edu/dri_press.

Risk & Rigor

A Lawyer's Guide to Decision Trees for Assessing Cases and Advising Clients

Marjorie Corman Aaron

DRI Press
Saint Paul, Minnesota

To my husband David, and our sons
Joshua and Elisha, for the honor and joy of
making decisions and taking chances with you.

Marjorie Corman Aaron

March 2019

Table of Contents

Background and Acknowledgements

My own introduction to decision tree analysis began in 1988, shortly after joining Endispute, Inc., now JAMS ADR, Inc. Endispute had contracted with a Boston law firm to provide a workshop in decision analysis for their litigation department. Endispute's Eric Green, Jonathan Marks, and I were scheduled to teach it and so I had to learn it. We benefitted from terrific articles by Marc Victor, who deserves full credit for pioneering its use in ligation practice over the past 30 years. At Endispute, we often used decision trees as analytical and communication tools when mediating legal disputes.

At about this time, Boston attorney Morris Raker invited us to a demonstration of the beta version of the TreeAge software for decision tree analysis—software he developed with David Hoffer, the "teenage whiz kid down the block" in Brookline, MA. I remain grateful for having had the opportunity, not long after that, to sit with Morris Raker to build a particularly complicated Endispute case in TreeAge, producing a tree far more refined than we had scribbled on easel paper during the mediation. I have been using the TreeAge software ever since.[1]

Of course, as my grandfather used to say, "time marches on." The whiz kid David Hoffer interned at Endispute, then earned a JD/MBA at Harvard. In 1996, it was my pleasure to co-author a book chapter with him on our favorite topic—decision analysis for legal disputes. Morris Raker retired from his law firm in Boston and established TreeAge, Inc. in Williamstown, MA. While TreeAge was originally created for lawyers and litigation practice, its business has greatly expanded to the areas of health care and policy applications. A number of years ago, I was privileged to be hosted by Morris Raker on a visit to TreeAge in Williamstown to meet the TreeAge team. While the company has since been sold, Joel Sartori remains at TreeAge as the extraordinarily patient technical support expert I have relied upon over the years.

I owe a debt of gratitude to many other professional colleagues and friends for tolerating and encouraging my persistent belief in the value of decision analysis for legal practice, and for inviting me to teach it in various forms. Professor Michael Wheeler invited me to an early Program on Negotiation (PON) conference on analytical methods for negotiation and prompted me to write on the use of decision analysis in mediation. Professors Michael Wheeler, Jim Sebenius, and Howard Raiffa[2] also encouraged my 1993-94 work with John Hammond on decision analysis for the legal case used in the Harvard Business School Negotiation course. They also organized a spectacular short course module on decision analysis by George Wu, then at HBS and now at the University of Chicago. The late Howard Raiffa's PON lectures on Negotiation Analysis were highly mathematical, but they strongly communicated the idea that analytical methods can support excellence in practical negotiation and decision-making. And

[1] Marc Victor was also an original TreeAge adopter, as reflected in his articles, public seminars, and website: www.litigationrisk.com.

[2] Professor Raiffa passed away in the summer of 2016, at the age of 92. Though he would have been the first to say that his was a long, full, and rich life, I wish I had been able to send him this piece.

to me, that Howard Raiffa's boundless warmth and wisdom coexisted peacefully with his commitment to analytics in negotiation and decision-making disproved the false dichotomy of humanistic vs. analytical. Though known as the father of decision analysis, Howard deeply respected emotion, intuition, gut sense, and the idea that the method was valuable only as much as it was useful for people thinking through decisions that mattered to them.

My friend and colleague Dwight Golann deserves full credit for accepting a chapter on decision analysis for his 1996 book *Mediating Legal Disputes* (after asking for something else), and for collaborating with me in any number of writing projects on mediation evaluation and decision analysis since then. After the CPR Institute for Dispute Resolution's VP Susan Scott invited me to present the method at CPR's 1996 June conference, an informant (Dwight) leaked her comment anticipating the session would be "a real snore". Challenge accepted! It committed me to the effort to make all teaching on the topic both lively and grounded in practicality. I am ever grateful for that opportunity, her challenge, and Dwight's loyalty as a snitch.

After that, I began to present short lectures and longer workshops on decision analysis first in Boston and, since 1998, in Cincinnati, Ohio. At some point after joining the faculty at the University of Cincinnati College of Law, I started to sneak an introduction to decision analysis into a dispute resolution course, and then into my client counseling course. To my surprise, many students seemed to like it and asked if I might teach an "advanced' course, and so I did.

In truth, there is no better way to learn a subject than to teach it. Preparing that course forced me to dig deeper into the relevant literature, and also to articulate the subtler aspects of its application in practice. Inevitably, when we were working on a problem in class, a student would propose constructing the tree one way and I would say, "no, you wouldn't do it that way," but then struggle to explain why. I came to understand what types of problems the students found difficult and the questions I found hard to answer. A shout out is due to the students at Hamline and at North Carolina Central State University who stuck with decision trees during workshop courses in the summer term's heat. The panel mediators in the Western District of Michigan and the Middle District of Pennsylvania (especially Director Joseph Barrett and lawyer-mediator Grace D'Alo) are also owed great appreciation for holding me to step-by-step explanations and practical answers. It's fair to say that the "how to" portions of this book seek to address the basic questions, confusion, hesitance, skepticism, and resistance expressed by law students, lawyers, and lawyer-mediators first learning the method in my presentations over the years. Students in the Advanced Decision Analysis courses at UC Law deserve full credit for portions of the text addressing its application in the more complex cases we worked on in that class.

It would be wrong to neglect to mention several lawyers and friends whose enthusiasm for this method and for collaboration in teaching have enriched my practice and my classroom. Many years ago, Attorney Dan Klein took to decision trees based on my short presentation at a Harvard Law School mediation workshop, undertook his own deeper research, and made decision trees a central part of his practice.3 What an honor for my students when Dan taught an Advanced Decision Analysis class session via video conference!

I am indebted to former students, now lawyers John Bennett, Patricia Foster and Sarah Alford, who developed decision trees for fantastically complicated cases and have come back to class to speak about the method's usefulness for clients and lawyers. Attorney Patrick Lane, then at Procter & Gamble, deserves appreciation for teaching us how the P&G lawyers use this method to communicate with in-house clients in complex patent litigation. IP Attorney John Bennett recently shared the terrific decision analysis presentation he created for the Intellectual Property practice group at the Cincinnati Bar Association. And I owe him thanks for every time he has demonstrated to my students how this method enables better communication with clients.

Locally, I owe a debt of gratitude to Cincinnati's Potter Stewart Inns of Court and Attorney John Pinney for encouraging a fresh programmatic approach with experienced inside and outside counsel, focusing on the attorney challenges in delivering case assessment both with and without decision analysis. Not to be outdone by their rivals across the river, Kentucky Judge Candace Smith and the Solomon P. Chase Inns of Court graciously let me work them through the simple stuff and some particularly tough decision tree problems, with warm hospitality and a gift basket that included Kentucky's best bourbon.

On the research and editorial fronts, much appreciation is due to then UC Law students Lindsay Stueve, Kathryn Cornelius, Freeland Oliverio, and William Buchsbaum, who pored through journals, wrestled with footnotes and bibliography, tested software, found the tiniest typos on tree branch labels, and helped think through the text's logical order. UC Law professional staff Lori Strait and Martie D'Andrea deserve credit for getting manuscript into shape for initial outside review.

I cannot express sufficient thanks to Professor Michaela Keet and attorneys Richard Vangelisti, Mike Troop, and Dan Klein for the exquisite care with which they read this entire manuscript. Their constructive and thoughtful comments and suggestions contributed greatly to its value for all readers.

Back at the University of Cincinnati, the contribution of professional staff wizard, Jennie Edelstein, can neither be measured nor calculated. I will be forever grateful for her uncanny technical talents, cheerful willingness to insert trees, eye for detail, and editorial prowess. It is certain that Jennie's prodigious work and steadfast encouragement greatly increased the probability of this project reaching a final outcome.

Many thanks are also due to UC's graphic design artist, Margaret Weiner, and to my husband David Aaron, who both worked with me so thoughtfully on cover designs.

On the technology front, full credit goes to the University of Cincinnati's Michael Mimms, Multimedia Support Specialist extraordinaire, Kent Meloy, Director of Innovative Learning Solutions and Dr. Mark Konecney, Scholarly Communication and Digital Publishing Strategist, for their invaluable advice and patient hands-on assistance with video components of this project. Mark Konecny also earns permanent appreciation for encouraging my stubborn quest for a publisher that would not prioritize profit over disseminating content for common professional good.

I am lucky and honored to have found exactly the right publisher in Dispute Resolution Institute Press at Mitchell Hamline School of Law. DRI Press Director Sharon Press, Associate Director Kitty Atkins, and Administrative Coordinator Debra Berghoff all share a deep commitment to the importance of accessible publishing for our profession—for lawyers and clients, and for teaching and training lawyers to the highest standards of practice. I am grateful for Sharon's early endorsement of the project's value and her patience with my decision-making and queries along the way, and for Kitty's tireless and clear-eyed management. No doubt, however, we owe the greatest debt of gratitude of Debra Berghoff, master book designer and creator. Unflinching and ever cheerful in the face of 95(!) decision trees, 28 URL links and some pretty darned technical text, Debra produced draft after draft after draft. No graphic placement, spacing, or style detail that might affect clarity or aesthetics escaped her. Without Debra's fulsome dedication—her keen eye, software prowess, and wise counsel—this book would never have come to be. It has been a joy and a privilege to bring Risk & Rigor into the world with this incomparable and delightful team of colleagues at DRI Press.

Author's Note Regarding Complex Tree Images, Video Links, and Website

Readers may note that, in more than a few places, this book contains complex trees in which the font size of branch labels and numbers is quite small and thus difficult to read without a magnifying glass or other enlargement technology. For these trees, I thought it more important to show how a case can map to "many feathered" complexity, and still fit on a single page. Because the trees in this book will not be shown to real clients with real cases, the exact words and numbers on the branch labels don't really matter. Of course, if you were creating a similarly complex tree for a real client, it would be very important that the words and the numbers be large enough for both of you to read and discuss them. Thus, you might enlarge the complex tree on a screen projection from your computer, or zoom in on its branch clusters as you discuss the tree on the computer screen. Sometimes, lower tech works just as well. You might elect to print the tree over several pages and tape them side by side on a wall, or have the complex tree printed on large paper or poster-board.

Please note also that Chapter Three contains links to URLs for 28 video recordings. A complete list of these can also be found at the end of the book, immediately before the bibliography. In each instance, the video shows the process of hand-drawing a tree, segment of a tree, or calculating results for a problem described in the immediately preceding text. The narration and the quaintly primitive handwriting are by your author.

Finally, I am pleased to inform readers that, by the time of this book's publication date, a website at RiskandRigor.com will offer supporting materials on decision tree analysis and how it can be taught and used in practice. This website will also offer a broader array of resources to facilitate client communication and decision making in the face of risk, costs, and other consequences. Also, note that this text discusses certain decision tree software and useful data sources. These were current as of the print publication date. We all know change is inevitable. This is certainly true in the realm of software and data and data analysis. Please look to the website for updated references. And please send me an email if you learn of new resources to facilitate lawyers' use of decision tree analysis for assessing cases and advising clients.

Introduction

Forswearing Ambiguity of Purpose or Method

A client asks of his lawyer: What's it all worth? How much do I have to worry about a verdict so high that it will bankrupt my company? What type of investment in this litigation makes sense? What can we count on and what is uncertain about the way this case could unfold in the court system? How sure are you of your predictions? How many different ways could this turn out? What could happen to make the case jump the track? How and when will I be able to influence what happens in the litigation? How could the possible twists, turns, and demands of this litigation affect my business, my income, my professional options, my personal circumstances, or my family?

Less often articulated is the important question: How does the choice to file this lawsuit or continue to defend it compare to other ways that time, money, talent, and energy could be spent?

This text is an unabashed and full-throated argument for lawyers to use decision tree analysis when considering such questions and their responses and when discussing them with clients.

It's fair for a reader to ask: Why is it worth my time to learn how to do basic decision tree analysis (in the first half this book) and then plow through the challenges of more nuanced applications (in the second half)? Why should I? What would be lost if I were to put the book back on a shelf, or to close the e-book?

While there are certainly other legitimate ways to "slow think" or systematically analyze a legal decision problem, I would argue that a decision tree's visual map-like presentation as well as its mathematical calculations can prove invaluable for lawyers and clients.

On the mathematical side, once a client comes to understand that legal outcomes are uncertain, that client may understandably want to know: "What would a betting man do?" What's a logical way to think through risk and value?" A client's decision about settling or investing resources may rest upon an assessment of: "When all is said and done, what are the overall chances that this or that will happen to me or my business? A decision tree's computational capabilities, using the lawyer's considered numerical estimates, offer a way to answer those questions.

In my view, however, the holy grail of decision tree analysis is not only or even most often found in a decision tree's mathematical yield-the cumulative valuation whose logic and method are explained in this text. Instead, a decision tree's power is found in clearer and just plain better client communication and thus a better lawyer-client relationship. And it fosters a lawyer's more rigorously derived and thus more justifiably confident legal strategy.

Even in a relatively simple case, building its decision tree structure—in graphic form, on paper or on screen—helps make future abstractions of risk and possible outcomes real, and it shows them in sequential and logical order. Needless to say, building a decision tree is all the more helpful in a more complex case. The tree structure is the case map. It enables the client to see where the lawyer's discussion of motions, issues, liability theories, and damages ranges fit on that map, on the various paths to an outcome. A tour guide may describe a winding and treacherous road ahead, but the prospective rider will consider the journey more carefully if he sees it mapped on the terrain. Of course, it's helpful that a client can also show the map—the decision tree graphic of the case—to other important players, whether fellow executives or a concerned spouse.

As discussed further in Chapter 13, for the lawyer aspiring to a "fully informed client," each juncture or turn along the tree's branch paths is a natural invitation for client questions and discussion. As lawyers, many of us tend to talk quickly through complicated law and process; we wave with a broad stroke through legal theories or damages ranges. We may assume a client's familiarity with legal concepts and procedure, or that the client absorbed and remembered previous explanations. At minimum, building a decision tree for a client's case and discussing why it looks the way it does also forces us to slow down. The process facilitates slowing down to explain each risk and possibility and to wait for confirmation of client understanding before moving on to the next segment of the tree. Often, the exercise also helps the client create emotional distance from the case and the idea of settlement.

Yes, similar calculations can be done with a spreadsheet and other decision-making approaches can be useful. However, in my view, the full blown graphic decision tree is a singularly worthwhile exercise when the client's decision rests on understanding, acknowledging, and coming to terms with foreseeable risks and possible outcomes, tangible and intangible, as the case unfolds.

For a lawyer, very simple cases don't require a tree. We get that overall settlement value suffers in the face of a real threat of dismissal on an early dispositive motion, or a potentially valid motion to eliminate a fraud claim. However, for more complex cases, the process of building a tree enforces the discipline of considering more nuanced questions: Is summary judgment really just all or nothing in this case? Might different potential rulings on the motion impact evidentiary issues down the line? With a limited budget for discovery or experts, where should we invest dollars to maximize our client's chances of success or, at least, to maximize settlement value? What is the relationship between linked risks and outcomes?

There is simply no substitute for seeing the more complex and nuanced map of interplay between procedural questions, legal issues, and possible outcomes. Sometimes, mapping the case by building a tree facilitates a less-than-obvious decision such as where to file, when choice of law questions are complex and state laws and judicial or jury temperaments vary. The tree gives the lawyer a sense of the whole picture, of the ways different issues fit together in a complicated case. As litigation unfolds—an expert report proves disappointing, a fact witness is unassailable on deposition—adjustments to the tree's probabilities or sketched paths may be warranted. And seeing where the fortunate or unfortunate development fits helps us to avoid over-weighting or under-weighting its significance.

In sum, lawyers and clients benefit from rigorous, clear, and honest ways of reaching understanding, prediction, conclusions, and advice. And claims to analytical rigor require deliberate consideration of factual and procedural uncertainties and their probabilities, strategic choices and their impact, and a full range of potential outcomes and their likelihoods. A client should be able to see the case's possible pathways as they may be mapped in his lawyer's mind. There's great benefit to the lawyer's analysis being transparent and accessible for discussion with both the client and attorney colleagues working on the matter.

Skeptics of the method sometimes argue against the value of decision analysis in legal practice because it is built only upon imperfect numerical estimates of probabilities and damages. Yet, as will be discussed further, the more ubiquitous prose analysis has no greater claim of accuracy or perfection. Moreover, as illustrated in Chapter Ten, lawyers who foreswear formal decision tree analysis still inevitably estimate probabilities and outcomes when recommending settlement numbers or ranges to their clients, just subconsciously and not methodically. The words of Professor Howard Raiffa are wise and on point. In a post-retirement, reflective piece, "Decision Analysis: A Personal Account of How it Got Started and Evolved," Professor Raiffa wrote:

> *I'm reminded here of the complaint that it seems wrong to build a logical edifice on such imperfect input data, to which Jimmy Savage responded, "Better to construct a building on shifting sands than on a void." Here, the 'void' being no use of judgment inputs.* [1]

Arguments for incorporating decision analysis into legal practice are pointless unless the reader knows what it is and how to apply it. The method's fundamental premises, inviolable rules, gray areas, real limitations, and meaning must be understood. Truth be told, I hope that once lawyers fully understand decision analysis and how to use it, further argument will be unnecessary.

To that end, this text seeks to fully explain the method's logic and application for both simple and more complex legal cases, identify common mistakes and misuses, and provide "best practice" advice for basic and more subtle technical choices. It is also unambiguously aimed at more effective client communication through the use of decision trees. Why? Because, when done well, the method enables a lawyer to move intelligently from prose to a visual map of case analysis and predicted consequences, and facilitates that lawyer's discussion with a more fully informed client.

[1] Raiffa, Howard, "Decision Analysis: A Personal Account of How I Got Started and Evolved," Operations Research 50, no. 1: 10 (2002).

1

DECIDING WITH CLARITY BEFORE CLIMBING TREES

Decision Analysis—Definitions and Distinctions with Trees and Risk

Far outside of legal contexts, a field of study and practice known as "decision analysis" has existed for quite some time. There are textbooks on decision analysis directed primarily at business and policy students; universities now offer degrees in "decision science,"[1] a field that includes formal "decision analysis." In simplest terms, decision analysis applies accepted logical and analytical methods to decision-making tasks that involve choice, information, uncertainty, prediction, and various types of quantitative and qualitative data. It draws upon (and seeks not to violate) rules of probability within the field of statistics.

"Decision *Tree* Analysis" represents decision analysis using a graphic tree structure, with branches and more branches splitting off from these, eventually leading to end points. These branches are constructed to depict a sequential and logical flow from decisions, to their possible consequences, including the myriad of paths these may follow, and their eventual results. Mathematical probability assessments and values are assigned; paths of consequences, risk, cost, and gain flow down each branch of the tree.

In fact, decision analysis can be accomplished without building a visual tree structure, but using a spreadsheet or scratch pad format instead. The thought process and results should be the same. However, the visual aspect of the tree itself is an important benefit for most clients and lawyers.[2] As will

[1] A celebration of the "Golden Anniversary of Decision Analysis," dated the field's origin to 1964 and attributes it to two professors, Howard Raiffa from Harvard, who made great advances in applying statistical decision theory to real world problems, and Ronald Howard from Stanford (then on Sabbatical from MIT), who created an engineering approach to complex decision problems and called it "Decision Analysis."

See the archived blog article and interview at www.smartorg.com/golden-anniversary-decision-analysis-raiffa-howard-award-organizational-decision-quality/ and Raiffa, Howard, "Decision Analysis: A Personal Account of How It Got Started and Evolved," *Operations Research* 50, no. 1 (2002):10. Numerous works by Professor Raiffa and Howard are included in the reference bibliography. The method was introduced into the business community and business schools in the 1960s and 1970s, and into the public policy arena in the 1970s. Gold, David. *Valuing Litigation*. Unpublished manuscript.

Most writing on decision analysis in law practice has been in article form, with Marc Victor heading the field of writers and practitioners. Some law school texts on analytical methods include a chapter on basic and simplified discussion of topic. For additional published works on decision analysis in legal practice, see the reference bibliography.

[2] See Daniel G. Goldstein and David Rothchild's research paper titled "Lay Understanding of Probability Distributions," which found that laypeople's statistical intuitions are affected by the type of elicitation method used. Specifically, the authors found that eliciting an entire distribution from a respondent using a graphical interface,

be discussed later, without a tree, the method's communicative power is diminished. The lawyer who fails to use a tree format may also be at greater risk of failing to incorporate a significant element or to recognize certain interdependencies (irony intended). Indeed, the tree structure alone offers many of the method's benefits, without any mathematical calculations. Thus, this text primarily discusses and presents examples of the method using the decision *tree* form.

Within this domain, *risk analysis* focuses solely on assessing uncertainties and consequences that may flow from a decision. Particularly in litigation, risk analysis is the main show. Once a grievance occurs, the client is typically faced with at least two decisions: first, whether to sue or not and, second, whether to send a demand letter and seek negotiation. Once a lawsuit or an enforcement action commences, the major decisions may be relatively few: file a counter claim or don't, settle (for how much) or don't settle.[3] At this point, very little control remains with the lawyer.

Once on a litigation path, the repeated questions are: *What might happen next?* and, *What are the possible consequences?* When litigation involves visible strategic choices—whether to file in a certain forum or seek removal, whether to retain experts or call particular witnesses—and we map these on a tree, it is accurately called decision analysis. However, perhaps more commonly, litigation offers few major process choices. Lawyers use the method solely to identify uncertainties, assess risks, and estimate losses or gains they face but do not control. The term "risk analysis" is sometimes used to reflect this focus on uncertainty and risk. It seems safe to assume this was the reason Marc Victor, the first attorney well-known for applying (and writing about) formal decision analysis in the legal context, named his company "Litigation Risk Analysis, Inc."[4]

Within this piece, "decision analysis" includes risk analysis; it refers to the general method of analyzing decisions through logical and linked mathematical consideration of their certain or uncertain consequences. So as not to forget that the method can guide strategic decisions as well as risk assessments, "decision tree analysis" is often my phrase of choice when discussing how to build a tree that fairly represents a legal case, as well as how to understand, interpret, and communicate using the tree structure.

The Perils of Lawyering in Prose Alone

It's fair to ask: WHY decision analysis, decision tree analysis, or risk analysis at all? Haven't generations of fine lawyers assessed cases and counseled their clients without it?

It is of course true that, in high stakes commercial transactions or disputes, lawyers have long been called upon to write formal opinion letters or lengthy memoranda analyzing legal issues, dispositive or critical evidentiary motions, trial and settlement strategies, as well as expenditures, risks, and conse-

---

and then computing simple statistics on the graphical interface leads to greater accuracy. Goldstein, Daniel G. and Rothchild, David. "Lay Understanding of Probability Distributions" *Judgment and Decision Making* 9, no. 1: 1-14 (2014).

[3] This may be an over-statement. In fact, within litigation there are often decisions regarding choice of venue, whether to retain certain types of experts or to pursue certain avenues of discovery. As discussed in later portions of this text, the method can be helpful for such decisions.

[4] You can find downloadable copies of Marc Victor's many terrific articles at his company website: www.litigation-risk.com/.

quences.[5] At minimum, lawyers review and discuss with their clients the case's legal issues and possible twists and turns along a litigation or transactional path.

Rigorous lawyering has always required us to carefully consider questions such as: In what direction are the courts moving on this issue? Will the expert's findings support our theory of the case? Will a jury find the expert persuasive? Is our CEO likely to be an effective witness, or will his arrogance alienate a jury? If everything breaks our way, how high might the damages be? How likely are punitive damages and emotional distress? What if everything doesn't break our way? Which claim is more vulnerable? How much does it matter whether we file in state or federal court? Would it be better for our client to sue pre-emptively, or wait it out, on the chance the opposition might take no action? If we sue, what counter-claims can we anticipate?

It's hard to argue that a lawyer should not carefully consider such questions. They flow from critical concerns more generically categorized as: What are my client's rights and interests? What actions might we take, given those rights and interests? What might happen, if we decide to do this? What might happen next? Are those the only possibilities? What might be the consequences for the litigation, dealings with regulators, business revenues, or professional interests? What might the ultimate financial, personal, professional, or business impact be? What recourse would we have then?

Imagine a five or ten-page lawyer's memorandum to a client, or perhaps a fifteen to twenty-minute oral presentation to a client, that covers critical procedural and substantive legal issues, litigation decision points, potential rulings, critical evidence and experts, damages theories, and potential outcomes, as well as appeals. Imagine the lawyer diligently walks the client through questions he has considered, his analysis and conclusions.

Assume the analysis is clear, persuasive, and the client understands it all. The lawyer might explain: *The initial question is whether to file suit, and if so, in which venue. The first hurdle will be their statute of limitations defense. While we should defeat that, a recent ruling within this circuit is concerning.... We also need to consider whether the court will admit some crucial evidence on the fraud claim. If they are able to block that evidence, our damages upside is impacted. In any event, we will face a battle of the experts on this econometric causation question. Then the damages are a tricky call. Under our best theory, the damages could range from.... It's also possible that the jury could find for us, but on a different theory. That will depend on how convincing the data and the witness are. On the other theory, the jury could return an award of only....* [and so on].

After listening to the presentation or reading the memorandum, even if the client has absorbed every predicted twist and every logical thread (and that's a big if), he will of course still want to know: *"So what should we do? What's it all worth? What are we looking at here? Should we make a settlement demand? What's the lowest we should take? What are the chances of a home run, of having everything break my way?"*

In most cases, our legal system is tasked with connecting legal claims and defenses to monetary amounts. Yet, there's a strong black box quality to the labyrinth of reason, law, credibility, exclusion,

[5] See Heavin, Heather and Keet, Michaela, "The Path of Lawyers: Enhancing Predictive Ability Through Risk Assessment Methods," *Canadian Institute for the Administration of Justice* (2016): 2, noting that "a perception inside the legal profession that lawyers are not undertaking risk assessment for their client may impede lawyer from adopting new techniques and acquiring new skills that will help them improve their role s as accurate predictors of risk."

inclusion, and legal rulings that may or may not occur before a judge or jury arrive at the question of damages. For the client contemplating settlement in light of that labyrinth, what it's all worth in settlement is complicated. A wise settlement decision must incorporate law, logic, prediction, risk, emotion, tangibles and intangibles.

The most painstaking and comprehensive prose analysis review fails to yield a logically and transparently derived numerical estimate of settlement value because no math was involved. Thus, the lawyer can only answer the client's question—*What's it all worth?*—by pulling a number out of thin air, perhaps with a sigh, regretful shrug, or a wave of the arms. A worrisome disconnect between narrative and numerical advice seems unavoidable. But is it?

Mortal Mind As Measure of Tree-Worthy Complexity

When a case is relatively simple—procedurally, legally, and on the damages side—informal decision analysis occurs naturally. Imagine the simplest contract case: your client will win or lose; what's due (or not) under the contract is clear, and no procedural or evidentiary motions are anticipated. It's easy math; most of us can visualize and assess this one pretty clearly.[6] We all know that if the defendant's deposition yields his admission of a meeting of the minds on contract terms, the case value will go up. But, if his deposition testimony is problematic, case value will go down.

Most cases are not that simple.[7] In litigation, procedural and evidentiary uncertainties are the norm; damages are complicated due to the array of legal theories, anticipated evidentiary challenges, and eventual judicial rulings. Lawyer and client must make strategic decisions that impact a litigation's possible paths and outcomes in uncertain but estimable ways. In the regulatory arena, attorneys are called upon to assess regulators' attitudes, rulemaking processes and outcomes, and legislative initiatives and emendations. In transactional work, we negotiate terms allocating risks and benefits—environmental liability, subrogation, force majeure, third party breaches, and penalty provisions—leading to future positive or negative value for the client.[8]

[6] I am sometimes surprised at how helpful it is for the client to see even the simplest case as drawn in a decision tree. Many years ago, attorney Elayne Greenburg (now a professor at St. John's University School of Law), reported its usefulness for her divorce clients. I was recently struck by the way the simplest two-branch tree helped an unsophisticated plaintiff to think through his decision during mediation of his employment case.

[7] See the insightful discussion and further references on this point in Heavin, Heather and Keet, Michaela, "The Path of Lawyers: Enhancing Predictive Ability through Risk Assessment Methods," *Canadian Institute for the Administration of Justice* (2016): 7-8. They draw the link to Kahneman and Twersky's earlier, seminal research and Kahneman's System 1 and System 2 thinking in his recent and popular book, Kahneman, Daniel, *Thinking, Fast and Slow* (2011). That book characterizes System 1 thinking as automatic and effective for certain types of decisions, but System 2 or slow thinking, as requiring greater cognitive effort and attention and observes that System 2 thinking is required for more complex computations and decisions. As Heavin and Keet observe, [at page 8]: "Understanding when quick, intuitive thinking may be influencing behavior and resulting in inaccurate predictions is important for lawyers and their clients as techniques and tools can be developed to counteract these intuitive responses. Accordingly, if a lawyer's advice to a client is based on intuitive thinking, rather than a cognitively based risk assessment, the ability of the client make a truly informed decision is compromised."

[8] Even though litigation examples are prevalent both here and in most writing on decision analysis in legal contexts, it can be used in other areas of practice. In fact, business attorneys may be pleased to learn that their business clients may use this method to evaluate business risk and opportunities. It is commonly taught in business schools, at least within MBA programs.

Once a case involves more than just a few procedural, legal, or evidentiary uncertainties or strategic decisions, we mortals lose the ability to assess their individual and cumulative impact on the case. We can't keep track of all possible twists, turns, and probabilities, nor can we relate our descriptions of what might happen to cogent advice about case valuation.

When the circumstances and uncertainties are many and the stakes high, shouldn't lawyers aspire to counsel clients based on more careful and systematic analysis of possible paths to success or failure? Not surprisingly, the balance of this text is dedicated to that aspriation—rigor in legal practice and fully informated clients.

2

Logical Premises—Fiction, Meaning, Method, and Practice

Consider this old SHOE comic strip and its dialog between two characters:[1]

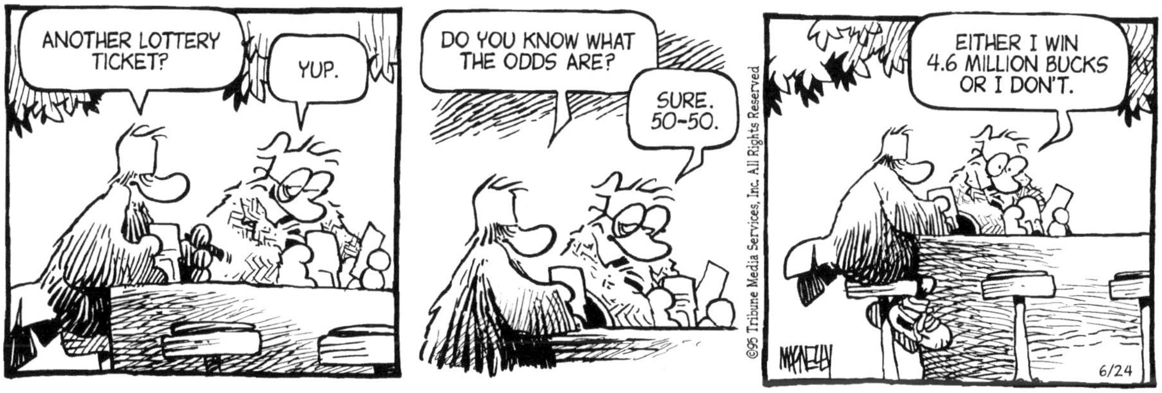

Is that accurate? Are the odds of winning the lottery in fact 50/50? The answer, of course, is no. Assuming $4.6 million tickets were sold at $1 each, the odds are 1 in 4.6 million. But does it matter? Not really. After all, only a dollar is at stake. Plus, one could argue that the pleasure derived from anticipating a possible win—those lovely daydreams of what to do with millions of dollars—are worth more than the single dollar investment. The uncertainty is the fun.

Being a party to litigation is akin to having a lottery ticket. However, unlike lottery players, clients don't generally derive any pleasure from the process or the wait. The defense client's lottery is entirely negative; the question is whether his ticket will yield losses and, if so, how much. In litigation, decision tree analysis can be thought of as a method for assessing the discounted value of the client's ticket—in support of his decision to settle by selling or buying it.

To arrive at the ticket's overall discounted value, the method's basic logic—its mathematical operation—is to multiply possible outcomes (costs and gains) by the probabilities of their occurrence. Most of us already use this logic in large and small decisions. For example, we will pay more for a car that has a low risk of breaking down, and less for one with a high chance of significant repair costs. When choosing between two investments of equal price, we choose the one we believe more likely to rise in value, or we seek a price discount for the one we believe has greater risk of failure. If I enter a lottery

[1] ©1995 Jim MacNelly Distributed by King Features Syndicate, Inc. Reprinted with permission.

limited to 100 tickets, for a $100,000 prize, each ticket might fairly be priced at $1,000 ($100,000 x the 1% chance of a win).

If all cases were that simple, no tree structure would be necessary to organize and calculate the discount. Discounting the possible result by its probability would be a one-step operation: a single percentage multiplied by its chances. The problem, of course, is that we rarely, if ever, encounter a case so simple: one in which even a single probability assessment is absolutely accurate and the anticipated award amount is exactly right.

In litigation, decision analysis applies the same logic and method—discounting to each possibility by its probability along a litigation path. Its power is in teasing apart our analysis of the ways a case might unfold as it moves through a series of uncertainties. For example, decision analysis allows us to separately consider the probabilities of winning or losing motions to dismiss, motions for summary judgment (full or partial), motions *in liminie*, adoption of distinct liability or damages theories, and different ranges of damages. The method then permits us to see the successive and cumulative impact of all of these risks in the form of a discounted value calculation—the weighted average of all possible outcomes at each stage of the analysis. The method's ability to display the distribution of possible case outcomes and their likelihoods and to map the many different paths a case might take often proves more valuable for lawyers and clients than a discounted value calculation.

Situated in Fiction, But Not Alone in Our Imaginary Land

In reality, *I will win 4.6 million bucks or I won't*!

And, in reality, your client will win or lose some amount, and the case will (usually) only be tried once.

It is just plain true that the method's mathematical operation rests on a fictional premise: that the analyzed event will occur many, many times, and thus its average result matters. This fiction can be heard in the way we often phrase the questions: *"If this case were tried a hundred times, in how many of them do you think a jury would find liability? If a hundred juries found liability, how many times do you think they would be mad enough to award punitive damages?"*

Is there a world where it would only make sense to measure a settlement offer against your decision tree analysis' discounted value number? Imagine a company client faced with defending a hundred virtually identical claims to be heard before a hundred different juries. At the outset, a decision tree analysis was performed using accurately predictive probabilities and damages figures, verified by the end results in each case. In other words, the lawyer predicted a 60% chance of liability finding, and indeed, sixty of the cases resulted in liability finding; the lawyer predicted that in 20% of the plaintiff's verdicts, punitive damages would be awarded, and that is indeed what happened. For such an imaginary set of cases, the discounted value yielded by the initial decision analysis would equal the average of all of the verdicts.

If the defense client had offered that discounted value amount to each plaintiff, and each plaintiff had accepted the offer, the defense client would be in the same financial position as he would be after all of the claims were heard and decision rendered, EXCEPT for attorneys' fees (if these were not included). In fact, if accurately estimated attorneys' fees were included in each case's cost figures, then the discounted value number—offered to each plaintiff—would equal the average of all case costs (fees and damages award included). The defendant would fare better financially only to the extent that one or more plaintiffs would accept less than the case's discount value.

In truth, most cases will only be tried once. Your client will win or lose this one case only once. And the damages will be a single number, not a distributed range of numbers. In fact, it's almost certain that the one-time case result will not be the discounted value number yielded by decision analysis.

Then why or why not use decision analysis in cases with real clients and real stakes?

First, at minimum, by requiring us to deconstruct the factors that may influence a case's eventual outcome, the method requires us to think carefully.

As Professor Howard Raiffa, a revered father of decision analysis, wrote:

> *The spirit of decision analysis is divide and conquer: Decompose a complex problem into simpler problems, get one's thinking straight in these simpler problems, paste these analysis together with a logical glue, and come out with a program for action for the complex problem.*[2]

Commitment to this forced decomposition also forces lawyers to slow down, to carefully consider instincts, hunches, research, estimates, and conclusions. When a lawyer reviews and discusses with his client each branch of choice and uncertainty and each probability estimate, the black box quality of the lawyer's analysis and advice dissipates. Thus, the method offers a careful, clear, and effective way to communicate with a client. It can de-escalate client emotions. In fact, these benefits may be gained even without mention of discounted value or probability distributions. The decision tree has value as an analytical roadmap, more accessible in a visual, graphic form than via memorandum or oral presentation.

But this discussion dodges the question for mathematical calculations within decision analysis. Given its fictional premise, how legitimate is it to perform arithmetic to derive a discounted value—the weighted average of possible outcomes—or to calculate the probability of each possible outcome within a distribution range?

In fact, many clients *do* find meaning and welcome direction from these mathematically derived data points. They are comfortable with the idea that we decide to play or not, or to bet a certain amount or not, according to the odds, even if only betting on one race or one round of cards. We all understand that probabilities are just that: there's no certainty. And we regularly make decisions around single events based on probability judgments.

Some clients find an intellectually and emotionally comfortable resting place at the data point generated by decision analysis—the discounted value of the probabilities applied to net costs or gains. While the dollar amount may be higher or lower than hoped for, their comfort derives from the method's logical consistency with the way they generally make decisions.

Think of a case with terribly high exposure, but a relatively low chance of success due to a threshold legal issue, in addition to significant uncertainty as to a liability finding. Must the client pay (or only accept) \$3,000,000—a number all acknowledge as reasonable for the injuries—if liability were clear? Or should the client offer (or accept) \$50,000—the future costs of litigation only—because the chances of

[2] Raiffa, Howard, *Decision Analysis: Introductory Lectures on Choices Under Uncertainty*, (1968): 271. I am indebted to Professors Heavin and Keet for reminding me of that wonderful quote in their article "A Spectrum of Tools to Support Litigation Risk Assessment: Promise and Limitations," 15 *Canadian Journal of Law and Technology* 265, (2017): 270. See the bibliography for reference to a subset of relevant work.

a defense verdict on the threshold legal question or on liability are so high? We seek guidance on what might be a reasonable number, somewhere between $50,000 and $3,000,000. We want to feel that if we paid more or accepted less, it wasn't as a result of fear, powerlessness, grief, anger, or violating a duty to protect the company's coffers.

Finally, in defense of the method's mathematically generated single discounted value number and array of possible numerical outcomes: don't lawyers traditionally recommend a settlement value, and discuss the range of the client's exposure? The answer is yes. And when lawyers do so, aren't they essentially, roughly, translating prose analysis to unnamed numbers in their heads, lowering the recommendation for vulnerabilities, raising it for perceived strengths? Yes, again. But, when it's intuitive—all in our heads—our thought process is hidden. And it almost inevitably lacks thoroughness and rigor. We may gloss over significant sub-issues, and we aren't capable of reliably relating a complex set of issues to the whole value.

The decision analyst follows the same time-honored process of case evaluation, only more transparently and, I suggest, more rigorously. He identifies uncertainties to be encountered and decisions to be made along the way, puts in estimated probabilities for possible but uncertain branches along the tree's paths, and includes considered estimates of possible outcomes.

In short, unless we oppose lawyers suggesting any numerical settlement value or ranges of potential exposure, it makes no sense to oppose the use of decision analysis as one method of generating numbers for clients to consider.

Misconstrued Meaning and Misplaced Moral Imperatives

Meaning is never an intrinsic characteristic of its source; meaning is generated by humans. Given its fictional premise, a decision tree's calculated result does not "mean" the settlement value, unless and until we choose to make it so. There exists no moral imperative for a client to "accept" decision analysis' results as a normative settlement rule, no biblical or philosophical text references the notion that a decision-maker is obligated to be influenced by the weighted average of possible trial outcomes in a legal dispute. The decision-maker is entirely and rightfully free to accept or reject the idea that "reasonable settlement" is defined or even guided by the odds of desirable and less desirable fates.

Another equally legitimate approach might ignore the odds (even granting their accuracy) and choose to act in a manner that is consistent with one's identity—in a way that "feels right." So, a business owner is entitled to say: *I didn't discriminate, or commit fraud, or cause an injury, and I am not going to pay the party who has accused me of that. I don't care about odds or chances: they do not influence my decision.* It is, of course, the lawyer's obligation to ensure that his business owner client understands the risk and recognizes the potential consequences for his business and its other employees. Having done so, the lawyer (and if it has gone that far, the mediator), must respect the client's self-determination enough to accept his way of making a decision.

In too many mediations where decision analysis is used, mediators and lawyers assert that the clients or opposing counsel are "unreasonable" when they reject the settlement in a target range suggested by its mathematically generated value. Innumerable articles on the use of decision analysis in litigation and mediation do refer to it as "*the* settlement value." Admittedly, the decision analytic language convention names it the "Estimated Monetary Value,"—shortened to "EMV,"—or "the discounted value" of the case, when used in a legal context. And, as a mediator, one reason I introduce decision analysis into settlement discussions is the hope that one or both parties will thereby feel comfortable settling in, or closer to, that range.

Just *offering* the mathematical results should cause no discomfort for the tree-builder or the client. Whether called the EMV, discounted value, or roll back number, it is no more and no less than the weighted average of the possible case outcomes. That's all. What's troubling is the tendency to ascribe greater or normative meaning to this number, as if it "should" determine settlement value. This number, as well as the distribution of outcomes and each of their associated probabilities, are nothing more and nothing less than data points.

The values of honesty, neutrality, and respect for self-determination prescribe against lawyer or mediator making any other claims regarding the meaning of those data-points. They are not entitled to push for settlement as "right" or "just" at or about the data point that is the EMV. If there is a moral imperative here, it is that no mediator or lawyer should judge harshly or pressure the client who ascribes it no greater meaning.

Where the Method is Meaningful, We're Obligated to Get it Right

The lawyer is obligated to bring the same level of legal knowledge, research, and experience to decision tree analysis as to a traditional, prose-form analysis of his client's case. The lawyer is also obligated to apply decision analytic methods soundly—in ways that do not violate fundamental axioms in probability and statistics—while fairly representing the case.

For that reason, this text is dedicated to enabling lawyers to become comfortable with technical elements for competent application of decision tree analysis in both simple and more complex legal cases. We begin with basic "How To's" that can also be found through various books, articles, and websites. However, I hope that readers who are less than comfortable with math and probability will appreciate this text's deliberate attention to explaining the concepts that underlie the method.

At the risk of revealing a punch line from the "How To's" chapter, the questions that need to be considered in formal decision analysis are quite repetitive and simple: *What is in your control at this stage, and what is not? If you make that decision, what immediate consequences would flow from that? What could happen next? Are those the only possibilities? Did we miss anything? And what might happen, or what might you decide to do after that?* Finally, you will reach questions at the anticipated end points about what the jury or judicial decision-maker might decide. In addition to thinking through the logical paths of possibilities and consequences, you must consider how likely each one is to become reality.

Thus, a commitment to mastering this method is not a paean to mathematical imperatives. Even the client who will accept his lawyer's advice on faith is entitled to believe that the lawyer's recommended settlement, expenditure for experts, and strategic litigation moves were derived from careful analysis of their costs, benefits, and risks. Business executives are called upon to analyze a product's market and to project revenues and costs as the basis for strategic business decisions. Why not lawyers?

Moving beyond the basics, my central purpose is to raise and address some more subtle but important questions that arise for the decision tree builder in a legal context. Sometimes, whether to add or subtract a tree branch or a layer of branches and the order in which uncertainties are accounted for can be difficult and consequential decisions. In some cases, simplifying or representing complexity (through pruning or adding branches or layers of branches) can distort the results and diminish the power of the analysis. Based upon years of working with decision trees in legal disputes, I offer some insights into how to make those choices. Not surprisingly, my advice is rendered in the language of trees, branches, and nodes generally used in this analysis.

Value for clients entirely aside, decision tree analysis facilitates lawyers' greater rigor when it forces us to map and consider the possible paths along which a case may unfold. As I hope you will eventually agree, that makes it well worth the effort.

3

How To's

Starting with Generic and Abstract Playing Fields

This chapter sets forth the basics of decision tree analysis and their roots in probability theory. It leads the reader though a series of abstract "games" and then some simple legal problems designed to demonstrate how to use the method. Those already comfortable with decision trees may wish to skim this over or skip to Chapter Four's discussion of common errors, including prescriptions against distortion of your analysis.

Conceptually, in order to build a decision tree you must:

1) Define the decision: What's the problem? What are the choices? For our purposes, we'll assume that the decision is whether to settle for a stated offer. Or, better yet, to decide the lowest or highest dollar amount at which you would settle a legal claim.
2) Identify the possibilities: What might happen if I decide on one course of action or another? In litigation, identify all of the (foreseeable and) possible procedural and evidentiary twists and turns, as well as their possible consequences, flowing through to various possible ways the case could end.
3) Judge the likelihood: What are the chances that each of these considered possibilities will come to pass? What's the chance of summary judgment, the chance that the critical evidence will be found inadmissible, the chance that the jury will find fraud, and the chance that the damages will be trebled?
4) Figure the net gains or costs—the outcomes or (positive or negative) "payoffs" at the end of the road: What will the net effect be if it works out this way or that way? In litigation, the attorney's fees and other costs incurred from the present to the end of the case must be subtracted to yield a net figure. On the defense side, they are subtracted from \$0—in the event of a defense verdict—or from a negative number—the damages award the defense will be obligated to pay. Thus, if liability is found, costs make the defendant's net loss a larger negative number.
5) Mathematical operations: A more careful description of the way the math works will be found later in this chapter. Sufficed to say here that only arithmetic is involved. Probabilities along a path are multiplied to learn the cumulative probability of each possible outcome. To find the discounted value or EMV, each pay-off is multiplied by its cumulative probability and these are added together. The EMV is simply the weighted average value of all possible outcomes.[1]

[1] As will be explained in more detail, the math can be done either from left to right or right to left on the tree, both visually and in fact. The final EMV will be the same, but seeing the operation's flow in the other direction tends to yield different insights. Each, or both, may be important in different cases and client circumstances.

The Power of Cumulative Probability

Decision analysis is built upon the foundation of probability theory, and its observation that probabilities are cumulative: whenever you have to jump through more than one hoop, and the success of each jump is not 100% certain, the probabilities of each jump must be multiplied.

Drawing upon the much used example of a standard, unweighted coin and a completely fair, unrigged coin toss, we all know there's a 50% chance (.5) that it will come up heads and a 50% chance that it will come up tails on each toss. But, what if I want to know how likely it is that the coin will land on heads twice in a row - in each of the two coin tosses? Then I am asking, what is the total or "cumulative" probability of both successive coin tosses coming up heads? What if I will win $10 if and only if that happens?

In fact, the two coin tosses could generate the following four possible combinations of heads and tails:

First toss	Second Toss
Heads 	Heads 
Heads 	Tails 
Tails 	Heads 
Tails 	Tails 

Clearly, "Heads, Heads" is only one of four (25%) of the possible combinations. Thus, the chances are 1 in 4, or .25 (25%) of that first winning two-heads combination.

That's how successive and thus cumulative probabilities work. If there's a 50% chance of an unweighted, two-sided coin toss coming up heads each time, then the overall probability that it will come up "heads" twice in a row is 25%. That is the first 50% probability (.5) multiplied by the second 50% probability (.5). 50% x 50% = 25%. (.5 x .5 = .25).

The set-up and the results are the same if we switch the context to a litigation with one procedural hurdle, then a simple yes or no liability question, and a specified damages amount. If there were a 50% chance of surviving summary judgment, and a 50% chance of a liability finding, these would yield a cumulative 25% chance of a damages award in the specified amount. 50% (survive summary judgment) x 50% (liability verdict with damages award) = 25%.

Given that all uncertainties in litigation don't seem to be 50/50—or equally weighted in one direction or another—it makes sense to consider the example of a deck of 100 cards, constructed to include, say 30 red cards (hearts or diamonds) and 70 black cards (clubs or spades).

If I draw three separate cards (but put each back after each draw, so as not to disturb the proportions), what are the chances that I will draw three red cards—hearts or diamonds—in a row?

To perform the analysis, each probability along each path is multiplied and each path's cumulative end probability is multiplied by that net end number. For a deck in which we know 30% of the cards are red, the answer is .3 x .3 x .3 = .027. There's a 2.7% chance of drawing three red cards in a row.

And the chances of first drawing a black card—club or spade—and then two red cards? This would set up as: a 70% chance of a black card, then a 30% chance of a red card, followed by a 30% chance of a red card.

The answer is .7 x .3 x .3 = .063. There's a 6.3% chance of drawing a black card first, and then 2 red cards.

Exercise 1- Weighted Coins for Litigation

Another way to think about it is to go back to the coin toss, but imagine that the coin at each juncture is weighted in accordance with our assessment of strengths and weaknesses. Imagine that the summary judgment "coin" is weighted toward our client's side; we've estimated an 80% chance it will come up heads. And, we are also somewhat confident of a liability verdict, estimating a 60% chance of prevailing at trial.

How would you calculate the cumulative probabilities?

Readers are invited to watch the video, and all of the videos that follow, via live link in an e-book or at the listed url. This first video narrates through the steps of a hand drawn calculation. Or you may wish to skip to the text below, describing the calculation and providing the answer.

Video 01: http://dx.doi.org/doi:10.7945/C22T3D

The cumulative probability of success with BOTH weighted coins is .8 x .6 = .48, or overall, a 48% chance that we will collect the damages award. Using the method's logic, from the plaintiff's perspective, we would multiply the anticipated (net) award by .48 to arrive at the litigation's discounted value.

Now, imagine a litigation in which the plaintiff estimates an 80% chance of surviving summary judgment and a 60% chance of winning $125,000 ($150,000 less $25,000 in attorney's fees). Application of the method in the case is shown below.

This url or video link narrates through a hand drawn application of the method in the case. The text explanation can be found below it.

Video 02: http://dx.doi.org/doi:10.7945/C2Z41T

We have already multiplied .80 x .60 =.48. Thus, we know that the overall chance of getting to any verdict award is .48 or 48%. We would then multiply .48 (the chance of a verdict award) x $125,000 (the anticipated amount of the verdict award), to get to the discounted value of $60,000. If the plaintiff accepts this way of thinking about value, and if he is without risk aversion or emotion, he might be indifferent between a settlement at $60,000 and proceeding down a litigation path. The method is not magic; it simply operates by multiplying each probability along the way to arrive at a cumulative probability for that outcome.

Exercise 2—More Weighted Coins in Sequence

Just to add some more complexity and reality to our imaginary, sequential coin tosses: imagine that a first coin is weighted to create an 80% chance of coming up heads on the first toss and a second coin is weighted to create a 60% chance of heads on the second toss. Now, let's add another layer to the game: we will win $125,000 if we get heads on the second toss, AND double that—$250,000, if we get heads on the third toss. Let's assume the third coin is weighted 75% toward coming up tails. But if only the third toss lands as "tails," we'll still keep the $125,000. (Before that toss, all other "tails" get us $0.)

Well then, what are the cumulative probabilities of ending up with $125,000, or with $250,000, or with $0?

The next video demonstrates how the calculation would be done, as explained in the text below it.

Video 03: http://dx.doi.org/doi:10.7945/C2T99B

Let's look at $250,000 first: we still have an 80% chance of heads on the first toss, and a 60% chance on the second toss, but now we have 25% chance of heads on the third toss. Only that combination yields $250,000. So, the cumulative probability of winning $250,000 is 80% x 60% x 25% = 12%. (.8 x .6 x .25 = .12)

Now, what's the probability of winning $125,000?

Once again, the next video demonstrates the calculation, also explained in the text below it.

Video 04: http://dx.doi.org/doi:10.7945/C26M5B

To calculate the probability of winning $125,000, the math is the same on the first two tosses, but it's 75% on the third toss. So, you have to figure 80% x 60% x 75% = 36%. (.8 x .6 x .75 = .36) (Remember the third toss only affects whether the winnings will be $125,000 or $250,000.)

And finally, what's the likelihood of getting $0 by the coin landing on tails in one of the first two tosses?

The calculation is explained and shown in the next video and in the text below it.

Video 05: http://dx.doi.org/doi:10.7945/C2PM5P

Well, we can actually end up with $0 in two ways: that first toss gives us a 20% chance of a $0. If that doesn't happen, then we may get there in two tosses, the first one would have to have been a heads—at 80%, and the second toss would have to be tails—at 40%, so 80% x 40% = 32% (.8 x .4 = .32). Combine the probabilities of our two paths to $0, and the probability of $0 is 52%.

A direct parallel would be a case in which plaintiff's counsel estimates an 80% chance of surviving summary judgment (or other preliminary dispositive motion), a 60% chance of winning on liability, and, if the jury finds liability, a 50% chance that they award double damages. (For the purposes of this example, let's assume a relevant statute permits this if the defendant's action was willful, etc.)

So, now we know the probability of results at $0 is 52%, at $125,000 is 36%, and at $250,000 is 12%. What's the weighted average—aka discounted value or Estimated Monetary Value (EMV)?

Before looking at the next video or the text below it, the reader is encouraged to give it a try.

Video 06: http://dx.doi.org/doi:10.7945/C2JX11

Multiply $250,000 x .12, to get $30,000; multiply $125,000 x .36, to get $45,000, multiply $0 x .52, and still have 0. Add these together: $75,000 is the answer!

For our legal case, it does NOT mean that a jury verdict is ever predicted to land at $75,000. Quite the contrary. It means that IF YOU WERE TO HAVE THE MISFORTUNE TO LITIGATE THE EXACT SAME CASE A HUNDRED TIMES, we are predicting a little bit more than half the time, you'll wind up with $0. The rest of the time, the results will be either $125,000 (36%) or $250,000 (12%). Assuming our predictions were accurate, and you added up ALL of the 100 results and divided by 100, to get an average, that average would be $75,000.

Scratch Pad Summary

That, in a nutshell, is the conceptual underpinning of risk analysis. The decision question is what to do in light of the possible risks and rewards and their discounted value. The idea is simple, as is the math. Still, it is also true that applying it in even a moderately complicated (two or three step) case can be challenging. It can be downright daunting where the case's procedural path, evidentiary issues, legal theories, and damages claims are just plain complicated.

What we've done so far is a "scratch pad" method of decision analysis or, really, risk analysis. In fact, calculations for a simple tree can be done on a scratch pad. Those inclined to spreadsheets will easily see that Excel does a fine job.

Now, a confession to ease the concerns of those less comfortable with math and formulas in this scratch pad format: this author tends to glaze over when reading math calculations within a paragraph. And, when doing the arithmetic on a pad or in Excel, with a separated box for each cumulative probability calculation, and then multiplication by the dollar amount, they seem disjointed. It's not intuitive to remember how and why they fit together. That is one reason I so strongly prefer to use a decision tree structure even for very simple cases. The math is the same, but the tree provides something to hang it on, to visualize how the pieces—the branches and ends—fit together. For even somewhat more complex cases, and for client communication and comprehension, there is nothing like a tree!

To that end, some tree-building conventions and advice are coming up next.

Symbolic Conventions for Trees

Experience teaches that the only way to become comfortable with the method is to experience it. Thus, this section first introduces a few commonly used tree building terms and their symbols, and then asks the reader to try a few tree-building exercises.

Here are some terms, symbols and graphic conventions you need to know:

Various Nodes and Branches

Critical junctures, turning points or end points on a tree are referred to as "nodes."

Decision Node and its Alternative Decision Branches

A "decision node" reflects a point at which a decision is to be made and is generally represented by a square. Assuming that more than one decision could be made at that decision node, decision branches should be drawn or inserted to its right (at least in languages read from left to right).

While it's pretty simple, this is explained and shown in the next video.

Video 07: http://dx.doi.org/doi:10.7945/C2F39V

The convention is to label or describe the decision branch across the top of its line.

A computer software-generated version is shown next [2]

---

[2] As suggested earlier, the software I have long used, and used to generate the trees in this text, is TreeAge, available at www.treeage.com. It was originally designed by Boston lawyer Morris Raker for use in litigation, although the website reflects the company's current emphasis on health care and health policy.

There is now a free, online decision tree software called Silver Decisions at SilverDecisions.pl. Developed on an EU grant by professors in Poland, it is an open source product. While a little bit clunky, law students and lawyers find it easy to use. This author is currently endeavoring to arrange improvements, using the open source platform. In the meanwhile, it works reasonably well for simpler cases and free is surely the best price.

Dan Klein of Klein Dispute Resolution offers an introductory decision tree analysis tool, limited to one probability on the liability question and a three point damages range. Thus it generates only a very basic tree. It is free at his website: www.decisiontree.kleinmediation.com/tree/generator.

As of this date, other software programs I've found that are designed to create decision or risk analysis trees include: Tree Plan, available at Treeplan.com, Precision Tree by Palisades Corporation, and DPL by Syncopation Software. Tree Plan operates as an add-on to Microsoft Excel and is less costly than TreeAge (particularly for the basic package). I make no claims to extensive experience with any of these. However, Palisades often offers instructional programs (at least on-line) for using their software. Information is available at www.palisade.com Syncopation Software's DPL Decision Analysis product appears to be well suited for assessing litigation risk.

Simple visual decision tree presentations can be made with Solutions, offered by SmartDraw at www.smartdraw.com, but it does not perform any calculations.

Other software that is related but not "pure" or classic decision analysis include: "CaseValue Analyzer," developed by Michael Palmer, and "Picture it Settled," developed by Donald Philbin.

I am indebted to Professors Heather Heavin and Michaela Keet at the University of Saskatchewan, College of Law for sharing a pre-publication version of their excellent article: "A Spectrum of Tools to Support Litigation Risk Assessment: Promise and Limitations," 15 *Canadian Journal of Law and Technology* 265 (2017). Their article

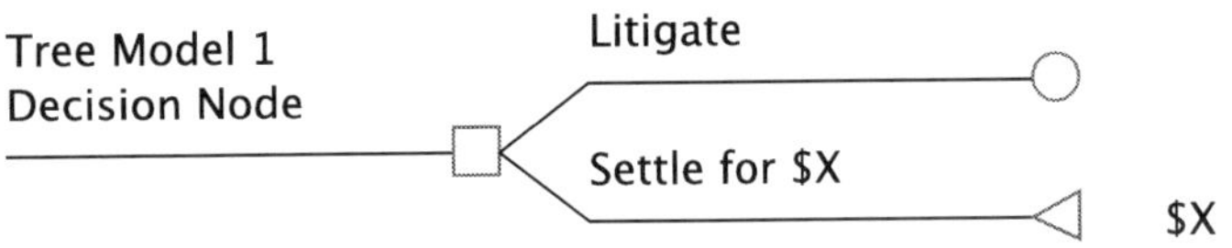

Chance Node and its Possibility Branches

A "chance node," represented by a small circle, as shown above, reflects a point of uncertainty, where we don't control what will happen next. Again, assuming that more than one possible thing could happen from that point, branches would be drawn to the right of the chance node, each representing one possibility. This is demonstrated in the video and shown in the tree that follows soon after in the text.

Video 08: http://dx.doi.org/doi:10.7945/C29D6K

The convention is to label each branch across the top of its line and to place its estimated probability underneath each branch line.

Of course, if there are more than two ways the case could go at this junction, then more than two branches should be included in the cluster.

A computer software-generated version is shown below. Note that this tree and the one that follows are intended to reflect only text discussion thus far. They are not "finished" trees as they stop without going past these two initial sets of chance nodes.

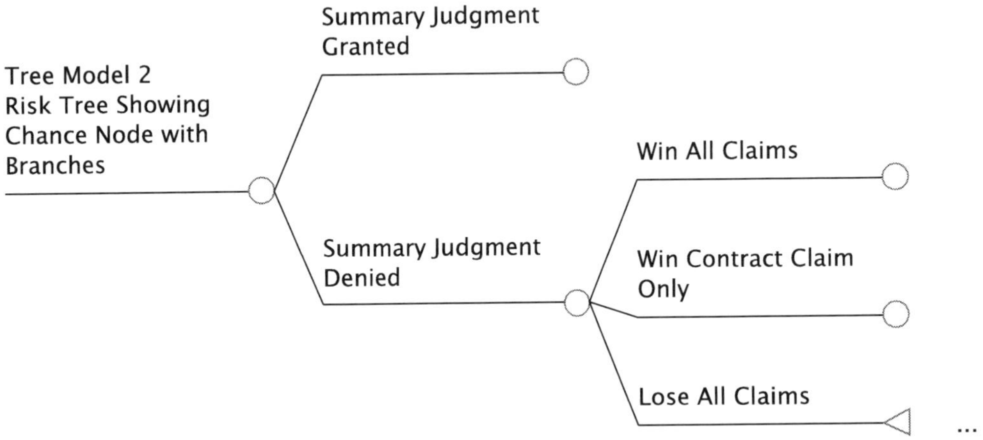

As discussed more fully later, after EACH chance node, the probabilities for each cluster of branches must sum to 100%.[3] If the total is lower, we've missed a possibility; if it's higher, we've overestimated the probabilities for at least one of the possible events.

---

discusses many of these software sources, particularly of Michael Palmer's Case Value Analyzer Methodology, and other non-traditional approaches.

Readers are encouraged to contact the author if they know of additional software for decision tree analysis.

[3] This is required by the laws of probabilities for "mutually exclusive and collectively exhaustive sets of events" like those of a specific branch cluster. Clemen, Robert T., *Making Hard Decisions: An Introduction to Decision Analysis*, (1996).

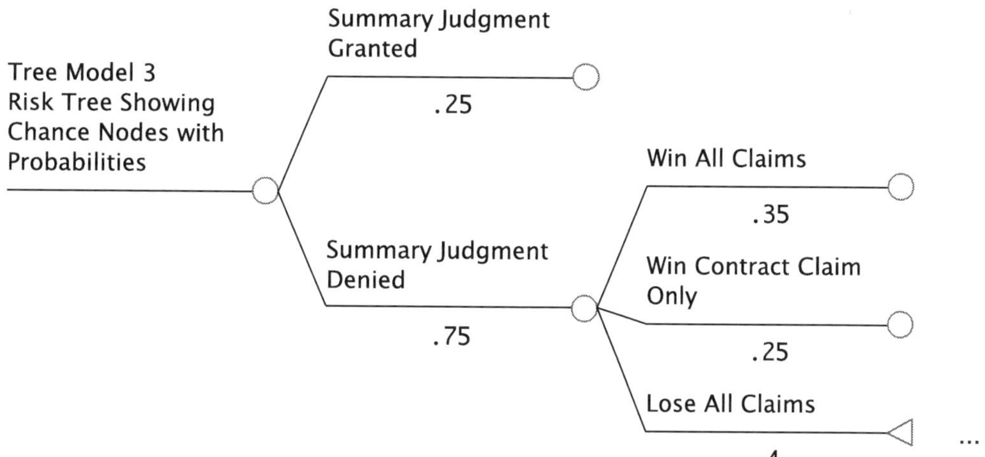

Terminal Nodes for Outcomes or "Payoffs" at the End[4] of Each Path

To the far right of the tree, at the end of each branch, there should be a "terminal node," represented by a triangle.

The following rather simple video explains and demonstrates placement of the terminal node.

Video 09: http://dx.doi.org/doi:10.7945/C25M4N

Usually, the "payoff" or net amount that will be lost or gained is written to the right of the terminal node.

The software-generated version follows.

Roll back to Estimated Monetary Value (EMV) a/k/a Discounted Value

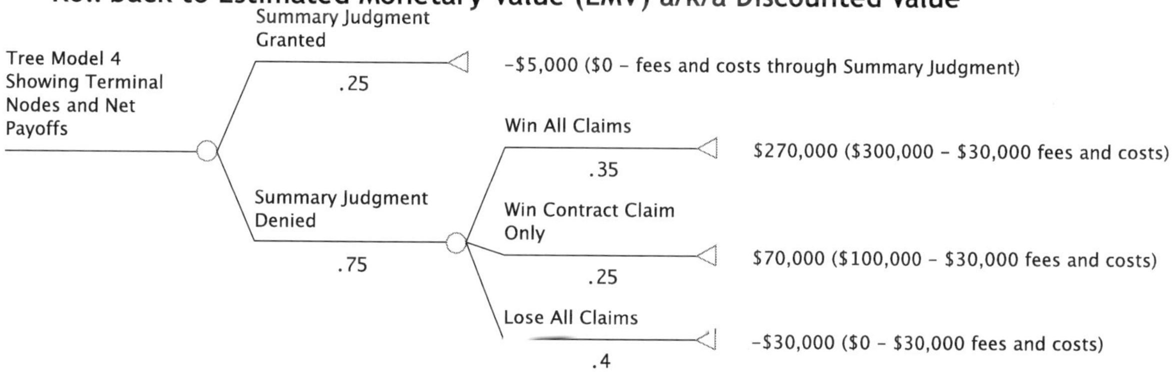

To "roll back" the tree is to calculate its discounted value by multiplying each possibility by its probability. As discussed earlier, in the literature of decision analysis, this is commonly referred to as the "Estimated Monetary Value" or "EMV." One way to "roll back" the numbers is to start at the far right of the tree and multiply each pay-off by the probability at that last branch, summing them at each cluster of branches, and then moving that sum forward as you multiply it by the likelihood of the next branch,

Lawyer Marc Victor, whose career has been in writing, training and consulting in decision analysis, further explains: "[T]he uncertainty must be capable of being resolved in at least one of the ways shown on the branches, in no more than one of the ways shown, and in no additional ways beyond those already shown." Victor, Marc B., "Interpreting a Decision Tree Analysis of a Lawsuit" (1998).

and so on, moving left after performing this operation at each layer of branches. The process moves from right to left.

The calculation can also be done at the right hand margin, by multiplying the probabilities from left to right along each path to obtain its cumulative probability, then multiplying each cumulative probability by the damages estimate at the end of the path, and then adding them up. Admittedly, this operation seems like the hard part. It will be unpacked, explained, and demonstrated quite thoroughly in the pages that follow.

The next video demonstrates how you might draw this tree and then "roll it back" by doing the math on the tree's form. Readers are encouraged to give it a try before watching.

Video 10: http://dx.doi.org/doi:10.7945/C21X2R

As explained above, the EMV or discounted value is the number yielded by the roll back operation. It is simply the weighted average of all of the possible outcomes, if the case were tried many, many (say 100) times.

The next tree is what the software generated image would look like, after the roll back.

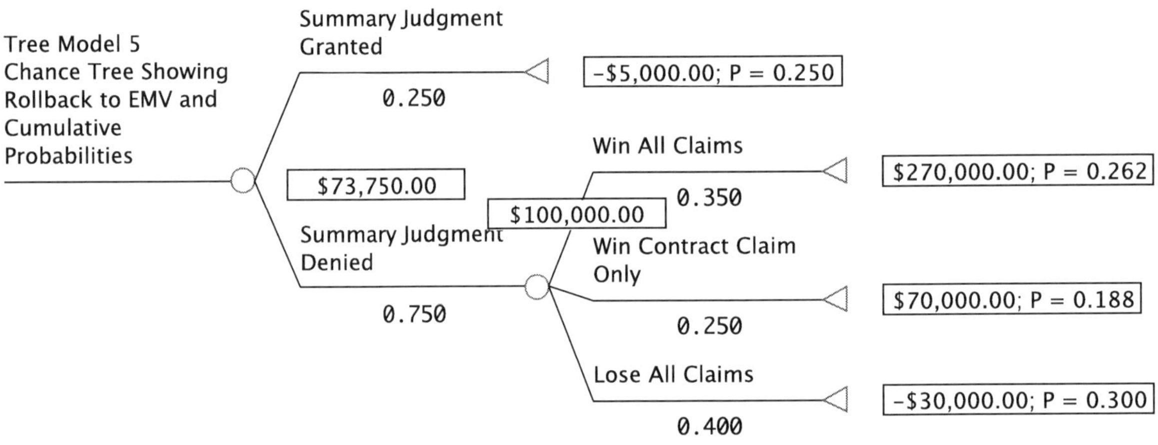

It's worth knowing and understanding the meaning of the $100,000 contained in the box on the left side of the branch cluster that comes after "Summary Judgment Denied." That $100,000 represents the sum of each possible outcome at the branch cluster to the right, multiplied by its probability. In other words, it is the result of:

- Multiplying the $270,000 "net outcome" or "pay-off" at the top terminal node by its 35% probability, which = $94,500;
- Multiplying the next terminal node net outcome of $70,000 by its 25% probability, which = $17,500;
- Multiplying the last terminal node net outcome of -$30,000 by its 30% probability, which = $12,000.

When you add these together, \$94,500 + \$17,500 + -\$12,000, the sum is \$100,000. Thus, the \$100,000 in that box is the EMV just at that branch cluster. Another way of thinking about it is that \$100,000 is the discounted value of the estimated net outcomes (damages or a defense verdict), if and only if you get past summary judgment. If summary judgment uncertainties are eliminated by the judges' denial of the motion, at that point in time, the EMV of the case would be \$100,000.

But right now, where summary judgment has not yet been decided, to get the overall current EMV, you have to account for the possibility of summary judgment. To calculate the current overall EMV, you would:

- Multiply the possible net outcome if summary judgment were granted, \$0 damages but -\$5000 in costs, by its 25% probability, which = -\$1,250; and
- Multiply the \$100,000 (representing the EMV of all branches to the right) by its 75% probability, which = \$75,000.

Add those together and you find that the EMV for the case at this point: \$73,750.

A reasonable and skeptical reader might ask: "Why multiply that \$100,000 by 75%? Didn't the \$100,000 already involve some multiplying? Yes. As we've seen, the \$100,000 was derived by looking at outcomes that might come *after denial* of *summary judgment*, multiplying each outcome by its probability. But remember, it's far from certain that we will get to that point. On this tree, we've decided there's only a 75% chance that will happen, because there's a 25% chance that summary judgment will be granted. Thus, we have to discount the \$100,000 value yet again, to account for its uncertainty—that the case is only 75% likely to get there.

As discussed in the video via link or url below, it's worth noting that each "P" on the far right hand side of the rolled-back tree refers to the cumulative probability of the outcome at the end of each possible path.

Video 11: http://dx.doi.org/doi:10.7945/C2X396

Having established standard terminology, symbols, graphics, and a few rules, it's time to work though some tree building examples, first for games of chance and then for litigation. The good news is that this text will walk through the math and roll back to the EMV many times again, enabling all readers to become entirely comfortable applying the method.

Encouragement for the Tentative

Those who remember encounters with word problems in elementary school math may also remember the awkward hesitation when first translating from verbal to symbol—math and graphics. Even when we understood the math operations, we might read a word problem, and have a moment or two of "oh gosh, how am I going to do that?!" before our brains could "see" how the words would translate to numbers and symbols. I hereby admit that, at the beginning, when tasked with constructing a decision tree for a case I could easily describe in words, it would suddenly feel like a great time to clean my office. And after that, I might start scribbling numbers on a pad, and then scratch out numbers that seemed in the wrong places or didn't fit together. Only after this bit of avoidance and pen-scratching would I tackle building the branches of the tree—the tree structure.

The truth is, with practice comes comfort and efficiency with word problems and decision trees. Now, I can build trees without much scribbling. It's all about practice. Hence, we move next to practicing with the tree format.

Playing Games On Trees

Before you start, an acknowledgment: the problems in Card Games #1 and #2 on the next few pages are quite similar to the problems used earlier to introduce the idea of cumulative probability and discounted value or EMV. The text asks the reader to try using a tree format to depict the decision or risk problem, and then provides suggested "answer" trees. These exercises are intended to familiarize the reader with where various components are placed and calculations shown in the "answer" trees. You will also see that, as the text moves through each of the Card Game problems, it begins to discuss issues of cost, timing, and risk tolerance. Those impatient with games may prefer to review the Card Game trees quickly, read the brief discussion of risk tolerance, avoidance, and emotion that follows, and then start the exercises that build trees for litigated case problems.

Card Game #1

Imagine that you have the opportunity to play a game of chance. To play, you must buy a deck of 100 cards that contains two card colors. Contained in the deck will be 50 blue cards and 50 red cards. Wearing a blindfold, you will pull a card from the deck. If you draw a blue card, you will win $100. If you draw a red card, you will win nothing.

Assume that the deck of cards costs $20.

You must decide whether to buy the deck or not. If you do buy the deck, then you will play.

The reader is invited to try to draw the tree and to roll it back. Of course, you are welcome to watch the next video, which demonstrates how to build the tree structure.

Video 12: http://dx.doi.org/doi:10.7945/C2SD79

Here's the neater, software-generated version.

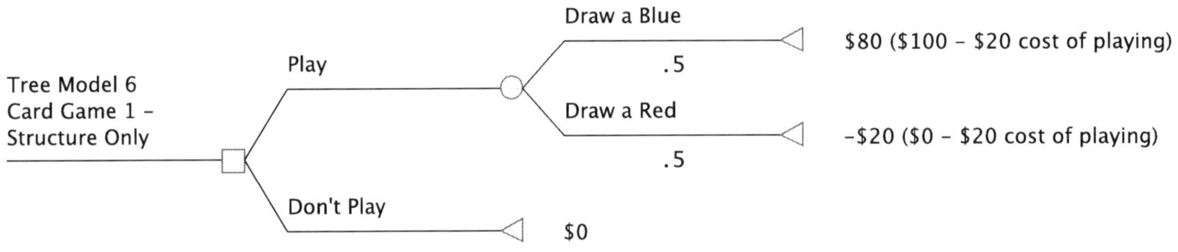

Now, here's a video that begins with the same tree and demonstrates how to go about the roll back calculations. For those who wish to skip the video, the text below it contains the explanation.

Video 13: http://dx.doi.org/doi:10.7945/C2NM40

Note that to roll back the tree, you start to the right of the terminal nodes, at the far right side. The numbers at the far right—used in the roll back calculations—must reflect the *net* payoffs. Thus, it's important to subtract the $20 cost of the deck from the payoffs earned in the game: $100 or $0. This makes the net payoffs at the two branches $80 and -$20. Multiply $80 x .5 (50% of the cards are blue) to get $40. Multiply -$20 x .5 (50% of the cards are red) to get -$10. Add the two together and the total is $30. That's the EMV of this very simple one-step tree.

Here's how the computer generated roll back would look.

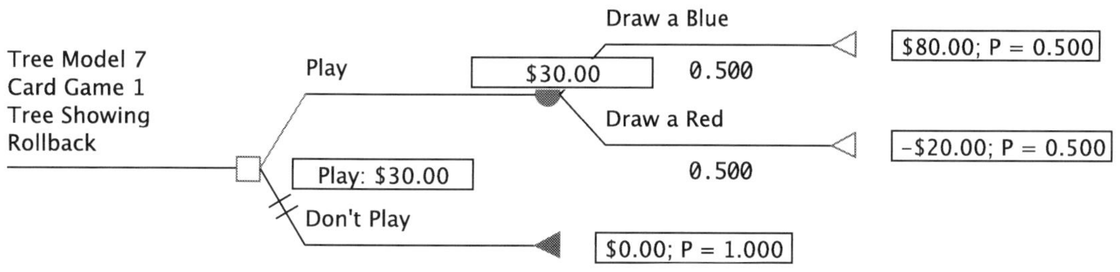

Remember, we haven't bought a deck for $20 yet. So, the question is whether it's better to do nothing—don't play at all and pay $0—or play the game with an EMV of $30 (after deducting the $20 deck cost from each payoff.)

Card Game #2

Now, imagine that a strolling magician with a standard deck of 52 cards wanders by. He assures you that it's a "regular deck" with half black suit cards and half red suit cards. Assume for now that it costs nothing to play the game. The rules are that he will hold the cards face down.

- If you draw a black suited card on your first try, and any red suited card on your second try, you will win at least $50.
- However, if the red suited card you draw on the second try happens to be a red heart (instead of a red diamond), your winnings will be $150.
- If you draw a red card on the FIRST round, you will lose nothing and gain nothing. However, you cannot go on to a next round. Game over.
- But if you draw a black card on the second round, you will lose $60. (Note, whenever you draw a card, you show it to the magician but then put it back into the deck, so the odds don't change.)

Before you draw the tree, just take a second to recognize that it's not so easy to picture the flow or do the roll back math in your head.

Here's how the tree would look.

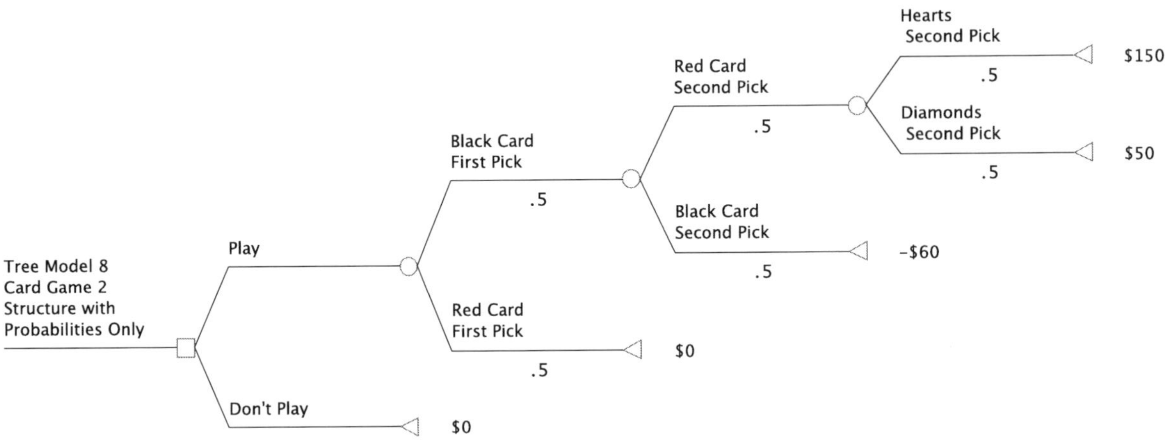

Video 14: http://dx.doi.org/doi:10.7945/C2HX3G

The next video reviews how the roll back would be done, and that's of course followed by a neater, software generated version.

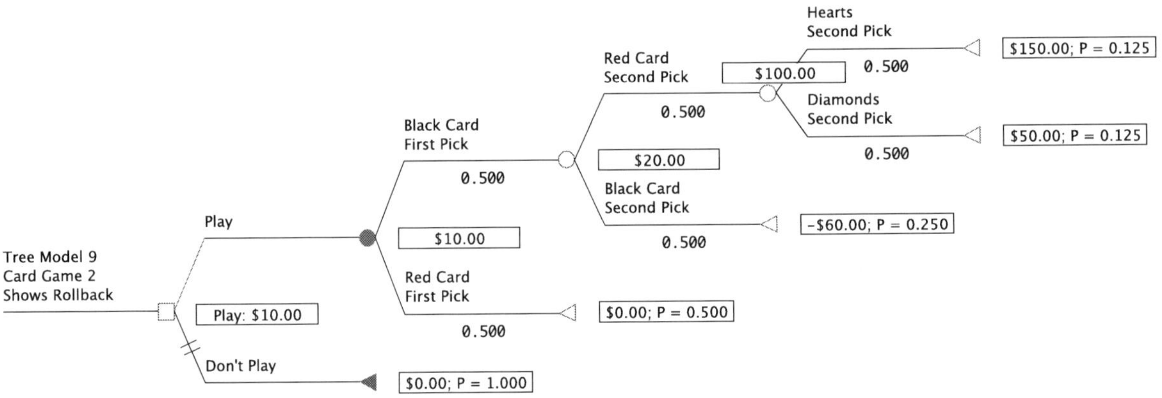

Video 15: http://dx.doi.org/doi:10.7945/C2D40G

The EMV is only $10. Maybe it would be worth playing if I wouldn't feel too bad about a possible $60 loss. What are the chances of losing that $60? The answer is 25%, reached by multiplying the probabilities along the black-suit-first-round and black-suit-second-round path of the tree: .5 x .5 = .25 (25%).

What are the chances of winning $150? To find that out, follow the path of possibilities and probabilities, from black-suit-first-round (.5), to red-suit-second round (.5), to the chance that it's a red heart instead of a diamond (.5). So the overall probability of winning $150 is 12.5% (.5 x .5 x .5 = .125).

What if the magician will require you to pay $10 just to play the game?

Here's the way you would construct and calculate the tree with after subtracting the $10 cost from the payoffs.

Video 16: http://dx.doi.org/doi:10.7945/C28D81

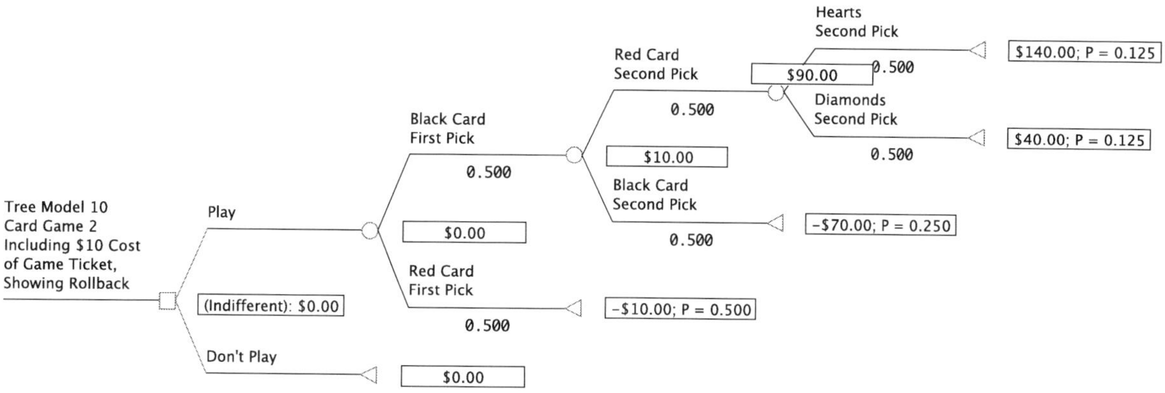

Here the EMV is down to ZERO!

Card Game #3

This game varies the cost of playing. This time, assume you have already paid an admission fee of $10 just to enter the booth and then you meet the magician before he sets up the card game. Now the rules are:

- There is no additional cost for playing a first round.
- If you draw a red diamond card in the first round, you will win $50 and you will be eligible to play a second round without additional payment. (It is your decision whether to play or not at this point.) In the second round, if you again draw a red diamond card, you will win an additional $500 (added to the $50 won in the first round). If you draw any other red card (presumably a heart), you will win an additional $250 (added to the $50 won in the first round).
- If, after that red diamond draw in the first round (winning $50), you decide to play again, and then draw a black suit card in the second round, you will lose $50. So, your yield will be a total of $0.
- If you draw a red heart card in the first round, you have to pay $20 in order to play a second round. If you draw a red heart again, you will win $100. If you draw a red diamond in that second round, you will lose $50.
- If you draw a black suit card in the first round, you win nothing. You may decide to play a second round, but that will cost an additional $100.
- If you drew a black suit card in the first round and then again in the second round, you will win $60.
- If you drew a black suit card in the first round and then a red suit card in the second round, you will win $1,000.
- You should assume a regular deck, with ¼ cards that are diamonds, ¼ hearts, ¼ spades, and ¼ clubs. And remember that we replace each card after drawing it, so the odds stay the same.

What would your tree look like? How about the roll back?

Before you build this tree, the author acknowledges that this sounds complicated. But if you build the tree methodically, it will be less difficult than it seems. The good news is that if you can do this one, you've made real progress.

The video below demonstrates how to structure the tree, before the roll back.

Video 17: http:.//dx.doi.org/doi:10.7945/C24M63

And here's what it would look like, generated on the computer.

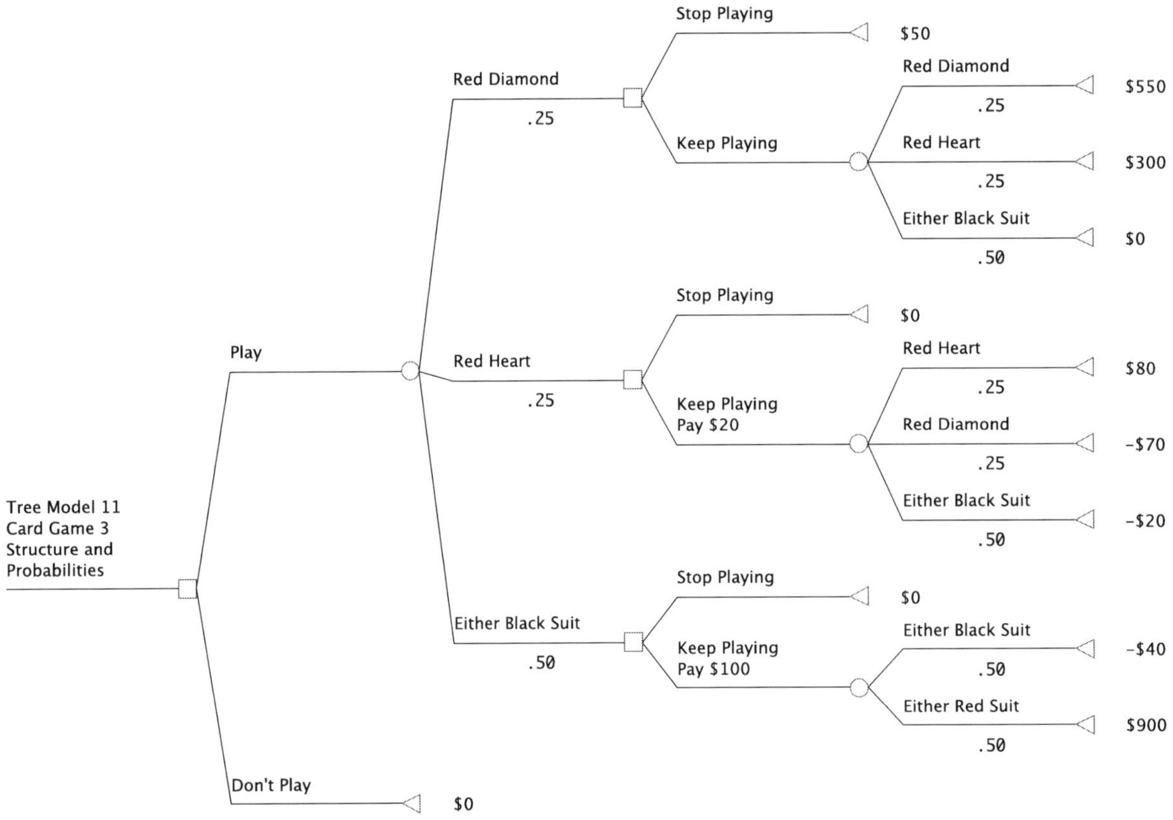

The next video works through a hand drawn and calculated roll back operation and its results. As usual, the neater software version follows.

Video 18: http://dx.doi.org/doi:10.7945/C20X2F

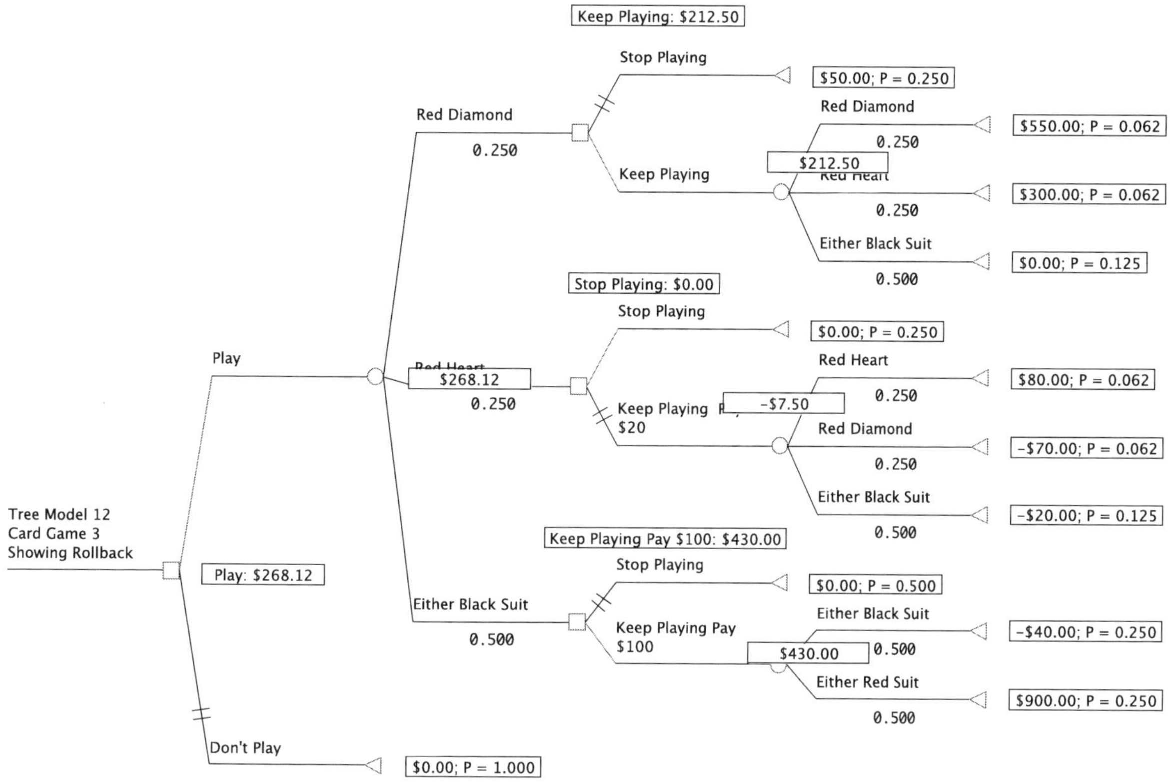

Note the two lines // intersecting some of the post-decision node branches on this tree. These are the software's way of communicating its recommendation not to choose that branch path. It assumes the recommendation will be followed and uses only probabilities along the other paths to calculate the EMV.

One question this may raise is: what about that original $10 paid to enter the magician's booth? Should it be added to the tree as a net cost? The answer is no! Remember, unlike the previous game in which we were deciding whether or not to pay and play, here the expenditure has already been made. It's a sunk cost. The only cost that should be subtracted from the pay-off is one we have not yet paid, but will incur along the way.

Card Game #4

Finally, the last game before practice problems on legal cases.

This time, imagine that same regular deck of cards. There will only be one round of play—one chance to draw from the deck. You may decide to play or not, but you do not have to pay to play.

- If you draw a red diamond, you will lose $100.
- If you draw a red heart, you will win $50.
- If you draw a black spade, you will win $200.
- If you draw a black club, you will win $200.

What would the tree look like?

The next two videos and printed trees demonstrate different ways you might go about building the tree.

Video 19: http://dx.doi.org/doi:10.7945/C2W416

The printed version is shown below.

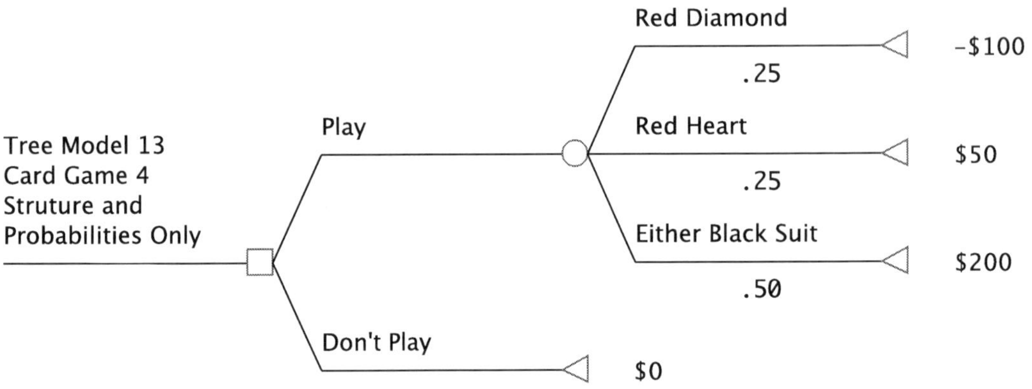

You could also have done it as shown in this second video.

Video 20: http://dx.doi.org/doi:10.7945/C2RD70

Now, here's the printed version of the tree.

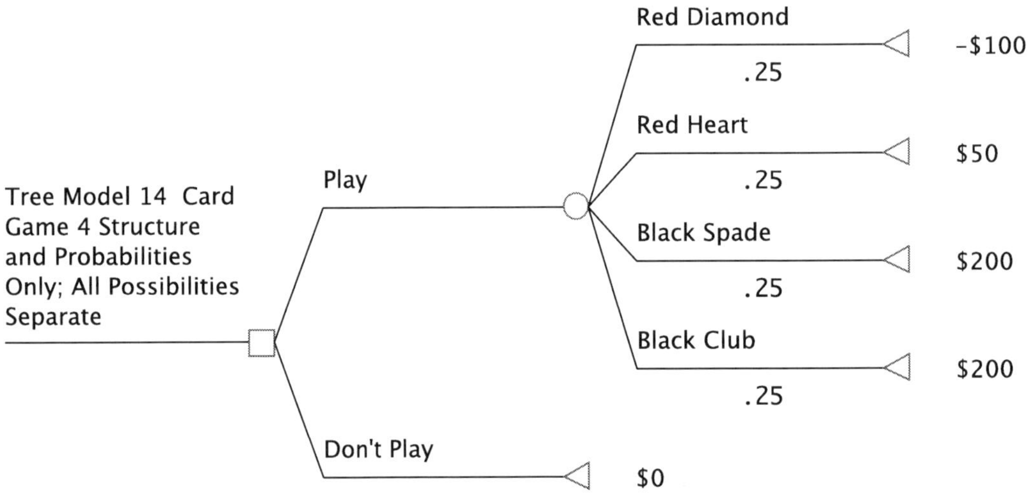

The next video demonstrates how you would roll it back to the EMV, on both trees.

Video 21: http://dx.doi.org/doi:10.7945/C2MQ3B

Note that the roll back results to the EMV are exactly the same as are the cumulative probabilities for each dollar amount. Either way is correct.

Here's the software-generated version showing the roll back operation.

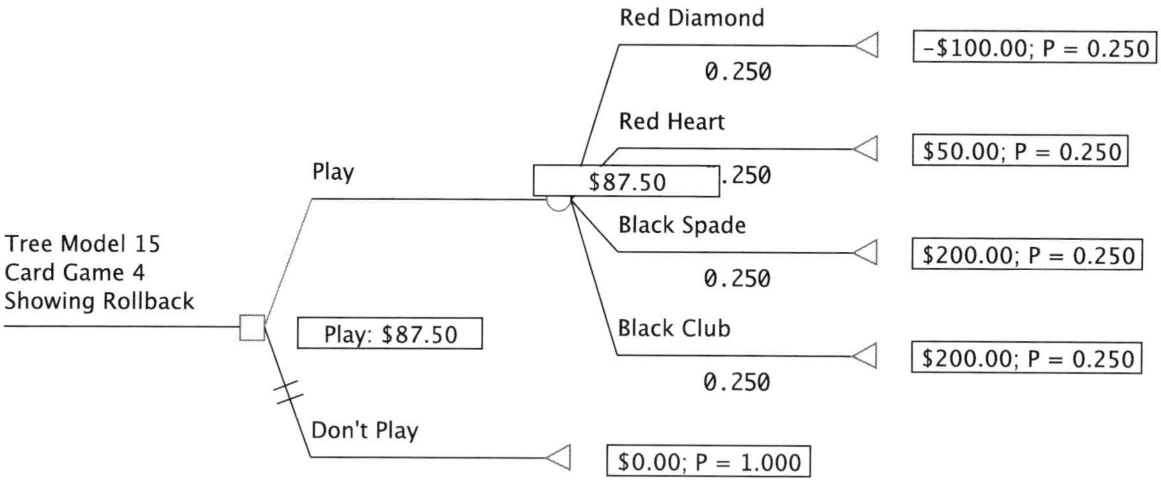

When is it okay or even better practice to collapse branches for a combined probability? T he answer is: when everything (costs, payouts and probabilities) AFTER that point would have been the same along each branch. Collapsing the branches (and combining their probabilities) creates a less cluttered tree. That's less important when we're playing card games, but more so when mapping the inevitable complexity of a real case.

Abstractions of Risk Tolerance, Avoidance, and Emotion are Real

Before we leave the realm of the abstract, it's worth considering how we might play differently or feel differently about playing, if the possible gains and losses were much larger. What if you could win or lose tens of thousands or hundreds of thousands, or more? And what if you could play each game hundreds of times and average the results?

Everyone's general, personal tolerance for risk is different. While most of us prefer certain gains over risky options, our break points differ. If presented with the opportunity to toss a coin or pick a card for the chance to win $10,000, I might be very happy to take $2,500 instead. Others might hold out for an offer of $4,000 or $5,000 or more.

Leaving aside personality driven attitudes toward risk, circumstances will affect our responses. Today, even I might be willing to risk a $500 loss for say, a $3,500 gain (the price of a modest vacation). If I lose $500, I won't be happy but I'll still eat. My response might have been different in student days. On the other hand, a decision between two alternatives where there is only an upside (win much or nothing) feels very different from a decision between two alternatives where you may win but also risk losses—an obligation to pay. Finally, our decisions would no doubt be different if we were to play a game many, many times and take the average (as an insurer might) versus one time only.[4]

[4] A brief additional discussion of working with risk aversion or risk tolerance can be found in Chapter Eight. More extensive discussion of risk preferences and risk tolerance and how these may be graphed and factored into decision analysis for an individual can be found in various books included in the reference and bibliography section, including (at least): Clemen, Robert T., *Making Hard Decisions: An Introduction to Decision Analysis* (1996); Raiffa, Howard, *Decision Analysis: Introductory Lectures on Choices Under Uncertainty* (1968); Raiffa,

Moving to Real Fake Cases

Imagine that you are plaintiff's counsel (in an hourly fee case), and you have explained the future litigation path to the client. The client then summarizes:

> Okay, *here's how I understand what might happen: If I win and get summary judgment in our favor, I will collect $300,000 in damages but I will pay $20,000 in attorneys' fees between now and then. If I lose on summary judgment but prevail on liability, I will pay an additional $40,000 in attorneys' fees through trial but will collect $300,000 in damages. If there is contributory negligence I will receive only $240,000 assuming 20% contributory negligence. However, if the defendant is bankrupt it will be a long time before I see a dime.*

Try to draw what the structure of the tree might look like, WITHOUT percentages, before peeking at the tree below:

Video 22: http://dx.doi.org/doi:10.7945/C2GX1D

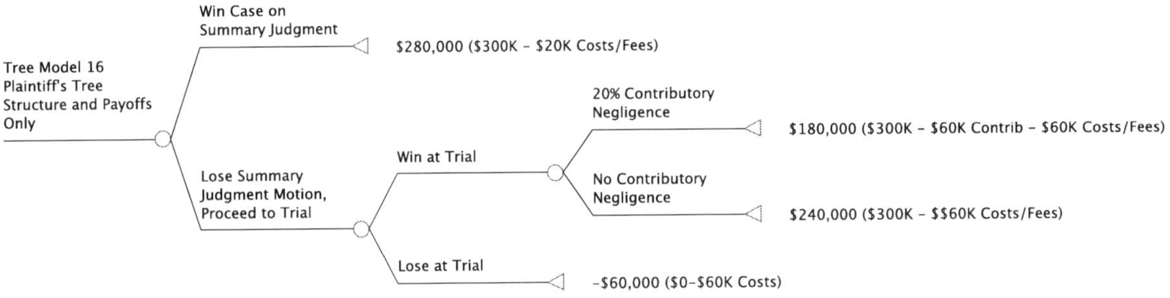

Next the client asks, "Well, what are the chances of all of this?" You respond:

> *Well generally, it's hard for a plaintiff to get summary judgment. Still, we have an okay chance, making it worthwhile to file because so much of the discovery evidence was uncontested. I do think you are very likely to win on liability, but I am concerned about some small but significant chance of a contributory negligence finding. And based on what I see of their balance sheet, the defendant's chances of staying afloat financially are pretty dismal.*

Here's what the tree would look like with the probabilities written in prose, first demonstrated and explained in the video and then shown with a printed tree.

Howard; Richardson, John; and Metcalfe, David. *Negotiation Analysis: The Science and Art of Collaborative Decision Making* (2007); and Hammond, Keeney, and Raiffa, Howard, *Smart Choices: A Practical Guide to Making Better Life Decisions* (1999).

Video 23: http://dx.doi.org/doi:10.7945/C2C68W

In fact, just seeing it mapped out this way, with prose instead of numerical percentages, may be very

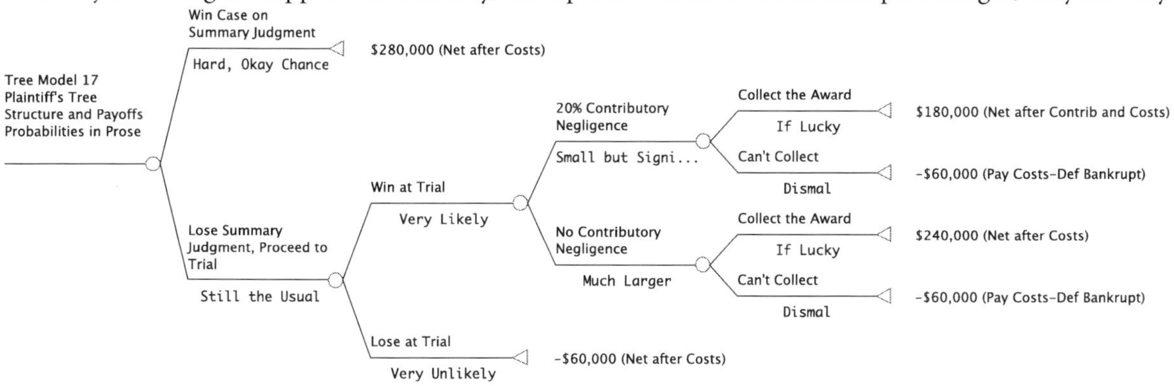

helpful to some clients.

But to do anything more with the tree, it's necessary to supply percentages for two reasons:

1) You can't roll back the tree, or even see the cumulative probabilities for each outcome without percentages along the way.
2) The prose will very, very often mean different things to different people. To you, "very likely" may mean 65%, but to your client, it may mean 85% or more. "Small but significant" may mean 25% to you, and 10% to your client, and so on. (Chapter Ten includes a more detailed discussion of this point.)

Percentages' Protection against Under or Over Inclusive Possibilities

As stated earlier, in order for decision tree analysis to have any claim to validity, the probabilities of the branches in each branch cluster following a chance node must sum to 100%, not more and not less. That's a hard rule, dictated by the rules of probability that are the foundation for a decision analytic approach.

After all, a chance node represents a significant juncture of uncertainty. When a future event is marked by a chance node, it means we know something will happen here, but we don't control it. Even as we seek impact, we still lack the power to determine what will happen. Thus, a chance node is followed by branches that represent POSSIBILITIES—the possible twists a case might take, the way a judge might rule on key evidence, the jury's decision to award punitive damages or not, etc. If probabilities assigned to these branches are lower than 100%, it means that we have underweighted or missed a possible branch; if the probabilities add up to more than 100%, then we have over weighted at least one branch and/or added a branch that should not be there. The branches must be mutually exclusive; their possibilities cannot overlap.

Consider the following example: could it be that, at noon today, there is a 40% chance of all sun, a 40% of complete cloudiness, and a 60% chance of mixed clouds and sun? That can't be right: these probabilities total 140%. For decision analysis (whether to bring sunglasses), we would have to ask the weatherman for separate probabilities of sun only, clouds only, and a cloud-sun combination that add up to 100% (assuming a 0% chance of precipitation).

Taking this into a personal injury suit, we can't have a 60% chance of a negligence finding, a 40% chance of a causation finding, and a 40% chance of a no liability finding. Negligence and causation are not mutually exclusive. But both are necessary. Thus, if there's really only a 40% chance that the jury will find causation, then there must be a 60% chance of no causation.[5] Moreover, if there's only an independent 60% chance of establishing negligence (for example, by failure to meet a defined standard of care), and a 60% chance of establishing causation—both are in doubt and both essential elements of a liability finding—then the total probability of liability is only 36%. [.6 x .6 =.36]

In my view, this mathematical rule of a 100% sum for each cluster of branches, combined with a careful deliberative process for estimating probabilities are strong reasons to eschew mere adjectives about likelihood and insist on percentages instead. Why?

First, when writing in prose and imagining what might happen next, it is easy to miss a possibility. Counsel might observe that summary judgment could be won or lost, but fail to notice a theory by which the judge could grant the motion in part. When sketching out a decision tree, the best practice is to ask: are these all the branches? Do they add up? Could there be another possibility? Have we missed something? Somehow, the act of drawing and seeing those branches arrayed on the page focuses our attention on what we might have missed.

Secondly, the method's requirement to use numerical probabilities tends to generate reflective dialogue, with oneself, a colleague, or the client. Saying "quite a strong chance" is easy. Saying "65%" suggests more care. And, it tends to inspire more care. When asking himself what he really thinks the percentage chances are of getting past summary judgment, the lawyer ruminates over the theories and arguments: "What have I missed? Why am I having trouble with percentages of summary judgment or not. Maybe it's not that simple. Let me look at their brief again...ahhh, I suppose it's possible possibile that the judge will take just that one argument seriously and grant partial summary judgment!" Through this process, otherwise neglected issues rise to the surface for thoughtful consideration.

Robust Structure With A Simple Approach

All that's required to build an entirely robust tree for a legal case is curiosity, patience, familiarity with the basics, and someone with thorough knowledge of the case (not necessarily the tree builder). Really, even the most complex tree can be constructed based upon the responses to a series of simple questions:

- What will happen next?
- What will happen after that?
- Is that the only possibility?
- What if that first possibility is the one that happens, then what?
- If you go to trial and liability is found, what are the likely damages?
- What will happen with a stingy jury, a reasonable jury, and a generous jury?

Even though the plaintiff and the defense may estimate different probabilities and damage numbers, the structure of the tree is usually about the same on both sides.

[5] See the section titled "Avoid a Natural Mistake of the Methodical", later in the chapter, for a word of caution regarding deconstructing separate legal elements of a claim or defense. It is important to structure a tree and estimated probabilities to be as consistent as possible with the way we anticipate a jury would approach its decision.

Below are a few simplified hypothetical legal case examples to practice drawing and rolling back a tree.

Simple Hypothetical—Plaintiff's Perspective

The parties will soon commence settlement negotiations in a simple case. Assume:

- If no settlement is reached, defense will move for summary judgment. Plaintiff has an 80% chance of defeating the summary judgment motion.
- Plaintiff has a 60% chance of winning at trial.
- If the plaintiff wins at trial, the damages award will clearly be $150,000.
- The plaintiff has a 1/3 contingency fee agreement. Expert fees are deducted AFTER deduction of the attorney's fee.
- Expert fees of $10,000 will be incurred after summary judgment motions through trial.
- If there is no recovery, the attorney knows he will not enforce the plaintiff's obligation to reimburse expert's fees (Assume the plaintiff has minimal surplus disposable income or savings).

Try to draw the tree and insert the probabilities and NET payoffs given. Then perform the roll back calculation to arrive at an EMV from the plaintiff's perspective.

The next video explains and demonstrates how to draw the structure, and is followed by the printed tree.

Video 24: http://dx.doi.org/doi:10.7945/C27D6Z

Now, here's roll back operation on the tree, first as a video and then in printed form.

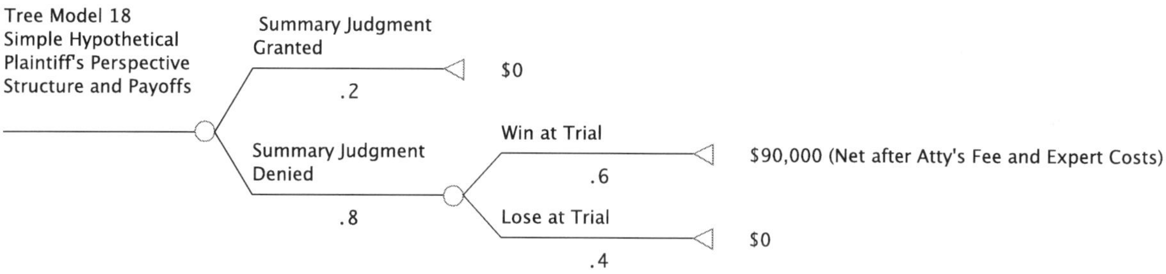

Video 25: http://dx.doi.org/doi:10.7945/C23Q42

As shown, because the plaintiff will have to pay the expert's fee and the attorney's fee (1/3) from the award, they should both be subtracted. The "Simple Hypothetical" states that the lawyer will not seek to

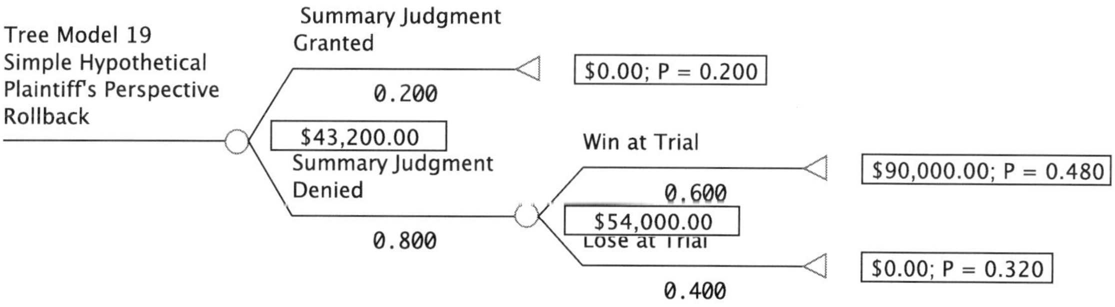

collect the expert's fee (which was advanced) if there is a defense verdict. So, it would only be deducted in the event of a plaintiff's verdict.

Simple Hypothetical—Defendant's Perspective

The parties will soon commence settlement negotiations in a simple case. Assume:

- Absent a settlement, defense will move for summary judgment. You estimate an 80% chance of plaintiff's defeating the summary judgment.
- You estimate that the plaintiff has a 60% chance of winning at trial (which means your client would have a 40% chance of no liability finding).
- If the plaintiff wins at trial, the damages award will clearly be $150,000.
- Significant discovery has been completed and $15,000 in fees have already been billed and paid.
- Defense fees from this moment through the summary judgment motion are estimated at $5,000.
- Defense fees *after* arguments on the summary judgment motion, through trial preparation and trial, are estimated to be $20,000.
- Expert fees of $10,000 will be incurred through trial (but after summary judgment motions).

Try to draw the tree and insert the probabilities and NET payoffs given. Then perform the roll back calculation to arrive at an EMV from the defendant's perspective.

A suggested tree structure and then the roll back are demonstrated and explained in the next two videos.

Video 26: http://dx.doi.org/doi:10.7945/C2ZX1R

Video 27: http://dx.doi.org/doi:10.7945/C2V70J

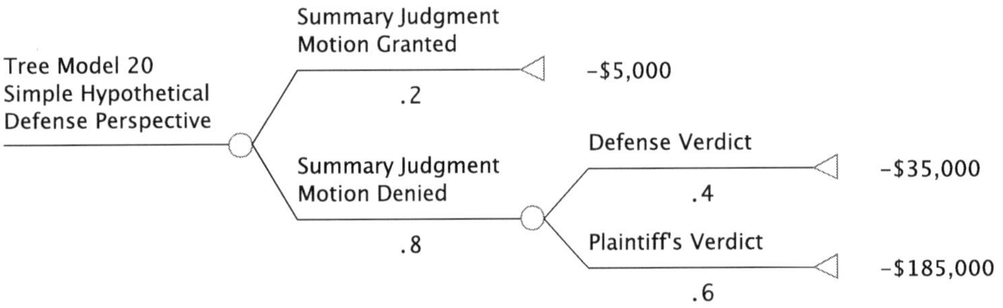

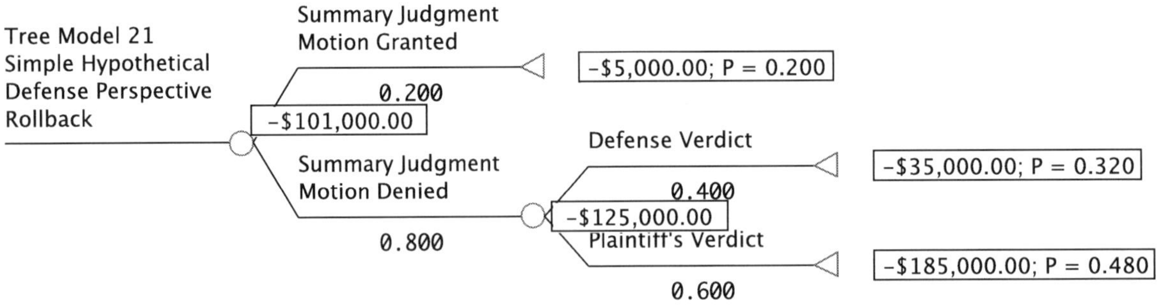

Note: the trees above keep past costs out and future cost in! ONLY fees and costs to be expended or received from the then current moment forward should be added to or subtracted from any anticipated award to arrive at the payout figure used for calculation. In other words, sunk costs—past expenditures on attorneys' fees—should NOT be included in the end payouts, even as negative numbers or losses. The same is true for attorney's fees already incurred, even if they haven't yet been invoiced or paid. They are still an obligation incurred before the tree's construction and any current decision. *The decision tree looks FORWARD in time, and asks what would be a good decision now, based on what will or might happen and its potential costs and benefits.*

Often, this is particularly important when working with the defense side (or any client who has already incurred attorney's and expert's fees). Psychologically or emotionally, they want to "count" these: they don't want to consider settling for any amount that doesn't seem to justify their expenditures. This psychological/emotional component is strong, real, and normal. But it doesn't change the logic (and good sense) that sunk costs should have no part in current decisions. In fact, explaining to a business client that this method "won't allow" past expenditures can be helpful. You are just following the rules of the method. And you can always write down the past expenditures somewhere on the page—just don't enter them onto the tree.

Closer to Reality

Try drawing and calculating a tree for this somewhat more realistic case problem below about an injury to a gymnast, titled "Balanced Trees on Balance Beams."

Balanced Trees on Balance Beams

You represent the defendant, American Steel Company, in a case involving the collapse of a civic center during a gymnastics competition. The plaintiff, Robin Lancer,[6] was a 12-year-old gymnast performing a balance beam routine at the time of the collapse. She suffered multiple injuries and was hospitalized for three days following the incident. She also suffered the emotional trauma of the event, particularly from watching her best friend (another talented gymnast) die as a section of the roof crashed upon her. Robin's lasting injury initially appeared to be to her wrist. Her primary care physician diagnosed carpal tunnel syndrome and Robin underwent surgery for the condition. Unfortunately, the surgery led to only marginal improvement. Based upon further expert review of Robin's medical records and the condition of her wrist, one expert has stated that he believes she suffered a disc injury in her back, which is causing weakness in her wrist and arm. The expert report discussing this analysis was provided to Robin and her counsel just days prior to the mediation. Robin plans additional tests regarding her medical condition, but all parties decided to go ahead with the mediation process. If the disc is determined to be causing or contributing to Robin's symptoms, she may or may not decide to have disc surgery, depending upon the precise diagnosis and physician's recommendations.

Robin sued American Steel Company under a strict liability theory—that its steel bars failed, causing the accident. American Steel Company brought in the concrete supplier, Acme Concrete, alleging that faulty mixing and an inappropriate installation of the concrete caused the accident—that there was

[6] Fact pattern derived from: Perry, Janet, G., "Counseling and Negotiation—The Settlement of Lancer v. American Steel," *Professional Responsibility for Lawyers, A Guided Course* (1991).

nothing wrong with the steel reinforcing bars. Acme Concrete is insolvent, and filed for bankruptcy protection prior to this litigation.

First, draw the neutral tree—get the structure. Then, supply some wildly hypothetical numbers that sound right to you. Do the calculations: roll back the tree to an EMV before taking a look at the author's version below.

Video 28: http://dx.doi.org/doi:10.7945/C2QD7P

As you can see, if there's any complexity at all, structuring the decision tree involves judgment. You may

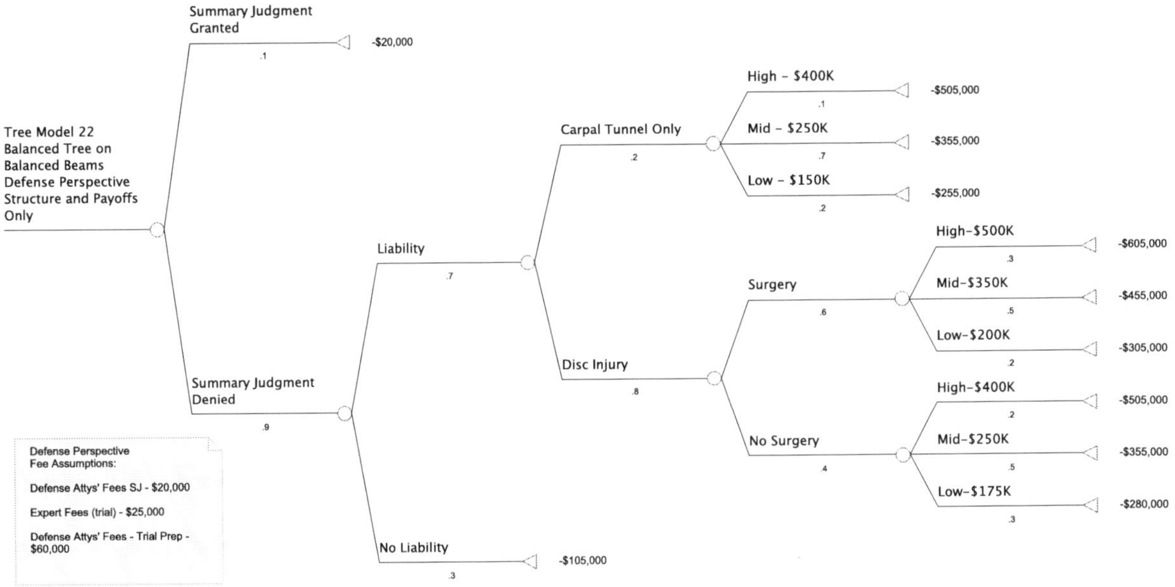

have created a different tree structure that is also a worthy map of the case, maybe better.

Focusing on the tree shown here, you can see that it boils the liability question down to whether (and the probability that) the defendant will avoid liability entirely. Because the other defendant is bankrupt, if this defendant is liable for 1%, he's on the hook for all of it. Building the parts of the tree structure related to jury findings and damages questions involves judgment calls too. As you can see, it branches in two directions where different factual findings will lead to very different damages calculations. So, if the plaintiff is found "just" to have carpal tunnel syndrome and not a back injury, some of the damages components would be very different (surgery vs. no surgery). These are legitimate possibilities (reflected as branches) to consider and discuss when structuring the tree. The version shown is just one cut at the problem. In a real case, the attorney's analysis—whatever it is—would direct the structure of the tree and the damages numbers. And that would of course be discussed with the client.

Here's how it would roll back to an EMV as well as the cumulative probabilities of each outcome. Given the number of calculations, it makes sense to move at this point in the text to the neater, computer-generated version below. The roll back operation and calculations are done in exactly the same way as shown in earlier hand-drawn examples on video.

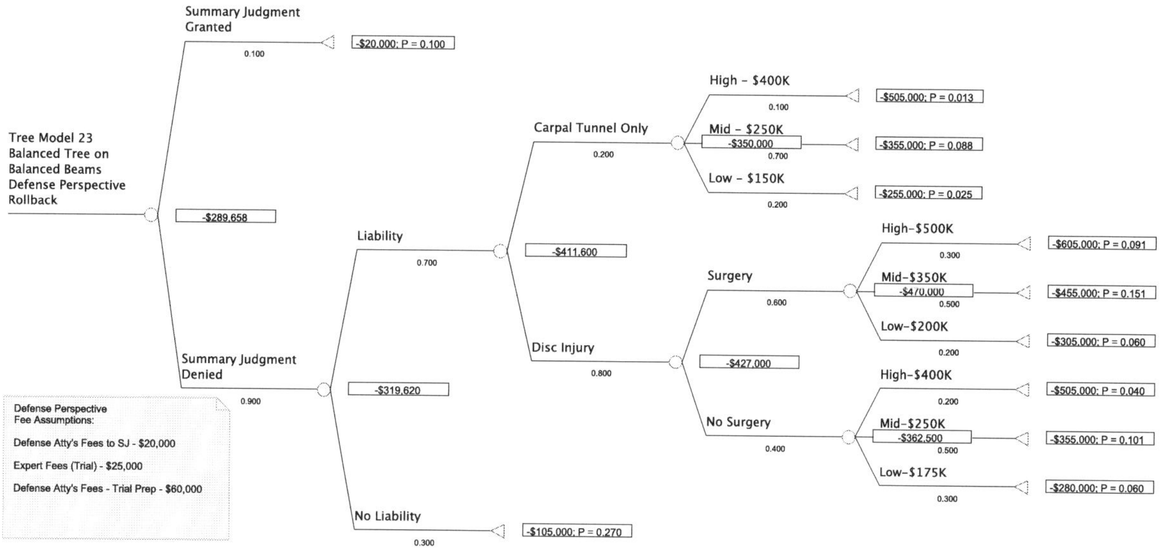

Avoid a Natural Mistake of the Methodical

One mistake many novice lawyer tree-builders make when constructing their first tree is to automatically start the tree by drawing separate branches for each requisite element of a legal claim. After all, we're trying to think carefully and methodically about legal doctrine. Our law school professor would ask us to recite the necessary legal elements.

Usually, these appear as a stacked set of branches. For example, in a personal injury claim, the plaintiff must demonstrate: duty, breach of duty, causation, and injury. So, the novice might instinctively begin by sketching out:

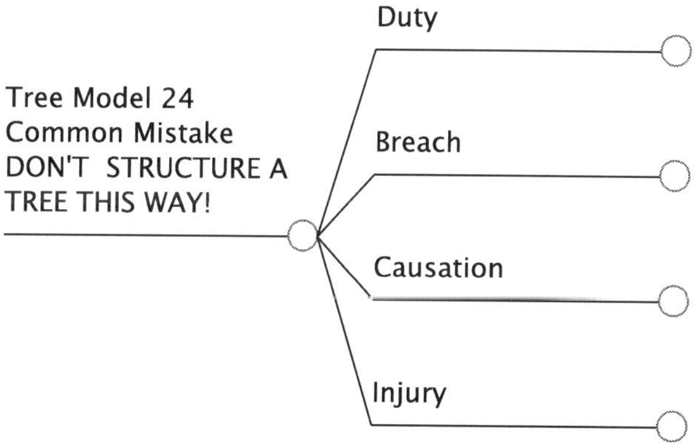

There are (at least) two problems with this approach. First, none of the individual branches lead you anywhere. Assume that duty will be established—then what? Then you also have to establish breach of that duty, then causation, then injury.

On a decision tree, each branch has to lead you to a next step, a next question. Even though they are the four prongs of a test for liability, that doesn't necessarily make them four legitimate branches on a tree.

Just as important, the branches and paths following a chance node must be mutually *exclusive.* Clearly, these are not. Indeed the opposite is true. We need all of them to succeed.

The fact that they are not mutually exclusive will become clear when you try to assign probabilities. If none of the prongs are in doubt—each will be assigned probabilities of 1.0 or 100%—making the total 400%. That can't be right.

More realistically, some of the elements will be quite certain—undisputed—and others not.[7] For example, consider a case in which a customer slipped and fell on carrot juice in a grocery store aisle. Assume it has been acknowledged that the store owes a duty to its customers. However, breach of that duty is very much in doubt: the store claims it had no notice of the spill, or the condition of the floor was perfectly fine. Let's assume further that causation is questioned, as the defense alleges that the plaintiff's injuries were entirely pre-existing, or that the reason she fell was her preposterously precarious shoes, not the floor. Her injuries and medical expenses are not in doubt.

Here's what you would see if you tried to assign probabilities to the branches, reflecting the fact that the duty and the injury were clear, but there's some uncertainty regarding breach of that duty (estimated 60% likely) and causation (estimated 70% likely).

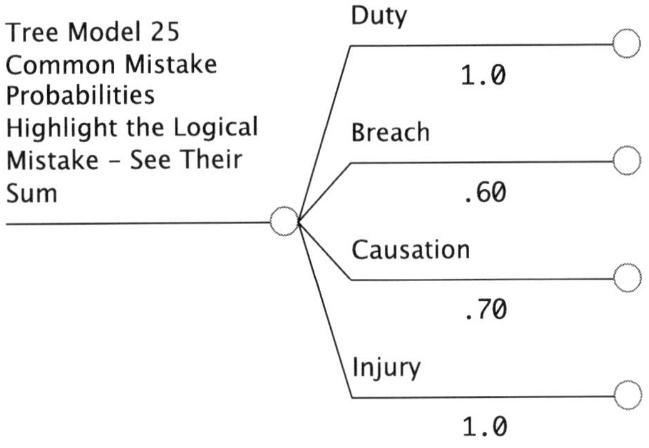

These add up to considerably more than 100%! Even if you include branches for only those elements in doubt—breach and causation—they do not (and need not logically) add up to 100% because they are not mutually exclusive.

As a technical matter, the required elements of a legal claim could be introduced as sets of branches that, together, address the liability question. Let's assume that summary judgment is not a concern (hasn't been raised or has been decided for the plaintiff). One could construct a tree using the contested elements of negligence as follows next.

[7] See the discussion in Heavin, Heather and Keet, Michaela, "Litigation Risk Analysis: Using Rigorous Projections to Encourage and Inform Settlement," *Journal of Arbitration and Mediation* (forthcoming): 15, suggesting that "allowing *de minimis* concerns to tip towards 100% prediction means that the lawyer can focus the risk assessment on true areas of uncertainty in the case."

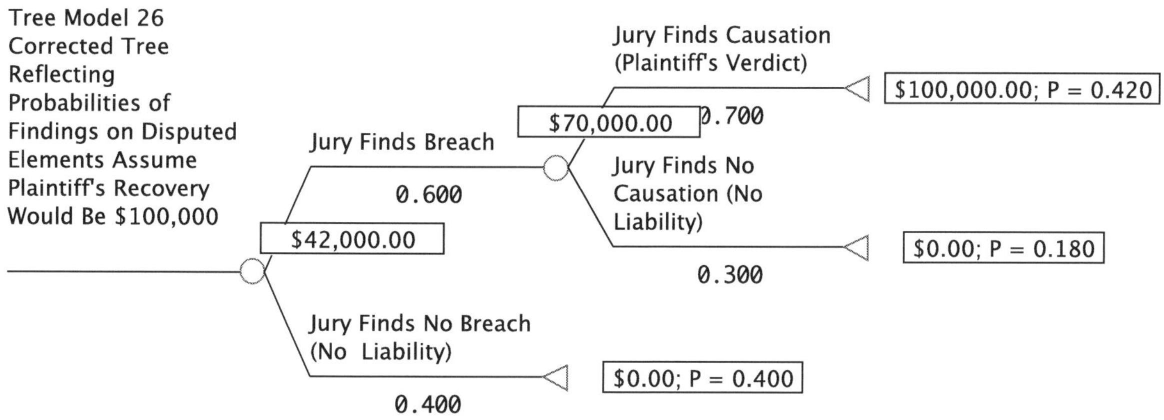

In this case, since you need breach of duty AND causation, the cumulative probability of liability would be only 42% (.6 x .7).

The question is: does that sound right? If the tree-builder lawyer REALLY thinks a jury will look at these questions entirely separately, and the same jury that finds breach of duty is still no more than 70% likely to find causation, then the 42% would be the overall likelihood of liability. Not pleasant for the plaintiff or her lawyer to hear, but the mathematical result of cumulative probability, appropriately applied.

On the other hand, plaintiff's lawyer may be right to argue that this is a distortion because the jury will not view elements separately but will more holistically decide whether the defendant grocery store is liable. Or, he may argue that, even if the jury works through each element of the claim, as instructed, the jury that finds breach of duty, is far more likely to also find causation than "just any" jury. In other words, the jury that finds breach of duty may be 90% likely to *also* find causation—putting the cumulative probability of liability at 54% (60% x 90%).

The Natural and Optimal Order of Things

A not-always-obvious choice for the tree builder is how to order sets of branches on the tree. Following basic junctures within the case timeline is natural, easy, and good practice. So, if motions to dismiss will be filed before motions for summary judgment, branches mapping possibilities for the motion to dismiss would naturally come before, or to the left of motions for summary judgment.

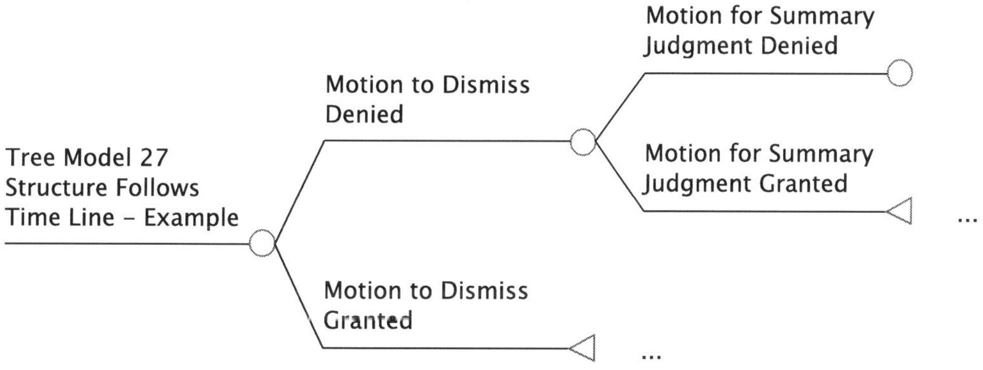

The same would be true for specific critical uncertainties in discovery (if you choose to put these on the main tree). These would unfold earlier in time than any ruling on a summary judgment motion. Indeed, they would likely impact the strength of the motion, or perhaps the chance that one will be filed.

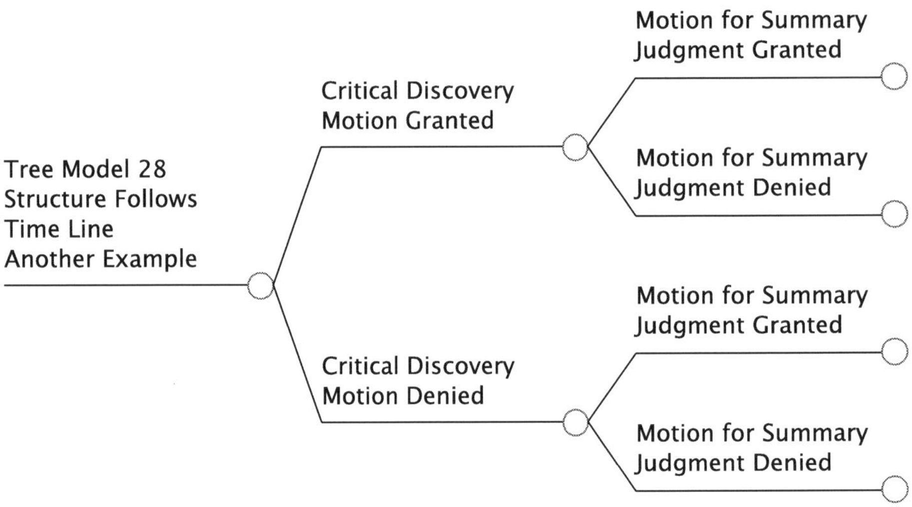

Though "earlier in time" is a helpful criterion for ordering the various sets of branches, it is often not operative. We don't know the order in which a judge or jury will consider the evidence and theories in a case. Indeed, "jury deliberation" has a black box quality. Unless the jurors are asked to consider and answer particular, directed questions, it's hard to say how they actually sift through what they have seen and heard.

Timing aside, it's important to consider two additional criteria for deciding whether a set of branches —really a set of grouped possibilities—should come earlier or later, meaning further to the left or next to the right, along the paths of the tree.

The first criteria of what possibility will *influence* what comes next. For example, in a wrongful death case, the judge's decision on a preliminary motion to disallow bifurcation of the liability and damages phases of a trial would impact the evidence admitted, and the likelihood of liability finding. Similarly, in a business case, the results of a motion to exclude certain parole evidence may influence the likelihood that the jury will find liability, find fraud, and award high damages within a range. After all, that is why the defense would move to exclude this evidence—because of its impact on the jury's decision making. Thus, in either case, the motion would come before, or to the left of branches assessing likelihood of liability.

The same could be said when building a tree in an early phase of litigation, when you don't yet know what the results of experts' analysis will be, let alone how strong or weak (subject to legitimate attack) their conclusions will be. Depending on the case particulars, the strength or weakness of the expert may affect the chance of liability, the chance of the jury's embracing a particular theory, the likely damages range, or all three. Thus, the set of branches outlining the possible results of the experts' analysis would appropriately be placed to the *left* of liability findings and damages.

Of course, it's also true that the motion to bifurcate, the evidentiary motion, and the experts' results will all have come earlier in time in these cases than jury deliberations on liability. When deciding to order among those three, the question is which sets of possibilities will influence the others.

A related but not quite identical criterion for placement is whether one set of branches of tree branches should affect the tree builder's *predictions* about branches that will come after it. In other words, the different branch paths don't directly impact the jury's or the judge's decision, but they do suggest different assessments of probabilities and damages by the tree builder. For example, in a case involving theories of fraud and breach of contract, if a jury were to find fraud, then the tree builder would be wise to think there's a high likelihood that they disliked the corporate defendant and want to punish him. In a personal injury case, if the jury finds contributory negligence, the tree builder might more heavily weight the possibility that they will not land at the high end of a possible damages range (even before contributory negligence proportions are subtracted).[8]

Thus, the order of the sets of branches might be thought of as seeking to map out alternative logical/emotional flow or narratives the jury might adopt. "If, then" becomes the operative question. If this happens—if it turns out that the jury thinks this way—then would that affect my predictions of what else that same jury might think and decide to do? That ordering of "if then" provides wisdom as to the order of your branch sets.[9]

A Question of Clarity

Sometimes, there is no foreseeable causal or predictive relationship between various possibilities. Assume a question about whether the jury will award emotional distress damages (and how much), or a question about whether the jury will award punitive damages at all and, if so, how much, at 2X or 3X the base (according to statute). Assume further that it's just about impossible to figure out how the two relate to one another. A jury awarding multiple damages might be more stingy on emotional distress, from a sense that some amount is too much. Or, it might be that punitive damages suggest jury anger and the angry jury will also be happy to award high emotional distress. We have no idea. In what order should these be placed on the tree? I suggest using whatever order will be more clear and less unwieldy.

Consider a tree that shows possible high, medium, and low base damages, and then different levels of punitive damages: $0 or punitive damages at two or three times a base amount.

[8] See discussion of linked events, information, or decision-maker's findings that may impact subsequent probabilities or predictions in Chapter 11.

[9] Imagine a case in which, after all evidence has been submitted, the defense makes a motion to dismiss a fraud claim on legal grounds. If even the somewhat conservative judge rejects the motion, that might inspire the defense to reassess the likelihood of the jury finding fraud. (Yes, if the judge dismisses it, there's a 0% chance of fraud damages.) Assume that in a vacuum and before the ruling, the defense had considered the fraud claim extremely weak. The judge's ruling, and perhaps his comments, might be a source of feedback that should inspire defense counsel to reassess.

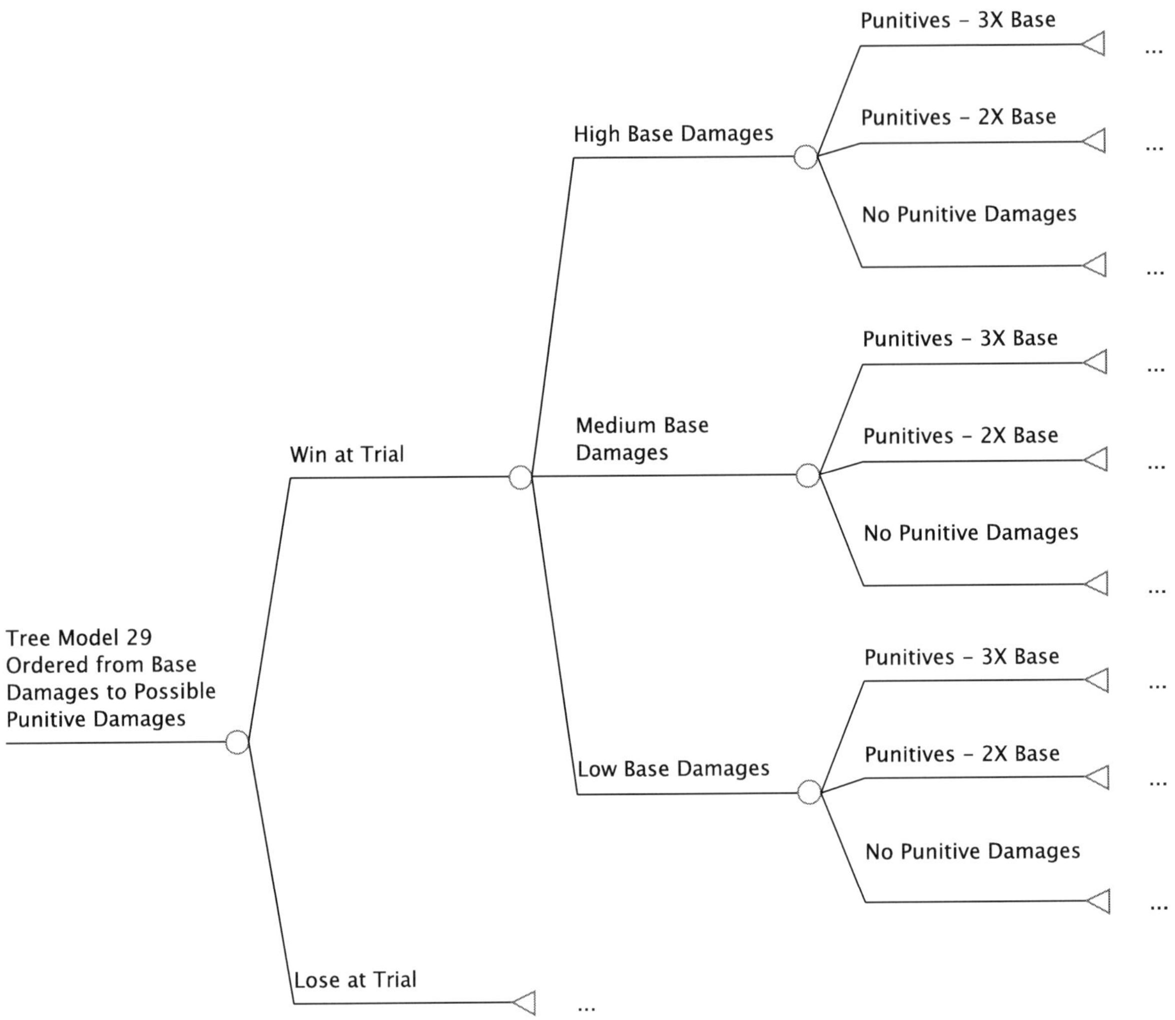

Next is a tree for the same case, with the branch clusters sequenced differently.

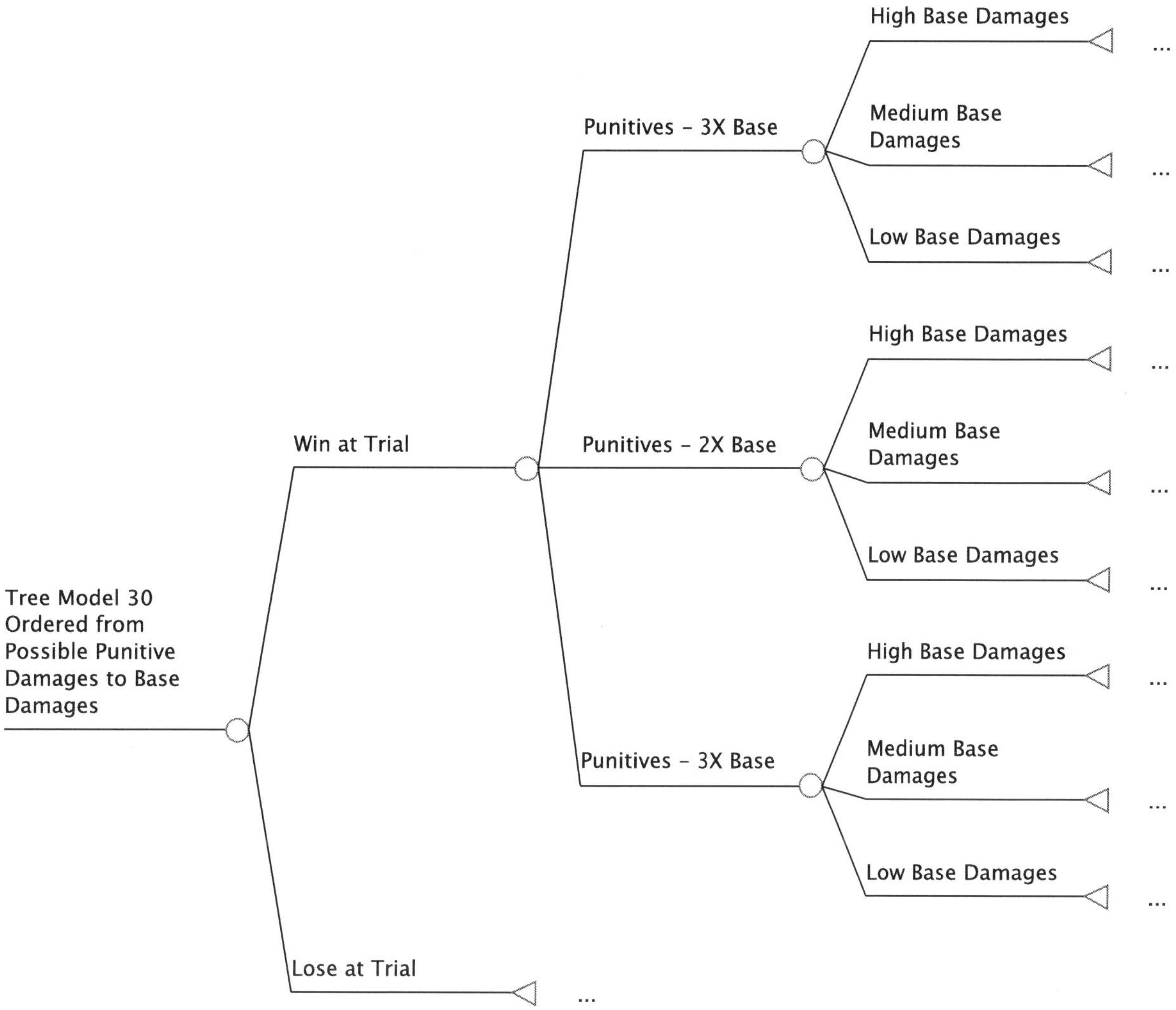

I might suggest opting for the second of these two trees as it more clearly shows where the end numbers come from: we see the high, medium and low base and then their multiplication where punitive damages are assessed. In other words, it may flow better with the lawyer's narrative explanation to his client. This is a close call. Perhaps our "right answer" is to use the presentation order that flows with the narrative, highlights issues being discussed, and enables the client to easily see where those end numbers come from.

Final Words on the How To's and When

If you've worked through all of the problems and absorbed the advice on tree structure in this text thus far, you're no longer a novice. You've got the basics. As you have seen, decision tree analysis requires us to deconstruct possible twists in various possible litigation paths, and how those twists impact what might come next. A more complex case takes time and will have more layers of branches, but the method and the logic are the same. And it's important for your tree to map your best sense of how the case might unfold. Uncertainties should not be ignored, inflated, or disingenuously placed. The tree is to be measured against what sound, experienced, and nuanced legal analysis would tell us in prose form.

Before we leap from basic method to practice, it's fair to address the question of when a lawyer can or should begin sketching out a tree for a case. The answer is that there's no time like the present, once the basic shapes of the case have come into focus. However, just as one's prose description of a case and its challenges and uncertainties shift over time, so should the tree. Unexpected twists in discovery may give rise to unanticipated motions. An expert deposition may legitimately lead to a change in your prediction of damages, or of the chances that damages will fall in a high or low range.

I intended this project to teach the basics for competent use of this method in legal practice, and also to move beyond basics toward its sophisticated application in more complex cases. In fulfillment of the latter goal, the pages that follow offer suggestions for best practices, highlight common errors and distortions to avoid, discuss some more subtle, technical judgments, and provide advice on using the method for communicating with clients.

4

Rigor Requires Refinement

A Mistaken, Inaccurate Map Leads Us to Unintended Places

Many years ago, I had the opportunity to teach a mediation workshop for a group of federal court mediators. As part of the workshop, I introduced decision trees, focusing primarily on litigation risk analysis. I was pleased when the court's ADR administrator later told me that many of the mediators used the method quite regularly after the workshop and considered it a valuable tool for mediation practice. A few years after that, I was invited back to teach a workshop focusing on other mediation topics but also to include a segment on "advanced decision analysis," building on what had been covered before. Recognizing that some of the mediators were new, and not all would have attended the previous workshop, we started with a reprise of the introductory material early in the morning. To my surprise, just about all of the mediators, including the alumni, showed up for the reprise. And to my chagrin, I learned that many had been using decision tree analysis only in highly simplified and less than rigorous ways since that initial session. While they found the method useful for facilitating movement and communication in mediation, I found out that they were using slap-dash distorted maps and plug-ins that failed to represent the case being analyzed. As the teacher, this was a humbling disappointment. In my view, a distorted risk analysis may be worse than none at all if we put faith in its distorted results.

These were intelligent lawyers, seeking to use the method to analyze and communicate as neutral mediators about litigation risks and consequences, possible costs and gains. Their goal was not distortion but honest analysis; their constraints were of time and discomfort with structuring a more complicated tree and the accompanying math. These two constraints work together: with little time, people are understandably less comfortable tackling a complicated tree. I learned that, even if the basic premises are understood, people just plain need practice and experience applying the method in more complicated cases. Practice yields greater confidence in our ability to adequately represent the essential twists, turns, and uncertainties in a complex litigation. That confidence eliminates undue worry that it will take too long or that its math will be too daunting.

The discussion that follows is in response to that lesson. It identifies common errors and sub-optimal choices, explains how these distort the analysis, and suggests better practice choices.

Structural Over-Simplification and Its Dangers

The single most common and problematic practice is over-simplifying the tree structure. Some simplification is inevitable—no decision analysis or litigation risk analysis can or should include chance nodes or branches for every theoretical and subtle shade of eventuality. Yes, the judge could suffer a stroke, hurricanes happen, a fire drill could interrupt the proceeding, a trial exhibit might vanish. Strange things can and do happen, but unless reasonably foreseeable, their appearance as nodes and branches will serve only to confuse and to obfuscate.

A decision tree is *over*-simplified when it fails as a structural representation of a case's logical and sequential flow: when it omits major and consequential turning points of uncertainty and decision. If there's a credible motion to dismiss or another dispositive motion, a motion for partial summary judgment (or an argument on summary judgment that could lead to partial but not complete dismissal), or a motion to exclude important testimonial or documentary evidence, these must be reflected in the structure of the tree. While damage awards are just about always uncertain, or estimated within a range, *which* range you define has everything to do with what will be "in" the damages. Will the judge award front pay as well as back pay, or back pay only? Will the jury find emotional distress, or not? Will they find the evidence supports a punitive damages award, or not? Where the damages range is situated on the tree may determine which damages components will be included.

Let's consider a hypothetical employment age discrimination case. Assume that most of discovery has been completed, but no dispositive motions have been filed yet. The defense attorney called a law school classmate who recently mentioned having attended a workshop session on decision tree analysis. The defense attorney explained that he would buy lunch, heck, even a fancy dinner, for his assistance in thinking about what might be reasonable settlement for his client, using a decision tree. The novice tree-builder classmate interviewed the defense attorney about the case, and learned the following:

- The defense plans to file a motion for summary judgment alleging that undisputed facts support a finding that the plaintiff left voluntarily. The plaintiff claims constructive discharge, and that her superior's so-called warning was really a message that her termination was in process.
- The plaintiff was 45 years old at the time she left the company, and has not found comparable re-employment in industrial product design.
- If summary judgment is denied, she would seek to introduce evidence of the obvious emotional impact this had on her while she was working there, as evidence of the defendant's intent. The defense will file a motion *in limine* because the emotional distress is not recoverable under the age discrimination statute. They will also say the company's actions weren't causally related and will try to use her psychiatrist's report and the report of their expert to say that her psychological distress had been ongoing, caused by childhood abandonment and her abusive ex-husband, but not by the job.
- If the case goes to trial, liability will, of course, be a hotly contested issue. The company's defense will be that the plaintiff quit; she was not terminated. In any event, her subpar performance warranted the poor performance review and written warning, and would justify her termination.
- The plaintiff will testify that her leaving was forced, and other witnesses will corroborate this claim with reports that her superior said "She's history." The plaintiff will also introduce evidence that most of the designers and executives who left the company within the last 3 years were older than 40, and they were replaced by much younger designers at lower salaries. The defendant will contest these numbers, arguing that many of the older designers quit. The plaintiff will claim they were forced out. The defendant will point to inadequacies in the plaintiff's work, which she will contest. She will say that her superiors changed design specifications constantly,

in a deliberate effort to set her up for failure. She claims evidence that they secretly laughed at the tricks and mind games they were playing. The defendant's HR manager will claim that they hired only designers with high computer graphics skills, and these tend to be younger.

- Liability aside, the now 47-year-old plaintiff seeks front pay for at least 5 years, and back pay for the two years since termination (her salary was $100,000 plus benefits worth $30,000 for total compensation of $130,000 per year). She claims to have been diligently looking for work, and notes that the entire industry remains depressed, even post recession. Of course, the defense alleges failure to mitigate, arguing that the market for services is global (and often online) and the plaintiff has only looked locally. Defense counsel refuses to imagine she would get front pay for as long as 5 years. He acknowledges it could be as high as 4 years, but thinks much shorter periods of time would be more likely, if she gets any front pay at all.
- Under federal age discrimination law, the plaintiff is not permitted to get "compensatory" damages—for emotional distress or to punish the defendant. However, the plaintiff will no doubt suggest that a jury will give her additional damages on a finding that the discrimination was intentional and egregious. This rests upon the theory that the company's management schemed to create cause for termination by diminishing the plaintiff's performance record. Testimony by the plaintiff and her former assistant suggest that her supervisor chuckled over how he had "confused the old lady" by changing design specifications, and he often denied what were the original instructions, or fabricated missed assignments. They knew how upset all of this made her. Of course, the supervisor denies this.

A much-too-simple and, frankly, unworthy way to think about this case would be:

"Win or lose summary judgment; never mind the motion in limine because it doesn't affect the summary judgment motion; win or lose at trial; damages high medium or low. And, remember that whether or not the motion in limine was granted could affect the likelihood of a verdict as well as the damages. We'll factor that in."

Here's the much-too-simple tree reflecting that thinking.

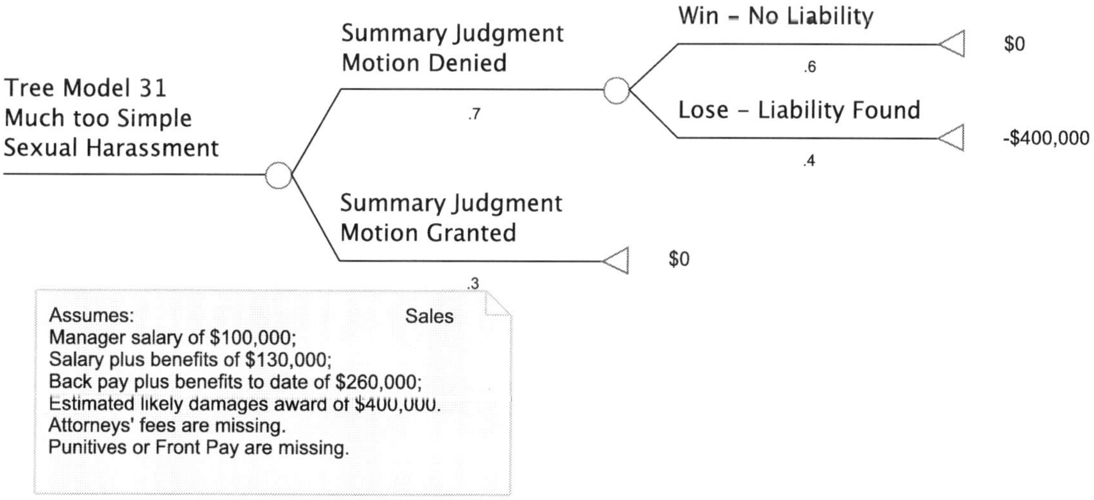

Following that much-too-simple structure, even the novice tree-builder might ask the defense lawyer to consider probabilities[1] and payoffs in a dialog, by asking: "What are your chances of getting the case thrown out on summary judgment? Let's assume the defense lawyer would initially say 40% or even 50%, but after the conversation about the leanings of the assigned judge, he would agree that 30% is more realistic. They would then talk about how the case could be won or lost, where the evidence is weak and strong, whether the motion *in limine* (regarding the plaintiff's emotional state) could affect liability or just damages. Finally, the tree-builder asks: "When you sum it all up, what do you think the chances are of a defense verdict?" The lawyer says, "I have a strong case," and eventually estimates 60%, recognizing there's still significant risk a jury will side with the plaintiff employee, and against the company.[2] They talk for a while about front pay, back pay, possibility of the plaintiff's described emotional state impacting a finding of intentionality and liquidated damages.

The classmate then asks for the defense lawyer's best estimate of likely damages. He replies: "Well, two years of back pay, including benefits, would be $130,000 x 2, so $260,000. I'll bump that up to $400,000 or so because it could be a bad day for us. The $400,000 reflects my opinion that all of the other baloney—front pay, liquidated damages, etc.—is so unlikely that it shouldn't be a big factor and certainly shouldn't drive the settlement."

Here is what that tree would look like, rolled back to reflect the EMV and the probability distributions.

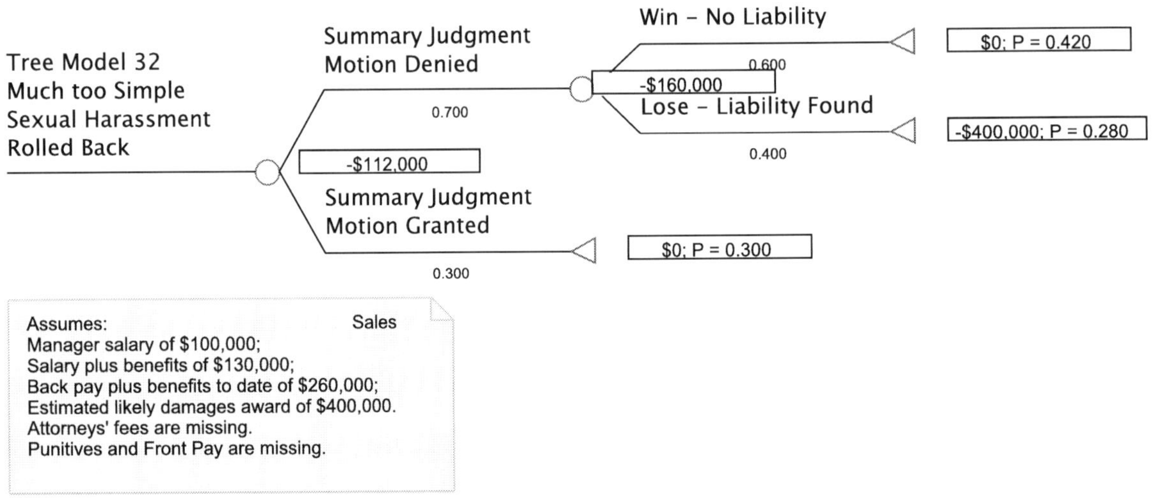

Note that the EMV is $112,000, and the only damages number presented is $400,000.

Imagine that the tree builder flashes back to the recent decision analysis workshop and says: "No, we really have to put in a range—we can't just pick one number. Defense counsel says, "Okay, then use a low damages number of $150,000 because the woman had not tried to mitigate, a 'medium' damages

[1] This section focuses on the tree's structure and the next on outcomes or payoffs. Chapter Nine provides an overview of impediments to unbiased probability estimates. Later portions of that chapter, as well as Chapter Ten, offer some best practices for thinking through or eliciting probability estimates.

[2] This hypothetical example involves purely hypothetical percentages.

number of $260,000, and a high of $500,000." He estimates a 40% chance of the low number, a 40% chance of the mid-range number, and a 20% chance of the high number.

Here's what the tree would look like.

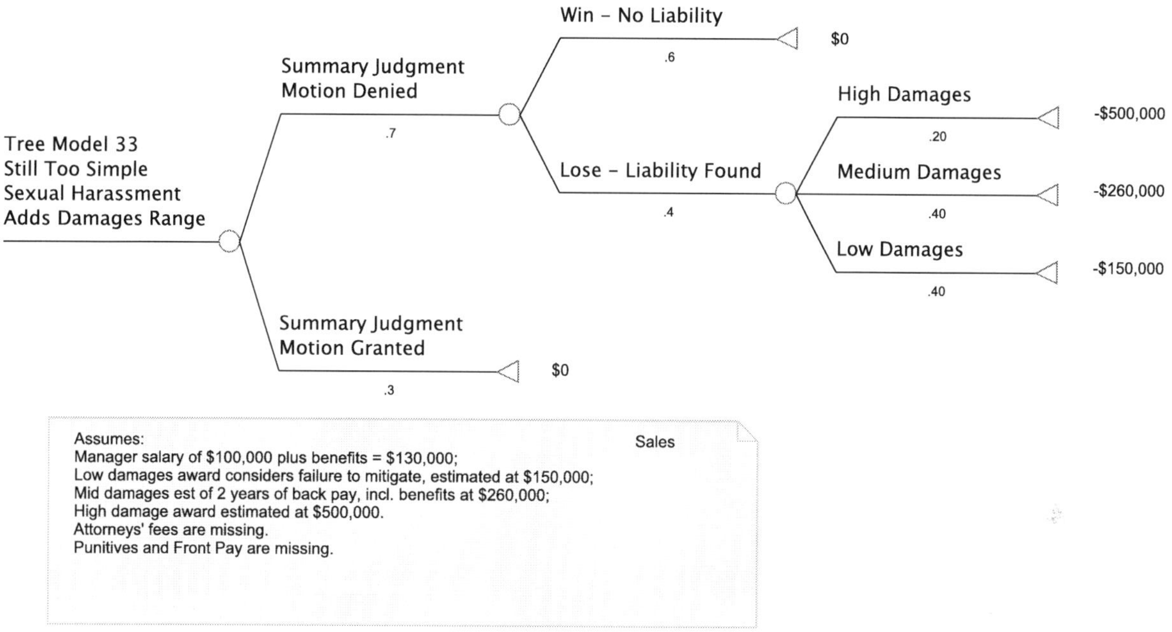

The next tree shows the roll back. Note that the EMV is lower because the attorney has more heavily weighted the lower damages range.

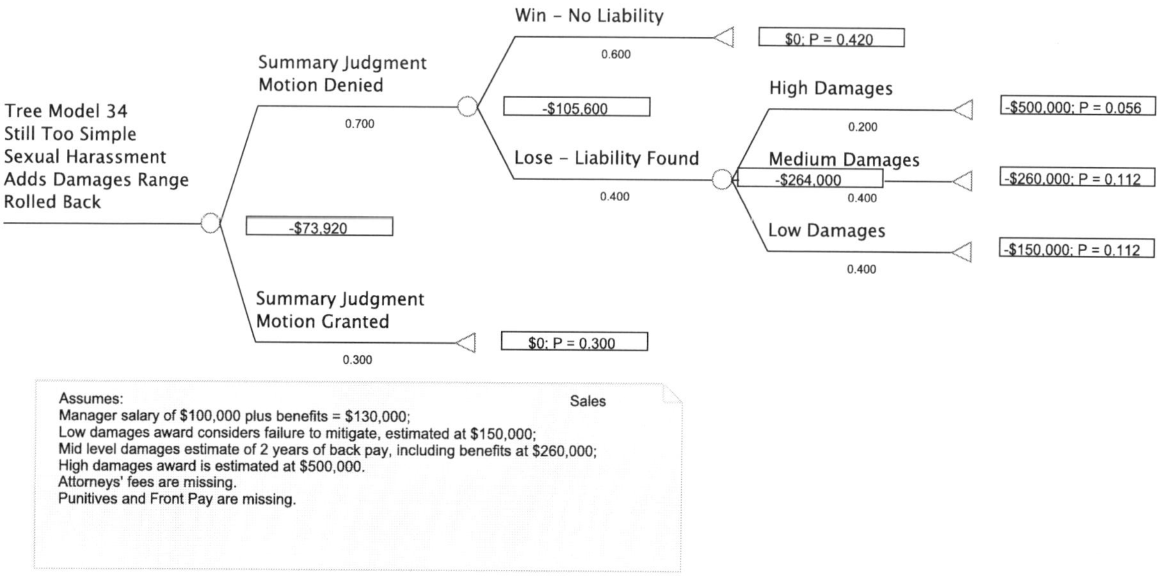

If the tree builder has another flash back to the decision analysis workshop, he might ask and learn that the defense lawyer's attorney's fees from now through summary judgment will be $10,000 and through trial (inclusive) at $75,000. (We're assuming that investigation and discovery are complete.) Using the Lodestar[3] approach to damages, the plaintiff's attorney will no doubt collect at least $100,000 for her work through trial, if the plaintiff prevails. These would add to the defense costs. The revised tree, with costs added is set forth below.

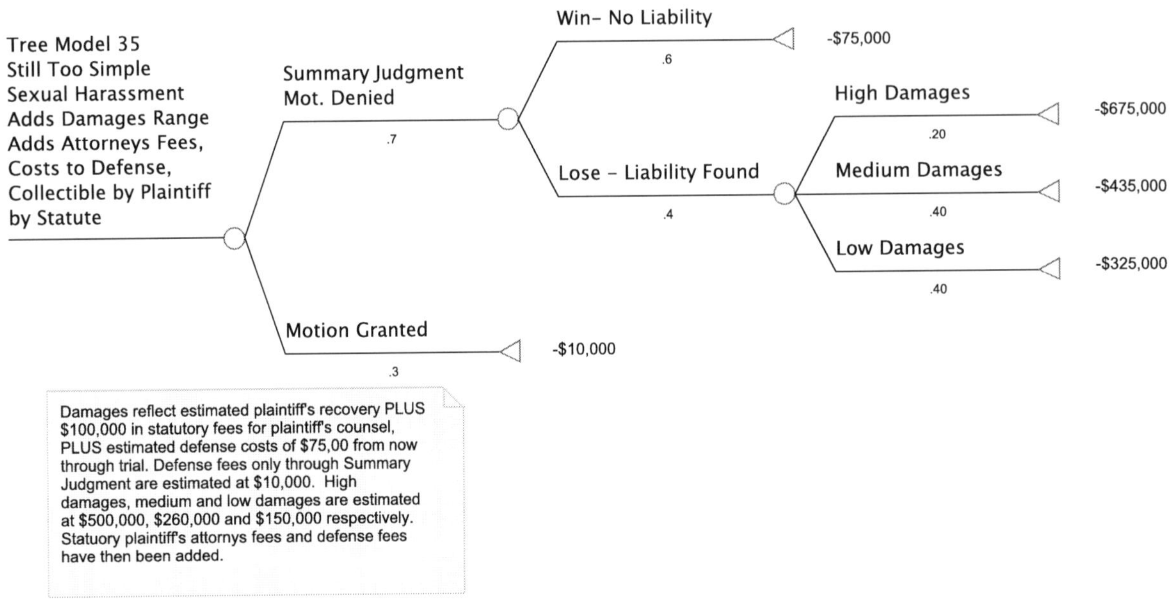

We see that now, when this tree is rolled back, the EMV has begun to creep up, in a way that bears greater resemblance to reality.

[3] "The lodestar method of calculating attorney fees is a two-step process. First, courts multiply the hours an attorney works by the attorney's hourly rate—this process yields the lodestar—and then courts adjust the lodestar up or down "to reflect the characteristics of a given action." Brooks, M.; Phillips Jr., R.D.; Connolly, T.; Feldman, R.; and Mamaysky, I. "Calculating Attorney Fee Awards," *GP Solo* (March 2010). This article is available at www.americanbar.org/content/newsletter/publications/gp_solo_magazine_home/gp_solo_magazine_index/magratten_phillips_connolly_feldman_mamaysky.html.

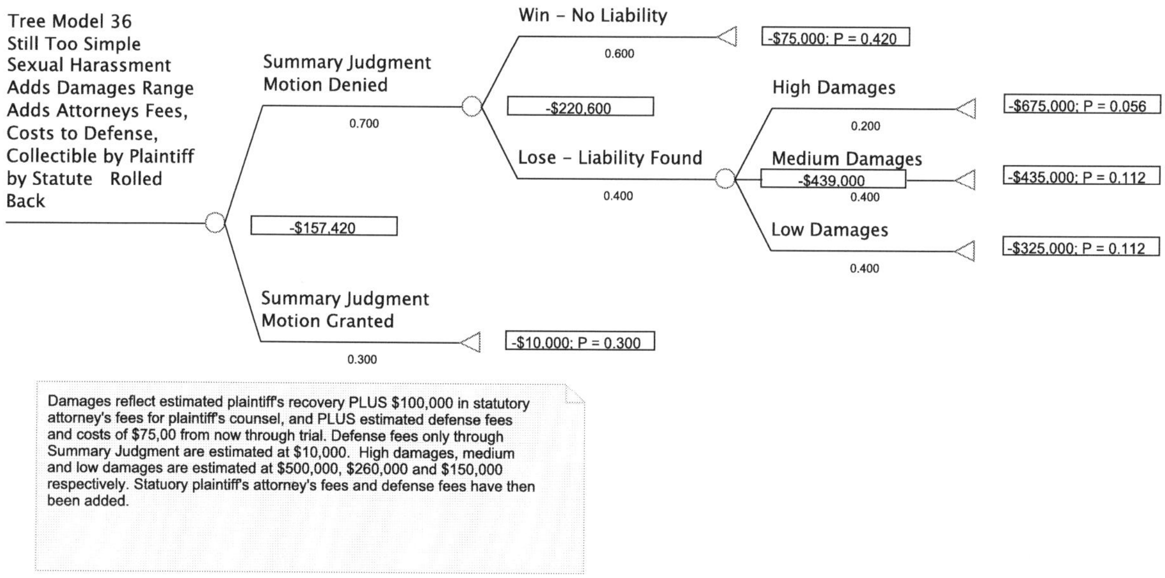

Isn't this good enough, or is the tree still "*over*-simplified"? From the defense perspective, doesn't the story boil down to this: "There is a shot at ending the case before trial; there will be a finding on liability or not; and there will be costs and fees and possibly a range of damages at the end of the day"?

To consider whether the tree's still relatively simple structure is a virtue, wisdom suggests looking to process, and then to results. We recognize that good process generally leads to good or at least understandable results. When the process is lacking, we anticipate the opposite. When I listen to the imaginary dialogue between the defense lawyer and his tree-builder classmate, and look at the tree, I see lapses, or gaps, both in its structure and in the way probabilities are derived.

Let's consider the structure first. In fact, there are multiple junctures of uncertainty, or turning points at which a third party's decision or action will impact what happens in the case. Thus, the tree should begin with a chance node, and branches for summary judgment—granted or denied—as this one does.

However, we also know that if summary judgment were denied, defense counsel would file his motion *in limine* before trial to block the plaintiff from introducing any evidence of her emotional state while working at the company.[4]

When the motion *in limine* is incorporated, the tree would look like the next one, up to the chance nodes and branches at "liability/no liability."

[4] At the risk of stating the obvious: if you begin the tree with both motions, with sequential, separate branch layers, each leading to a separate liability chance node, and if damages theories and estimates involve any additional complexity, the tree will become quite large. For discussion with some clients, you may want to break the presentation into separate trees – one that tracks the possible outcome of each motion. In some instances, you may want to present the full, extremely complicated tree as one (hard to read) visual. That makes the point that the case is complicated, that the client's desired outcome is one of many, and getting to that outcome will require threading several needles in just the right and lucky ways.

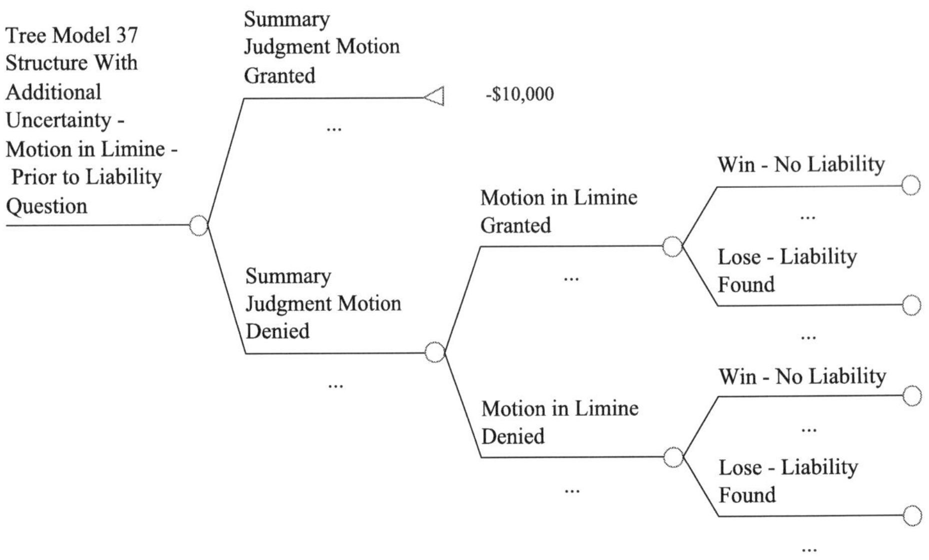

And, as we'll see in the more complete tree, if viewed as a factor that might impact *overall* jury sympathy, the motion *in limine* results could also impact the chance of a liability vs. no liability finding. Certainly, evidence of the emotional impact of company actions on the plaintiff during her tenure would impact the likelihood of the jury finding intentional discrimination and awarding liquidated damages.

A more complete tree would reflect different paths the case might follow if the motion *in limine* is granted or denied. It would also reflect the truth that the damages award may be back pay only, or back pay plus front pay. If front pay is awarded, there's discretion in the time period permitted. If the court decided to permit evidence about the plaintiff's emotional state, there's a greater chance of liquidated damages.

Next is what a not-so-simple and, in my view, more accurate tree might look like.[5]

[5] As indicated earlier, these two relatively complex trees as well as certain others that come later in the text are obviously difficult to read. The font size and the image had to be reduced to fit them on the page. Because the tree depicts only a hypothetical case and no real client is involved, I chose to make the image fit the page. It is not important to read the precise words or number to understand the principle being discussed in the text.

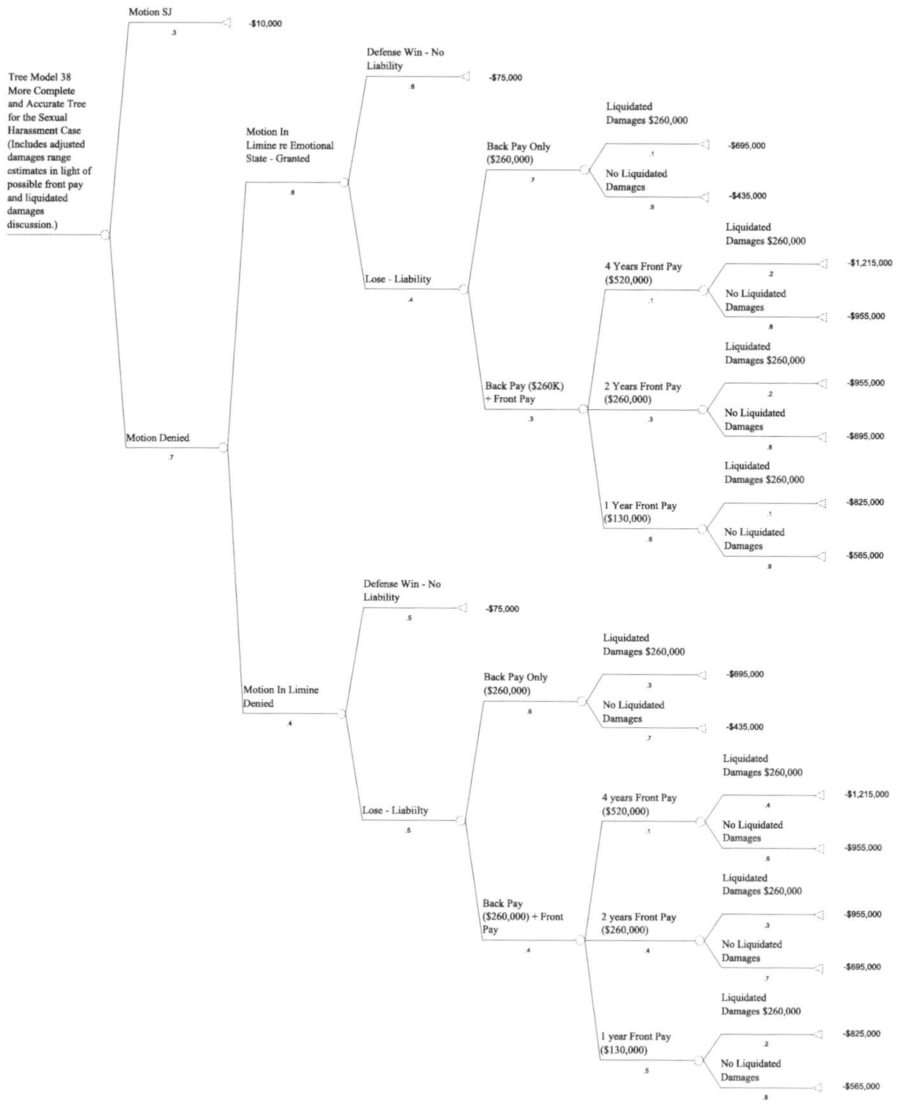

And next we see the tree rolled back and its calculated results.

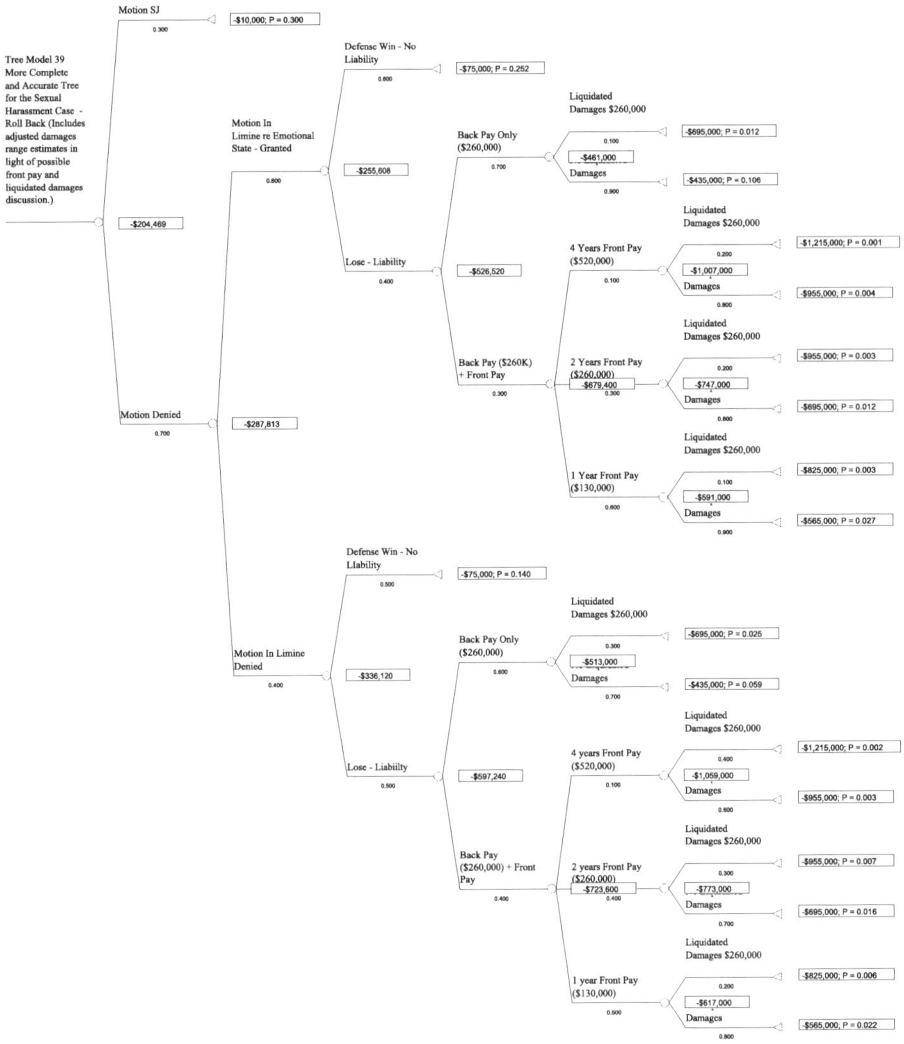

Note that the damages estimates in this tree include the following numbers and calculations: Back pay is set at $260,000.

The range for front pay has been estimated at 1–4 years. One year of front pay is $130,000. Two years would be $130,000 x 2 = $260,000. Four years would be $130,000 x 4 = $520,000. These estimates were used for the range despite plaintiff's claim for 5+ years of front pay.

Under federal law, there are no compensatory damages, but a jury may decide to award "liquidated damages" in the amount of back pay. It could be argued that some of the other estimates—the top of the front pay range at 4 years, for example, and some of the probabilities—are too conservative. However, this segment still draws upon an initial and hypothetical discussion with defense counsel.

As you can see, the EMV of $204,469 is significantly different from the EMV in our simpler trees. More important is that it shows vastly different ranges of possible outcomes, from a low of $455,000 to a high of $1,215,000 (based upon a low damages award of $260,000 and a high damages award of $1,040,00 plus plaintiff's and defense attorney's fees of $175,000).

It's fair to say that if our tree-builder takes the time to sketch out this tree structure, and then discusses various damages components with his classmate, their assessment of the case will be far more rigorous. And that rigor will inform defense counsel's subsequent discussion with his client.

5

DECISION RULES WHEN DECIDING HOW MUCH TO BUILD OUT

It is true that a reasonably accurate map of reality can become mighty large and intricate. There is indeed a tension between seeking to represent complicated realities and making the tree comprehensible. Particularly where client communication is important, it may not be helpful to create and present a monster tree, scary in its profusion of branches and far-flung, wispy ends.[1]

The difficult question is: when to conflate or collapse branches or branch layers into one, and when to keep them separate? I recommend basing that decision on whether the results of a given uncertainty may significantly impact assessments along subsequent paths to the right on the tree. If the ruling on a motion for change of venue will significantly impact the applicable law or process or the nature of the jury pool in identifiable and significant ways, that motion deserves a chance node. If a motion to dismiss would eliminate claims that carry particular penalties or require costly expert and discovery expenditures, that motion also merits a chance node.

When deciding whether to create a chance node for an evidentiary motion or any other post-filing-but-before-trial motion, consider whether the ruling will significantly "change the movie" the jury will see at trial. If jurors learn of the company's prior SEC infractions (even if unrelated) are they more likely to believe that apparent corporate collusion was mere coincidence? Won't jurors who hear testimony about prior sexual harassment episodes in the company be more inclined to find corporate awareness of a hostile work environment? Imagine a suit brought by an ailing and aging plaintiff injured in a ceiling collapse case. If jurors learn that his much younger wife married him quite recently, and she is a former prostitute, aren't they less likely to render a high award for loss of consortium to her or even high damages to the plaintiff? It seems fair to anticipate that this type of information would "change the movie" —the story in the case presented to the jury.

Extending a movie analogy: it's true that, to some degree, small slices of dialog and panoramic screen shots all affect the audience response. Even if a screen shot is altered and the dialog adjusted in a scene or two, the pre-release and post-release audiences will have seen basically the same movie.

[1] As discussed earlier as well as in later sections, in some high dollar, legally and factually complicated cases, the monster tree is a must. High stakes patent litigation is particularly prone to large trees due to numerous and distinct legal hurdles involved in many cases. The same may be said of much complex litigation. There, the wise choice is not to simplify the tree, but to present an overview and then to deconstruct and present its component parts with care. On the other hand, as suggested in the preceding note, at least starting with a visually complex tree may be an important part of communicating with your client.

However, if a critical scene is added, a major character dies early, and the plot changes, the two audiences have seen a much different movie and can be expected to react differently.

Back to the question of whether a particular uncertainty "deserves" its own chance node, or should just be folded into the mix, Ask yourself whether the resolution of that uncertainty, e.g., the ruling on the motion, means the jury will see a very different case presentation. If so, separate chance nodes and subsequent branch clusters are indeed warranted.

No doubt, adding chance nodes and branches toward the left hand side of a tree—near its beginning—almost inevitably means that the tree will become a large one. Think of a real tree in the forest with a large branch split near to the bottom of the trunk. Each branch will have sprouted its own set of more branches, and branches off of those; at the end of each we'll see many twigs. Back to decision trees in legal cases that start with multiple chance nodes to the left of "liability/no-liability." Each branch must trace a path through preliminary motions and other uncertainties to liability/no liability and beyond. Simplification by eliminating or ignoring a specific legal ruling or procedural twist is legitimate (indeed encouraged) *only* if it has little or no significant effect on probabilities and outcomes anticipated to follow down the line. Of course, strategies that don't alter a reasonably and necessarily complicated tree but do simplify its presentation are to be applauded. (Some simplification suggestions can be found later in this chapter.)

Damages, More Complexity, More Branches, and More Arithmetic

Often, the devil is in the damages.[2] You may remember that the tree-builder for our over-simplified tree (in Chapter Four) initially asked: "At the end of the day, what do you think would be the high, medium, and low numbers for damages, if there is a plaintiff's verdict?" That's not a bad question for a case where one might expect a damage award to fall anywhere on a continuous distribution range—where no separate, possible but uncertain factors would yield higher likelihoods of certain points, or clusters of points along the ranges. Thus, in a personal injury case, where liability is at issue, plaintiff's medical treatment

[2] Of course, some evidentiary motions may be inevitable at trial. I draw a distinction between pre-trial and during-trial evidentiary motions here primarily because settlement decisions are often made before trial. And, while it's often true that a trial may include many evidentiary motions, a single such motion tends to be less significant than a motion brought before trial. Put more simply, when either party's lawyer gets wind of the experts and evidence the other side will proffer at trial, and believes it critical to prevent them, pre-trial evidentiary motions are filed.

In the best of all possible worlds, from a settlement perspective, the court would hear and rule upon these motions well in advance of trial. Once having lost a critical evidentiary ruling before the trial date, the losing party could reassess their negotiating position, and reopen settlement discussions.

The unfortunate reality is that pre-trial motions are often ruled upon immediately pre-trial, when the witnesses are prepped and ready, the players committed to the trial process. Still, I gently suggest that, as a matter of intellectual clarity, these chance nodes should be separately reflected on the tree. After all, they lay bare the architecture of paths to more and less favorable outcomes, particularly in this case where defense success on the motion might entirely bar the plaintiff's emotional damages claim. However, in a tree that is highly complex in structure without chance nodes for an evidentiary motion, ruled upon immediately pre-trial, or during trial, I can see the argument for folding that uncertainty into an overall probability of liability or no liability. One option would be to capture its effect in a sub analysis, deconstructing that probability assessment, as discussed later in this chapter.

expenses and lost wages are known, there's been testimony about pain and suffering, and punitive damages aren't possible, damage award estimates may well fall along a continuous distribution range.[3]

However, in the employment case discussed earlier, the initial "high, medium, low" question was too simple. Really, there will be different damages ranges depending upon whether the jury finds intentional discrimination, whether the judge awards front pay (and for how long), and whether the jury awards liquidated damages. If the judge decides against front pay, and the jury awards back pay plus liquidated damages, that path will lead to an entirely different range than front pay, plus back pay, plus liquidated damages. The jury that learns of the plaintiff's emotional state and finds intentional discrimination is a different jury—a different set of actors, persuaded differently—than the jury that says back pay only and nothing more.

A way of thinking about when to break damages down further is to ask: is there something else—something specific—a binary, yes or no—that I could know about the jury's findings or logical path, that would greatly impact the damages outcome? If the answer is yes, then the tree-builder should consider separate damages branches. That is clearly true in an employment case where there's a separate actor-decision maker—the judge who will determine any front pay award. It's also true in other legal arenas. For example, in a business dispute alleging breach of contract as well as fraud, the possible fraud finding will require separate and different damages branches than the possible finding of breach of contract only. It may be that, under the breach of contract theory, there's some controversy over whether a liquidated damages provision should be enforced or consequential damages permitted. With this in mind, the portions of a tree depicting different legal theories and their damages in such a business dispute are shown next.

[3] Guidance is provided in Chapter Eleven about the mathematics and a good set of questions for deriving a continuous distribution range in a case such as this.

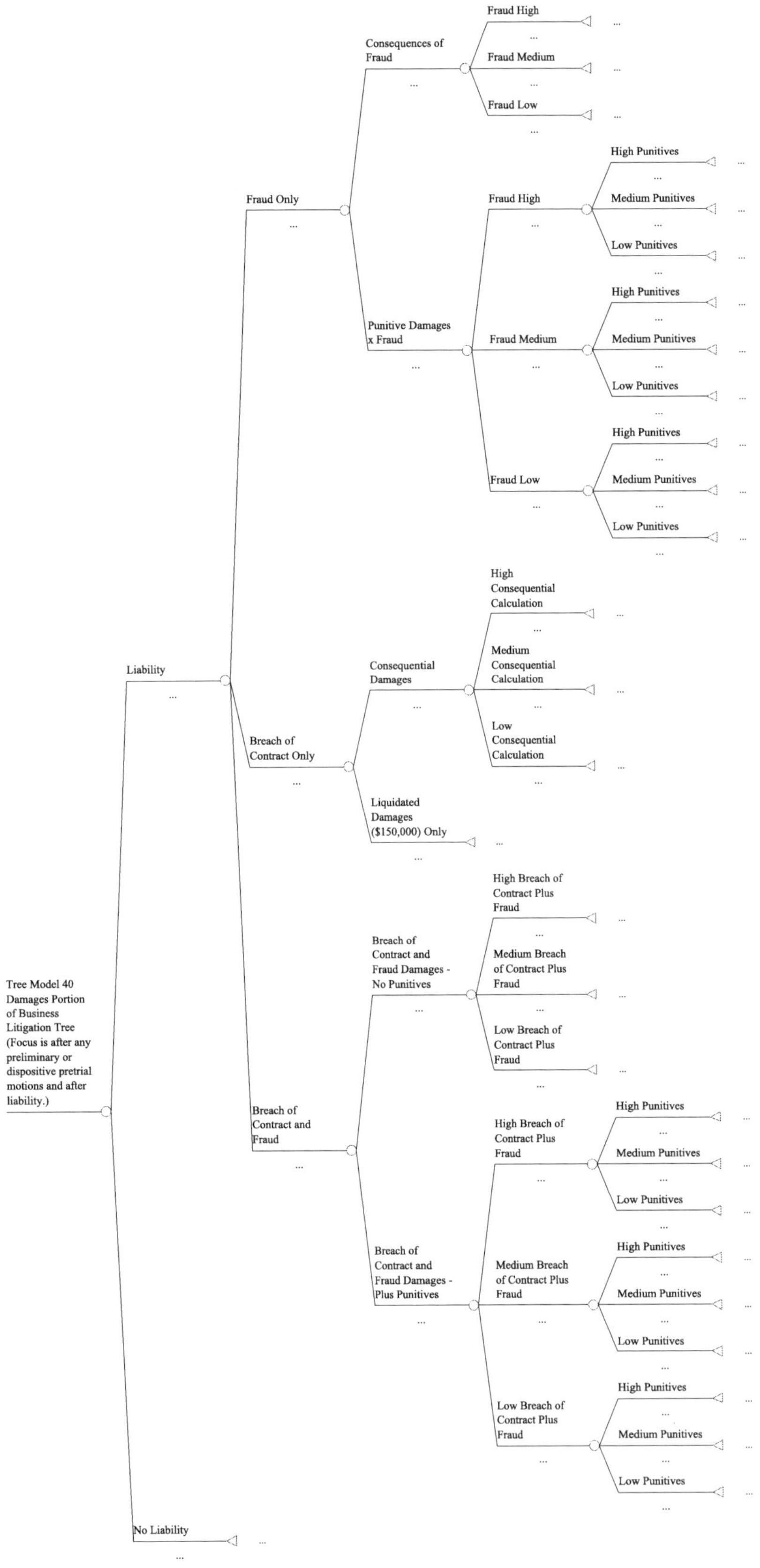

This tree is based on entirely hypothetical law and fact. It assumes liquidated damages of a set amount. It assumes that breach of contract and fraud theories are not mutually exclusive; both could be proven. It assumes that one can identify a range of quantifiable damages resulting from fraud separate and apart from a range of consequential damages from breach of contract. It also assumes that punitive damages will fall along some range, but are not constrained to apply a multiplier of other damages.

Note, finally, to the far, far right, in most instances, we do see branch clusters "high, medium, and low". That is because, at the end of these paths to damages (in some combination), there remains uncertainty —a distributed range of numbers along which a damages award might fall, with equal probability.[4] (The exception is the "liquidated damages only" path, where the damage amount would presumably be set in the contract.) In Chapter Nine, we will discuss techniques for setting and eliciting the range, consistent with principles of mathematics, probability and statistics, and psychology.

Branches Prompt Dialog and Rigor

The process of building a realistically complex tree for a reasonably complex case raises questions at every potential chance node and cluster of branches. The dialogue prompted—whether internal or with a colleague or client—may be the method's most important contribution. Mapping the case (via pencil or computer) forces you to consider: What are all of the possible uncertainties before trial? Which deserve a place on the tree? What might be their impact on the course of the trial? Are there only two possibilities at the dispositive motion stage: summary judgment granted or denied? Or could a judge grant partial summary judgment? If so, what claims would survive? How would the elimination of certain claims or theories impact case presentation? Would it eliminate or reduce the likelihood of an overall liability finding, of certain measures of damages? Or, would their elimination affect the damages range, and the probabilities of awards at extreme ends of the range.

Just as the act of structuring the tree prompts rigorous, thorough consideration of the possible paths of a case, it also reveals where strategic choices and resource allocation decisions will be made. We may have a choice of venue if we file suit: which would be optimal? If they file in state court, should we opt to file a motion for removal? Does it make sense for us to file preliminary dispositive motions? Is it worth retaining an expert on this issue? On damages? Does this depend upon their theory of the case?

The numerical probabilities for each branch at each juncture and net outcomes at each end point, if taken seriously, also requires careful consideration.[5] The lawyer must review the sources of uncertainty, the weights of arguments and facts predicted to tilt the probability scale in one direction or another. What are the strengths of the other side's facts—smoking gun documents, likeable witnesses, close time sequence?

What case law supports their legal theories? On your side of the case: will the jury understand your highly credentialed expert? Is it worth investing more time to work with the expert, if he is a critical piece of your case? What really is the highest damages amount the jury could award that the judge would not reduce? On the defense side: have you considered how the jury might feel about our company if everything breaks its way at trial? On the plaintiff's side: have you considered how a jury, unsure

[4] It is arguable that the end node at back pay only, no emotional distress, and no punitive damages, should be a single calculable number—lost wages and benefits. Fair point, theoretically. But, in real life, there may be controversy about efforts to mitigate, about lost bonuses or overtime. We are still discussing structure and not numbers, but I can't resist noting that defense attorney's fees should be added as costs, as well as plaintiff's attorney's fees (owed by statute). They would impact the range and there would still be some uncertainty as to attorneys' fees the court would find reasonable. This would most likely be resolved in a post trial hearing. Note also that I have not included any reference to an appeal or its chances, etc.

[5] More detailed discussion of impediments to unbiased estimates are found in Chapter Nine and suggested best practices for the process of estimating and discussing probabilities are in Chapters Nine, Ten, and Eleven.

about liability or unimpressed by your client's mitigation efforts, might come up with a verdict much, much lower than what you're claiming?

In Chapters Nine and Eleven, we'll review best practices for estimating probabilities and damages in ways that minimize distortion by psychological biases. What should be clear is that the process of estimating probability and damages along each path on the tree demands thought and rigor.

Consider the Jury Verdict Form's Impact[6]

If possible, before estimating the likelihood of a liability finding, the decision analyst should consider the jury verdict—the questions it will ask the jury to address. Let's assume the jury will understand the judge's formal instructions that, in order to find liability, both causation and negligence must be found. Where the jury will be given only a simple general verdict form, should the decision analyst assess the probabilities of each separately, and multiply them to get the cumulative probability of a liability finding? Probably not! After all, when jurors return verdicts on general verdict forms (without addressing specific questions), experience suggests that, despite the legal distinctions, the jurors act on a gut sense of what's right—of the justice they want to bring about. If you don't believe they will assess the negligence and causation issues separately, but rather, holistically, then your probability estimate should be holistic. It should reflect the way you believe the jury would approach the question.

In federal courts, it's common for juries to return their verdicts in the form of answers to special interrogatories. Special interrogatories are designed to cabin decision-making sloppiness by compelling juries to make separate findings about legally separable issues, e.g., to address separate components of multi-element claims or defenses one component or one element at a time. The jury is asked to determine, separately for each issue, whether the party bearing the burden of proof has met its burden. To assess probabilities, the decision analyst should ask the parallel questions: what is the likelihood of the jury answering yes, to each and every one of the questions required for a liability finding?

No binary advice is offered here. It depends on how you believe a jury, given separate interrogatories, will think about their answers. Most of us make decisions based on emotions, on what we want, and then justify our decisions with reasoning and argument. If that's true, then even the interrogatory jury form may not lead to perfect, open, *independent* deliberation on each question. Underlying favor or disfavor toward the plaintiff may color jury deliberations on each interrogatory.

Apply Gut Sense and Reality to Cumulative Probabilities

When Path and Math Disconfirm Gut Sense—Insight or Distortion?

Imagine a discussion with plaintiff's counsel about a pending case. He begins by saying: "My gut tells me this case is a strong one! I think our chances are very good on that ridiculous summary judgment motion. We are also quite strong on getting the medical expert in, and that will help our chances on liability. And even without the expert, it's more likely than not that we win. And if we win, we clear $150,000 with no contributory negligence; I'd say reduce it by a third if the jury finds contributory negligence."

[6] This section is either excerpted or paraphrased from: Aaron, M. and Brazil, W., "Shaking Decision Trees for Risks and Rewards," *Dispute Resolution Magazine*, 22, no. 1 (2015): 12-18.

When pressed to think about the way these factors fit together and to provide estimates for a decision tree, plaintiff's counsel estimates: a 75% chance of surviving summary judgment, a 60% chance of the desired expert evidence being admitted. He acknowledges that whether the evidence is admitted would affect the chances of liability and estimates these as 65% if the evidence is admitted, 51% if it is not, and in either event, a 50% chance of the jury finding contributory negligence in the range of 1/3, or approximately 33%.

Here's the structure of the tree, reflecting the stated probabilities.

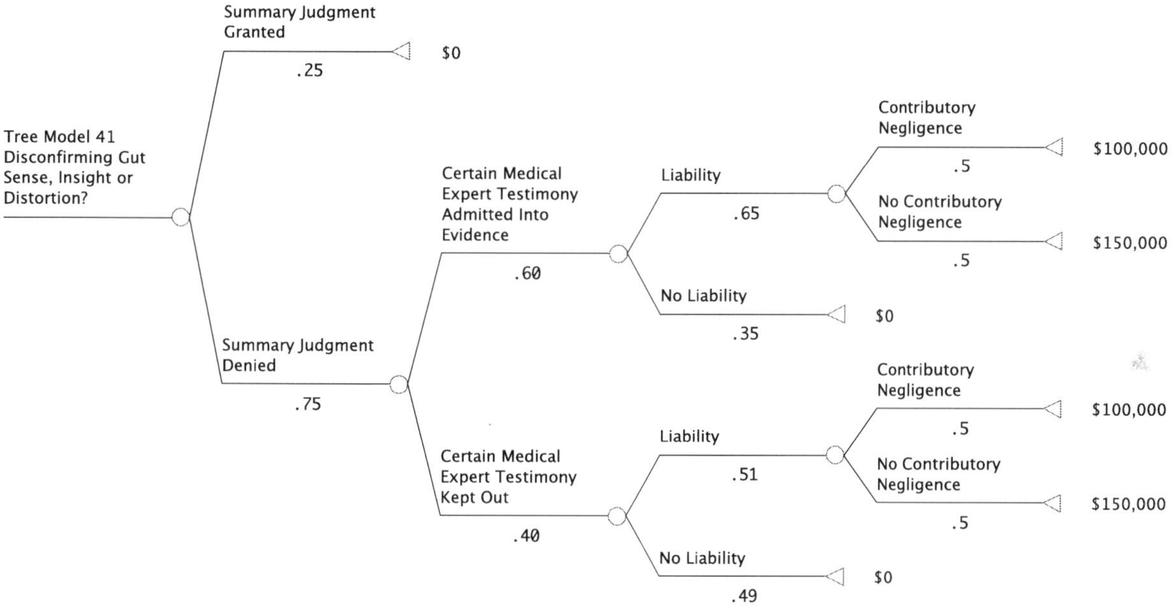

In fact, as you can see below, even though based on plaintiff's counsel's estimates, when the tree is rolled back and cumulative probabilities calculated, the results can be disappointing.

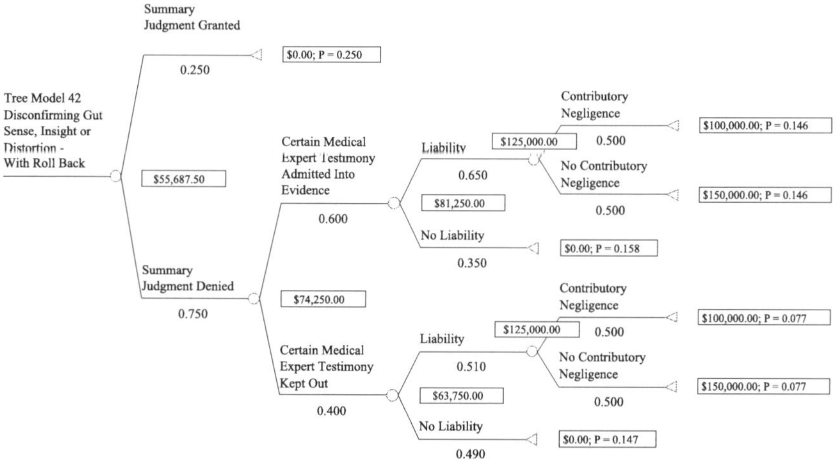

From the cumulative probabilities on the right side, we see an overall likelihood of any recovery by the plaintiff at 44.5%, and the chances of recovering the full $150,000 at 22.3% (.077 + .146).

"Wait a minute," protests the plaintiff's lawyer, "according to your decision tree analysis and your cumulative probabilities, the total chance of my client winning $150,000 is, give or take, 22%? And the overall chances of winning anything are 44%? My gut tells me our case is stronger than that! These numbers are too low!"

If the cumulative probability of a particularly important result—say, liability or a desirable damages award—ends up far, far from a lawyer's gut sense, should we look to the gut or the math as the distortionist? The answer, of course, is that we should re-examine both, with some care.

In truth, one of the strongest reasons to use decision analysis is that our "gut" sense or the lawyer's intuitive calculator is not capable of determining cumulative probabilities for each possible outcome in a reasonably complicated case, let alone one that is highly complex. Yet, we would all acknowledge that, in rare instances, everything or nothing will break our way, and reality is more often a dastardly combination of positive and negative breaks. And each time the cue ball encounters another ball in play, our point total heads up or down.

The decision tree should be structured to represent, as accurately as possible, a map of the paths along which the case might flow. Uncertainties should be estimated at critical junctures—particularly where a decision-maker or other actor will impact the path of the case. Where the tree fairly captures the lawyer's informed analysis of the uncertainties and their probabilities and yet, the cumulative probabilities of desirable and undesirable outcomes contradict the lawyer's gut sense; it's time to silence the gut and consider arithmetic's counsel.

Yet the gut should be a critical check on the structure of the tree. Sometimes, the tree-builder is seduced (or seeks to distort) by the lure of over-complexity—by deconstructing uncertainties in an unrealistic way. It is true that the more layers in a tree—the more branch clusters along its path—the more cumulative probabilities reduce the likelihood of each possible final result.

Disavow Distortion Disguised as Greater Diligence

An over-eager or disingenuously diligent decision analyst asks a savvy and appropriately skeptical lawyer:

"What is the likelihood of proving each of the four required elements of liability? That the jury will take seriously the defense claim of a waiver and use that against the plaintiff? Or, what is the likelihood your star witness will perform well? That the jury will have too many skeptics?" The analyst then multiplies these percentages to yield a suspiciously low cumulative probability of success. We are right to suspect this analyst is a shill for the defense!

Yes, all of these will have to fall into place for a liability finding: the elements must be proven, the waiver testimony discredited, the witness be credible, and the jury somewhat sympathetic. But if you break them down, and assign even a high probability to each one separately, the probability of a liability finding will be severely reduced when the multiplication is done. And the savvy lawyer would be right to favor his gut sense that a jury is highly likely to find liability. Many of these factors may influence a jury—the decision-maker—but it may be true that their decision will be made holistically. In this case, on the question of liability: clean and simple structure may be a more accurate map.

As always, our reference point is informed, thoughtful prose analysis of the case. Does the tree fit? Does it reflect our best judgments about how important uncertainties may break, in what directions, and what impact these may have as the case unfolds over time? If not, then by all means, use good lawyerly instinct and wisdom to reshape the tree, and rethink the probabilities. If so, the wise lawyer may want to discuss that original tree and its cumulative results with his client.[7]

Choosing to Walk it Back: Resolving Realism, Complexity, and Confusion

Having staked a righteous claim in the fully branched, fully developed tree school of decision analysis, I am amenable to compromise. Especially when compromise on complexity reduces confusion and insignificantly affects the outcome, compromise may be the favored choice. It is true, after all, that when a tree sprouts branches upon branches, twigs upon twigs, the whole thing just looks like feathers. Shamelessly continuing the analogy, we are tempted to brush the feathers away with a wave of the hand or a frustrated breath. Unreadable, the endlessly complex trees tease and annoy us with the idea that they might have value, but it's hard to pin them down, read, and gather what insight they might offer.

Here are a few ways to "slim down" the number of branches, without sacrificing accuracy.

Logically, while building the tree, I tend to think and then draw by asking "what could happen next"—supply binary (or three or more) answers—and "if that, then what?" ...and so on. For example, I might sketch branches reflecting the most basic uncertainty: will the jury find "some liability or no liability." Then, assuming involvement of a co-defendant, on the "some liability" branch, I would next ask whether it would be a shared liability (with the co-defendant) vs. solely liable, and so forth. Here's what that portion might look like, including a similar approach to the question of contributory negligence: None or some? If so, how much? The attempt to think carefully, step by step, is shown by the way the branches are drawn.

[7] An affirming and elegant discussion of the need to balance "methodological rigour and intuition" can be found in Heavin, Heather and Keet, Michaela, "Litigation Risk Analysis: Using Rigorous Projections to Encourage and Inform Settlement," *Journal of Arbitration and Mediation* (forthcoming):4-6.

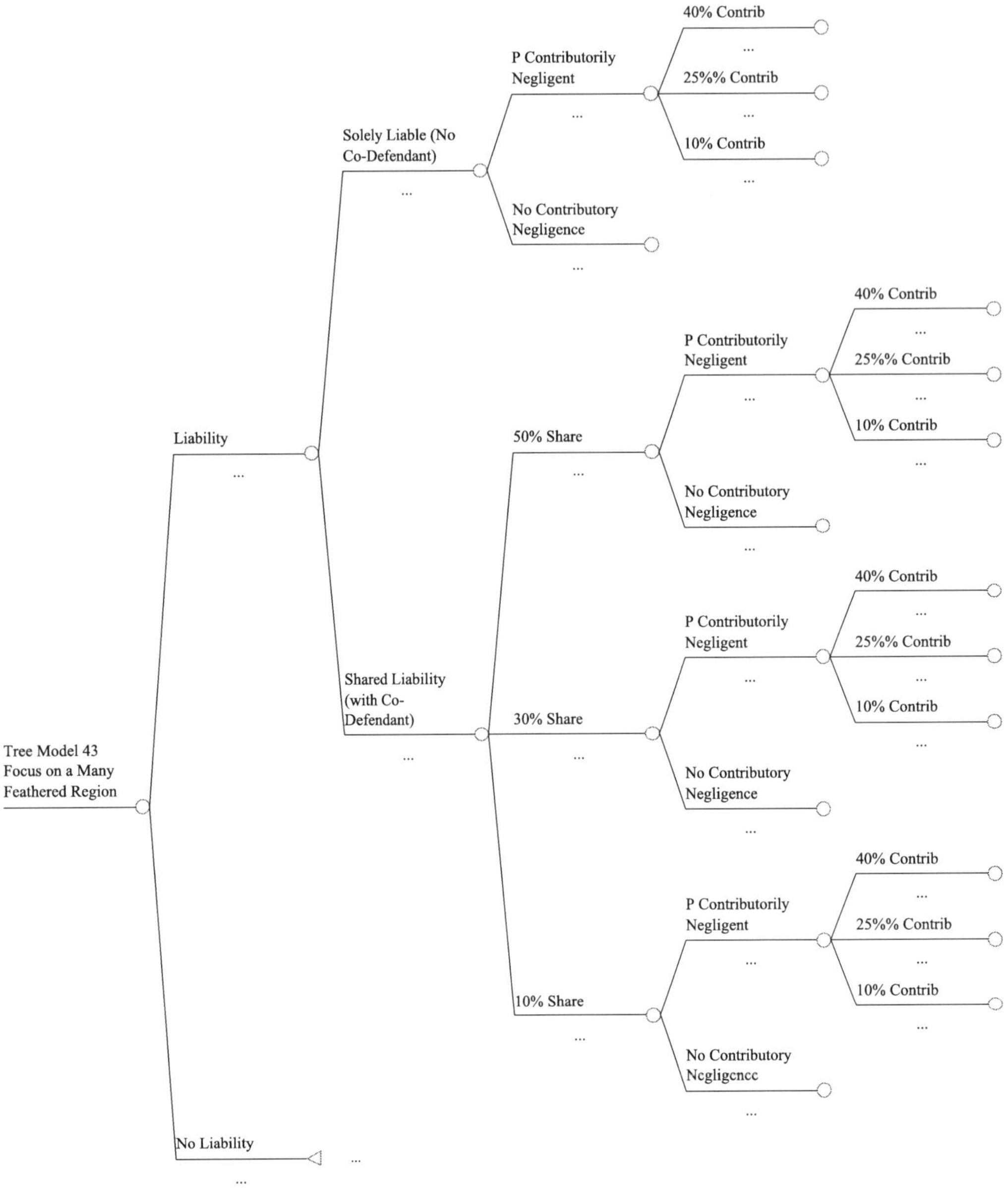

Then shown below, the tree can be "pruned" by collapsing the branches to recognize that, really, I've concluded that three outcomes are possible on the question of liability: no liability, shared liability, and sole liability.[8] They can be represented by three branches emanating from a single chance node, instead of two successive chance nodes. A similar adjustment can be made on the question of contributory negligence: rather than two successive questions or nodes, we might line up all of the possibilities- various estimated levels of contributory negligence, starting with 0 (none).

[8] See Professor Howard Raiffa's original discussion of how to think about pruning in Raiffa, Howard, *Decision Analysis: Introductory Lectures on Choices under Uncertainty*, Addison-Wesley, (1968): 242-243 and 267.

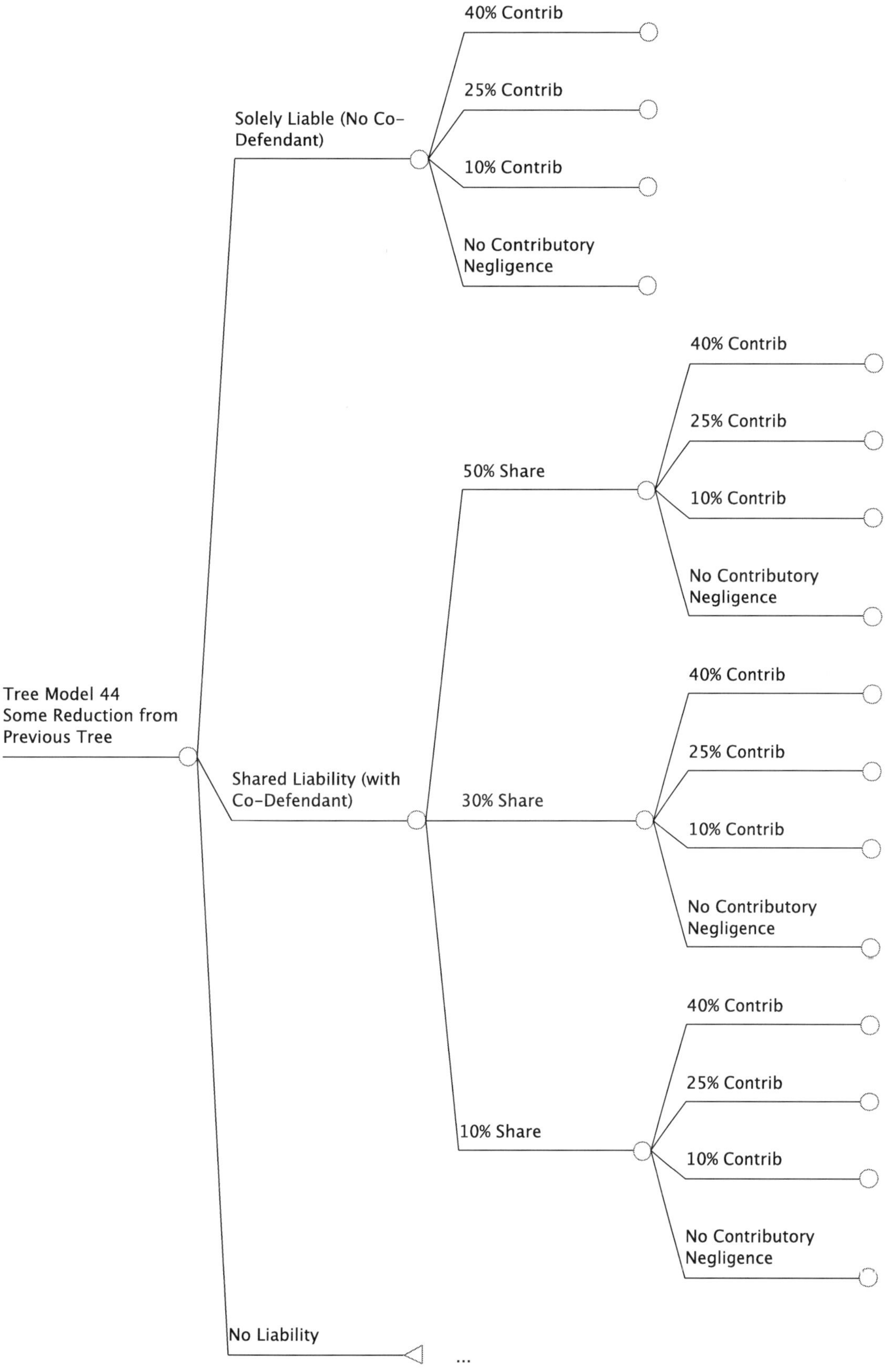
40% Contrib
25% Contrib
Solely Liable (No Co-Defendant)
10% Contrib
No Contributory Negligence
40% Contrib
25% Contrib
50% Share
10% Contrib
No Contributory Negligence
40% Contrib
Tree Model 44
Some Reduction from Previous Tree
25% Contrib
Shared Liability (with Co-Defendant)
30% Share
10% Contrib
No Contributory Negligence
40% Contrib
25% Contrib
10% Share
10% Contrib
No Contributory Negligence
No Liability
...

A note of caution is important here, and will be echoed in Chapter 11 regarding best practices for considering or eliciting subjective probability. That is because research shows people will assign probabilities differently, depending upon the way these questions are asked and depicted on a tree, even though theoretically, the probabilities should be the same.[9]

In other words, if one is asked: "What are the chances of a plaintiff's verdict, and if so, what are the chances of shared or solo liability?[10] they might estimate a 70% chance of liability and a 50% chance of shared liability vs. solo. This would mean that overall (after cumulating the probabilities), they estimate a 30% chance of no liability, a 35% chance of shared liability, and a 35% chance of solo liability. Yet, if the question is asked differently: "We know there are three possibilities: defense verdict (no liability), shared liability, or solo liability. What's the probability of each?", people will allocate the percentages differently.

Since we are in the realm of subjective probability, and we can't test our probability estimates in repetitive jury trials, it's an open question as to which method would prove more accurate. However, instinct tells me to favor the first, more deconstructed probabilities, as it forces the lawyer-estimator to walk forward from the world in which liability/no liability is undetermined, and only then consider how the jury might allocate the blame.

Best practice may be to try it both ways, and think carefully about which probability assignments seem "more right." Given that our task is to simplify the tree, these "alternative sketches" are best done on a scratch pad. Once the tree builder is satisfied with the probability best assigned to each possibility, he can put it in the right place on our streamlined tree.

For the Practical Arborist, Guidelines to Go By

Fair questions for the serious tree-builder lawyer are: "what are the guidelines?" And, "what's a reasonable way to go about deciding where to prune layers, where to combine branches, and where to retain the original "true" depiction of the case within the tree structure?" The suggestion provided above is easy because, assuming care with probabilities, it doesn't really affect the structure (beyond cosmetics) and shouldn't change the outcome at all. Let's consider some criteria for different ways of growing, pruning, and trimming trees:

1) If the original tree fits on a page, and your client can follow its logic and its paths, I see no reason to simplify for its own sake. If your client's major concern is the distribution of outcomes, you can easily create a separate chart showing the probability for each outcome, or the cumulative probability of outcomes greater or lesser than certain dollar amounts.

[9] It is also true that when people are asked to think and assess the separate probabilities about possible paths to an [unfavorable] outcome, the sum of these probabilities tends to be significantly higher than if asked for a simple aggregate estimate of the probability of that outcome. The original experimental work is presented in Fischhoff, Baruch; Slovic, Paul; and Lichtenstein, Sarah, "Fault trees: Sensitivity of estimated failure probabilities to problem representation," *Journal of Experimental Psychology: Human Perception and Performance* 4 (1978): 330-334.
The consensus view that disaggregation leads to higher probability estimates, and collapsing components to lower estimates, is also summarized in Garthwaite, Paul H.; Kadane, Joseph B.; and O'Hagan, Anthony, "Statistical Methods for Eliciting Probability Distributions," *Journal of the American Statistical Association* 100, no. 470 (2005): 680-701.

[10] For the purposes of simplifying this example, I am assuming that solo liability on the co-defendant is not a possibility.

2) There may be some areas where you can see that much "feathering" (fine breakdowns of possible twists in the case), doesn't yield significant differences at the end of each path.

Imagine that your client has been sued for breach of contract in a business dispute. The plaintiff claims that a merger agreement was in place (though the written document was never signed), and your client breached the agreement when they opted to pursue a different business opportunity. Although the agreement contained a $2 million liquidated damages provision, the plaintiff argues that its language doesn't apply and that they lost profits in the amount of $10 million. The plaintiff also claims that, even if there was no contract, the defendant company was not acting in good faith during the negotiation phase, should have informed the plaintiff earlier of its decision not to go forward. As a result of the defendant's actions, the Plaintiff incurred $2 million dollars in reliance damages. Thus, there are disputes (and chance nodes) as to whether a jury would find there was a contract, and if so, whether a liquidated damages provision in the amount of $2 million should apply? And even if the jury finds no enforceable contract, there's a possibility of (hence a chance node for) $2 million in reliance damages. Thus, it might theoretically be legitimate to conflate the sets of branches leading to $2 million. Each probability would have to be added. I suggest the addition occur only after considering them separately.

Below is what the tree might look like before combining any branches.

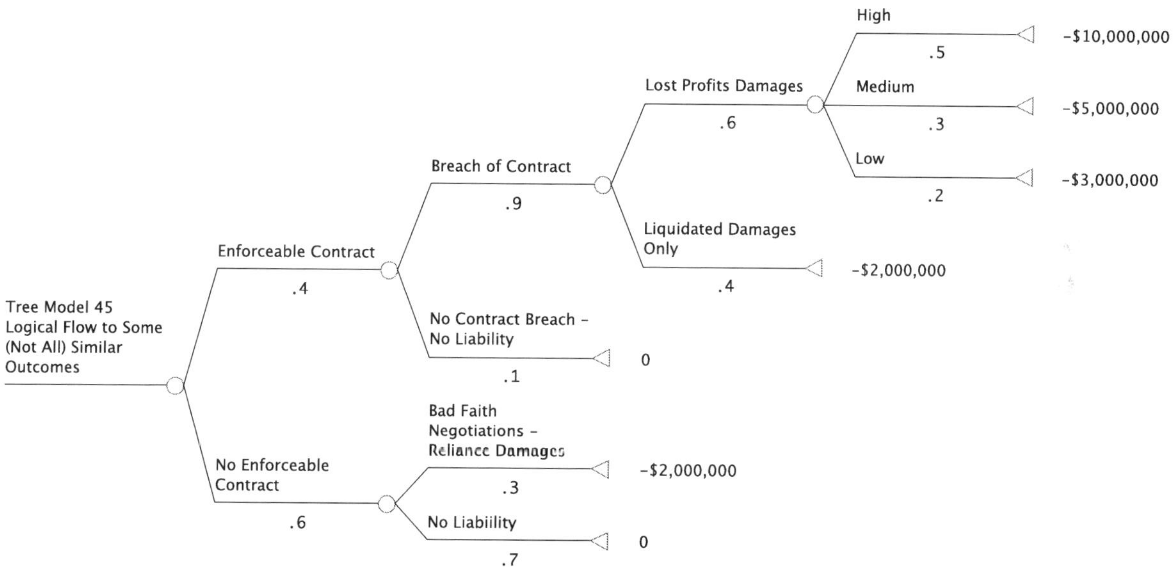

Next is an adjusted tree, that combines the two paths leading to $2 million in damages, and the two paths leading to a defense verdict.

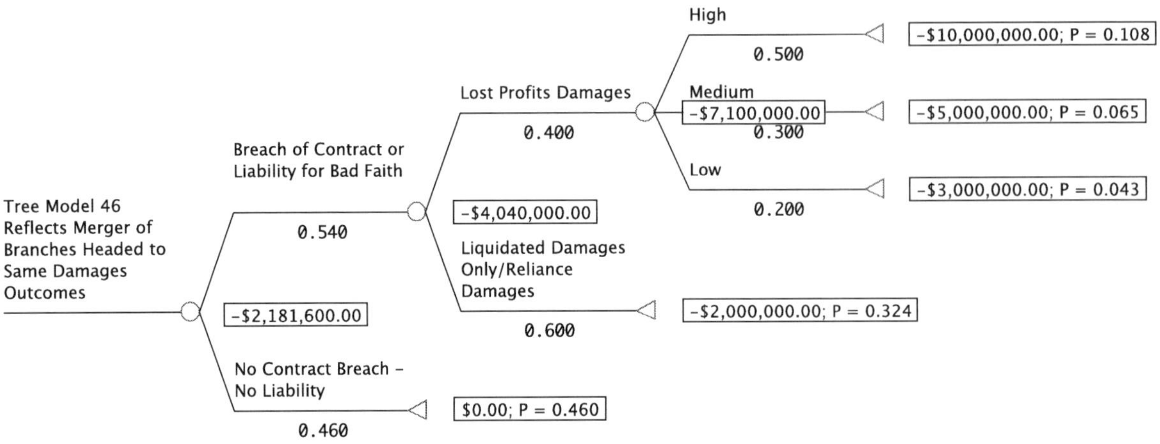

Please accept my note of some disapproval and, at minimum, cautionary advice: the reason NOT to set the tree up in this simpler way is that conflating seems to reflect muddied thinking. If one purpose of this method is to clarify thinking, to reflect careful reasoning (even where reasoning has to account for an emotional jury), trimming the tree in this way defeats that purpose. As suggested earlier, my inclination is to include complexity and the number of chance nodes that reasonably reflect reality. If that creates a messy or illegible visual, you can break the tree into sub parts for separate review and discussion. However, if you must merge branches, then DO take care to add each probability you would have applied to each separate branch.

With all due respect for legal logic and careful thinking, the question of impact can reasonably inform the tree builder's initial draft of the tree structure. A lawyer-tree builder may be inclined to consider and create separate branches for alternative claims or theories of the case. In the event of a motion to dismiss or motion for summary judgment, he might consider and create branches for alternative ways the judge might allow some portions of the case to go forward. If these alternative claims or theories lead to little or no difference in the evidence introduced, the likelihood of liability, or the measure of damages, then you may safely merge them in a well-considered final tree structure.

3) Particularly with regard to multiple branches for different possible damages theories and ranges, the client may be indifferent above or below certain break points.

Imagine that your client's business will be bankrupted by a judgment over $3 million. Assume that, if there were a fraud finding, it's at least 50% likely the damages award would be greater than $3 million. To that client, whether it's more likely to be $4 million, $5 million, or $8 million doesn't matter so much. But he does very much want to know the overall likelihood that it will end up at $3 million or higher. Or imagine that your commercial plaintiff client's business recovery will not be significantly impacted by a judgment of less than $300,000. He doesn't care to know at the low end, whether it could fall at a disappointing $100,000 or $200,000. But he might very much care about the upside: the probabilities of recovering an amount that would revive his business and its ability to move forward with credit and investment. In either case, you are free to prune branches and combine probability estimates without guilt in areas of little significance for your client's decision. [11]

Strategies for Both—Simpler Presentation and Complex Support Structures

Whether inside or outside corporate counsel, a lawyer representing a large company in an enormously consequential matter needs to be able to present a simple, compelling overview of a looming litigation so that the executive team and perhaps the board of directors are fully informed. The case will require commitment of resources; the marketing and PR departments may wish to undertake certain initiatives in anticipation of the litigation's impact (win or lose); research and development or the corporate acquisitions unit may want to seek alternative ways to produce the controversial product, free of patent claims. The corporate lawyers and compliance department will need to understand the case analysis for the purposes of SEC filings and shareholder notice.

Just as in a prospectus or shareholder's report, an executive summary makes sense when presenting decision analysis in oral or written form. For that, a readable single page tree (even enlarged) may be best. Or you might opt for a two-page presentation, one showing the structure of the tree leading up to liability determinations and one showing the structure of uncertainties regarding damages. If you want everyone on the same page, it has to be a page that all can understand.

Yet, in view of the stakes and resources that have been or should be expended to assess and improve risk at critical case junctures, thorough analysis is warranted. This is no time to give details short shrift. Thus, I strongly recommend that the tree-builder lawyer create subtrees for elements impacting liability and damages that could not be separately highlighted in the "executive" tree. These subtree analyses are what yield the probabilities or damages reflected in the executive tree.

Proffering the Probability Subtree

Consider a case in which the trial court's rulings on one or two critical and complicated motions *in limine* will significantly impact the likelihood of liability. To put that into the main tree, with all subsequent branches, would add a great deal of visual complexity. Remember, each of those initial "left side" branches must be followed by all of the case's possible paths toward liability and damages.

Instead of presenting the various motions *in limine* branch clusters on the main tree, you might create and provide a back-up in the form of a "probability subtree" showing the ruling's anticipated effect on the likelihood of liability, and the probabilities assigned to each ruling. This subtree serves to explain how you derived the probability estimate for liability in the summary tree. As shown on the next tree, it permits the elimination of a tangle of preliminary motions before two simple liability or no liability branches.

[11] The TreeAge software includes a helpful "over under" feature for precisely this type of question. From the menu under "Analysis," you can "ask" the total probability of results under or over a given dollar amount.

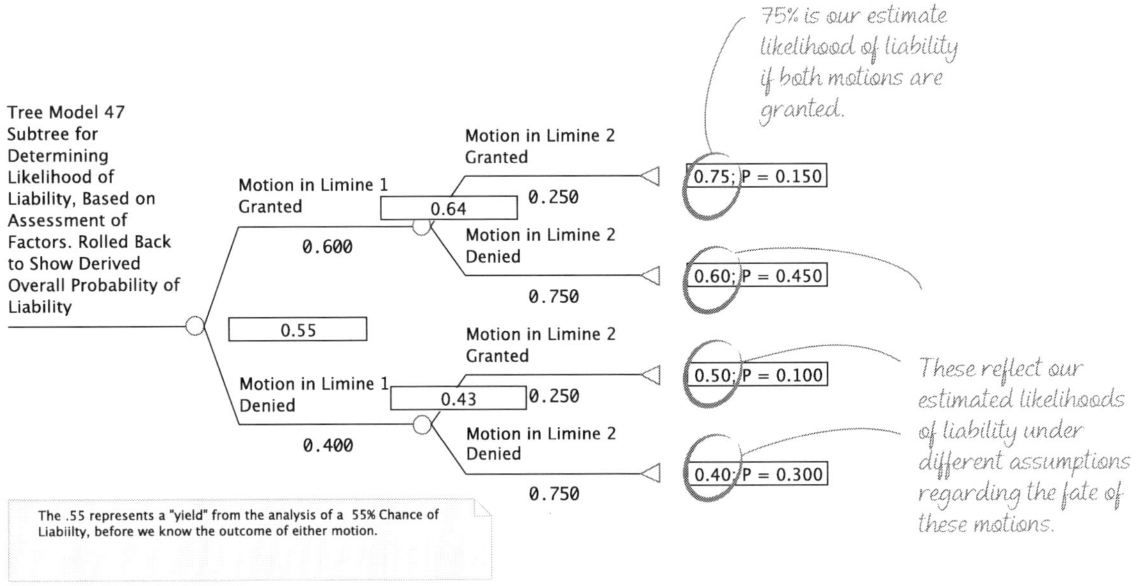

It's important to recognize that the percentages at the end are estimated probability OUTCOMES. This subtree is intended to assist us in deriving the probability of liability that will appear on the main tree. Thus the top path along the branches reflects a judgment that IF the Motion *in Limine* #1 were granted, AND Motion *in Limine* #2 were granted, the likelihood of a liability finding would be .75 or 75%. The .6 below the "Motion *in Limine* #1" branch reflects someone's estimate of a 60% chance of that Motion *in Limine* #1 will in fact be granted, just as the .25 under the "Motion *in Limine* #2" branch reflects someone's estimate of a 25% chance that it will be granted, and so on.

When these are rolled back, the probability "EMV" is the overall estimate of the chance of liability, derived from these separate assessments of uncertainties affecting the chance of liability. Thus, that 55% would be inserted in the summary or main tree as the chance of a liability finding.

Damages Without Details

On the damages front, you might put all of the damages analysis into a separate tree, roll it back to an EMV for damages, and then plug that damages number into the executive tree.

The very real danger, of course, is that the executive tree would NOT reflect the highest or lowest estimated damages number, but a weighted average of the damages numbers.

First, here's a wonderfully complicated tree, rolled back and with all of the motions, theories and potential damages displayed. The reader will note that the case story—the facts and legal analysis—is not presented here, though that would explain the cryptic references and abbreviations on various branch labels. The case story doesn't matter for our purposes: to illustrate an admirably complex tree and then how that tree can be simplified by "collapsing" damages subtrees.

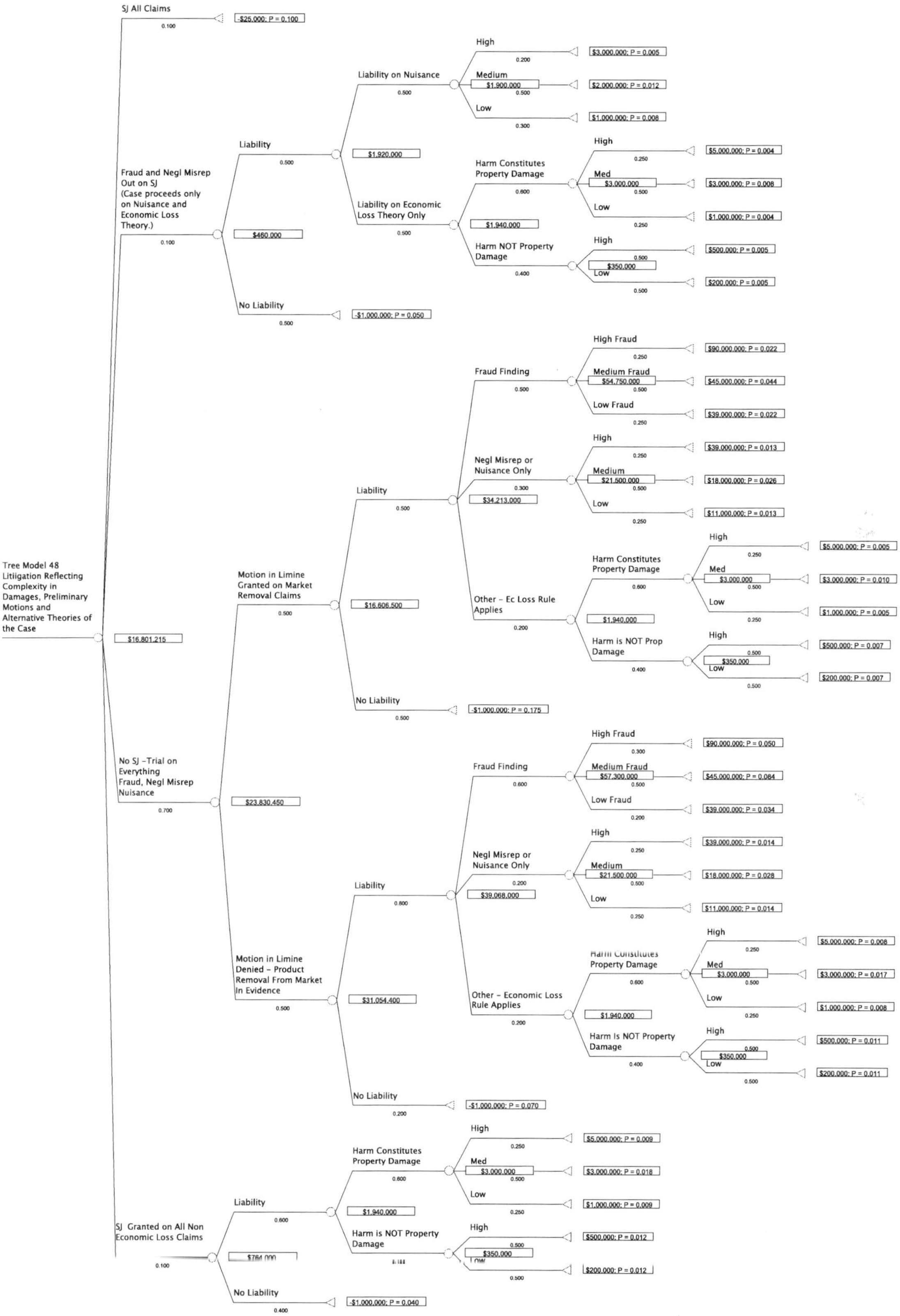
Tree Model 48 Litigation Reflecting Complexity in Damages, Preliminary Motions and Alternative Theories of the Case
$16,801,215
SJ All Claims
0.100
-$25,000; P = 0.100
Fraud and Negl Misrep Out on SJ (Case proceeds only on Nuisance and Economic Loss Theory.)
0.100
$460,000
Liability
0.500
$1,920,000
Liability on Nuisance
0.500
High
0.200
$3,000,000; P = 0.005
Medium
$1,900,000
0.500
$2,000,000; P = 0.012
Low
0.300
$1,000,000; P = 0.008
Liability on Economic Loss Theory Only
0.500
$1,940,000
Harm Constitutes Property Damage
0.600
High
0.250
$5,000,000; P = 0.004
Med
$3,000,000
0.500
$3,000,000; P = 0.008
Low
0.250
$1,000,000; P = 0.004
Harm NOT Property Damage
0.400
High
0.500
$500,000; P = 0.005
$350,000
Low
0.500
$200,000; P = 0.005
No Liability
0.500
-$1,000,000; P = 0.050
No SJ -Trial on Everything Fraud, Negl Misrep Nuisance
0.700
$23,830,450
Motion in Limine Granted on Market Removal Claims
0.500
$16,606,500
Liability
0.500
$34,213,000
Fraud Finding
0.500
High Fraud
0.250
$90,000,000; P = 0.022
Medium Fraud
$54,750,000
0.500
$45,000,000; P = 0.044
Low Fraud
0.250
$39,000,000; P = 0.022
Negl Misrep or Nuisance Only
0.300
High
0.250
$39,000,000; P = 0.013
Medium
$21,500,000
0.500
$18,000,000; P = 0.026
Low
0.250
$11,000,000; P = 0.013
Other - Ec Loss Rule Applies
0.200
$1,940,000
Harm Constitutes Property Damage
0.600
High
0.250
$5,000,000; P = 0.005
Med
$3,000,000
0.500
$3,000,000; P = 0.010
Low
0.250
$1,000,000; P = 0.005
Harm is NOT Prop Damage
0.400
High
0.500
$500,000; P = 0.007
$350,000
Low
0.500
$200,000; P = 0.007
No Liability
0.500
-$1,000,000; P = 0.175
Motion in Limine Denied - Product Removal From Market In Evidence
0.500
$31,054,400
Liability
0.800
$39,068,000
Fraud Finding
0.600
High Fraud
0.300
$90,000,000; P = 0.050
Medium Fraud
$57,300,000
0.500
$45,000,000; P = 0.084
Low Fraud
0.200
$39,000,000; P = 0.034
Negl Misrep or Nuisance Only
0.200
High
0.250
$39,000,000; P = 0.014
Medium
$21,500,000
0.500
$18,000,000; P = 0.028
Low
0.250
$11,000,000; P = 0.014
Other - Economic Loss Rule Applies
0.200
$1,940,000
Harm Constitutes Property Damage
0.600
High
0.250
$5,000,000; P = 0.008
Med
$3,000,000
0.500
$3,000,000; P = 0.017
Low
0.250
$1,000,000; P = 0.008
Harm Is NOT Property Damage
0.400
High
0.500
$500,000; P = 0.011
$350,000
Low
0.500
$200,000; P = 0.011
No Liability
0.200
-$1,000,000; P = 0.070
SJ Granted on All Non Economic Loss Claims
0.100
Liability
0.600
$1,940,000
Harm Constitutes Property Damage
0.600
High
0.250
$5,000,000; P = 0.009
Med
$3,000,000
0.500
$3,000,000; P = 0.018
Low
0.250
$1,000,000; P = 0.009
Harm is NOT Property Damage
High
0.500
$500,000; P = 0.012
$350,000
Low
0.500
$200,000; P = 0.012
No Liability
0.400
-$1,000,000; P = 0.040

Now here's a simplified version of the tree, with various damages branch clusters "collapsed"—not showing. (The TreeAge software allows you to collapse subtrees at any point, but still rollback the tree to derive its overall EMV. The roll back is calculated using the damages numbers that were at the terminal nodes, even though they are not visible.)

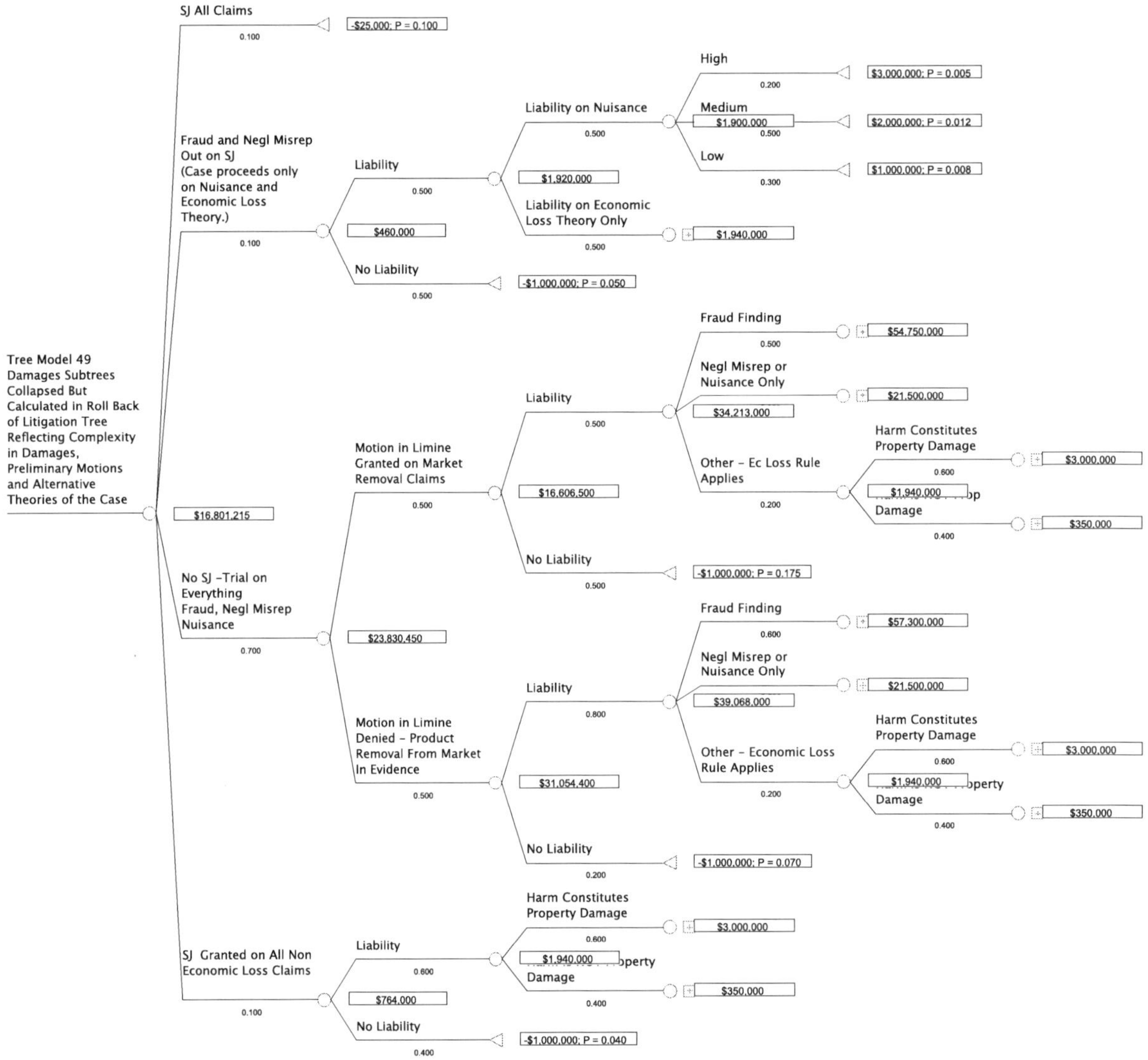

The danger of focusing your client discussion on a visually simplified tree, with collapsed damages subtrees and branches is that it fails to alert the client to the full possible range of numbers. This is particularly dangerous where the range of possible damages is wide. After all, the damages range represents the outcomes that might indeed impact your client. Thus, a visually simplified tree, pruning back the damages ranges, makes sense for a discussion of procedural uncertainties and legal theories. However, that should be followed by a separate examination of the damages subtrees. Despite their invisibility, they form the basis for the rollback.

I'd also suggest a page that graphs or lists all of the possible outcomes and their likelihoods. Here's what a graph of the probability distributions might look like.

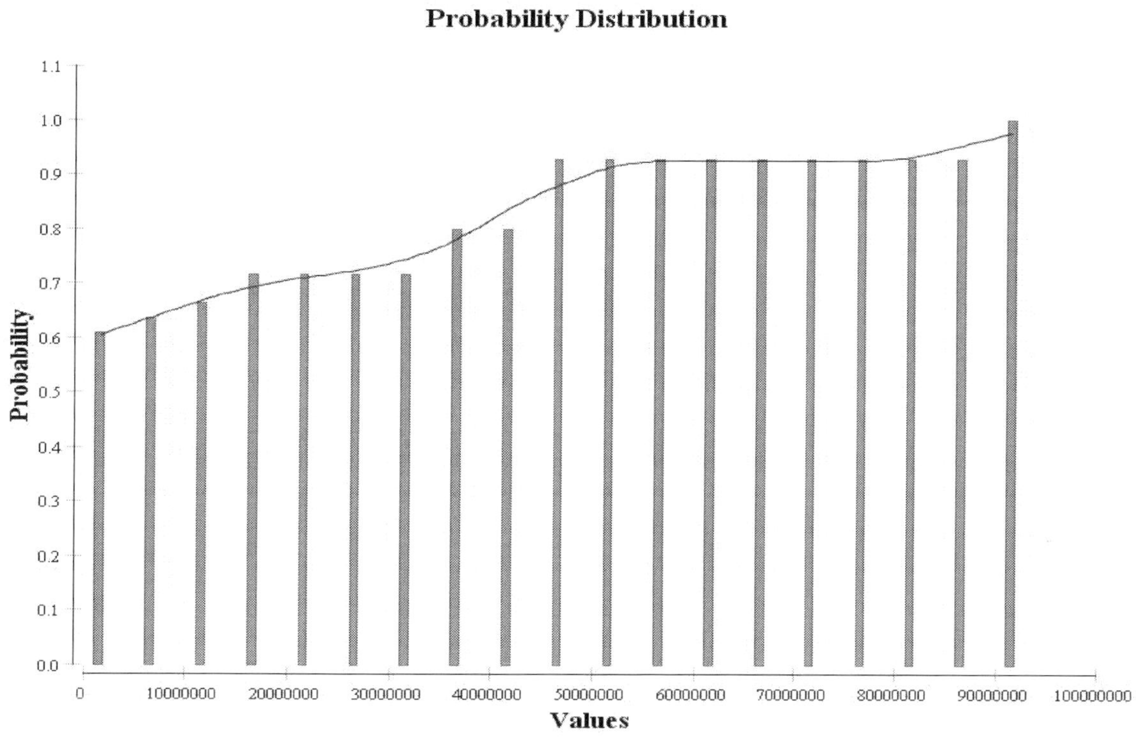

A more precise breakdown, derived from the full tree (Tree Model 48), might be helpful if presented to your client in this way. (This could also no doubt be generated on a spreadsheet.)

Possible outcomes	Total Probability	From these path probabilities
$90,000,000	7.2%	.022, .050
$45,000,000	12.8%	.044, .084
$39,000,000	8.3%	.022, .034, .013, .014
$18,000,000	5.4%	.028, .026
$11,000,000	2.7%	.013, .014
$5,000,000	2.6%	.009, .008, .005, .004
$3,000,000	5.8%	.005, 008, .010, .017, .018
$2,000,000	1.2%	.012
$1,000,000	3.4%	.009, .008, .005, .004, .008
$500,000	3.5%	.007, .011, .012, .005
$200,000	3.5%	.007, .011, .012, .005
-$25,000	10%	.10
-$1,000,000	33.5%	.05, .175, .07, .04
TOTAL	99.9% (.1% under 100% due to rounding loss)	

Another way of thinking about it is to highlight that your analysis reflects a 27.7% chance of a verdict between $39,000,000 and $90,000,000; an 8.3% chance of a verdict that is either $18,000,000 or $11,000,000 (or in between), an 11.3% of a verdict between $1,000,000 and $3,000,000, and so forth. On the other hand, there's a 43.5% chance that the verdict would result in $0 recovery and significant attorney's fees and costs. The discussion with your client would focus on the numerical ranges of greatest significance to his business.

Separate Confusion of Counterclaims

Counterclaims can be counted upon to present visual confusion, depending in part on how they fit logically and thus, where they should be placed in the tree structure. While you may wish to build the counterclaim's tree structure separately, the various probabilities for branches of the counterclaim will inevitably be impacted by events and evidence in the main case. In other words, given that the cases are related in real life, it makes sense to relate the two trees.

In some cases, there is a straightforward logical inconsistency between finding in favor of the plaintiff in the main claim and in favor of the defendant-claimant on the counterclaim. The jury can accept the narrative and case theory of one side or the other, not both. You can fashion a tree structure that is more manageable.

By way of example let's take a case between a custom software developer and a business client. Assume that no dispositive motions are filed: it appears clear that the trial will be fact intensive, and all material facts are hotly disputed between the parties. The structure of the tree toward the left side might look like this (branches relating to damages, which would be toward the right side are omitted for now):

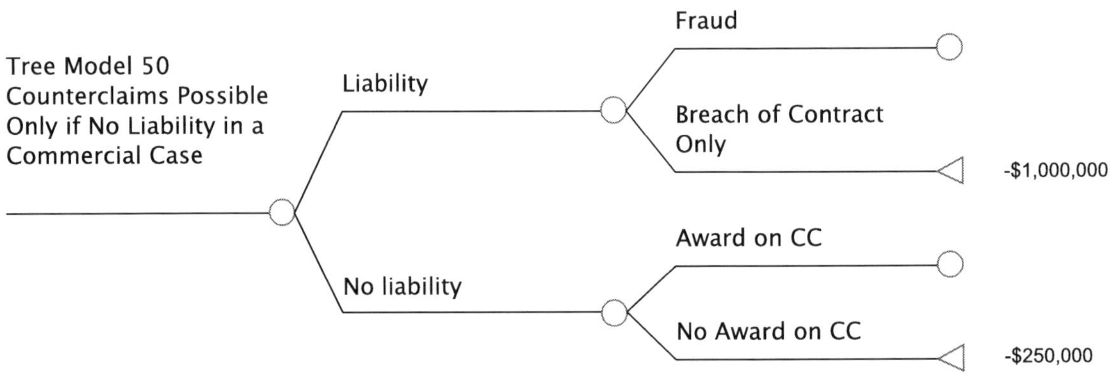

Where a jury could logically rule in favor of the plaintiff on the main claim and also in favor of the defendant on its counterclaims, building this possibility into the tree is just plain more complicated. This should not be surprising, given that this type of counterclaim presents a more complicated thought problem for any lawyer, with or without formed tree analysis. The difficulty is thinking about whether to structure the tree in three main sections: the first branch would be "verdict for plaintiff only"; the second would be "verdict for defendant-counterclaimant only;" and the third would have to be "liability for each on each claim."

It might look like this next one.

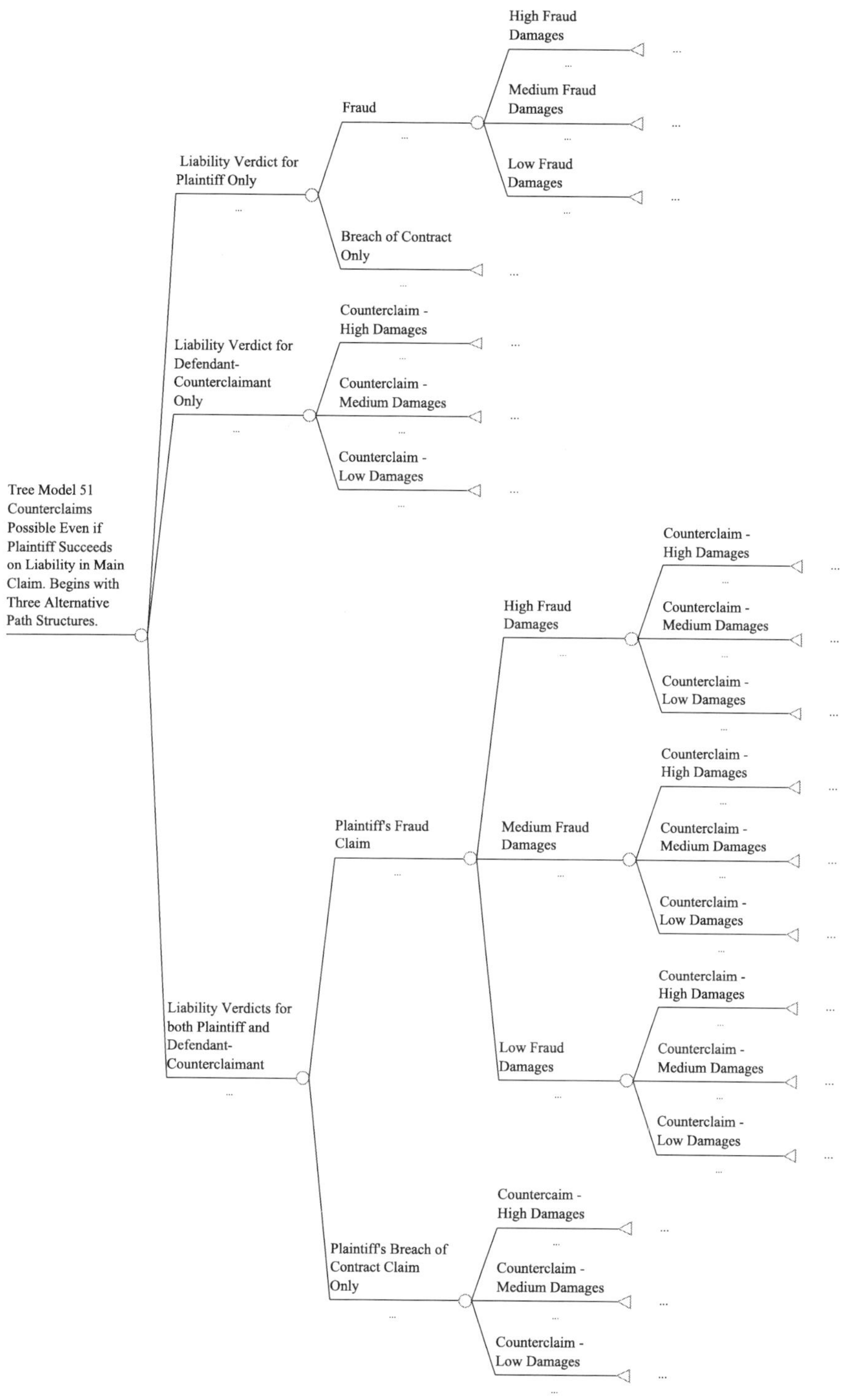

The problem with structuring the tree this way is that it may not capture the impact or reasoning along what we think of as the jury's path. To look at the three segments separately seems wrong. After all, the jury that would have heard evidence and experts and finds the defendant liable for breach is a very different jury from the one that does not. And those two hypothetical juries are likely to view the evidence on the counterclaim in entirely different ways.

For that reason, it would be logical to create the decision tree for the main case and at the far right side, after what would otherwise be the terminal nodes (where payoffs are calculated), to insert a series of branches representing the counterclaim. Then, as you follow the counterclaim branches, you would insert probabilities that make sense in light of what the jury decided with the main claims.

Imagine that the next tree reflects the structure of the counterclaim (deliberately somewhat simplified).

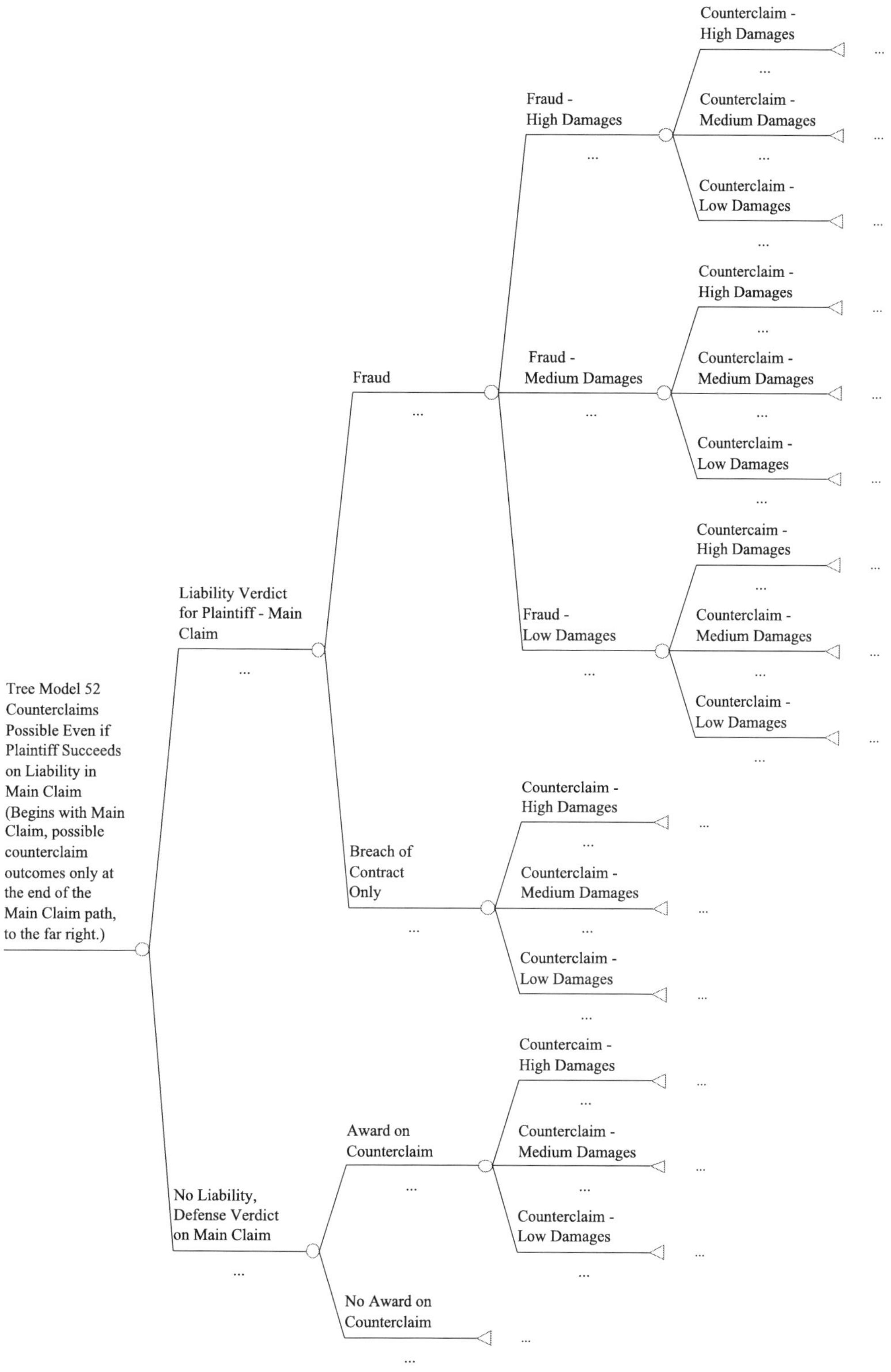

Again, this tree assumes an obvious, single amount of damages on a breach of contract theory alone, based on the contract terms and uncontroverted evidence.

Note that inserting this tree at the far right end of our main tree would VERY quickly create a feathery mess, unreadable without a magnifying glass, enlarged printing, or many pages put together. And, if the main tree has any complexity itself, the tree-builder lawyer will be stuck plugging in the subtree, over and over again, moving down the right-hand side. And he would be tasked with making sure that the probabilities and payoffs on each inserted subtree are consistent with its place along the path.

Assuming the tree builder is admirably patient, he will then have to manage pay-off figures that include the main claim and the counterclaim. One problem is that this will tend to obfuscate the separate distribution of possible outcomes from the main tree, and from the counterclaim.

Even if the tree-builder is indefatigable and enthusiastic about the exercise, the client is likely to glaze over. What does it all mean? One of the purposes of a decision tree approach is to map what might happen, so we can see possible paths to the end of the case. At some point, when the tree is overly complex, we lose the ability to see. The visual message that "it's complicated" is clear, but what to do with that remains a mystery. We are lost in the forest.

Perhaps, then, the lawyer is wise to create a separate, simpler tree, with paths that are easy to see and understand, and probabilities confirmed by more detailed sub-analysis.

6

Structure Through to the Net (Outcomes)

As the reader knows, on the right-hand side of the tree are the possible story endings—the outcomes. It's important to work with *net* outcomes or *net* payoffs—*after* subtracting amounts to be expended from amounts that may be won. Our task in constructing a decision tree, even one focused on litigation risk analysis, is to consider what decision to make in light of all possible outcomes and their respective probabilities, and in light of costs to get there.

It would be foolish to choose one path over another because it leads to a larger pot of gold, without also counting the gold coins I will lose (or theoretically gain) along that path. If my game ticket will win $1,000 or $2000 or $3000, or maybe $0, I might be willing to sell that ticket at a certain price, depending upon the probabilities. But if I have to pay $250 or $500 for a ticket to play, I might be willing to sell the ticket for a much different amount. And, if I will value or take pleasure in the game itself, my ticket price will also be different.

Some have criticized the application of decision analysis to legal cases because users—mediators and lawyers—fail to account for costs, risk aversion, or other intangibles.[1] In reality though, this criticism is of misapplication of the method. This author cringes to learn of those who purport to use decision analysis and yet completely ignore costs, intangibles, and risk. Any respectable textbook or article on decision analysis will explicitly require that its calculations include consequential costs from the time of the analysis going forward. Software (TreeAge) invites the tree-builder for legal cases to create payoff formulas, contemplating that attorneys' fees and other costs will be subtracted from the plaintiff's anticipated positive "payoffs" and added to the defense's potential negative payoffs.[2] Unless the actual costs—lawyer's and experts' fees—will be entirely insignificant in comparison to the litigation's stakes, there's no excuse for omitting costs from final outcome estimates to which analysis will be applied.

This section highlights the importance of structuring the "pay-off" as a net number and offers advice on how to do it. That net pay-off should include anticipated damages (positive or negative, depending upon who will be paying and who receiving) minus the costs of getting *from the moment of decision to that end point.* At a minimum, if the outcome is measured in dollars, then the dollar costs should

[1] Aaron, Marjorie and Brazil, Wayne, "Shaking Decision Trees for Risks and Rewards," *Dispute Resolution Magazine* 22, no. 1 (2015): 10-18.

[2] Technically, estimated verdict amounts should include any statutory interest and should adjust future payoffs by discounting for time value of money. Particularly in the days of higher general interest rates and when final judgment is far in the future, the tree builder is encouraged to calculate the time value of the future monetary award. A somewhat less-technical approach can be excused—skipping the present value discount, for example—in a time limited mediation or for a lawyer reluctant to hike his bill. As always, the relevant question is whether the difference will be significant.

be subtracted. Thus, as the lawyer tree builder works his way to the end point of the various paths, he should not only ask: "What is the best estimate of this damages amount?" He must also ask: "What will the attorneys' fees and the experts' fees be between now and then? What other expenditures will the company have to make from here on in?" These questions should be built into the process, set out as blanks to plug into the arithmetic formula for deriving end values, before rolling back the tree.

As a best practice, intangible and less direct but consequential costs and gains should also be included. While some intangibles are more easily translated to dollar values than others, it is generally worth some effort. Chapter Eight in this text suggests some ways to consider intangibles in the analysis and client discussion.

Within Range of Significant Net

Many, if not most, litigated cases fall within a dollar value range such that including attorneys' fees and other costs in net payoffs makes a significant difference in the economics of the decision. Consider how many of your cases involve potential outcomes that are less than $500,000, with attorney's fees and costs projected at $50,000 or more. Imagine that, when you roll back and boil down the decision tree analysis—WITHOUT calculating fees, at the far right side of the tree, there's an overall 40% chance of $0 award (via 20% chance of summary judgment, and 25% chance of the defense prevailing at trial, if summary judgment is denied. Assume a very sympathetic plaintiff). This would yield a 60% overall chance of a defense liability, with a 20% chance of verdict at $100,000, 20% at $250,000 and 20% at $500,000. That tree would roll back to an overall EMV of just under $170,000. (It would be $170,000 exactly but for the assignment of a probability of .334 to the median branches, instead of .333, or 1/3, to make the probabilities at each branch sum to 100%.)

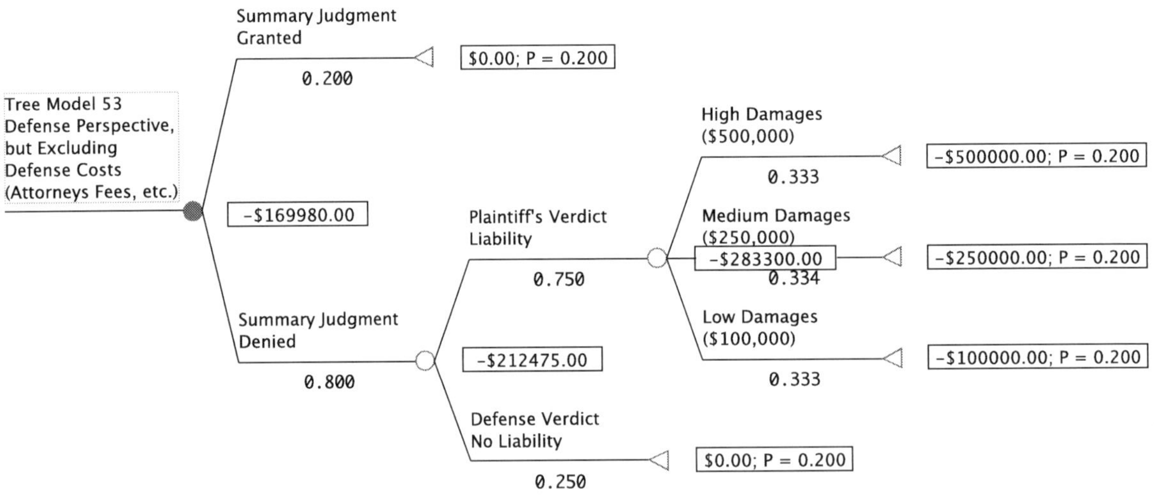

Now, take the same tree and add in the cost of attorneys' fees and costs at $50,000 if the case goes to trial, but only $20,000 if the case is dismissed on summary judgment.

That same tree would roll back to an EMV of approximately $214,000, as shown next.

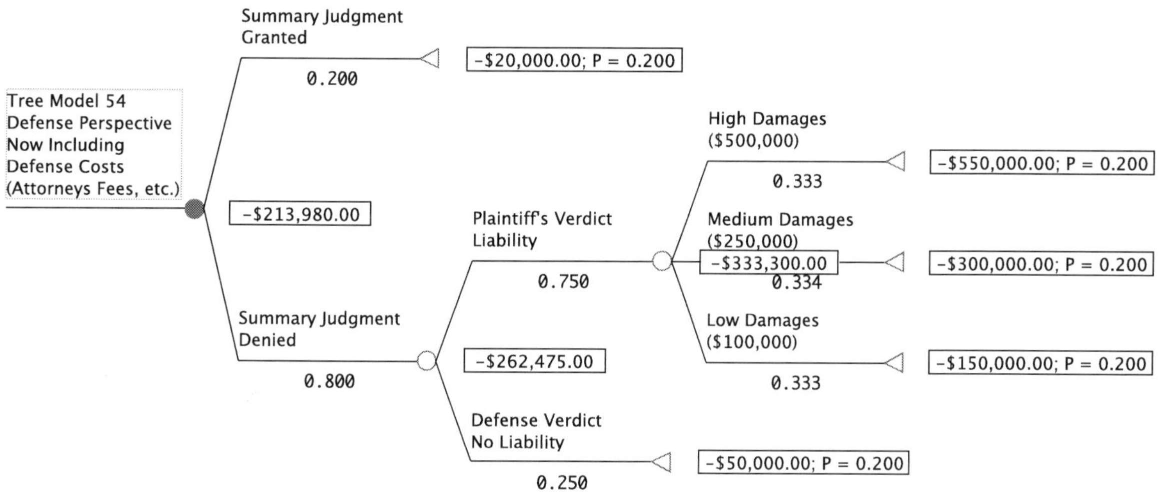

Obviously, my attorneys' fee estimate may be too conservative for labor-intensive cases with many depositions, much witness preparation, and expensive experts.

The EMV would be approximately $256,000, assuming $100,000 in costs and fees (from the date of decision) through trial, $30,000 through summary judgment, as shown next.

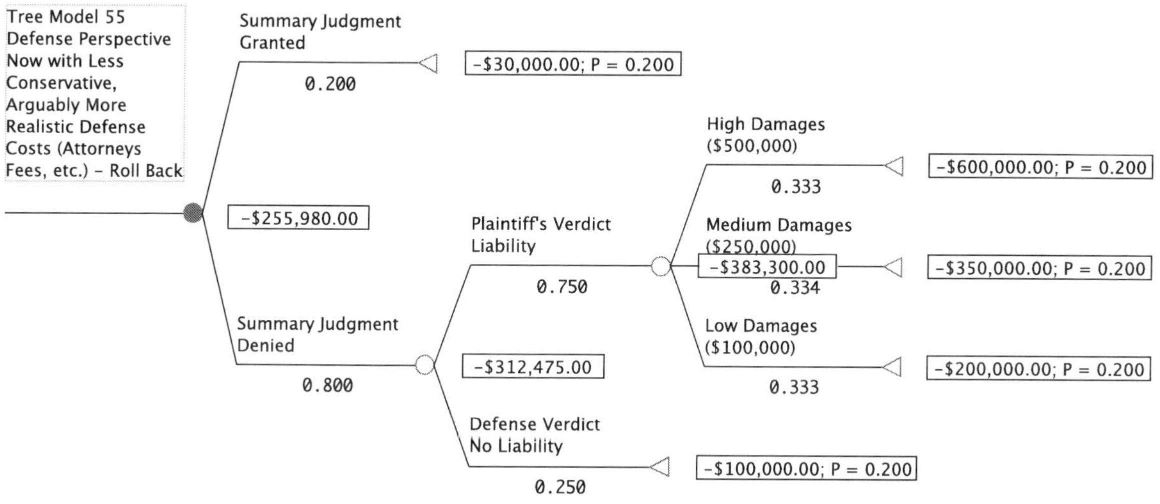

On the plaintiff's side, wherever the plaintiff is responsible for attorney's fees at an hourly rate, including those fees in the calculation has a parallel, if not more dramatic impact. Using the same hypothetical case, the plaintiff's EMV would be $170,000 without including fees and costs.

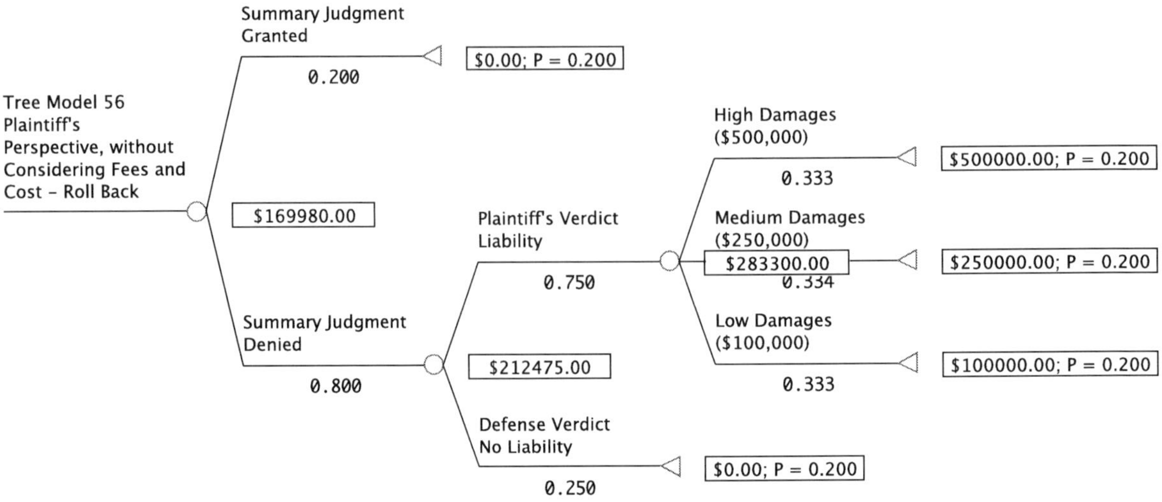

Without showing yet another tree, I hope the reader will accept that, if the plaintiff's estimated fees and costs were estimated at $50,000, the EMV would be approximately $126,000.

What if $100,000 is a better estimate of the plaintiff's attorneys' fees and other costs? (Assume $30,000 through summary judgment and $100,000 through trial.) There the results are dramatic: the plaintiff's EMV is reduced to approximately $84,000, as reflected on the tree below.

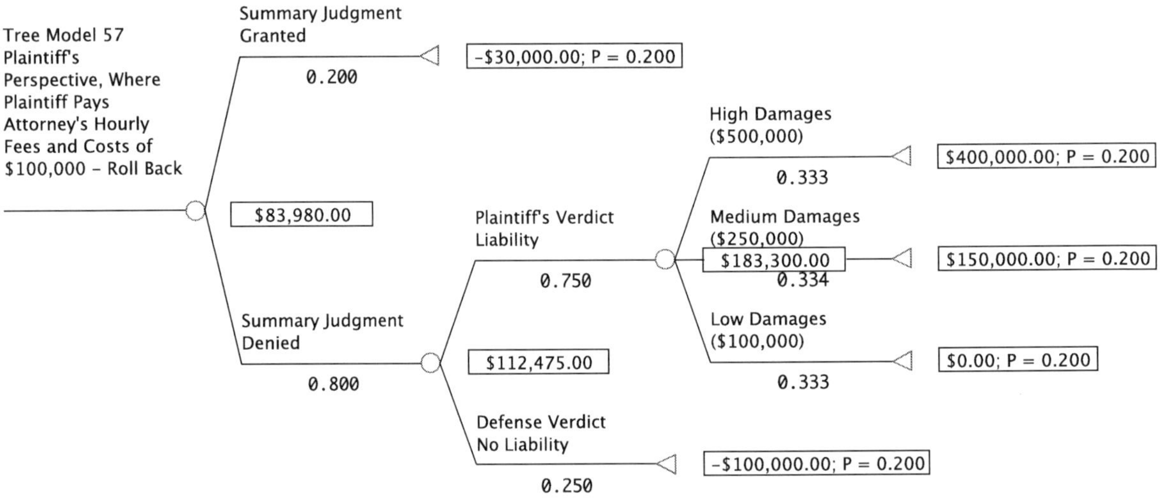

Not surprisingly, the impact of adding or subtracting fees and costs into the net payoff weakens as the potential award range grows. For rare cases involving potential exposure or gain in the millions (or multiple millions), with fee and cost estimates a small percentage, they become a less critical element of the computation.[3]

[3] Pushing people toward settlement is not the purpose of this piece. Thus, I have refrained from inclusion of musings about how cost and fee estimates may become motivations for settlement even in large cases. For readers in the role of settlement counsel or mediators, it is worth thinking and asking about.

Here's one last illustration, using a hypothetical case in a not-so-unusual dollar range.[4] Imagine that there's a potentially dispositive preliminary motion, with a relatively low chance of success. The plaintiff could win damages within a certain range, or the plaintiff could succeed on some type of fraud or punitive claim or any theory that would, at minimum, enable the plaintiff to collect her attorneys' fees from the defendant, as well as double damages. Let's assume that if the plaintiff wins on liability, the base damages would be $75,000, $200,000, or $350,000, depending on how the evidence comes in and what the jury believes. Now, let's assume further that defense costs will be approximately $30,000 through the dispositive motion (including discovery, which is only partially complete), and an additional $70,000 through trial. Finally, let's assume that plaintiff's counsel's "reasonable fees and costs" through trial would be $100,000.

Here's what the tree would look like from the defense perspective WITHOUT considering anyone's costs or fees. Note that the EMV is $172,000.

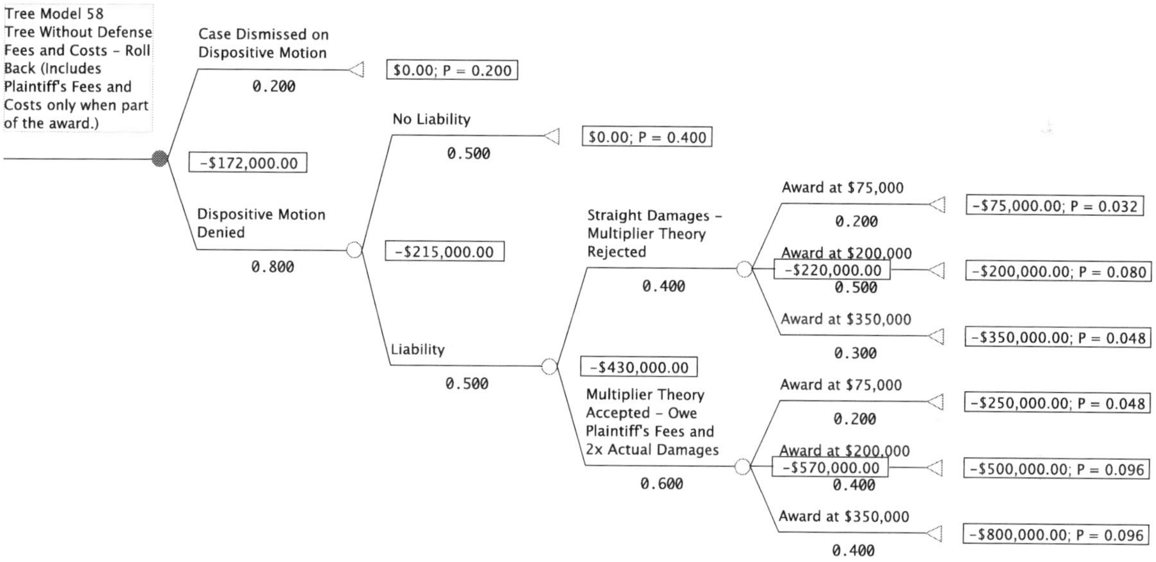

The next tree shows what it would look like AFTER including costs and fees the defense would be responsible for paying. Note that the EMV is -$258,000.

[4] Aaron and Brazil, 16-17.

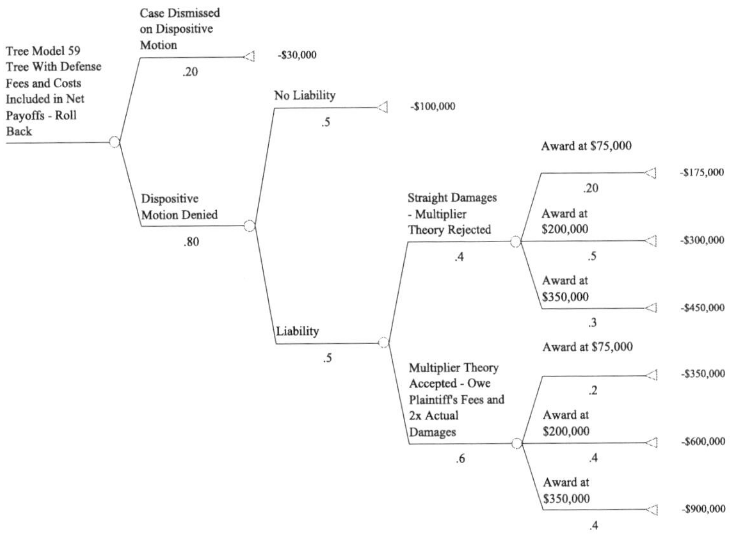

For the defense client who chooses to be guided by this analysis in making settlement decisions, it would be misleading to omit these fees and costs. They will be real when incurred, and will come out of cash reserves just as the judgment will. In fact, the costs and fees will come out sooner.

Shortcuts Risk Shorting Communication Value

The weary lawyer or mediator determined to build a decision tree for a client's case might ask: "Why can't I build the tree without costs and just SAY to my client, 'Of course on top of that will be your fees and costs in $X amount'...?" Theoretically, he can and that would be better than nothing. But one important reason to include those fees and costs in real net pay-off numbers is known as "measurability bias."[5] Humans tend to ascribe too much weight to what is measured and counted, and too little weight to what is not. Take something out of numbers, and we are less likely to assign it importance when making a decision. This is a problem for intangibles that are hard to measure and count and yet really will matter to the client. Given that costs and fees are estimable, numerical, and thus countable, excluding them from end "pay-off" values creates an unnecessary distortion.[6]

Consider the following hypothetical regarding the measurability bias in action. The defense's business representative reports to his boss: "Our lawyer's decision tree analysis pointed to a logical settlement value in the range of $350,000, with a worst case damages number of $750,000, a low estimate of $150,000 and a 40% chance of a defense verdicts. Of course, he also said we should consider the fees and costs that could be in the $100,000 range." I can just hear the client asking for corporate authority to settle for $350,000, or $300,000 or less, focusing on the EMV as stated, and the idea that less is a

[5] See: Hall, Brian and Staats, Trent, "Do the Numbers Get in Your Way?" *Negotiation* 7, no. 11 (2004).

[6] Some tree builders may be tempted to take the short cut of subtracting total fees and costs from the Estimated Monetary Value, in other words, AFTER the Roll back.

If those fees and costs will be exactly the same—no matter what the result—this would be fine. However, where an early dispositive motion could end the case with lower fees, as in the example above, we would be OVER weighting the costs and fees to subtract their total from Estimated Monetary Value. Moreover, in the example above, the defense tree should only count plaintiff's estimated fees on branches where they would be due—branches reflecting plantiff's win on more punitive theories.

bargain or a strategic negotiation win. Costs are just as real a part of any outcome. Leaving them out of the EMV analysis falsely diminishes their reality and their force. The client may elect to set different settlement limits and aspirations, if presented with an EMV of at least $400,000, based on net payoffs that include those costs.

The other common and problematic practice is to subtract or add the costs on top of an EMV calculated from payoffs without costs. This results in mathematical inaccuracy in any case where attorneys' fees and other costs will differ depending on the case's path. Imagine that the decision analyst lawyer represents the defendant company in an employment discrimination case with a 20% chance of summary judgment. The attorney's fees through summary judgment would be a fraction of the attorneys' fees and experts' costs to be expended if the case goes to trial. The EMV or roll back number for the entire "value" of the case—the weighted average of all possible outcomes—includes a 20% discount for the possibility that summary judgment will be granted and the plaintiff will collect $0. Thus, subtracting the *full* estimated fees & costs overweighs them and distorts the EMV, as is evident when you compare Tree Model 60 and Tree Model 61.

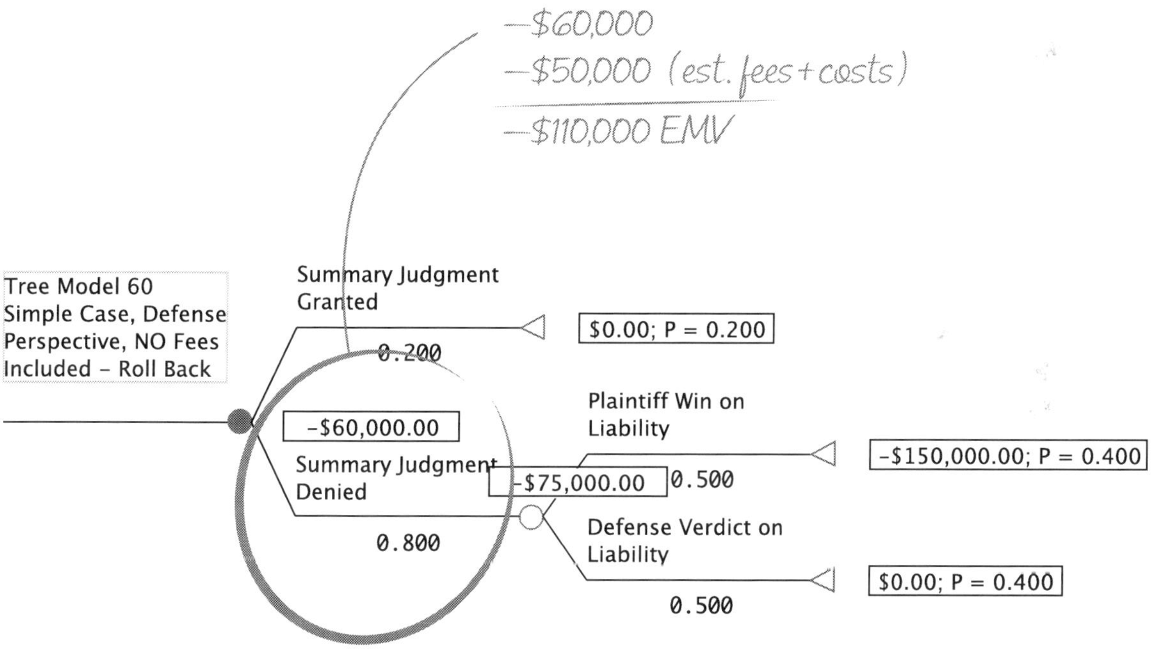

As shown on the next tree, when accurate fees and costs are placed at each end point, they are weighted appropriately within the analysis.

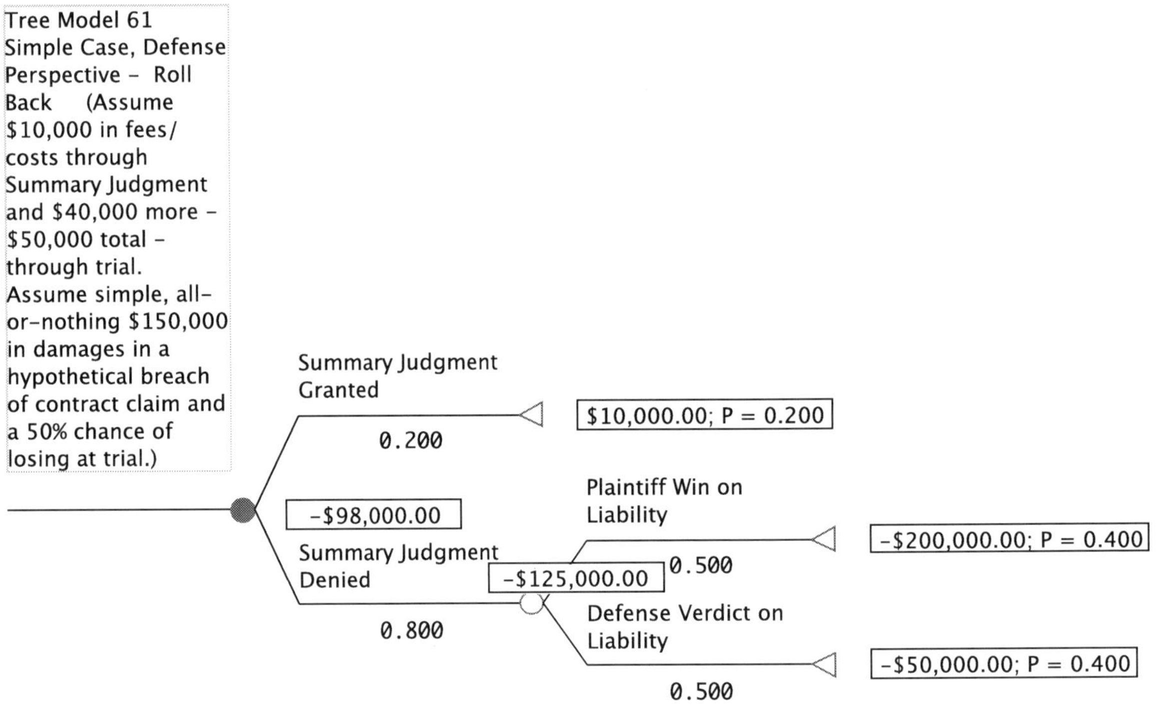

The EMV is $98,000, when attorneys' fees are included on the tree. The "pay-off" or, for the defense "payment to be made" numbers at the right of the tree include the $50,000 in fees. Thus, the $200,000 at the terminal node is comprised of a $150,000 award plus 50,000 in attorney's fees.

On the other hand, if (and only if) fees and costs will be the same no matter what, it shouldn't matter whether you calculate an EMV and then subtract fees and costs or enter them in the net payoffs and then roll back the tree.

Anticipate Occasional Resistance

The lawyer decision analyst, especially one who deals with clients, may predictably raise at least two objections regarding the inclusion of future fees and costs in net payoffs. The first is that many clients feel resentment at having costs and fees used "against" them. And mediators or other settlement proponents may indeed push parties for higher or lower settlement offers when fees and costs increase or decrease the EMV. However, this shouldn't be permitted to compromise the tree's accuracy as a map of the case and its consequences.

It is also true that some lawyers resist providing an estimate of future legal and expert fees and other significant costs of litigation. This is unfortunate. It's simply not sound practice to ignore these costs, as they will be real, and presumably, would impact a client's decision from a business or financial perspective. The decision analyst can observe that while litigation costs should be accounted for if the analysis is to reflect reality, they need not be disclosed to the other side. Even where they influence an internally set "reservation price" for negotiation, they need not dictate initial negotiation offers to be presented externally. Moreover, if the other side has also counted its own costs and fees, these should similarly affect their receptiveness to reasonable settlement offers or demands.

The Rule Against Sunk Costs, in Perpetuity

A second objection, often raised by clients, pushes in the opposite direction: toward including ALL costs and fees, not just those to be expended between now and resolution of the case. To a plaintiff without a contingency fee arrangement, attorneys' fees and costs are part of the harm; they are consequences of the defendant's unlawful action. They want all attorneys' fees and costs to be part of damages, including those incurred to date. When considering a settlement offer, they measure it against likely damages recovery *plus* attorneys' fee expenditures to date. On the defense side, they would prefer to *reduce* (even an EMV based) settlement offer by their full attorneys' fee quotient to date.

As the experienced lawyer knows, this dynamic —a desire to recoup expenditures—runs deep and is often expressed with or without decision analysis. However, except in cases where attorneys' fees are indeed recoverable, it makes no sense to add past expenditures into settlement demands. These are sunk costs, for both sides. In fact, these expenditures are what made the case ready for the analysis and potential settlement.

One benefit of using a decision tree is the ability to say to a client: "Unfortunately, the rules of decision analysis don't permit us to include past costs here. It's just not allowed. We want to make sure our decision tree is clean, accurate, and in accordance with the decision analysis method. We can certainly write them on the chart or in a notation box. They are what enabled our settlement position and bargaining power today."[7]

[7] See discussion of using decision tree analysis to communicate with clients in: Aaron, Marjorie, "Finding Settlements with Numbers, Maps, and Trees," in Moffitt, Michael and Bordone, Robert (eds.), *The Handbook of Dispute Resolution* (2005).

7

Reality of Quantification for Intangibles

The positive or negative value of the consequences of many decisions are neither anticipated nor quantified. Yet, experience in real legal disputes reminds us that the "intangibles"—the unquantified consequences not covered in a damages award—may prove the most consequential.

A recent research study that included interviews of corporate counsel found that corporate clients recognize litigation's consequences as including costs of organizational distraction, internal time of valuable people pulled away from profitable work, costs of electronic data and discovery requirements, business relationships and reputation, in addition to the costs of lawyers and experts. As the researchers observed: "Corporate clients may view these concerns as extremely important, and worth factoring in, even if not easy."[1] While their research focused on a corporate context, their observation rings more generally true: litigation or other legal entanglements often have more intangible but no less impactful consequences for the parties than legal fees and monetary awards.

It's fair to say that there are two types of such intangibles: those easily monetized as direct costs or gains, and those not.

Direct Time as an Easy Monetizer

For all clients, and some lawyers too, litigation is fundamentally a distraction. It takes them from their businesses, their professions, and their normal non-litigation lives. Company lawyers speak of litigation as a "cost of doing business," but it is also a cost taken from other business activities. The only difference between outside attorneys' fees and expert costs, and internal company litigation-related costs is that the former are "out-of-pocket." Yet, if the internal costs are real, it makes sense to calculate them as well, to the extent possible and feasible.

This is relatively easy to do for one aspect of executive and staff involvement in the litigation—their raw time. Lawyer and client can estimate the hours of management and staff time required for depositions, document discovery, witness preparation, and trial testimony and multiply by inputted hourly rates. Thus, if two lower level employees will have to spend 100 hours going through boxes of materials, and their salaries are approximately $40,000 per year ($20 per hour); the cost to the company would be $2,000. Of course, if the IT department will be required to run massive electronic and data searches, their hourly rate will be much higher. A high level executive, salaried at $360,000, costs the company

[1] Heavin, Heather and Keet, Michaela, "The Path of Lawyers: Enhancing Predictive Ability through Risk Assessment Methods," *Canadian Institute for the Administration of Justice* (2016):19. Heavin and Keet note [at page 20] that without systemic methodologies which cover all relevant factors and put results in concrete terms, clients are arguably left to make decisions without the best available information."

$180 per hour. How much of that executive's time will be spent in depositions, witness preparation, and testimony?

When a lawyer-tree builder is considering the net costs and payoffs with a company client, it is worth discussing the professional and staff time demands that litigation will impose on the business.[2] Ask for approximate salaries; make some calculations. These would be subtracted from the net payoff on the corporate plaintiff's side and increase the net negative payoff number on the defense side.[3]

Sometimes, "bean counting" the person-hours is not worth the time spent on the exercise, as the total is not significant within calculated net payoffs. Even where the drain on personnel time might be significant, the client may be just as happy with a rough cut plug-in number (saving time in the discussion). Just ask: "What would it be worth to not have your staff working on or worried about this?" Or, "What's a guestimate of the cost of this distraction?"

Monetizing Financial Impact, Beyond the Hourly

For a corporate client, depending on the nature of the industry, the dispute, and its timing within their business cycle or product launch schedule, the consequences of litigation may be felt far beyond direct personnel time.

Sometimes, the tree-builder lawyer is advised to inquire more broadly, with questions such as:

- *If this litigation continues, and particularly if the other side were to prevail, do you have a sense of the budget increase your public relations department will seek to achieve damage control, or resurrection of public image?*
- *Is the company planning any initiatives, such as pursuing an acquisition or other new opportunities, or courting a suitor for its own acquisition, that would be impacted by this litigation? Is there a disclosure issue for a potential investor, in a securities filing, or in accountants' reports? How problematic or how costly would disclosure be?*
- *Would the impact be felt whether or not the company is successful in the litigation, or only in the event of a loss? Can the impact be quantified in dollars? How might it be reparable? Assuming nothing is certain and future predictions are inexact, can we consider a range? Is timing critical for estimating impact? Should we think more carefully about when discovery and depositions are likely to occur, when the trial date would be, and when to anticipate a verdict?*

[2] The astute reader may note that if the company would be paying many if not all of these salaries in any event, these should not be counted as litigation costs. That's true. However, the approach fails to consider the opportunity cost: how these employees' time would otherwise benefit the company. Their time multiplied by salary rates should be a minimum measure of this value. The true opportunity cost of diverting their time, attention, and energy could be much greater.

[3] Arguments for considering the cost of time when applying decision analysis in a legal context are made by: Prestia, Paul, and Samaras, Harrie, "Beyond Decision Trees: Determining Aggregate Probabilities of Time, Cost, and Outcomes," *Alternatives to the High Cost of Litigation,* (2010). As readers would no doubt anticipate, I quarrel with their suggestion that conventional decision analysis requires "augmentation" to include it. Basic texts on decision analysis plainly state the requirement to consider time and its costs, including the time value of money. By way of example, see Clemens, Robert T. *Making Hard Decisions: An Introduction to Decision Analysis* (1996), on the topic.

On the individual plaintiff's side, particularly in any employment-related case, you might ask the impact of the litigation on the likelihood of the plaintiff finding a new job:

- *While the litigation is pending, what do you think the chances are of being hired within the next 6 months or a year? [Say 25%] What about after the litigation is ended? [Say 75%]*
- *So, assume that the litigation process will run for a year or 18 months beyond today, is it fair to say that the litigation itself may cost additional lost income? While that lost income would theoretically become part of back pay damages at trial, it will be additional loss if you are not successful. And perhaps more importantly, it tells us that an important consequence of the litigation is that it puts your career on hold, and that costs you in the long run.*

Individual or small business litigants might be asked to estimate the cost of lost consulting days or time off from work in a new job.

Here are some helpful catch-all questions:

- *Assume the discovery process would run through Y date, and the two-week trial will be Z months from now. Imagine that an always accurate crystal ball revealed that the company will not prevail in the litigation, and the damages awarded against the company will be $X. How much more would it be worth to the company to avoid going through the process at all?*
- *Or, looking at it more optimistically, if the crystal ball determined that your side will prevail and will receive reasonable damages, how much less would you take in order not to go through the entire process? What would that be worth in dollar terms?*

At the risk of stating the obvious, when the litigation carries the risk of injunctive relief of any kind, honest efforts should be made to quantify the consequences of both favorable and unfavorable injunctive relief. For example:

- *What will it cost the company if it is ordered to cease or recall product sales?*
- *What will it cost to redesign packaging and advertise this redesign?*
- *What will it cost to liquidate a property or other commercial interest?*

For the defendant in an employment case:

- *What costs would the organization incur if the judge ordered the plaintiff's reinstatement? [Put differently: How much would the HR manager beg you to pay, after a reinstatement order, to settle and avoid reinstatement?]*
- *Would a key employee or top salesman opt to leave if the plaintiff were reinstated? How much would that cost the company?*

Obviously, when representing the former employee-defendant in a non-compete case, counsel should ask his client to estimate the costs of a potential injunction against competitive work within a certain time and geographic range.

Monetizing Linked Business Impact

Consider a software development company that sues its large corporate customer for failure to pay for development services. Prior to filing suit, there was undoubtedly much wrangling over the scope of work, disputes about deliverables, and cross-accusations of failure to live up to contract terms. The software company's General Counsel might have analyzed litigation risks, assessing the likelihood of prevailing on breach of contract and recovering the amount due, plus perhaps the claimed value of their additional work, or of prevailing only on a reliance claim but not breach of contract.

When the corporate customer counterclaims for breach, alleging deficiencies and delays in the software provided, the General Counsel will also create a decision tree for the counterclaim. In fact, a smart second-guesser could argue that the General Counsel should have considered the possibility of a counterclaim when constructing his initial tree.

Simplified versions of these are set forth below.

The first Tree Model (62) reflects the main claims. Note that it does not include attorney's fees or costs that would reduce the net payoffs. However, it is fair to say that these fees and costs would be the same at the end of every branch path on the tree (at the terminal nodes).

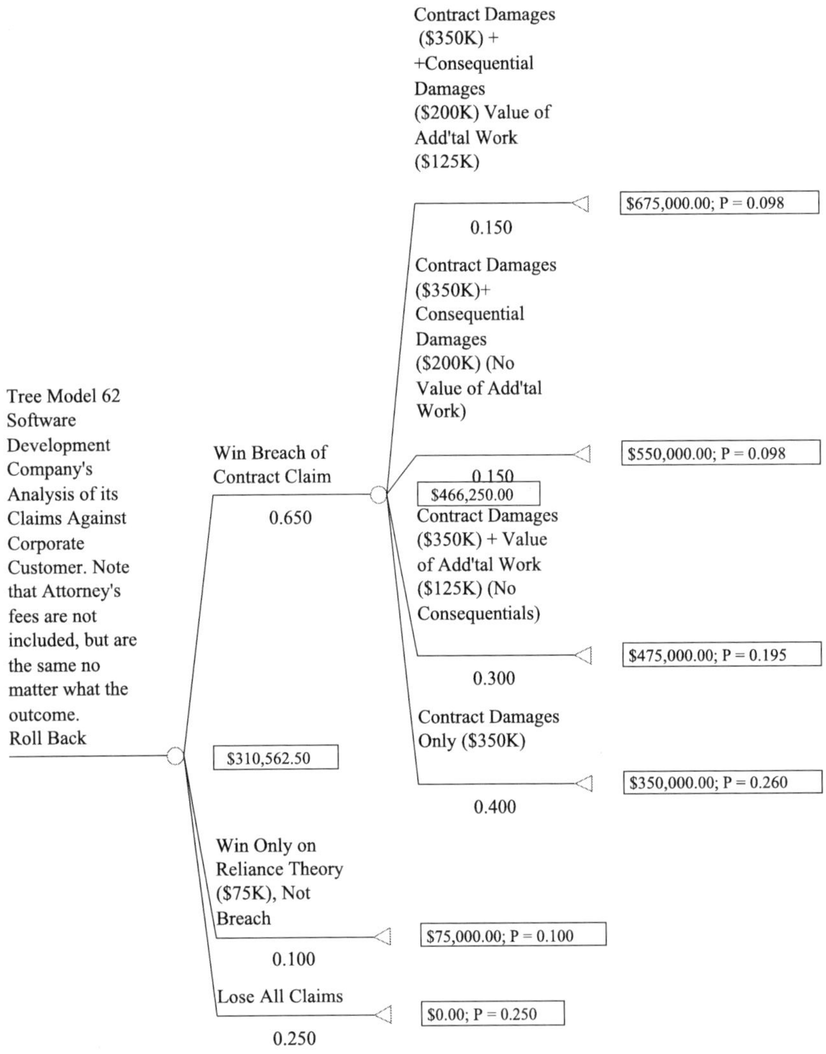

The next tree maps the vendor's main claim, this time with estimated attorney's fees and costs deducted from net payoffs to the far right of each branch path.

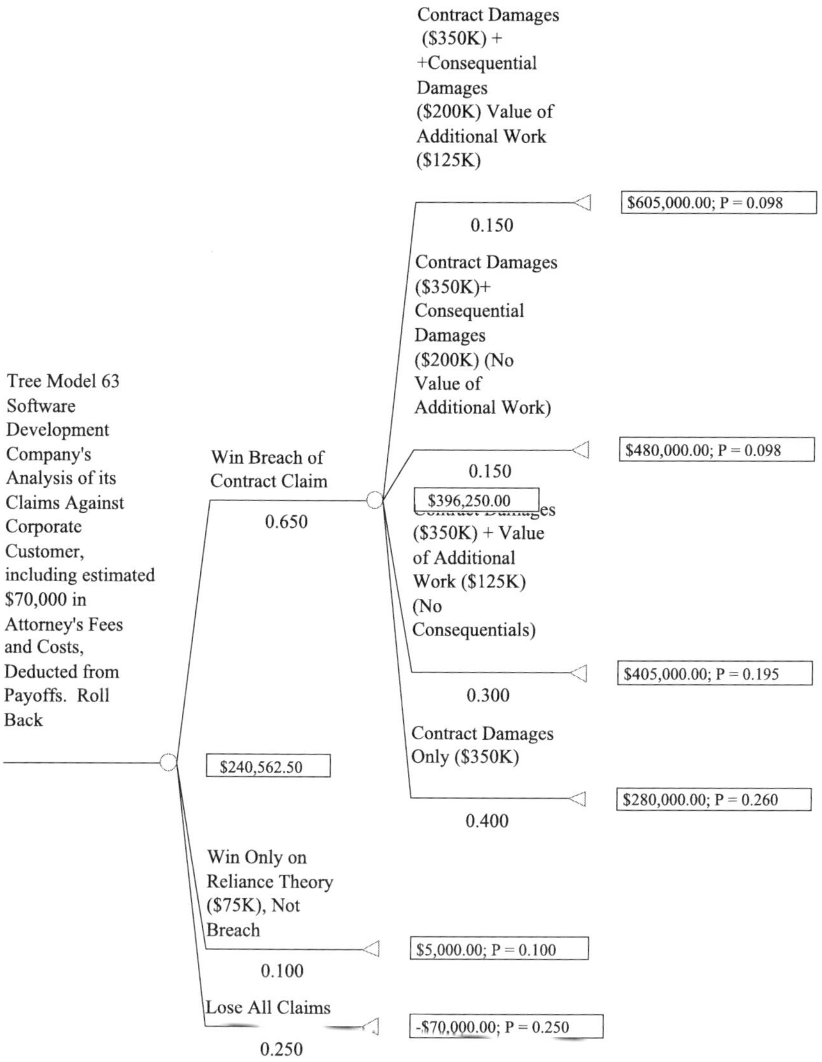

The tree that follows is a separate, simplified map of the counterclaim that the General Counsel might prepare.

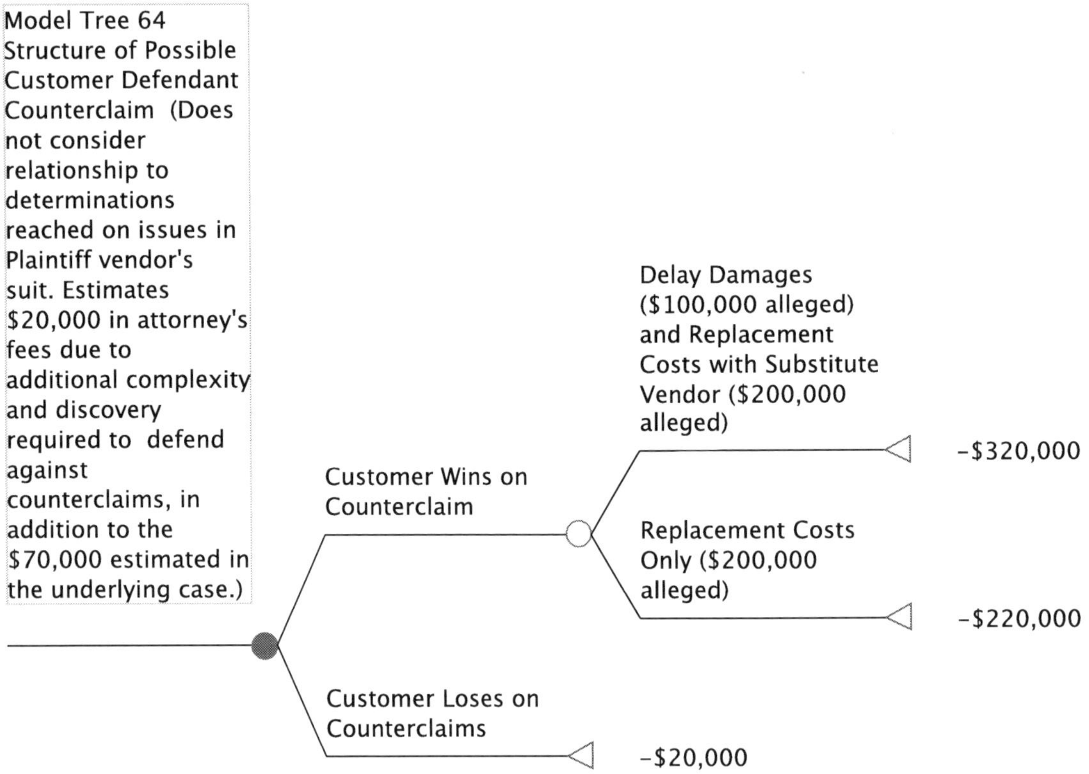

Last and surely not least, the General Counsel would be well advised to put the main claim and the counterclaims together as the more accurate and admittedly more complex picture of what might occur in the litigation.

Note that the estimates of various probabilities are affected by their place along the path. For example, the tree builder has assumed a jury that finds for the plaintiff on reliance claims is less likely to find for the defendant on its counterclaims than is the jury that finds against the plaintiff on all counts.

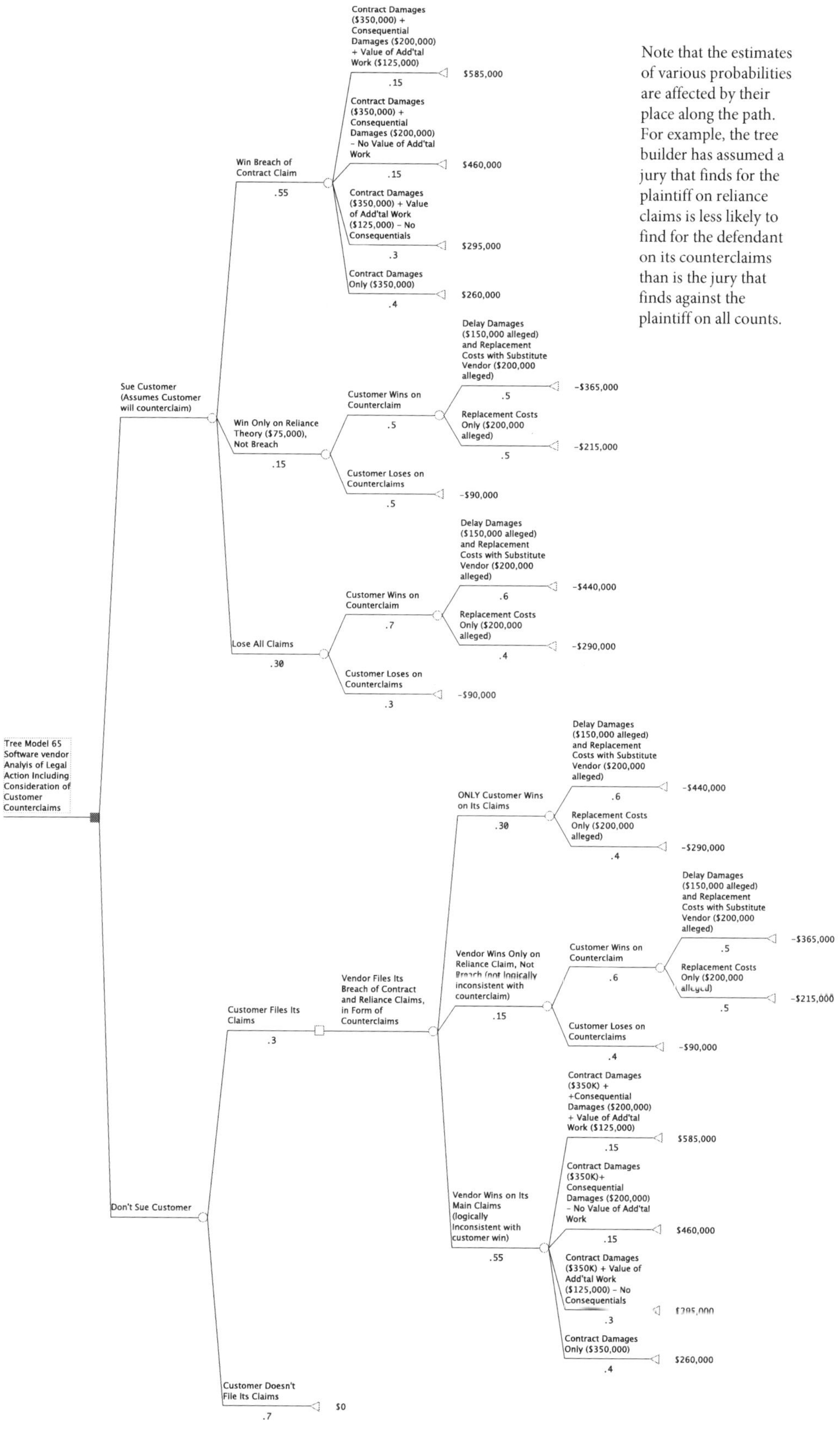

What's missing? We might note (as was true in the real case upon which this is based) that the General Counsel failed to consider any other contractual or business relationships between the parties. What if the corporate customer is a subdivision of a larger company? How many current or potential contracts for software services might be involved? What are the cancellation provisions in those contracts? What is the likelihood that this software company will retain the larger company's other business, or obtain new business? Might there be a larger impact within the industry?

Assume that the General Counsel is hard-nosed and brave, but not reckless. He is not scared off by a mere possibility that they might lose some business, with this customer or elsewhere. He will not run from the case if this is a vague, irrational, or exaggerated fear. Yet, wisdom tells us when certain fears are realized, the consequences are entirely real, and quantifiable.

Sage advice is to attempt to think carefully about and then attempt to quantify what that impact would be. The tree-builder would be wise to sit down with his client, do an inventory of current contracts and their termination provisions, and estimate the stream of new business and potential future contracts the other company may command. Without pretense to precision, an intangible damages subtree could easily be sketched, as reflected on the next tree.

When reviewing this tree, please note that it assumes major contracts, valued at $2.5 million, which include a 60-day notice provision for termination. All of the contracts can be terminated without cause, with payment of any additional hours expended since the last contract payment. It assumes and includes an estimate of a cumulative $1 million left in current contracts. It also assumes and includes maximum potential annual future flow of business from the parent company and all subdivisions of $1.2 million. That's a total potential of $6 million over five years. It might be fair to discount that by 50%, recognizing that they would not necessarily get all of this business, even without this dispute. The tree above thus includes a 50% chance of a loss of $3 million in value as a result of filing suit.

It's worth remembering that if this decision tree were being constructed AFTER suit has been filed, the opportunity to win back future business might have been lost. Or, it would be much more difficult to retain this business than if the tree had been built before taking legal action.

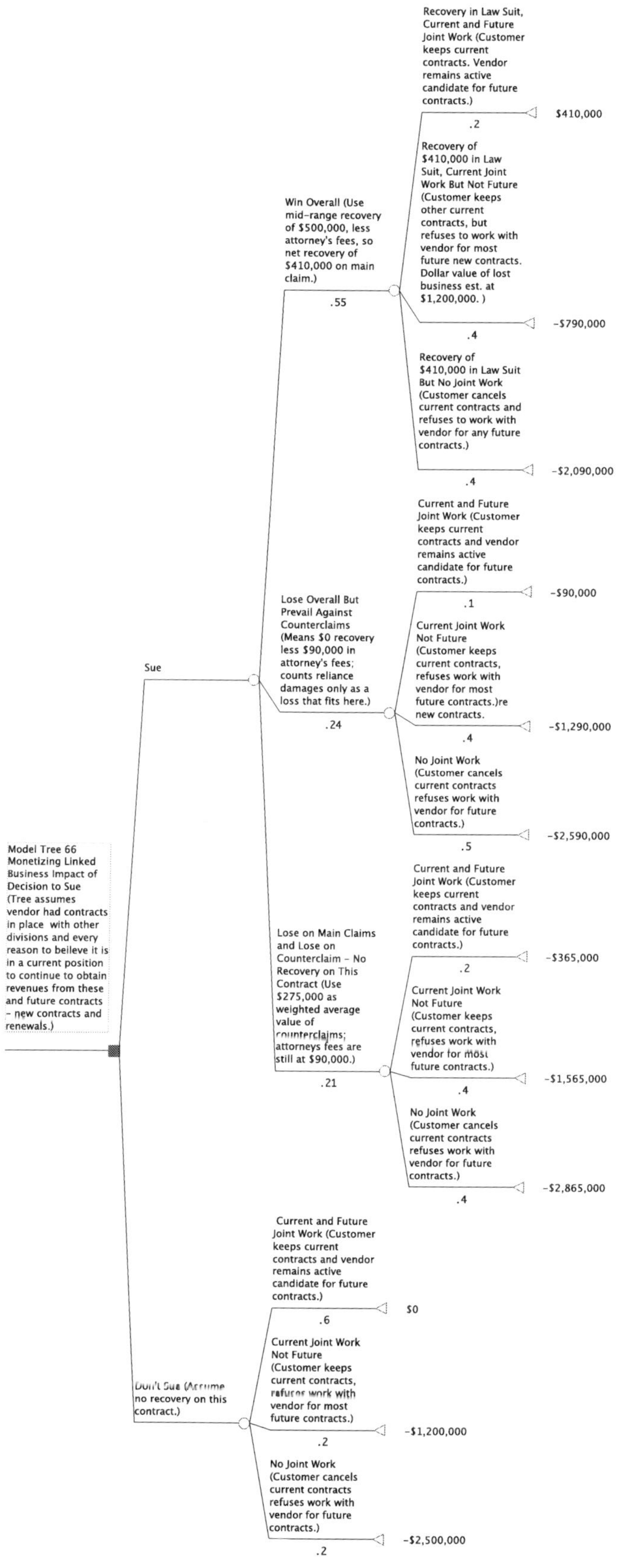
Model Tree 66 Monetizing Linked Business Impact of Decision to Sue (Tree assumes vendor had contracts in place with other divisions and every reason to beileve it is in a current position to continue to obtain revenues from these and future contracts - new contracts and renewals.)
Sue
Win Overall (Use mid-range recovery of $500,000, less attorney's fees, so net recovery of $410,000 on main claim.)
.55
Recovery in Law Suit, Current and Future Joint Work (Customer keeps current contracts. Vendor remains active candidate for future contracts.)
.2
$410,000
Recovery of $410,000 in Law Suit, Current Joint Work But Not Future (Customer keeps other current contracts, but refuses to work with vendor for most future new contracts. Dollar value of lost business est. at $1,200,000.)
.4
-$790,000
Recovery of $410,000 in Law Suit But No Joint Work (Customer cancels current contracts and refuses to work with vendor for any future contracts.)
.4
-$2,090,000
Lose Overall But Prevail Against Counterclaims (Means $0 recovery less $90,000 in attorney's fees; counts reliance damages only as a loss that fits here.)
.24
Current and Future Joint Work (Customer keeps current contracts and vendor remains active candidate for future contracts.)
.1
-$90,000
Current Joint Work Not Future (Customer keeps current contracts, refuses work with vendor for most future contracts.)re new contracts.
.4
-$1,290,000
No Joint Work (Customer cancels current contracts refuses work with vendor for future contracts.)
.5
-$2,590,000
Lose on Main Claims and Lose on Counterclaim - No Recovery on This Contract (Use $275,000 as weighted average value of counterclaims; attorneys fees are still at $90,000.)
.21
Current and Future Joint Work (Customer keeps current contracts and vendor remains active candidate for future contracts.)
.2
-$365,000
Current Joint Work Not Future (Customer keeps current contracts, refuses work with vendor for most future contracts.)
.4
-$1,565,000
No Joint Work (Customer cancels current contracts refuses work with vendor for future contracts.)
.4
-$2,865,000
Don't Sue (Assume no recovery on this contract.)
Current and Future Joint Work (Customer keeps current contracts and vendor remains active candidate for future contracts.)
.6
$0
Current Joint Work Not Future (Customer keeps current contracts, refuses work with vendor for most future contracts.)
.2
-$1,200,000
No Joint Work (Customer cancels current contracts refuses work with vendor for future contracts.)
.2
-$2,500,000

Monetized Results Straight to Payoffs, or as Close as You Can Get

Why should tree builders focus on monetizing consequences? As discussed earlier, the answer is: "measurement bias." The human psyche tends to "count" things that can be measured, and to undervalue that which cannot. Indeed, a primary purpose of decision analysis in litigation is precisely to ensure that consequences of chance and decision are counted, with appropriate discounts for their probabilities. To name payoffs and probabilities in numerical terms, rather than describing them as "big wins" or "less than likely," is to measure them.

Life has a habit of yielding hybrids: outcomes partially stated in dollars, and partially not. One job offer includes a relatively high salary of $X, with two weeks of vacation, two significant extra benefits, stable work structure and some opportunities for slow advancement. The other job opportunity has a lower salary, with four weeks of vacation, a few additional and attractive benefits, greater informality and opportunities for faster advancement. Research suggests that many will take job #1, and later become frustrated and dissatisfied. At the time of the decision, they seem to over-value terms that were easily measurable, and undervalue terms that were not.[4]

The same is often true for parties in litigation: the plaintiff may seek a high dollar settlement and reject a lower dollar offer that includes additional, clearly valuable terms where their value is unstated in dollars. They tend to measure the dollar number sought versus the dollar offered, and disregard or discount heavily the significance of other terms. In the settlement context, the simple antidote is to monetize—to estimate the dollar value of the additional terms, and include these within the calculations of the entire offer's value.

Consider the hypothetical mediation of an employment dispute between a pharmaceutical company and its salesman. In the course of discussion, the plaintiff has stated his strong interest in pursuing a physician's assistant degree, as well as keeping his company car and laptop computer. Which presentation of this identical offer is more likely to be accepted?

a) $150,000 payment plus out-placement services, tuition reimbursement for matriculation in a physician's assistant degree program, keeping the company car and laptop computer,

Or

b) Total value of $225,000, which includes a $150,000 cash payment, $50,000 for tuition at the physician's assistant degree program, the $22,000 blue book value of the company car, and the $3,000 price of the powerful laptop.

Most plaintiffs will be happier when the offer is presented as in (b) above. Not surprisingly, the opposite is true for the defendant company's representatives. Fair dealing and fair questions would have required communication of these numbers to the company in the course of the negotiations. Nevertheless, when meeting with company representatives to seek the firm offer, a settlement proponent or mediator is advised to present it as in (a) above: "$150,000 payment, plus tuition reimbursement, plus company car,

[4] Hall, Brian and Staats, Trent, "Do the Numbers Get in Your Way?" *Negotiation* 7, no. 4 (2004).

plus the computer." Even though the company representatives should know the (at least approximate) total cost, a "yes" decision is more likely if its $225,000 price tag is not highlighted.[5]

While I hope the reader recognizes the value of a decision analytic method for making wise decisions, it should be recognized that part of the method's value is in forcing us to see what's in the sausage. Particularly where decision trees are drawn, the branches, probabilities, payoffs-outcomes, and distribution of those pay-off-outcomes are clearly visible. The tree-builder, the lawyer, and the client can all visually follow the various paths.[6] At the end nodes, they are confronted with imagining that how the case could play out in any and all of these ways—with the dollar amounts of liability and costs shown at the far right—as the payoffs at the end nodes.

Of course, for those receptive to the idea of using the EMV to inform decisions, the calculated roll back to the EMV is meaningful. If "non-monetary" but valuable or costly terms are excluded from the net-payoffs, they are obviously not in the EMV.

Imagine a decision tree built by the defendant company's lawyer in a commercial contract case that does not include any fees or costs. Assume the simplest case, where the balance of the contract owed is $200,000, and the question is whether the plaintiff fulfilled their end of the bargain or not, and thus whether the defendant was justified in withholding payment.

For the purposes of this example, and as reflected in the tree below, let's also assume that the defense's evidence against liability is pretty strong.

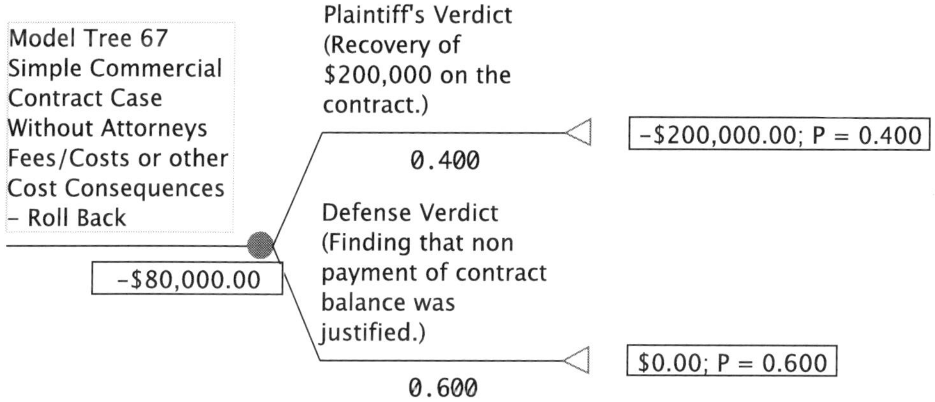

Next, imagine the same case, rolled back, after adding in estimated attorneys' fees and costs of $40,000. This is admittedly lower than in some recent examples. It assumes the case is legally straightforward.

[5] Tversky, Amos and Kahneman, Daniel, "The Framing of Decisions and the Psychology of Choice," *Science*, 211, no. 30 (1981). For additional and accessible explanations of Prospect Theory, risk aversion and loss aversion, see Plous, Scott, *The Psychology of Judgment and Decision Making* (1993); Kahneman, Daniel and Tversky, Amos, "Prospect Theory: An Analysis of Decision under Risk," *Econometrica* 47, no. 2 (1979): 263-91. The fact that the risked loss will take place in the future undoubtedly causes it to be discounted as well. See Frederick, Shane; Loewenstein, Geoge; and O'Donoghue, Ted, "Time Discounting and Time Preference: A Critical Review," *Journal of Economic Literature* 40, no. 2 (2002): 351-401. For experimental research demonstrating the application of prospect theory in legal settlement contexts, see Guthrie, Chris "Framing Frivolous Litigation: A Psychological Theory," *The University of Chicago Law Review* (2000).

[6] While a spreadsheet approach to the calculation will yield the same numerical results, that visual presentation seems less powerful to me. For those accustomed to and persuaded by the power of spreadsheets, my preference need not apply.

Still, there would be discovery and many corporate witnesses to defend on deposition and prepare for trial.

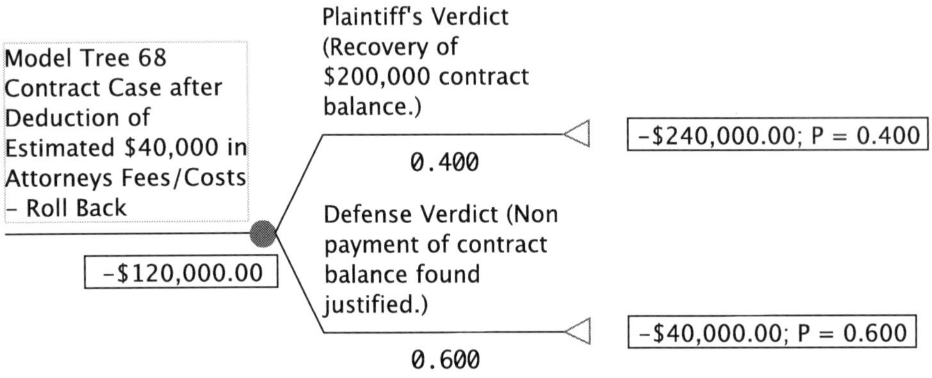

Next, here's the same case, but after including costs of executive and staff time estimated at $30,000. (This is based on ten executives with time valued at $1,000 per day, for two days each, plus at least twenty days of staff time in complying with discovery). The tree also reflects a consequential increase of $50,000 to the public relations budget.

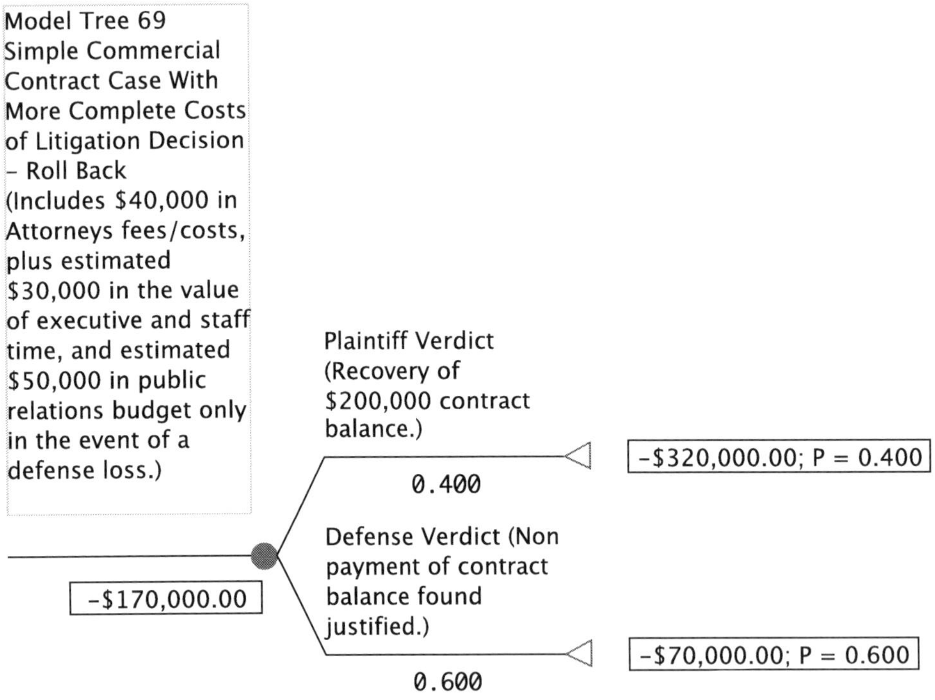

Can't We Just Talk About it?

Why not just create the tree and calculate the net pay-off with only experts' and attorneys' fees, yielding an EMV of $120,000, and then add, orally or by written notation on the tree: "plus ten days of executive time and twenty days of staff time, plus a $50,000 increase to the PR budget?" As stated earlier, the post roll back EMV and the end pay-off numbers are what stick in our minds. Thus, if these fail to include real financial consequences, their impact on the decision may not be commensurate to their reality.

While firm about the truth of this assertion—that including financial consequences should be included in payoffs and this calculation—I hereby offer a back-up plan. If it's not feasible to estimate and include these financial consequences in the payoffs, DO at least *write* them on the tree document. At the risk of micromanaging, I suggest placing them on the tree as near to the end node/payoff notations as possible. And, with an arrow pointing to the EMV, clearly note that the EMV does not take into account the following financial consequences. Of course, references to these financial consequences should include their numerical value. It's less compelling to write: "This EMV does not include executive and staff time, public relations, or opportunity costs," than to write: "This EMV does not include $30,000 in executive and staff time, $50,000 in expenses related to public relations: total of $80,000, without other opportunity costs."

As discussed earlier, estimating consequential costs can be reasonably straightforward when it involves multiplying estimated executive and staff time by the salary value of that time. Other categories of costs will be just as real when incurred but require deeper and wider inquiry to be fairly estimated. The tree-builder lawyer's purpose is not dire warnings of exaggerated cost numbers, but rather to elicit understanding of the actual projected impact on business or professional expenses and revenues. The exercise is an attempt to solidify and monetize what might happen, in honest, real ways. After all, the $50,000 required for remedial public relations is just as real a business expense as the $20,000 spent on fees, costs, or damages award.

Monetizing consequences would be just as important, arguably moreso, for the client salesman, unhappy at his treatment by his employer but subject to a non-compete agreement. Imagine that this client recently received an offer from a competitor and came to a lawyer for advice. He may have some good defenses against the non-compete: claims for breach of contract due to deliberate management actions and broken promises on compensation. Theoretically, he could assert these claims independently. He has a number of different choices, each with potential consequence. For example: he could leave the current job but elect not to compete for the requisite period; or he could leave and go to the competitor company (which may or may not take up his defense.) If so, his current employer could file for injunctive relief and the competitor company may or may not take up his defense or rescind the offer. He could also turn down the offer and stay at the current job. Under various scenarios, he could assert his breach of contract claims.

It's a complicated decision. The dollar reductions in family income will be felt just as severely as litigation costs if that former salesman is enjoined from competing in the territory and is unable to find work, or works and rents an apartment outside the territory. In my view, the plausible decision tree shown below, demonstrates the obvious benefit of drawing and discussing it with the client. And, looking to the terminal nodes, it's easy to see the value of estimating and recording predictable financial costs and gains with each of the client's choices.

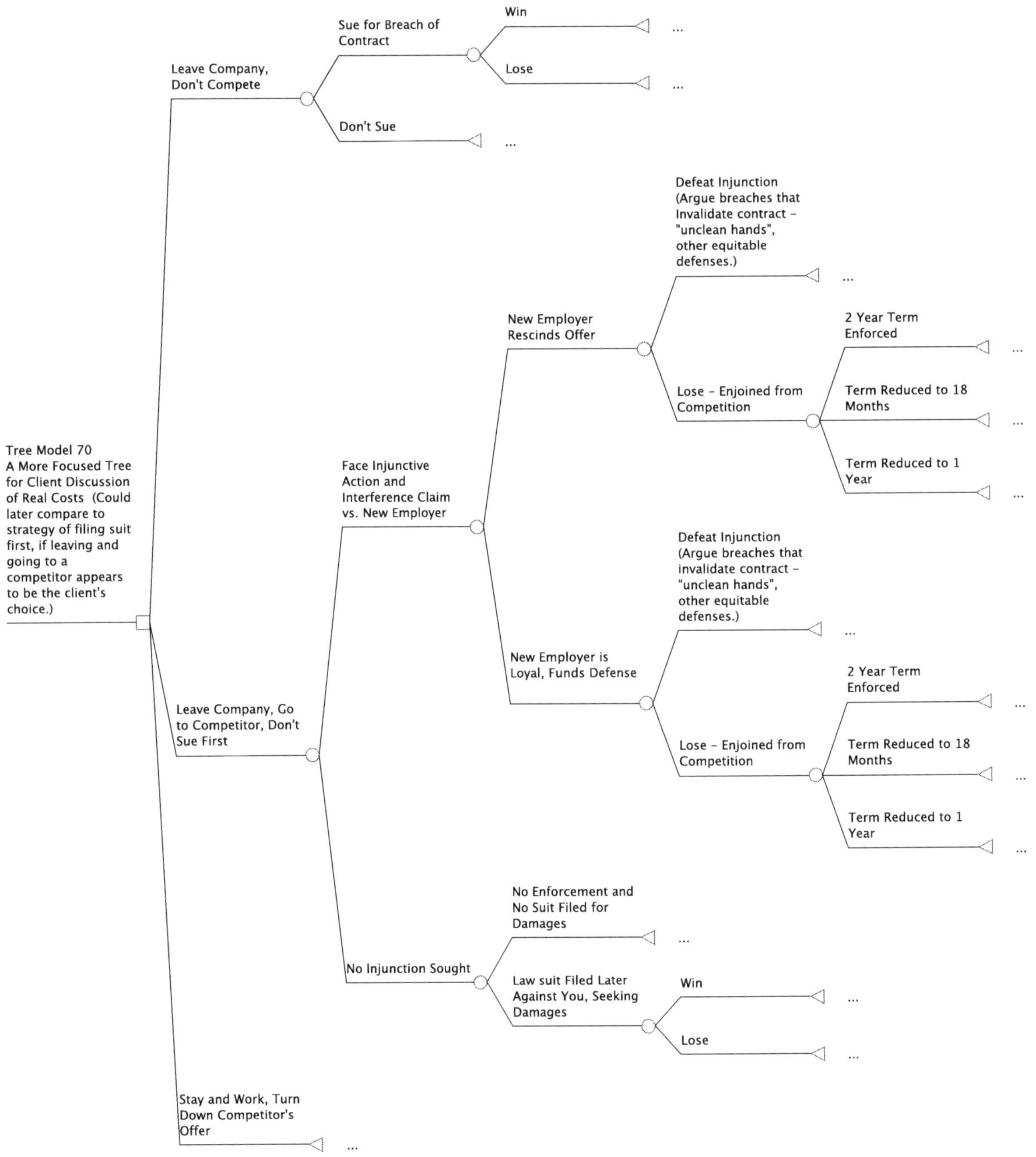

The perfect need not be the enemy of the good. Even if a perfect estimate of financial consequences is not possible, a good faith effort at a reasonable estimate is good enough, and better than excluding that cost entirely from the net outcomes.

8

Even More Intangible Non-Monetary and Still Important Consequences

Even a committed and creative estimator must concede that some very real consequences cannot be measured in dollars. Money isn't everything! Fortunately, human beings are not narrow rational economic actors, solely motivated by desire to maximize financial gain. A healthy range of intangibles, of values measured in emotional satisfaction, relationships, pride, personal and professional narrative, comfort—all things that matter greatly to us—drive our decisions and are impacted by them. When a decision and chance (node) leads to opportunities, risks, losses, and gains, their intangible consequences may be no less important. Indeed, these may be much more important.

For the tree-builder, there are at least four ways to work with true intangibles.

1) The first is to ignore them when building the tree. The lawyer-as-counselor would still raise the question of intangible but real human consequences of a client decision: *How will the other employees feel? What will the community reaction be? What will be the professional or family impact?* The tree-builder lawyer would explain that the decision tree simply maps the path of the litigation and calculates a dollar EMV and various possible monetary outcomes. The decision tree informs consideration of what the litigation might mean for the client, his colleagues, family, patients, customer, etc., but it only measures risk and monetary outcomes—not the other important but terribly consequential non-financial impacts.
2) A second way to work with intangibles is to use the outcomes end of the tree to prompt questions about these non-monetary but important consequences. Though monetary value cannot be assigned, the lawyer tree-builder makes careful notation by writing these consequences to the far right of the tree, wherever they would occur.

   Let's take a look at this second way of working with intangibles by considering a client who seeks to take legal action against his family-owned company with multiple locations. The suit would necessarily include allegations of misconduct against various relatives in the company's leadership position. Your client owns shares in the company. No doubt, it would be worth asking about the litigation's impact on Thanksgiving dinners, on aging family matriarchs or patriarchs, or relationships between his children and their cousins, and other extended family members. How often do they interact? This thought experiment might lead the client to set aside or delay filing his claim. Or it may limit those named as defendants. Perhaps there will be value in foregoing an allegation that his father was complicit, or that his grandfather engineered a conspiracy. Does a direct claim against the father or grandfather really strengthen the case so much as to be worth how he would feel about it? To me, this entire discussion would suggest the wisdom of enormous efforts to reach a peaceful agreement within the family. The very act of filing suit may have such a poisonous impact as to render this impossible. That is another intangible value that may be worthy of weight and consideration.

Here's how the tree might be drawn.

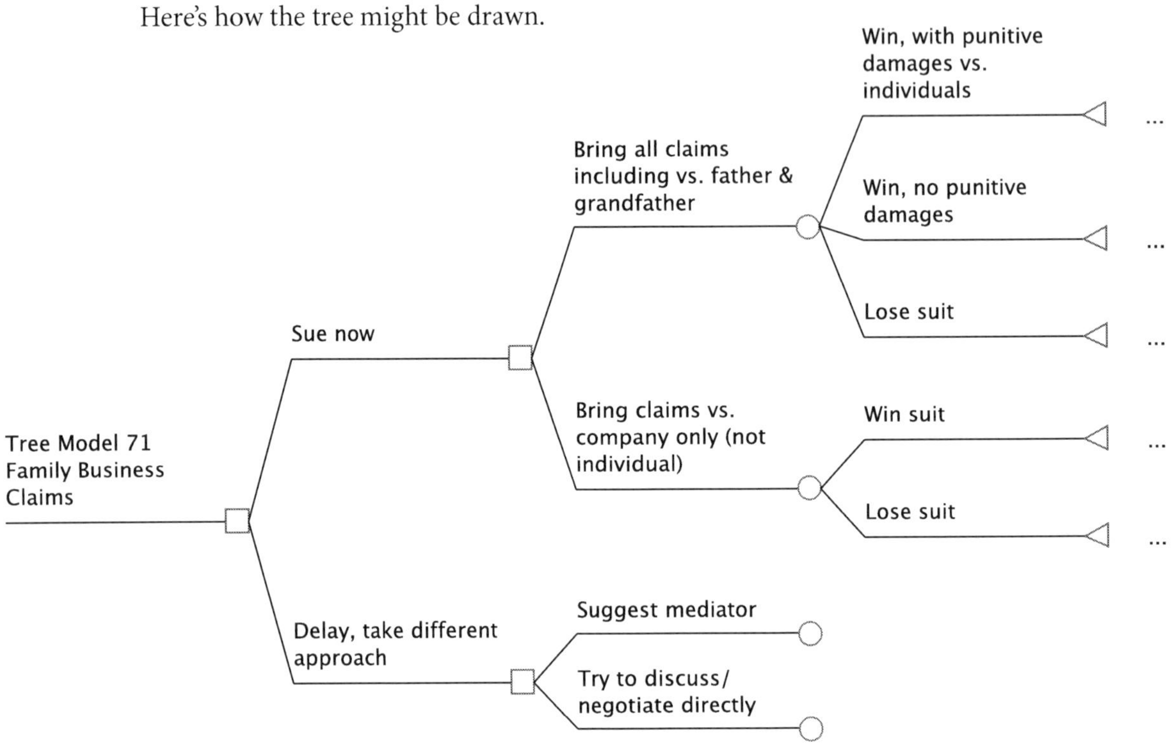

The considerations listed in bold face below are examples of what might be written to the right of the tree's terminal nodes on a yellow pad, a large flip chart or white board, or more likely, multiple charts, boards, or other enlargements. Client reflection and discussion might generate the text written under each category, such as the text which follows.

Net $ Impact/Outcome if suit is won with punitive damages
Recover your % share of company's lost income due to misconduct – $?
Recover punitive damages, likely multiple of lost income
[After est. 2 years' time]
-Pay $50,000 in attorneys' fees & costs
-lose share of parents'/grandparents' estates - wills change?

Net $ Impact/Outcome if suit is won, no claims involving punitive damages
Recover your % share of company's lost income due to misconduct – $? [After est. 2 years' time]
-Pay $50,000 in attorneys' fees & costs
-lose share of parents'/grandparents estate, wills change?

Net $ Impact/Outcome if suit is lost
- $0 Recovered
-Pay $50,000 in attorneys' fees & costs
-lose share of parents'/grandparents' estate - wills change?

Intangible Impacts of Filing Suit [any strategy, any outcome]
Family relationships break down further, including relationships with parent and grandparents
-no more family gatherings: holidays, weddings, graduations
-fractured/no interactions between your children & cousins
-discomfort at town/school events, any common friends
-town/neighbors/friends may take sides; social backlash

Intangible Impacts of Filing Claims against Father and/or Grandfather
-If file suit naming father and/or grandfather personally, asserting conspiracy claims, relationship break irreconcilable.
-If file suit without those claims, is the relationship break less likely to be irreconcilable?

Consequences of delaying, either negotiating, retaining a mediator
Control your own fate, not imposed
Save attorneys fees (though mediator may cost)
Process may preserve/mend relationship

At the end of each branch path, client and lawyer are invited to pause and consider: what would the monetary and emotional costs be if the case unfolds along this path? The thought exercise will make what is abstract and in the hypothetical future seem more real.

In our non-compete case from last chapter, similar questions would be asked: "What would it cost me if a judge were to grant the injunction so that I couldn't work in my industry for 18 months? Could we still cover the mortgage and the kids' activities? Is it worth incurring the lawyer's litigation costs? How will I feel if I make no change?" The client might predict that it's worth the risk of a brief injunction because his most valuable clients will return after that period. He might consider or pursue "Plan B"—a temporary employment interlude outside of the industry, or selling only non-competitive products at the new company—and estimate his earning capacity during the interlude. Even if the dollar estimates are far from certain, it's worthwhile to write them at the terminal nodes on the right side. And rolling back the tree with those numbers to learn both the EMV and the likelihood of the various possible outcomes may prove significant for the client's decision.

3) A third way is to make roughly estimated monetary adjustments to account for non-monetary consequences.[1] These can be broad or more specific.[2]

Thinking broadly, the decision-analyst could ask the client to consider what it would be worth to him, his family, or his organization not to go through this entire process. A way to frame the question is to ask: *Disregarding lawyer's fees and all of that, what if there were two ways to get to a final result. The first way, you and your employees [or you and your family] go through the litigation process, the depositions, documents, hearings and, say eighteen months from now, there's a trial, you and others testify, and then the jury says X—whatever they say. The second way, I could wave a wand and we'll just be faced with X—whatever it is. In other words, you can skip the entire process. What value would there be in NOT having to go through it all? How much would that be worth?*

Then, let's assume your decision tree begins with a decision node that has two branches, settle or litigate. If the "settle" branch ends with the other side's current offer (or the amount you think they would be willing to pay), the client's dollar valuation of NOT going through it could be added to the settlement payoff. Or, it could be subtracted from the end of the litigation payoffs (or added as a negative, for the defense side).

A note of caution: focusing on distaste for the process can be problematic, particularly when working with a defense client who already feels "extorted" by the process and its costs. There may be understandable resistance to your suggestion to focus on the unattractiveness of litigation as a reason to pay more.[3]

It may be perceived as fairer to focus on a particular real but intangible impact of a litigation decision. For example, imagine that your client owns a business that is a member of a closely-knit trade association. He has a potential breach of contract claim against another business in

---

[1] For a clear and careful presentation of a way to evaluate non-monetary consequences, see: Hammond, John S.; Keeney, Ralph L.; and Raiffa, Howard, *Smart Choices: A Practical Guide to Making Better Decisions* (2000).

[2] Professors Heavin and Keet reference the importance of assessing impact on the client and note that it is often missing from risk analysis tools. See Heavin, Heather and Keet, Michael "Litigation Risk Analysis: Using Rigorous Projections to Encourage and Inform Settlement," *Journal of Arbitration and Mediation* (forthcoming): 8.

[3] While I have asked clients to estimate the value of "not going through it," I appreciate their resistance to that being used against them, in a way, by subtracting it from or adding it to negative payoffs. With all due respect for measurability bias and inclusive payoff numbers, this is one where it seems better just to record the number on the margin—as a plus for settlement or a negative for litigation. It's recorded on the page and becomes part of the discussion.

the organization. He believes the other business shorted the quality and quantity of goods delivered on the contract. This was very costly to your client who had to find quality replacements on a rush basis to fulfill his contract with a major customer. There have been some "friendly" discussions about the problem, but the other business owner has offered a "pittance" in settlement.

In addition to mapping the legal claims, probabilities, and hard costs, you may wish to discuss any subtle impact on other trade association members' willingness to do business with him in the future. Can the client put a price on that—or on his desire to avoid it? Perhaps it cuts the other way, perhaps filing suit has the additional positive value of communicating a warning against shorting the quantity or quality of an order. This answer will likely depend on the offending trade member's reputation within the association. Indeed, your client may wish to communicate proactively with other members to preempt negative rumors and backlash. Whatever your discussion yields, it may be possible for your client to put a positive or negative dollar value on the impact of his decision to take legal action. If so, that may be included at the appropriate outcome node. Or, as in the example above, it could at least be written on the tree page.

Technically, it is also possible to assign a dollar value to purely emotional or relationship-based consequences of a decision. I hereby admit that this option makes me uncomfortable, but I offer it for those less uncomfortable with translating the value of emotional or personal relationship values to dollars.[4] After all, our legal system routinely asks juries to assign dollars to emotional distress, loss of consortium, and alienation of affection.

4) A fourth way to work with intangibles—utility analysis—involves assigning utility values to both financial and intangible factors, including attitudes toward risk must be referenced here. For some clients, and some highly consequential legal problems, it may be well worth the time and effort. It should also be noted that the initial steps in a utility analysis—assigning points, weights and preferences to different intangible factors—can be of great assistance to a client thinking through a difficult decision. Its value does not only derive from the capacity to plug utility values into a decision tree.

However, because I suspect only the smallest minority of lawyers or clients would ever take the time to do a full utility analysis, this text does not currently include a section on how to do one. (That may someday appear on the riskandrigor.com website on topics related to this book, currently in the planning stages.) It is admittedly technical and somewhat time consuming. A description of this method can be found in a number of the reference sources included in this text's bibliography.[5]

[4] See the option of converting both money and intangibles to utility values, discussed briefly below this section.

[5] A less technical explanation can be found in Hammond, Keeney, and Raiffa, Howard, *Smart Choices* (2002): 131-153. For more in-depth discussion of utility analysis among the references contained in this book's bibliography, the reader may consult the original Raiffa, Howard, *Decision Analysis: Introductory Lectures on Choices under Uncertainty* (1968); or Clemen, Robert T. *Making Hard Decisions* (1996): 465-489.

About Risk, the Ever Present and Entirely Real Intangible

No doubt, decision tree analysis prompts the lawyer and client to thoughtfully consider and discuss risk. That is one of the method's primary values for client counseling and decision-making. As referenced in the "how to's" section, the distribution of possible outcomes in two cases (even with the same EMV) will suggest different decisions, depending on the client's aversion to or tolerance for risk. In simplest terms, one case's mathematical roll back to a $100,000 EMV may flow from possible outcomes that range between $125,000 and $175,000. (This assumes a 66% (2/3) chance of a liability finding and no preliminary dispositive motions). Another case's EMV may flow from a 40% chance of liability, but damages that have a 50% chance of clustering right around $375,000 and a 50% chance of clustering right around $125,000. If you look at the distribution of outcomes he would have an overall 20% chance of a verdict (plus costs) of $375,000, a 20% chance at $125,000, and a 60% chance of $0 dollars in liability.[6]

Different business clients will respond differently to these case scenarios. One client might note that, in the first case, he's probably going to lose so he might as well make a substantial offer. Or, if $125,000—$175,000 will not severely impact his business, he may decide it's worth rolling the dice. The same client might be greatly concerned about even a 20% chance of a $375,000 verdict: that might put him into bankruptcy, lead to lay-offs, eliminate a credit line, or preclude a major investment to which he is largely committed. The client might also acknowledge his general discomfort with risk.

The plaintiff in either case may also be strongly impacted by the distribution of risk. Some plaintiffs will be uncomfortable with even a 1/3 risk of $0 recovery (and still paying $25,000 in fees and costs). Others would take the 2/3 bet for $100,000, even with $25,000 in fees. But they would not be pleased to buy a $25,000 ticket with a 60% chance of $0, a 20% chance of $125,000 and a $20% chance of $375,000. A plaintiff may be risk averse because he needs to recover a minimum amount to keep his business afloat or to pay off debts. Dollars over that are great, but not worth the risk of $0.

The reader will not be surprised that those deep into decision analysis offer quantitative ways to account for risk aversion and risk tolerance. Their suggestions include deriving risk utilities by considering the difference in value between a certain dollar amount obtainable without risk, and the same dollar amount with risk.[7] While beyond the scope of this text, it is possible to develop a general risk profile or curve for a particular client, and use it for that client's decision analysis.[8]

In my practice as a neutral mediator using decision tree analysis, I choose not to quantitatively account for risk in either of these ways for two reasons. The first is prescriptive; the other is practical. First, I prescribe against quantitative adjustment to reflect risk aversion (or preference) on the tree because, in my limited experience observing this practice, it rather ironically tends to lead us to double count risk. Here is how this can happen: assume a tree built for the plaintiff, in which payoff numbers

[6] Note that, in an attempt to simplify, this example violates the requirement of including costs. Assume $25,000 in attorneys' fees (and other costs). They would raise the EMV to $125,000 in both cases, as the fees would be the same no matter what the outcome.

[7] See Hammond, Keeney, and Raiffa, *Smart Choices* (2002), for a clear and simple discussion of utility analysis for outcomes that are intangible, a mix of quantifiable or tangible and intangible, and considering different levels of risk as an element of utility.

[8] Once again, on the topic of deriving a client's risk profile, readers may consult the original Raiffa, Howard, *Decision Analysis: Introductory Lectures on Choices under Uncertainty* (1968), or Clemen, Robert T., *Making Hard Decisions* (1996): 465-489.

have already been reduced to adjust for their associated risk. Then the tree is rolled back to reflect and EMV and a range of outcomes. Still, the plaintiff tends to look at the tree, see those numbers, and then think, "but it's risky," and adjust down again. The strict decision analyst might respond by noting: "Yes, it is, and we've already counted that on the tree." Somehow, that idea doesn't feel real, but the actual risk still does. Hence, the impulse to discount for risk yet again.

The second reason I intentionally neglect the quantification of risk utilities or attitudes before rolling back the tree is practical. The client's eyes, and perhaps mine, would no doubt glaze over. "What again are we exactly including in the pay-off numbers again? Oh yes, estimated damages awards, attorney's fees, expert costs, monetized value of the employees time… and now what else?" That's where I draw my line: short of quantifying and accounting for a client's attitude toward risk *within* the tree and its mathematical analysis.[9]

Make no mistake: it is critically important for the client to think deeply about risk; how he understands it; how he will feel about it over time; how he would or would not be able to manage extreme but possible results; and what steps he could take to reduce risks or minimize their impact. Reckoning with risk is one of the benefits of using decision tree analysis with a client. However, my practice is not to inject it into the tree, but to step back from the tree and let the client consider the tree's reflection of risks ahead. The goal is to strengthen the client's ability to make a wise decision in light of the way he feels about these risks.

[9] With some exceptions, in many circumstances I also draw it after including estimated costs and fees, but before some of the other intangible factors, and sometimes before other categories referenced in the earlier discussion of non-monetary consequences. It depends on client patience, the overall complexity of the tree to that point, and the desire to highlight some of these elements rather than fold them in.

9

Psychology's Important Interlude Pernicious Impact on Subjective Probability and Payoff Predictions

Decision tree analysis is only as sound as the judgment that informs its subjective estimates of probabilities and dollar outcomes. These estimates are, by definition, inexact. No one can accurately predict the future all of the time. Presumably, an expert is valued because her education and experience mean that her estimates, though unavoidably subjective will be more accurate, more of the time. The lawyer is the expert on law and legal process. Thus, decision analysis in a legal context has reason to rely on a lawyer's best judgment given the facts and the law in the particular case. We cannot expect more or less than that.

Still, lawyers are human. A robust body of research establishes that humans—lawyers included—are subject to psychological impediments that distort or block access to what otherwise might be their expert judgments. As these impediments can affect any prediction or estimate, it seems most efficient to describe them in this interlude. My intent is to provide a common foundation and sensibility for later discussion of challenges, choices, and best practices in assessing and eliciting subjective estimates of probabilities and outcome predictions.

Reckoning with the Psyche's Impediments to Sound Prediction[1]

Thoughtful, informed, and deliberate analysis is a best practice for just about any endeavor, with possible exceptions in romance and immediate danger. In the context of analyzing legal problems, best practices must be designed around what are very common, well-known impediments to optimal analysis.

[1] Much of this discussion is drawn liberally from Chapter 5 in Aaron, Marjorie, *Client Science: Advice for Lawyers on Counseling Clients Through Bad News and Other Legal Realities* (2012), which includes references to important primary and secondary sources. Too much experimental and empirical research exists confirming the power of human bias in decision-making to cite it here. This discussion of psychological biases includes citations only for highly specific references. Those who wish to delve deeper into the impact of bias, and indeed, other ways that psychology impacts lawyers' thinking, are encouraged to read: Robbennolt, Jennifer K. and Sternlight, Jean R., *Psychology for Lawyers: Understanding the Human Factors in Negotiation, Litigation and Decision* (2013). Research specific to lawyers' decisions regarding settlement and trial can be found in Randall, Kiser, *Beyond Right and Wrong: The Power of Effective Decision Making for Attorneys and Clients* (2010), drawing upon research reported in Kiser, Randall L.; Asher, Martin A.; and McShane, Blakeley B. "Let's Not Make a Deal: An Empirical Study of Decision Making in Unsuccessful Settlement Negotiations," *Journal of Empirical Legal Studies* 5, no. 3 (2008): 551-591.

Another important piece of research at the top of this non-exhaustive list is: Goodman-Delahunty, Jane; et al., "Insightful or Wishful: Lawyers' Ability to Predict Case Outcomes," *Psych., Pub. Pol'y. & L.* 16, no. 2 (2010):133 -157.

What are these impediments? It's fair to group them into two broad categories, even if not entirely unrelated: (1) egocentric and partisan perception biases and (2) the tendency to anchor on an initial number or position. They impede optimal analysis because of their power to distort, bending one's thinking and conclusions away from clearheaded, unbiased, unanchored versions. Some elaboration on these impediments and their impact on decision-making is provided below, as well as ways to counteract or adjust for them.

Egocentric and Partisan Perception Biases

Most of us are partial to ourselves, so it seems right to discuss egocentric biases first. One of the most robust findings in psychology is that people tend to have inflated, optimistic, positive assessments of themselves and their own likelihood of success.[2] Particularly relevant for the lawyer-tree builder, even professionals tend to be overly confident that their better-than-average intelligence and professional skills will bend the odds in their favor. Research indicates that this effect worsens when a decision must be made under time pressure.[3]

Back to decision trees: when assigning percentages to branches on his decision tree in a case, the lawyer will consider how he would frame the argument on summary judgment or build his case through witnesses or in summation at trial. The client will think about his own role as an important witness. Particularly where their performances will directly impact a critical juncture, egocentric biases may lead to distorted probability estimates. We forget that the other side's lawyer has won a few cases in his time or that their key witness might also be described as charismatic.

[2] Garrison Keillor, originator and recently retired host and star of Minnesota Public Radio's much beloved radio show (broadcast nationally through NPR), *Prairie Home Companion*, long told weekly stories from his Minnesota hometown, "Lake Wobegon, where the women are strong, the men are good looking, and all of the children are above average." Given Mr. Keillor's retirement, the "above average" quality of Lake Wobegon's children may not be as universally recognized in the future as it is today. Author Kathryn Schulz refers to this as "the Lake Wobegon Effect" in *Being Wrong: Adventures in the Margin of Error* (2011): 106; see also Dunning, David; Heath, Chip; and Suls, Jerry M., "Flawed Self-Assessment: Implications for Health, Education, and the Workplace," *Psychological Science in the Public Interest* 5, no. 3 (2004); Dunning, David et al., "Why People Fail to Recognize Their Own Incompetence," *Current Directions in Psychological Science* 12, no. 3 (2003): 83–87 (describing research that indicates most people are not adept at judging their limitations and greatly overestimate their own talent and expertise). This footnote discussion is also drawn from Aaron, *Client Science*.

There are simply too many sources confirming that "experts" in a field are generally subject to the same range of cognitive psychological biases in estimating probabilities and outcomes and in confidence levels as non-experts, though sometimes to lesser degrees. One antidote is repeated feedback such as weather forecasters receive on a daily basis. A good summary of the research through 1980 is found in Lichtenstein, Sarah; Fischhoff, Baruch; and Phillips, Lawrence, "Calibration of probabilities: The state of the art to 1980," in Kahneman, Daniel; Slovic, Paul; and Tversky, Amos (eds.), *Judgment under uncertainty: Heuristics and biases* (1982): 306-335. It's fair to say that the vast majority of subsequent published experimental research confirms experts' susceptibility to anchoring, the representativeness heuristic, over-confidence, tightness of range and all the rest, even if tempered in some instances.

[3] Study 2 of Epley, Nicholas; Boaz, Keysar; Van Boven, Leaf; and Gilovich, Thomas, "Perspective Taking as Egocentric Anchoring and Adjustment," *Journal of Personality and Social Psychology* 87, no. 3 (2004): 327–339.

Entrenchment by Judgmental Over-Confidence

A Chinese proverb wisely observes: "To be uncertain is to be uncomfortable, but to be certain is to be ridiculous."[4] Yet, the egocentric bias known as "judgmental overconfidence" is prevalent in human psychology. Assume a defense lawyer predicts his summary judgment motion will succeed. If he claims to be "ninety-five percent sure", judgmental over-confidence is likely exerting its influence. He has made a predictive (and optimistic) judgment and he is also confident of that judgment. Research confirms that attorneys tend to be overconfident about often inaccurate predictions.[5]

Tree-builders should be aware that overconfidence tends to increase after making a judgment or committing to a choice. The classic experiment at a Vancouver racetrack makes the point. Experimenters asked prospective bettors about their level of confidence before and after placing bets on their favorite horse. The bettors were more confident after betting; yet the horses had not gotten any faster![6] After making a strategic litigation or settlement choice, lawyers and clients may become more confident. We will no doubt reassess after new information or important pre-trial rulings. However, these adjustments are often insufficient, again due to perception biases, overconfidence, and the power of anchoring (the latter to be discussed shortly).

The Lawyer's (or Client's) Partisan Position

Separate from egocentrism, our partisan positions cause us to filter information and then evaluate it differently than a neutral party would.[7] We fall prey to "biased assimilation of information" and "selective perception" of the information acquired. In short, we are inclined to absorb and value information supporting our positions and discount or ignore countervailing evidence.

A plethora of research shows partisan perception bias

It's important to know that lawyers are subject to this bias notwithstanding professional obligations to be "objective".[8] Most are not particularly competent at predicting how a neutral decision-maker—judge, jury, or arbitrator—will rule. In a landmark study comparing trial attorneys' predictions and later reported trial results, University of California Professor Elizabeth Loftus and Leiden University Professor Willem Wagenaar found that, as a whole, the attorney participants were over-confident and inaccurate

---

[4] Aaron, *Client Science*, 154.

[5] Loftus, Elizabeth F. and Wagenaar, Willem A., "Lawyer's Predictions of Success," *Jurimetrics* 28 (1988).

[6] Knox, Robert E. and Inkster, James A., "Postdecision Dissonance at Post Time," *Journal of Personality and Social Psychology* 8, no. 4 (1968): 319-323.

[7] One explanation is that people perceive and interpret the world through knowledge structures or "schemas." These affect what we observe and remember. Failure to observe what runs counter to our schemas may rise to "unintentional blindness." For further references and more detailed discussion, see Chapter 5 in Aaron, *Client Science*, 143-144.

[8] Goodman-Delahunty, et. al., "Insightful or Wishful," 133-157.

When assessing probabilities of favorable rulings by a judge or jury, the decision analyst should be aware of a study finding that socio-political attitudes biased the way state court judges and law students evaluated research on capital punishment. It seems that knowledge of an assigned judge's social and political leanings may be a significant factor in your assessment. Redding, Richard E. and Reppucci, N. Dickon, "Effects of Lawyers' Socio-political Attitudes on Their Judgments of Social Science in Legal Decision Making," *Law and Human Behavior* 23, no. 1 (1990): 31-54.

predictors. More highly confident lawyers were not more accurate.[9] A later study confirmed that lawyers' predictions about winning or losing on liability were barely more accurate than chance.[10] Not surprisingly, the author's law school class annually demonstrates partisan perception bias, with wide divergence between defense and plaintiff sides' average estimates of the chances of liability in a business fraud case.

Experience is no antidote; it may even exacerbate the problem. Two separate studies found lower calibration between prediction and results among lawyers in practice for more than thirty years.[11] Accuracy reached an average plateau somewhere between six and ten years of practice and continued to thirty years. We can only speculate as to why. Perhaps senior lawyers become entrenched on one side of the practice, handle more difficult cases, or become more over-confident. To all lawyer-readers over fifty, this is a peer's respectful word to the wise.

Further research establishes that the partisan role, not the law degree, is what diminishes our accuracy.[12] This suggests that, where possible, it would be wise for a professional uninvolved in the case (even if it's an in-firm lawyer) to serve as the tree-builder and/or to actively engage in critical dialogue with the lawyer estimating probabilities for his own client's case.

The Bias Blind Spot

Even if aware of such biases, we tend to believe our own judgments are less susceptible to bias than others'.[13] Given the prevalence of optimistic and egocentric biases, this "bias blind spot" is no surprise. After all, we also see ourselves as above average and thus more objective, less self-interested and more moral. It is also consistent with the psychological phenomenon known as "naïve realism": people's tendency to believe their own understanding of the world as simply accurate and conclude that others' views stem from bias or ignorance.

---

[9] Goodman-Delahunty, Jane; Granhag, Willem A.; and Loftus, Elizabeth F., "How Well Can Lawyers Predict Their Chances of Success?" Unpublished manuscript (1998), cited in Koehler, Derek J.; Brenner, Lyle; and Griffin, Dale W., "The Calibration of Expert Judgment: Heuristics and Biases beyond the Laboratory" in Gilovich, Thomas; Griffin, Dale W.; and Kahenman, Daniel (eds.), *Heuristics and Biases: The Psychology of Intuitive Judgment* (2002). These sources are also cited in: Kiser, Randall, *Beyond Right and Wrong*, 56 n. 37, and in Aaron, *Client Science*, 156, n. 56. See also: Loftus and Wagenaar, "Lawyer's Predictions of Success."

[10] Goodman-Delahunty, Jane et al., "Insightful or Wishful."

[11] For more complete discussion, see Kiser, Randall, *Beyond Right and Wrong: The Power of Effective Decision-Making for Attorneys and Clients* (2010) and the initial research article the book builds upon: Kiser, Randall; Asher, Martin; and McShane, Blakeley,"Let's Not Make a Deal: An Empirical Study of Decision Making in Unsuccessful Settlement Negotiations," *Journal of Empirical Legal Studies* 5, no. 3 (2008): 551–591.

For a shorter summary, see Chapter 5 in Aaron, *Client Science*.

[12] In the influential book by Kelvin Jr., Harry and Zeisel, Hans, *The American Jury* (1971), the authors reported on research in which more than 500 judges in 400 civil jury trials recorded their opinions of the cases' difficulty and how they should be decided, before learning the jury verdicts. Judges agreed with the jury's verdict 78 percent of the time. Kiser makes the point that this 78 percent agreement is higher than most expert-to-expert agreements in other fields. Kiser, *Beyond Right and Wrong*, 18. When they disagreed, judges would have ruled for the plaintiff 10 percent of the time and for the defense 12 percent of the time—a statistically even balance. Many other studies have yielded strong findings of judge and jury agreement.

[13] For an extended discussion and influential research into the bias blind spot, see Ehrlinger, Joyce; Gilovich, Thomas; and Ross, Lee, "Peering in to the Bias Blind Spot: People's Assessments of Bias in Themselves and Others," *Personality and Social Psychology Bulletin* 31, no. 5 (2005): 680-92.

Judgmental Anchoring

Judgmental anchoring—a previously considered number's influence on a numeric judgment—also critically impacts best practices for decision analysis. Much like an anchor pulls a boat in its direction, our first number—that first guess or reference point data, even if obviously wishful—pulls our subsequent numerical judgments up or down.

It's fair to say that anchoring is another one of the most robust, consistently demonstrated phenomenon in research on psychology and decision-making, across a variety of domains.[14] It doesn't matter if the anchor number is plausible or implausible, is known to be from a partial or impartial source,[15] or is entirely irrelevant to the problem. Novices and experts alike are subject to anchoring, in both laboratory and real-world experimental conditions.[16]

I can't avoid temptation to describe the first demonstration of anchoring, as it illustrates the concept in its purest from. In 1974, Professors Amos Tversky and Daniel Kahneman performed their classic experiment,[17] in which a "Wheel of Fortune" type roulette wheel was spun in various business school classes. The wheel had secretly been preset to the number 10 or 65. The students were asked to estimate the percentage of African countries in the United Nations. For classes in which the roulette wheel spun to 10, the average estimate was 25 percent and for classes in which the wheel spun to 65, the average estimate was 45 percent. Clearly the preset wheel numbers were powerful anchors, despite their obvious irrelevance to the question.

My own and law professor colleagues' numerous informal anchoring experiments consistently confirm what a psychology professor would anticipate: the phenomenon is alive and well among lawyers and law students. Each year in my client counseling class, I ask law students to estimate damages and recommend settlement for an employment discrimination case. The case is described in some detail on a document that also references an unrelated personal injury case with vastly different awards. Each year, the students' damages estimates and recommended settlements are strongly anchored by the numbers in the unrelated personal injury case. Similar informal experiments with experienced counsel yielded the same results: damages estimates and settlement recommendations were strongly anchored by numbers in a logically unrelated case. Why does anchoring work? It has been suggested that when someone is anchored, they selectively search for and activate information consistent with it.[18] And, even

---

[14] See, Smith, Andrew R. and Windschitl, Paul D., "Biased Calculations: Numeric Anchors Influence Answers to Math Equations," *Judgment and Decision Making* 6, no. 1 (2011): 139-146, and George, Joey F.; Duffy, Kevin; and Ahuja, Manju, "Countering the Anchoring and Adjustment Bias with Decision Support Systems," *Decision Support Systems* 29, no. 2 (2011): 195-206.

[15] See Chapman, G.B.; and Johnson, E.J., "Incorporating the irrelevant: Anchors in judgments of belief and value.," in Gilovich, Griffin, and Kahneman (eds.), *Heuristics and Biases: The Psychology of Intuitive Judgment.* For comprehensive discussion and citation to numerous sources on this issue, see Epley, Nicholas, and Gilovich, Thomas, "The Anchoring and Adjustment Heuristic: Why the Adjustments Are Insufficient," *Psychological Science* 17, no. 4 (2006): 311–18.

[16] Smith and Windschitl, "Biased Calculations," and Whyte, Glen, and Sebenius, James K., "The Effect of Multiple Anchors on Anchoring In Individual and Group Judgment," *Organizational Behavior and Human Decision Processes* 69, no. 1 (1997): 74–85.

[17] Tversky, Amos and Kahneman, Daniel, "Judgment under uncertainty: Heuristics and biases," *Science*, New Series 185, no. 4157 (1974): 1124-1131.

[18] Epley and Gilovich, "The Anchoring and Adjustment Heuristic" (citing to numerous sources).

if we adjust from that anchor by considering additional information or arguments, we resist or underweight these in comparison. Thus, we tend to adjust insufficiently.

It doesn't require much imagination to see how a lawyer conducting decision analysis in his client's case could be anchored by his own or his client's partisan perception biases in estimating liability percentages. Imagine the tree-builder putting the question to a defense lawyer: "So, what are the chances of winning that summary judgment motion and knocking out this case?" Without much thought and with some bravado, the lawyer may throw out a number, "I'd say 80%." When discussing the probability of a plaintiff's verdict, the defense client or lawyer may say, with exasperation, "ZERO percent—5 percent—it shouldn't be more." Before any reasoned discussion, an anchor has been set in place. Surely, intelligent people adjust for new information!? It would seem reasonable to think that intelligent people undergo thought processes to adjust from an anchor, whether internally or externally generated. Unfortunately, a considerable body of experimental research agrees and confirms that, while people tend to adjust somewhat, their adjustments are generally insufficient to achieve accuracy.[19]

Anchoring, Adjustment, and Underestimating Damages

Not surprisingly, psychology impacts our estimates of possible outcome values in a similar way. Mediators will attest that it's not uncommon to hear counsel estimating likely damages in the same case, roughly as follows: Plaintiff's counsel asserts: "The jury will most likely come back at $500,000 in our case—that's what I see as the mid-point." Yet, in the other caucus room, defense counsel reassures his client: "If we do lose, a verdict wouldn't be more than $150,000 or so." For them to arrive at these widely divergent numbers (based on shared factual information), some combination of optimism, selective perception, or biased assimilation of information is operating in at least one, if not both rooms. Their estimates may also have been influenced or anchored by external numbers:[20] the newspaper report of a million-dollar verdict in a fraud case or one lawyer's experience with a stingy jury's low verdict in a personal injury case. Whatever the source, these articulated numerical estimates then become anchors affecting subsequent movement, expectation, and decisions.

Evidence of Defense Blind Spot and Underestimation[21]

Research suggests that defense lawyers are particularly prone to underestimating dollar amounts of damages exposure.[22] A comprehensive 2008 study comparing final settlement offers and demands and trial results in 5,653 civil cases found that, while plaintiffs were somewhat more often mistaken about

[19] Scholars seem to agree that the limits to adjustment are what might be thought of as the "outer edge" of the judge-estimator's reasonable range, but from his own (biased) perspective only. Imagine a lawyer has been asked to judge the likelihood of winning the case. He names "65%" as his best guess. Internally, perhaps unconsciously, he feels that a reasonable range is 55% - 75% (still with 65% as his best estimate point). As he learns more information, or is asked to consider arguments or perspectives of the other side, he will adjust, but only to the edge of his (biased) range—only to 55%. For more information on the insufficiency of adjustments, see Epley and Gilovich, "The Anchoring and Adjustment Heuristic."

[20] See Epley, Nicholas; Keysar, Boaz; Van Boven, Leaf; and Gilovich, Thomas "Perspective Taking as Egocentric Anchoring and Adjustment," *Journal of Personality and Social Psychology* 87, no. 3(2004): 327-339.

[21] "Word to the Wise" section is excerpted from Aaron, *Client Science*, 157-158.

[22] Kiser, Randall, *Beyond Right and Wrong*, drawing upon the research originally published in Kiser, Asher, and McShane,"Let's Not Make a Deal."

winning on liability, the average gap between the last offer and the ultimate award was seventeen to nineteen times higher on the defense side than on the plaintiff's side. This strongly suggests widespread defense failure to recognize damages exposure in the event of a plaintiff's verdict, or, at least, failure to account for that exposure in case valuation and settlement offers.

Experimental research also supports the observation that defense lawyers tend to estimate low jury awards, at least in the personal injury area.[23] In one experiment, plaintiffs' and defense lawyers, judges, and jurors were presented with descriptions of personal injury cases and asked to rate the severity of the injury and an appropriate level of award. (Liability was not at issue.) The results: when respondents had no partisan stake in the outcome, there was considerable consistency in the way they analyzed injury severity and thought about awards. However, the largest deviation was found between defense lawyers and all other participants. Defense lawyers tended to rate described injuries as less severe, resulting in lower awards.

I cannot resist noting that unpublished data generated in my annual law school negotiation course suggests that defense tendencies to under-estimate damages exposure begin early. As reported earlier, when law students and their business school clients estimate the likelihood of a plaintiff's verdict in a case of alleged breach of contract and business fraud, both sides display typical partisan perception bias. More striking is that defense-side estimates of damages in the event of plaintiff's verdict have averaged between 10% and 25% of the plaintiff side estimates—four to ten times lower—based upon the SAME spreadsheet numbers on business revenues and projections, etc. My suspicion is that the trial attorneys as well as the law students and clients tend to conflate the likelihood of a defense verdict and the measure of its consequences. In other words, they internally discount any very, very large number by some certainty that it will not happen. It's a hidden double discount. They fail to think through what the highest dollar verdict might be if the jury finds liability and all aspects of the trial go badly.

All of this leads to some important advice for the defense side in particular: beware of unrealistically low verdict estimates. Don't conflate the likelihood of a defense verdict and the measure of its consequences. Remember that your hundredth personal injury claim will be the jury's first. What might the award be if, against the odds, a jury, judge, or arbitrator rules against your client? One mediator (not to mention the defendant) still ruminates on the $40 million-dollar jury award in a case where, in a mediation caucus with the defense, the notion of damages exposure beyond a few million had been waived away as "silly." Don't fail to consider the worst-case scenario.

On Exposure and Wider Range

Even in opinion letters or case assessment discussions devoid of formal decision tree analysis, defense lawyers are appropriately called upon to estimate "worst case exposure" and plaintiff's lawyers are asked to say how high or low the award could be.

Leaving bias aside, our entirely normal tendencies are to describe these ranges too narrowly; we fail to imagine all possible outcomes.[24] In short, we are prey to the general "tightness of range" prob-

[23] Wissler, Roselle et. al., "Decision Making About General Damages: A Comparison of Jurors, Judges, and Lawyers," *Michigan Law Review* 98 (1999): 751 & 805.

[24] Prior research regarding over precision caused by failure to adequately consider all possible outcomes of an event is discussed and a method to mitigate the failure was proposed and tested by Haran, Moore, and Morewedge

lem identified by Professors Raiffa and Alpert in 1969. In their classic experiment, large numbers of Harvard Business School students (all familiar with decision analysis!) were asked to provide extreme range estimates for five independent categories or "almanac type" information, including the "percentage of students (who drink) and who prefer bourbon to scotch," and the "number of eggs produced in the United States in 1965." The subjects were divided into four subgroups: one was asked to estimate numbers at 1% and 99% of the range, the second group at .1% and 99.9%, the third at the extreme ends of the verbal range "minimum possible value" and "maximum possible value," and the fourth group at "astonishingly low" and "astonishingly high."

The experiment sought to learn how large the "surprise index" would be. Or, stated more accurately, it was designed to see how well calibrated our estimated ranges are to actual ranges. Theoretically, there "should" have been only 2% surprises—a surprise index of 2—outside of the actual range—in the first group, and .2% for the second group. (Remember that at either end of a 1% and a 99% range, 1% of results would be lower and 1% would be higher, a total of 2% of results outside the parameters of the range.) In fact, Raiffa and Alpert's experiment yielded a surprise index of 46 for the 1%/99% group and 40 for the .1%/99.9% group. The other two groups had surprise indexes of 47 and 38. This paper spawned a vast number of additional, related experiments and literature on the question of calibration and expertise when subjective probabilities and numerical range estimates are required.[25]

In summary, overwhelming evidence establishes that when we ask people to assess ranges using fractiles—markers at particular percentage points along a range of possible outcomes—they come up with ranges that are too tight. To see what this means in practice, imagine that we ask the following questions to an experienced trial lawyer acting as a neutral consultant in a personal injury case:

- Name a jury verdict number that is at 99% of the possible range; you are confident that if liability were certain and the case were tried 100 times—the verdict would be lower than that number, 99% of the time.
- Can you answer the same question, but at 75%, then at 50%, 25% and finally, 1%?

The research predicts that the lawyer-expert's numerical estimates would set out a range that is too narrow for each segment, and particularly at the extreme ends.[26] In other words, the range would not be well-calibrated to realities.

Of course, in a litigation setting, even these realities are theoretical. There is no almanac data; this case will not be tried 100 times. And yet, research as well as anecdotal evidence suggests that lawyers are too often "surprised" by jury awards outside of ranges they had seen as possible.[27] The author ruefully recalls two recent cases in which jury verdicts came back at multiples of the defense's and the mediator's

---

in their article, "A Simple Remedy for Overprecision in Judgment," *Judgment and Decision Making* 5, no. 7 (2010): 467–76. Their experiment involved weather predictions, and the method they called SPIES (Subjective Probability Interval Estimates) required judges to consider a full range of possible temperatures, broken up into intervals, and then assign probabilities to each interval (with total probabilities not to exceed 100).

[25] See Alpert, Marc and Raiffa, Howard, "A progress report on the training of probability assessors" and Lichtenstein, Fischhoff, and Phillips, "Calibration of probabilities: The state of the art to 1980," in Kahneman, Slovic, and Tversky (eds.), *Judgment under uncertainty: Heuristics and biases*, 294-305 and 306-334.

[26] Epley, Nicholas and Gilovich, Thomas, "Putting Adjustment Back in the Anchoring and Adjustment Heuristic: Differential Processing and Self-Generated and Experimenter-Provided Anchors," *Psychological Science* 12, no. 5 (2001): 391-396.

[27] See Kiser, et. al, "Let's Not Make a Deal," 566-568, 585-586, and 589-590.

highest estimate. Thus, all are advised to play with imagining the worst and the best of all possible outcomes (depending on your perspective) and testing their impact on the decision tree.

The good news is that some but not all studies indicate that training, cautionary instruction, and particularly feedback as to accuracy may reduce the problem.[28] So, for example, weather forecasters tend to have high calibration rates because they receive feedback on their predictions literally every day. Unfortunately, the bad news is that most trial lawyers don't receive such frequent feedback.

Raiffa and Alpert's further research to determine the impact of new information and training on people's range estimates is relevant to the tree builder seeking to elicit legal analysis that encompasses all legitimately predictable verdict ranges.[29] Their work shows that when new information enters the picture, people do expand estimated ranges, but not enough. When people adjust, we move incrementally, grudgingly, and often insufficiently from where the anchor has set in our emotional, psychological mud.[30]

Elicitation for the Full Possible Range

Given all of this, what questions should a tree-builder ask when setting up ranges on a tree?

This question—about which questions to ask—lands us in realm of "elicitation" studies in the field of statistics. These studies posit that there is an "expert" who possesses knowledge and a legitimately formed opinion. The analyst's challenge is to elicit in a way that faithfully yields the expert's opinion.[31] This is a challenge because experts too are prey to the same psychological heuristics and biases as the rest of us. Successful "elicitation" is designed to mitigate the impact of these heuristics and biases and thus their distortions of the expert's true opinion. Elicitation research seeks to learn how the analysis-elicitor—can best design questions and dialog for successful elicitation.

[28] Classic articles asserting the effectiveness of feedback on accuracy include: Lichtenstein, Sarah and Fischhoff, Baruch, "Training for Calibration," *Organizational Behavior and Human Performance* 26 (1980): 149-171; and Kioriat, Asher; Lichtenstein, Sarah; and Fischhoff, Baruch, "Reasons for Confidence," *Journal of Experimental Psychology: Human Learning and Memory* 6 (1980): 107-118. A good summary is also provided in Lichtenstein, Fischhoff, and Phillips, "Calibration of probabilities: The state of the art to 1980," in Kahneman, Slovic, and Tversky (eds.), *Judgment under uncertainty: Heuristics and biases*. See discussion of the research and of their experiment in providing feedback in the form of accurate answers to initially posed questions in Arkes, Hal; Christensen, Caryn; Lai, Cheryl; and Blumer, Catherine, "Two Methods of Reducing Overconfidence," *Organizational Behavior and Human Decision Making Processes* 39 (1987): 133-144.

[29] Alpert, Marc and Raiffa, Howard, "A Progress Report on the Training of Probability Assessors," in Kahneman, Slovic, and Tversky (eds.), *Judgment under uncertainty: Heuristics and biases*, 294-305. Increasingly available databases that provide access to jury verdict for all state and federal courts (including patent litigation) may also offer a reality check on dollar ranges that have been awarded in past cases. Some of these databases and analytic services are discussed more fully in this text's Chapter Eleven.

[30] Overprecision resulting from a failure to adequately consider all possible outcomes of an event is described in and tackled by Haran, Uriel; Moore, Don; and Morewedge, Carey, "A Simple Remedy for Overprecision in Judgment," *Judgment and Decision Making* 5, no. 7 (2010): 467–76.

[31] Garthwaite, Paul; Kadane, Joseph; and O'Hagan, Anthony, "Statistical Methods for Eliciting Probability Distributions," *Journal of the American Statistical Association* 100 (2005): 680-701. The authors write that: "Elicitation is the process of formulating a person's knowledge and beliefs about one or more uncertain quantities into a (joint) probability distribution for those quantities." This piece is also available through Semanticscholar.org at https://www.semanticscholar.org/paper/Chapter-1-Elicitation-Garthwaite-Kadane/d213d8252de5f77a55980ee8e15eb16506f31a4c.

For decision analysis or risk analysis in a legal context, the "elicitor" could be the non-lawyer decision analyst, a tree-builder lawyer or mediator; the expert(s) could be the lawyer on the case or a lawyer or former judge called in to consult on the merits. Presumably the lawyer (or legal team) would be the most knowledgeable about the facts, evidence, witnesses, legal issues and so forth.[32] As a practical matter, the tree-builder and the expert may often be the same lawyer.

How then, is the tree builder best advised to ask the lawyer (even if it's himself) about his estimates of a possible jury verdict range in a way that avoids or mitigates "tightness of range"?

One option is for the tree builder to ask that the lawyer, in effect, establish the quartiles. In other words, ask: "Is there a verdict amount that's 'smack dab' in the middle, a point at which you would predict the actual number would be lower half the time, and higher half the time if, hypothetically the case were tried a hundred times?" That becomes the median.[33]

Those who have studied psychology or absorbed lessons in this "Interlude on Psychology" may be concerned about the anchoring effect of that median number. Fair point. In fact, that mid-point number is likely to serve as an anchor. For that reason, it's best to avoid naming a mid-point before thorough consideration and discussion of the facts, evidence, emotions, and law that will impact a verdict in the case.

The reason to elicit the number is that some research suggests somewhat less over-confidence—less anchoring close to the mid-point number and somewhat wider confidence ranges—when the expert generates that number, than if it was externally introduced. Still, given our awareness of the strong tendency toward anchoring and tightness of range, some skepticism seems warranted.

On the other hand, depending upon his or her role, the tree builder may deliberately choose to introduce or suggest the median point (or any other points) in hope of an anchoring effect, even recognizing a tightness of range concern. Consider the mediator tree builder, who may fairly be characterized as "negotiating from the middle." The mediator may want to name a (neutrally assessed and neutrally motivated) number and ask if that might be the median jury verdict. Perhaps the mediator's suggested numbers will mitigate the lawyer's tendencies toward partisan bias, at least in naming the midpoint.

Whatever the stated median, the next question might be: "Assume a verdict number higher than that, at what number would we likely be 'halfway up the high side?' In other words, at what number would 75% of the verdicts be lower and only 25% higher?" and so forth, until reaching the farthest ends of the range—99% and 1%.[34]

[32] Of course, in practice, tree builder may also be the lawyer in his client's case. If so, elicitation is reflexive: the tree builder's dialog is with her own lawyerly self.

[33] See Block, Richard and Harper, David, "Overconfidence in Estimation: Testing the Anchoring-and-Adjustment Hypothesis," *Organizational Behavior and Human Decision Processes* 49 (1991): 188-207.

[34] In fact, this author has been introduced to quite a hyper-technical body of research literature on elicitation of expert opinions as to probabilities, values, and ranges so as to avoid their common psychological biases and judgment errors. By way of example (and to mine their references), see Garthwaite, Kadane, and O'Hagan, "Statistical Methods for Eliciting Probability Distributions," Fischhoff, and Phillips, "Calibration of probabilities: The state of the art to 1980," in Kahneman, Slovic, and Tversky (eds.), *Judgment under uncertainty: Heuristics and biases*, and Winkler, R.L.; Hera, S.C.; and Baca, R.G, "The Quality of Experts' Probabilities Obtained Through Formal Elicitation Techniques," Center for Nuclear Waste Regulatory Analyses (1992).

Another option would be to start by eliciting extreme ends of a hypothetical range: "What jury awards are the highest or the lowest you could imagine?" You might ask the lawyer to name an extremely high hypothetical award amount at which he is 99% sure the actual award will be lower or to name an extremely low award amount at which there's only a 1% chance it would ever be lower. Then, and only then, would the tree builder ask the lawyer to estimate the probability of numerical points or chunks within that range, or to estimate the 50% median.

Theoretically, to avoid common conservatism, the elicitor could also name some extreme numerical points and ask if they could fairly be considered at 90%, 95% or even 99% of the range. Of course, that assumes the elicitor is better equipped to predict the extremes, which may not be true.

Research suggests that before eliciting numbers or percentages, it's important to engage in thought exercises for both unfavorable and favorable extremes.[35] Much time should be spent discussing and listing the many factors that might break for the other side—"What would the perfect storm look like?"—and then all of the ways things could go well.[36] In short, before making any numerical or percentage estimates, do imagine the circumstances that might give rise to extreme outcomes in either direction. This thought exercise is likely to lead to fewer "surprises" in the form of actual results that fall outside of the anticipated range.

Value and Risk of Frames[37]

This interlude's final segment on "Value and Risk of Frames" offers insights from psychology for communicating with clients about decision trees numerical inputs and calculated values in legal settlement contexts.

The way a lawyer frames choices to a client can greatly influence the client's response. If a choice is framed as a loss, we are more likely to choose a risky alternative; if it's framed as a gain, we are more likely choose to keep it rather than risk it. Of course, most choices can be seen from multiple perspectives. Whether described or felt as a loss or a gain depends on expectations, goals, and context.

These insights derive from an impressive body of research in the field of psychology. Original credit is due to Professors Tversky and Kahneman, who first articulated the now widely accepted, tenets of "prospect theory[38]" regarding the ways most people respond to risk, gain, and loss:

---

[35] This advice derives from studies regarding scientific data and quantifiable, knowable outcomes of numerous tri als. The problem is that one recommendation—for the elicitor to state the known or knowable extreme numerical ranges and ask the expert to name the percentage likelihood of outcomes along those ranges—is not realistic in our context. This author is doing the best she can to extrapolate advice from some of this literature, or at least to avoid bad advice.

[36] See Flannelly, Laura and Flannelly, Kevin, "Reducing People's Judgment Bias About their Level of Knowledge," *The Psychological Record* 50 (2000): 587-600. This is just one among many reports of experimental research demonstrating that active consideration of the counter-arguments, negative factors, or the opposite view tends to reduce biases and over-confidence.

[37] This discussion of Prospect Theory and its application for client counseling is largely excerpted or paraphrased from Chapter 5 in Aaron, *Client Science*, which contains a vast number of citations. As is true for the balance of this interlude, readers are also directed to the Sternlight and Robbennalt, *Psychology for Lawyers*.

[38] Tversky, Amos and Kahneman, Daniel, "The Framing of Decisions and the Psychology of Choice," Science 211, no. 4481 (1981): 454. For additional explanations of Prospect Theory, see Plous, Scott, *The Psychology of Judgment and Decision Making* (1993); and Kahneman, Daniel and Tversky, Amos, "Prospect Theory: An Analysis of Decision Under Risk," *Econometrica* 47 (1979): 263-291.

1) People tend to be risk-averse as to significant gain.

Once we have gained something we are often loath to give it up in favor of a relatively strong chance of getting more. Preference for the "bird in the hand" over the "bird in the bush" is the operative aphorism. This is true even when the "rational" choice—in terms of mathematically discounted value—is to take the risk. Thus, most people prefer a sure gain of $240 over a fifty percent chance of winning $500. Different people's breakpoints will be different. I might settle for $175, or even $150, or less. Others might take no less than $200, and be comfortable with rolling the dice. And a few will insist upon every penny of the mathematically discounted value that is $250, or even more.

2) People tend to be risk-seeking as to significant loss.

We hate to pay up and declare defeat right now. When people are given a choice between a 75% chance of losing $1,000, or just paying $750 (or, I suspect, $740 or even $700), most will choose to roll the weighted dice. We would rather not choose loss, particularly current loss, if it can be delayed.

It turns out that tables are turned for insignificant gains and losses. When an offer is extremely low, we become risk seekers, choosing to roll the dice for the long shot high dollar win. Consider a $10,000 offer, based on 5% chance of $200,000. If the offer was a mere pittance to the client (no impact on cash flow, etc.), he won't experience regret at its loss. And he might like to put the defense to the test. On the other side, people would rather pay a bit more than discounted value to avoid the small chance of enormous loss. Thus, a defense client faced with a 5% chance of that same $200,000 loss might be willing to pay more than the economically rational $10,000. Why? People are sometimes willing to pay a premium for certainty and peace of mind. And we are motivated to avoid regret. The defendant may be happy to over pay a bit (more than discounted risk value) to avoid entirely the fear of having to pay $200,000, particularly if that would severely impact his business or career.

3) People tend to prefer positively framed choices—certain gains from a reference point—over choices involving risk.

Affirming the expression "a bird in the hand beats two in the bush": most of us an opportunity for sure gain over a chance to win considerably more, if that chance comes with the risk of winning nothing. As discussed earlier, when offered $100 as a no-risk gain or the chance to play a coin toss game with a 50% probability of winning $210, $220, or $250 (or perhaps more), most people will choose the $100. If potential winnings are high enough, most of us would indeed accept the risk and toss the coin. The important observation is that the exact 50% discounted value would not usually be the indifference point. That's particularly true where the scale of the numbers becomes higher and we would anticipate great regret over turning down a high "bird in the bush" number and then losing at the risky game.

4) People tend to prefer choices involving risk over negatively framed alternatives—certain losses from a reference point.

Experimental research in legal contexts and more broadly has established Prospect Theory's validity: whether an offer is framed positively as a gain or negatively as a loss from a salient reference point impacts the likelihood of its acceptance or rejection. Literature in law and psychology is replete with examples, so I've opted to stick to the early, classic experiments on point.

First, Professors Kahneman and Tversky gave subjects two sets of choices between alternative programs to combat an outbreak of a dangerous disease which originated in Asia expected to kill 600 people. The first group was asked to choose between Program A that would save 200 people and Program B that would have a 1/3 probability of saving 600 people and a 2/3 probability of saving no one. A second group of respondents were asked to choose between Program C, in which 400 people would die, or Program D, that would have a 1/3 probability of no one dying and a 2/3 probability that 600 people would die.

Professor Max Bazerman later conducted a similar experiment[39] in which participants were given parallel choices regarding a financially troubled company, with three manufacturing locations and 6,000 employees, 2,000 at each location. First, participants were asked to choose between Plan A, that would save 2,000 jobs and one of the manufacturing plants, and Plan B, that would have a 1/3 chance of saving all of the manufacturing plants and all of the jobs. Next, they were asked to choose between Plan C that would result in the loss of 4,000 jobs and 2 two of the three 3 manufacturing locations, and Plan D, that would have a 2/3 chance of losing all of the manufacturing plants and all of the jobs.

In both experiments, the vast majority chose Plan A, and then Plan D. If you read the problem carefully, this makes no sense. Plans B and D are the more risk-seeking. So, internally consistent risk seekers should choose B and D. Plans A and C have certain outcomes. Those who prefer certainty should prefer these plans in both instances. Why do people choose inconsistently? The answer is in the framing: Plan A is framed around the positive—SAVING lives or KEEPING jobs, so it is preferred to B. But Plan C is framed around the negative—CERTAIN LOSS of lives or jobs—and so taking risk with plan D is preferred. The identified reference point determines the frame—whether you view an option as a loss or a gain—and that impacts your decision.

All lawyers should be aware of Prospect Theory and how word choice may influence clients in one direction or another. Yet, it's true that if the lawyer, empathizing with his client, emphasizes loss from a targeted settlement, the client is less likely to accept it. Consider this well-meaning but negative framing by the lawyer: "Well, I know we talked about a possible verdict at trial of $500,000 to $600,000, with a lot of risk. And that's why we had a targeted settlement at $300,000 or so, when we met before the settlement conference. But unfortunately, it looks like the most we can get the defendant to pay is $195,000, that's $100,000 or so less. But if we don't take that, we'll have to roll the dice."

Prospect theory and abundant research tell us that a client is likely to respond differently if the lawyer says: "I know a frustration we've had is that the defense hadn't offered us a dime before today. And I know we talked a lot about the risk of a defense verdict, in which case you would not get anything; your lost wages and other expenses wouldn't be covered. On the other hand, this offer of $195,000—maybe we can get it up to a round $200,000—would just be yours—no risk, under your control, and it would

[39] See Bazerman, Max, "The Relevance of Kahneman and Tversky's Concept of Framing to Organizational Behavior," *Journal of Management* (1983): 1-3; and summary and sources cited in Aaron, *Client Science*, Chapter 5. Note that countless additional experiments—too numerous to cite here—have confirmed the basic tenets of Prospect Theory.

cover expenses and more. Payment could no doubt be processed in a week or so. Or, we could turn it down, say no, and roll the dice."

These reference points—expectations, target numbers, out-of-pockets, the last offer before mediation—will be familiar to any litigator or mediator involved in settlement discussions. As it happens, decision tree analysis generates an array of different and potentially salient numerical points, including the final EMV or discounted value, the EMVs at various intermediate branch clusters, and sometimes, within the range of possible outcomes tied to cumulative probabilities.

As discussed later, these can become reference points around which to frame an offer. "Higher than the EMV" may feel like a gain or a great deal for the plaintiff; "$X lower than the EMV" can be framed as a great deal for the defense. It can also be characterized as a currently "owned" opportunity, a gain that will be lost after summary judgment is denied, when the EMV (and the plaintiff's position) will clearly be higher.

The Representativeness Heuristic Distorts Reality

"In making predictions and judgments under uncertainty, people do not appear to follow the calculus of chance or the statistical theory of prediction. Instead they rely on a limited number of heuristics which sometimes yield reasonable judgments and sometimes lead to severe and systematic errors."[40] One of these heuristics is "representativeness." The more a person or circumstance is "representative" of what I'll call an archetype, the more we are likely to predict their fit with an archetypical story or outcome. This is true even where logic and evidence tell us that story or outcome is rare.

In Kahneman and Tversky's classic experiment, sixty-nine subjects were asked to consider the percentage of all first year graduate student in the US that were enrolled in each of nine fields of specialization. This question generated a set of "base rates"—an estimated distribution of graduate students across different fields. A second group of sixty-five subjects were presented with a personality sketch of "Tom W" and asked how similar Tom W was to the typical graduate student in each of the following nine fields of graduate specialization. A table was generated indicating how close or how far Tom W was from being "similar" to a typical student in these fields.

Finally, a predication group of 114 psychology graduate students was given Tom W's personality sketch,[41] and told that it was written during his senior year in high school by a psychologist on the "basis of projective tests". Those graduate students in psychology knew this type of test to be highly unreliable (particularly from high school). And yet, more than 95% of predictors judged Tom W more likely to study computer science than humanities or education, even though there were many, many more graduate students in these fields. In 1973 or so, the time of this research, 20% of graduate students were estimated to be in Humanities and Education, 17% in Social Science and Social work, 15% in Business Administration, and 12% in Physical or Life Sciences—to name the major categories. Only 7% of graduate students were estimated to be in Computer Science. Yet, our predictors of Tom W's field ranked the

[40] Kahneman, Daniel and Tversky, Amos, "On the psychology of prediction," in Kahneman, Slovic, and Tversky (eds.), *Judgment under uncertainty: Heuristics and biases*, originally published in *Psychological Review* 80 (1973): 237-251. This section's summary of the representativeness heuristic is based upon and drawn from Kahneman and Tversky's chapter, referenced in this note.

[41] In fact, following the prediction, the predictors were asked to estimate the likelihood of such a projective test being accurate. They rated the accuracy as 23%—holding such tests in low esteem.

likelihood of his being in computer science as much higher, despite the overall "base rates" or prevalence of other fields, because Tom W's personality profile matched or "represented" their characterization of a computer science student. This was true even where they knew personality profiles to be unreliable.

This experiment, as well as similar subsequent experiments, established a very strong correlation between similarity and prediction. The more a subject was similar to, or "representative of," a certain category or type, the stronger people's prediction that he belonged.

\What makes this a problem? And how does it relate to probability estimates for decision tree analysis in a legal case? Fair questions! The "representativeness heuristic" is a problem because it makes us inaccurate predictors under accepted rules of probability. Representativeness causes us to ignore the impact of base rates—the overall likelihood or prior probabilities—on the probability we seek to estimate.

Explanation of Bayesian Bedrock as Back-Up for Prescriptive Advice

To include an explanation of Bayes' Theorum, or not to include it? That was a question your author debated. Whether to skip this rather technical, even intimidating topic so as not to lose the more typical lawyer reader, or to include it to maintain some credibility with the statistically astute?

After much internal deliberation, I decided to include it with the caveat that non-mathematically inclined readers can skip it without guilt. All you really need to know is: mathematics and statistics provide analytical proof that the representative heuristic tends to distort our subjective probability judgments; and work with base rates can adjust for this distortion.

If, and only if this prelude discussion has managed to intrigue you, please do consider the following discussion of Bayes' Theorum and its role in subjective probability.

Bayes' Theorem is yet another bedrock rule of probability theory. Also known as Bayes' Rule, it can be thought of as a formal rule about the optimal—mathematically accurate—way to revise probability assessments in light of evidence. It states that accurate prediction requires us to take prior probabilities into account, as well as "conditional" or "posterior" probabilities. When Kahneman and Tversky write that "people do not appear to follow the calculus of chance or the statistical theory of prediction," they are pointing to our common failure to follow this rule when formulating subjective probability estimates.

Bayes' Theorum or Rule can be and often is expressed via mathematical formula. Fortunately, it can also be illustrated with a decision tree.

Imagine we know that 60% of all successful entrepreneurs have MBAs and 40% don't. Suppose 20% of unsuccessful entrepreneurs have MBAs and 80% don't.

Suppose 5% of all entrepreneurs are successful. What proportion of MBAs who are entrepreneurs are successful? The answer is NOT 60%!!!

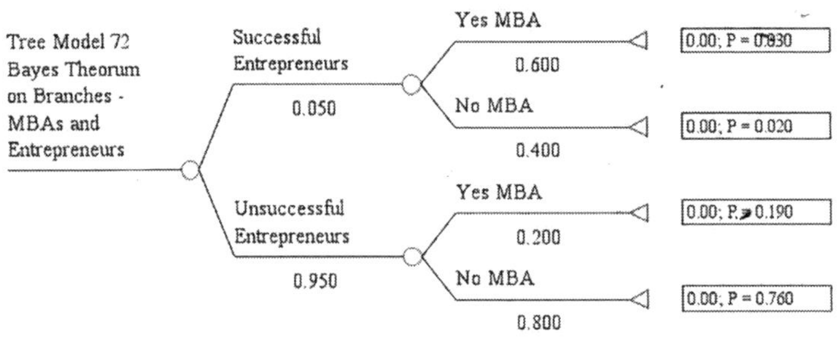

To answer the question: "What % of MBA's who are entrepreneurs are successful?", we look to the tree and observe that a total of 22% of entrepreneurs have MBAs—the 19% who were unsuccessful, plus the 3% who were unsuccessful. But our question asks the proportion of the successful to the total with MBAs, and that is the 3% successful/ the 22% total = 13.6%.

3% of entrepreneurs who have MBAs are successful	3	=	13.6%
22% of entrepreneurs have MBA's (19% +3%)	22		

Consider the following hypothetical example within the realm of assessing the probabilities of legal case outcomes in which a lawyer may tend to use representativeness as a factor.

In an age discrimination case in which the plaintiff absolutely fits the image of "saintly and sympathetic," the lawyer's estimate, influenced by the representativeness heuristic, might be that she is 75% or 80% likely to win.

Now let's imagine that only 40% of all plaintiffs win in age discrimination suits (The 40% has no claim to truth, but it will make the math easier.) Here is how Bayes' would apply:

40% of plaintiffs win. Of these, 80% appear to be saintly/sympathetic; 20% don't.
60% of plaintiffs lose. Of these, 50% appear to be saintly/sympathetic; 50% don't.

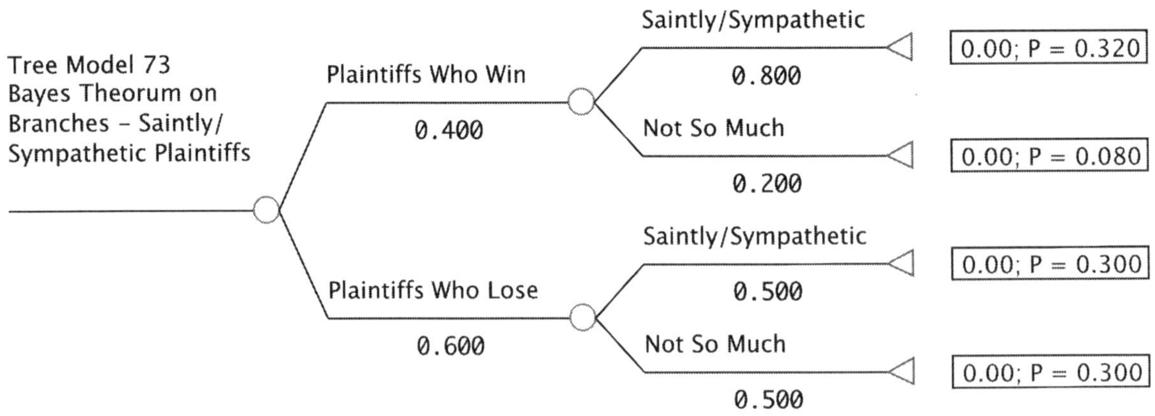

What are the chances that our saintly/sympathetic plaintiff will win?

Well, let's consider that:

- 32% win and are saintly/sympathetic
- 30% lose and are saintly/sympathetic
- 30% lose and are not
- 8% win and are not

Drawing from these results, we see that a total of 62% of plaintiffs appear saintly/sympathetic. Yet only 32% of those who win appear that way.

So, the chance of a saintly/sympathetic plaintiff winning is 32/62—just over 50%.

Put in more colloquial terms, there is a relationship between saintly/sympathetic and the likelihood of winning. If your client is representative of "saintly/sympathetic," it is appropriate to adjust your subjective probability assessment up from the base rate of 40%. But, it's a more modest bump—not nearly to 75% or 80%.

For certain types of statistical evidence to be introduced at trial, failure to understand, use, and explain Bayes' Theorem may be malpractice. Injustice occurs when the jury is misled by inaccurate or misleading statistics entered into evidence.[42] That is not our concern here.

The decision analyst and his client DO have strong interests in admittedly subjective probabilities based upon sound judgments and, to the extent possible, uncorrupted by psychological biases. Hence this discussion of the representative heuristic, Bayes' Theorum, and Chapter Eleven's suggestion to research and consider relevant base rates.

Promise, Power, and Practice in Probabilities and Payoffs

This "interlude" sounds an informed warning about lawyers' and clients' psychological tendencies when estimating probabilities and payouts and advises awareness of framing choices when communicating.

If we are such imperfect, biased estimators, what business do we have assigning probabilities and payoffs to decision trees?

For better or worse, it is as much our business to estimate probability and payoffs in numerical terms as it has traditionally been to evaluate a case in prose terms. A lawyer's traditional descriptive evaluation is no more or less subject to the psychological biases outlined earlier. Yet, this prose has long been relied upon to support recommendations and decisions regarding "reasonable" settlement ranges.

Of course, for a decision tree to be analyzed in full, or even used as a reasonably informative map, numbers can't be avoided. Even though numerical probability and outcome estimates are absolutely and unapologetically subjective, their use in decision analysis offers complete transparency. At the very least, corruption by psychological bias is more likely to be seen and critically questioned when reflected in numbers.

[42] The author hereby acknowledges some ambivalence regarding the decision to place a summary description of Bayes' Theorum in this section. On the one hand, it is linked to the representativeness heuristic; on the other hand, this interlude has been about psychology rather than numbers and probability theory. Fair point. Readers interested in further discussion of the topic are invited to consult just about any text on probability theory.

This interlude was intended to offer research insight and best practice advice for lawyers using decision tree analysis. My hope is that it will inspire humility, rigor, and reflection when we lawyers undertake the critical act of estimating probability and outcome in our clients' cases.

10

Affirming and Working With Subjective Probabilities

Lawyers analyze case law, statutes, and regulations, reach conclusions about legal and factual strengths and weaknesses, and advise their clients regarding certainties and uncertainties. Few lawyers' predictions come with absolute certainty; ambiguities and their consequences must be acknowledged and explained. Law school begins the process of acculturating lawyers to ambiguity and uncertainty as embedded in the legal system. If all laws, rules, and facts were clear and predictions about legal process outcome uncontroversial, legal analysis and its communication would be far less difficult.

Given that advising clients as to legal and factual uncertainties is an essential component of legal advice, it is not surprising that experienced lawyers become comfortable with that process. In face-to-face meetings, over the phone, on email or in a more formal opinion letter, lawyers walk clients through their analysis, explaining where the uncertainties lie, and how they assess the chances of success at each juncture. Phrases such as "highly likely," "quite possible," "just about a slam dunk," and "pretty good chance" roll off lawyers' tongues or keypads, with the reasoning supporting the phrase. Yet, if you ask them to assign a percentage, many lawyers resist, protesting: "I couldn't assign a probability percentage; it's too precise. No one can really do that: nothing is exactly this percent or that percent. If I just throw out a percentage, it's garbage in, garbage out. No client or lawyer should rely on a percentage number."

The entire enterprise of decision tree analysis for legal problems respectfully disagrees and invokes two sources of wisdom in support of that disagreement. The first one, referenced earlier, is:

> *"Let not the perfect be the enemy of the good."*[1]

Although probability percentages used in a decision tree are inevitably subjective and may not be perfect, they can be good approximations of the lawyer's judgment—the same judgment traditionally relied upon. In fact, there's no such thing as a knowably "perfect" probability in our legal context, given that its accuracy will never be tested through large numbers of identical trials in the same case.

---

[1] Other legitimate translations might be that the best or the better is the enemy of the good. Though this quote is generally attributed to Voltaire: *Le mieux est l'ennemi du bien*, Google answer informs us: That there are two citations for Voltaire's use of this phrase. Both citations are appropriate, since Voltaire wrote this phrase once in Italian and another time in French. The Oxford Dictionary of Quotations, Elizabeth Knowles ed. (5th ed. 1999), page 797, quotation number 11, provides this entry: 'Le mieux est l'ennemi du bien .... The best is the enemy of the good' Contes (1772) 'La Begueule' l. 2; though often attributed to Voltaire, the notion in fact derives from an Italian proverb quoted in his Dictionnaire philosophique (1770 ed.) 'Art Dramatique': 'Il meglio è l'inimico del bene'. See www.answers.google.com/answers/threadview?id=262796

Loftier philosophical and epistemological foundations aside, subjective probability percentages can and should be used for the following reasons:

1) *Clarity has greater virtue than covert operations.*

As discussed earlier, if lawyers express likelihood in verbal rather than numerical terms, they nevertheless inevitably and covertly use percentages to formulate their advice or case evaluation. Surfacing and articulating those percentages enables greater clarity of analysis, for the lawyer and the client.

2) *Acknowledged imprecision reflects professional judgment, given uncertainties.*

It is essential to know and acknowledge that named numerical percentages on a decision tree do not signify precision or certainty (nor do named damages figures). In fact, percentages chosen should be understood as approximations of the lawyer's gut sense. Moreover, the percentages inserted on a decision tree can easily be shifted up or down to account for high degrees of uncertainty, to test the impact of a shifting "gut sense" at any or all junctures.

3) *Informed process yields sound judgments as to percentage likelihood.*

While a percentage "just thrown out there" may have no value, decision tree analysis benefits from using percentages arrived at through a deliberative process structured to avoid common biases.

While expressed as rejoinders, these points are central to the case for using decision tree analysis in legal practice, and thus merit elaboration here.

On the Virtues of Clarity Over Covert Operations

Imagine that a group of lawyers are shown three different descriptions of the chances of success in a case, and asked to name a reasonable settlement (in view of that description) as follows:

- *This case is unassailable on liability. Damages will unquestionably be at $500,000. What is a reasonable settlement?*
- *I have a very strong case on liability and the damages proof is equally strong in support of a $500,000 award. What is a reasonable settlement?*
- *I have quite a good case on liability and my damages are likely to come in as high as $500,000. What is a reasonable settlement?*

I have administered this "test" countless times, to countless lawyers' groups as well as law students. Every time, I ask the group, by show of hands, "How many of you had settlement numbers that were highest for the first case, in the middle for the second case, and lowest for the second case?" All of them. It never fails. Thus, we see that lawyers do routinely discount case valuation based upon an internally generated percentage that corresponds to their meaning for "unassailable" or "very strong," "quite good" or "likely" and so on. The calculation is hidden, but it happens, using numerical percentages to adjust from valuation of the best to the worst-case scenario in dollar terms.

Clarity is a virtue in lawyer-client communication. If nothing else—even if no EMV or roll back calculation is performed—placing percentages on the decision tree provides clarity to the client about the lawyer's assessment. I remember a construction case mediated in a courthouse program, in which I had begun to sketch a decision tree mapping the structure of the case. I turned to the plaintiff's lawyer and said: "You said your client has a very strong case. Okay, then, what do you think the chances are that your client will prevail on liability?" The lawyer responded: "I do think this is a very strong case, I'd say 60%." The client was shocked, unhappy, and frankly, angry: "What do you mean? You've got to be kidding! When you've been saying I have a very strong case, I thought that meant 90%, maybe more. I never would have invested this much if I thought there was only a 60% chance of winning! I certainly would have offered to settle a long, long time ago, before spending all of this money." Lack of clarity led the client to make entirely different choices than he would have otherwise made.

One person's "highly likely" is another's "good chance." For some, "a good possibility" is merely "possible," worse than an even chance – 50%. For others, the "good possibility" is indeed good, significantly better than 50%. When making an introductory presentation on decision analysis, I always read a list of eight probability assertions to the group, so that everyone sees the words on screen and hears the same voice, volume, and inflection. It includes assertions such as: "You have an excellent case on liability!" "This case is shaky on liability" … "You should win this case".... and so on[2]. The listeners are asked to record what liability percentage they would mean, as the lawyer, if they made each assertion in the way I voiced it. I then survey the class responses for each assertion, to find the range between the highest and lowest assigned percentages. Here is a set of typical results:

Prose Probability Description Stated	Participants' Translations High % - Low%
It is very likely that X will win this suit.	90%-50%
X is likely to win this suit.	80%-50%
X should win this suit.	83%-35%
There is a good possibility that X will win this suit.	90%-50%
It is extremely likely that X will win this suit.	90%-75%
You have a very good case on liability.	80%-50%
You have an excellent case on liability.	98%-65%
Your case is shaky on liability.	55%-20%

As you can see, most often, the ranges are 25–30 percentage points wide. 20 points is relatively narrow; it is very rare to have ranges as low as 10 or 15 points. Ranges of 40 points or more are not at all uncommon. The obvious lesson is that although a lawyer intends to accurately communicate with his descriptive phrasing, the client's interpretation may be far from the lawyer's intended meaning.

From a legal practice perspective, wide discrepancy between probabilities intended and probabilities interpreted means the client is not fully informed. And it may unintentionally threaten client autonomy and self-determination around questions of risk. The owner of the small construction company de-

[2] Full credit to Jonathan Marks and Eric Green of Endispute, Inc., circa 1988 or so, who introduced me to this exercise; it works every time. The results in the table that follows was generated in a recent class or workshop I taught and are completely typical.

scribed earlier offers a client persona for elaboration. Let's assume that this client is risk averse by nature, has avoided large mortgages and other debt in his personal life, lives well within his means, and saves for retirement in his personal life. His modest 401K is invested in bonds and low risk mutual funds in blue chip stocks. He prefers to keep the bird in the hand, instead of looking to uncertain bushes. He runs his business in a similar way. He decided to file suit against a developer because his company had incurred extraordinary losses (and received only meager payment) on a large job. He strongly believed he and his employees were in the right and, in the initial consultation, the lawyer assured him of an extremely high likelihood of winning and recovering damages in the $250,000 to $300,000 range. Let's say the client invested $25,000 from the company's limited cash reserves in the initial filing and early discovery. Let's also assume that the lawyer is not terribly risk averse by nature. He allocates a substantial portion of his 401K to riskier stocks for their greater upside. He enjoys rolling the dice.

What if, after the document exchange and a few key depositions, defense counsel approached our construction company owner's counsel about the possibility of settlement? While explaining that he doesn't have complete authority, he indicated that he believed his client might be willing to offer $80,000 to $100,000 to settle the case. As is always true, the document exchange and a few key depositions raised a few concerns, but the plaintiff's lawyer still sees the case as "very strong" (60% in his mind). He communicates the settlement overtures to his client, as well as his assessment that they have a "very strong" chance of winning and recovering damages in the $250,000 to $300,000 range. The lawyer acknowledges that it will take another $25,000 in fees and costs through trial. If this were the lawyer's decision to make (even without any interest in the fees), he would go forward. After all, the midpoint damages range is $275,000—the net would be $250,000. If you discount that with a 60% chance of winning, the EMV would be $140,000 (when the cost of fees are factored in).

Given his personal risk preferences, he would not take a settlement at $80,000 or even $100,000. Thus, he will no doubt signal to the client that it's not worth pursuing settlement negotiations. Here's what the tree might look like in the lawyer's mind.

Tree Model 74
Lawyer's Assessment, Using Lawyer's Translation of Prose to Percentages)

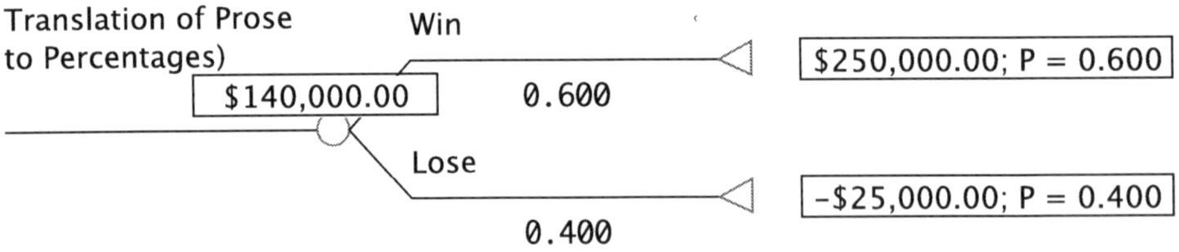

Let's say the client understands "very strong" chance to mean 90%. Discounting the $250,000 net using 90%, the EMV would be $222,500. Even if this client were quite risk averse and would accept a hefty additional settlement discount to avoid the risk of losing, and the need to deplete cash reserves by $25,000, he may nevertheless reject the $80,000—$100,000 as just too low.

Yet, if the same client had understood "very strong" to mean only 60%, his settlement point would no doubt be different from his lawyer's. With an EMV of $140,000, a 40% chance of getting nothing, and the requirement to spend precious cash, that client might well take 1/3 less to avoid risk and accept a settlement at $100,000 or lower. At the very least, he would think it worthwhile to pursue settlement discussions. Here's what the tree might look like in the client's mind.

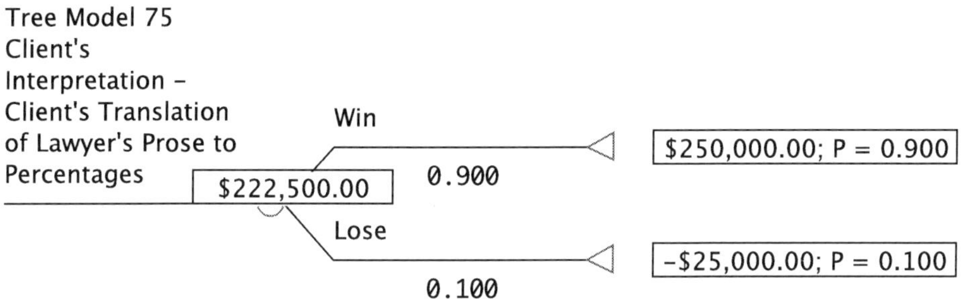

Accurately communicating legal analysis, offering legal advice, and wise counsel are all within the lawyer's role, and are entirely consistent with client autonomy and self-determination. The client must be well informed and free to reject the lawyer's advice (subject to legal constraints), and act in his or his company's best interest, as he sees it. However, lacking awareness of his lawyer's real assessment of risks, the client cannot be well informed. And by failing to articulate that risk assessment clearly, the lawyer may unwittingly impose his own risk preferences and risk tolerances upon his client. That would indeed be inconsistent with the proper separation between legal advice and client self-determination.

Disclaiming Precision, Owning Gut Uncertainty

The logic, method, and purpose of decision analysis strongly caution against claims to precision in its numerical inputs or calculated numerical outcomes—dollars or compounded probabilities. Even decision analysis aficionados readily and properly concede that its goal is to model a decision and its consequential uncertainties and possible outcomes, but perfect precision should neither be sought nor expected.

This is particularly true for decision analysis applied in legal contexts, where the analysis will not be subjected to proof and refinement after hundreds of trials. After all, when decision analysis is used to formulate public health policy, or to evaluate pharmaceutical treatment protocols or stock market strategies, we anticipate that the results will be recorded and the outcomes reviewed. In a decision analysis regarding whether to prescribe a cold medicine, we would ask: "If 100 people took this cold medicine, what percentage of them would see dramatically improved symptoms?" Presumably, a sample of 100 people or more would take the medicine, with various positive and negative results. Even if 55% of the sample saw positive results, we know that a second sample is unlikely to yield *exactly* a 55% success rate. A reliably precise success rate can't be predicted with certainty until a large number of samples have been taken from the target population. And still, the percentage recorded from any single small number sample is likely to vary from the overall "true" average rate.[3]

For decision analysis in a legal case, to assign a probability percentage for liability, we similarly ask: "If this case were tried a hundred times, what percentage of the time would there be a plaintiff's verdict?" In the simplest of cases, with damages set at $100,000, no costs to subtract, and liability probability of

[3] This is a basic fundamental truth in statistics and probability theory, available from any reputable text on the topic

70%, the EMV would be $70,000. We are positing that the plaintiff would win 70 out of 100 times. Just as $70,000 is the average of all of the trial outcomes, 70% is understood as the predicted win-loss percentage over time. As acknowledged at the outset, this question is premised on a fiction for the purpose of prompting the analysis. *That same case will not be tried 100 times.* Our sample size is one. Among the few certainties is that the case outcome will not be its hypothetical, fictional weighted average.

If the numerical percentages are not intended to be precise, then what are they intended to be? They are targets points used to express the lawyer's gut sense. Imagine that the lawyer states that surviving summary judgment is "nearly certain"—"a slam dunk", defeating the defense motion to exclude expert testimony is "highly likely", "chances are quite good" of a favorable jury instruction on a key point, and the other side's star witness "might possibly" crack on cross-examination. As demonstrated by the phrases to percentages exercise described earlier, we don't know what he means by these phrases. More importantly, we don't know (and perhaps neither does he) what impact it will have on case assessment if he later reassesses "nearly certain" summary judgment survival to "very strong chances" after reading their brief. How should the client play his hand if the other side's witness proves to be wonderfully disastrous at deposition? When percentages are assigned, we see how the lawyer's gut sense of how the risks are ordered, and how they change as the facts, legal theories, and other realities unfold.

Thus, when a lawyer assigns 90% to the chance of surviving summary judgment, 75% to the chance of favorable ruling on his expert, and 60% to the desired jury instruction, we understand that these are markers—subjectively placed along a range of strength—not precise or provable assessments. It is a way of communicating: "I am not 100% certain, but I am surer of this than of that, and even less so on this question." A helpful way to think about these markers is as target points placed along a continuum, as reflected on the next tree, with fuzzy circles reflecting degrees of uncertainty. Yet, as lawyers know, acknowledging uncertainty and ambiguity does not reflect lack of careful thought and analysis: quite the opposite.

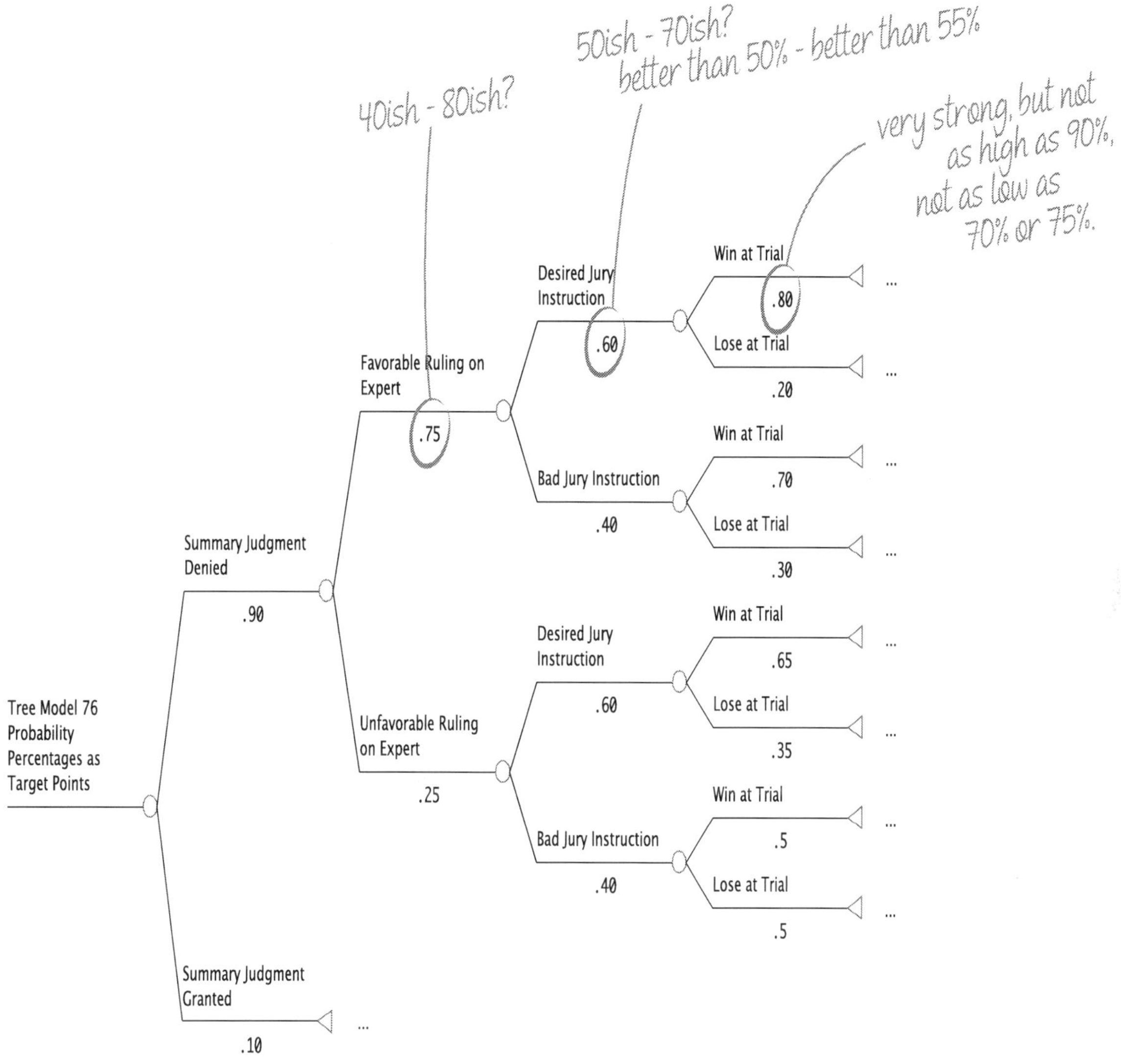

The obvious is also true: decision tree analysis requires us to use numbers—damages estimates in dollar numbers, and probabilities in percentage numbers. As a practical matter, without numbers, there can be no roll back calculation to an EMV and no calculation of the probability distribution of outcomes. Math and decision tree calculations are built on numbers.

Given that a numerical percentage is just a target point for expressing a lawyer's (or client's or mediator's) sense of relative confidence, it would be entirely foolish to argue that 88% is correct and 90% is not, or that only a 92% probability will do. One important benefit of percentages is that they are easily shifted to account for the reality of their subjectivity and imprecision. Decision analysis software, Excel, or even an arithmetic calculator makes it easy to play with any percentage.[4] Suppose the tree builder has named 80% as his estimated probability of success at a particular case juncture. It is easy and often wise

[4] Of course, there is nothing magic about software and calculators. Since the functions are plain arithmetic, anyone with patience, pencil, and paper can try the math using different probabilities.

to see what happens when the probability ranges between 78% and 82%, or 75% and 85%, as if drawing circles around that target point. Where the facts or legal standards are squishy, and the gut sense is unclear, a wider circle can be drawn. Of course, as the case develops over time, the method enables us to analyze the impact of shifts in our "gut sense" at any or all junctures.

Showing What If? Sensitivity Analysis Maps the Impact of Uncertainty Ranges

"Sensitivity analysis" is the technical term for the process of testing the impact of variance in a probability percentage or damages estimate. Essentially, it examines the "sensitivity" of the tree's results to this variance. The TreeAge software enables the user to easily graph this—to see what happens along a range of estimates. It can also be used to help decide whether actions intended to increase the probability of a favorable outcome—e.g. retaining a costly expert—are worthwhile, at least in terms of possible payoffs or EMV. [5]

To see the way sensitivity analysis can assist discussion of uncertainty and subjective probability, consider the case circumstances described in this paragraph, and then take a look at the next two trees and their graphed sensitivity analysis, from the plaintiff's perspective. Let's assume that the plaintiff's counsel wishes to retain a "fancy expert" on the theory that his report and testimony would improve the chances of a liability finding. Even though he hasn't yet formally retained the expert, much less seen his report, plaintiff's counsel has informally consulted with him—as prelude to retention—and explained the circumstances in the case. Though the expert was careful to say that he couldn't really provide an opinion without examining the evidence, he suggested a possible theory that would put liability squarely on the defendant. Plaintiff's counsel anticipates a defense motion to block this expert from testifying based on the argument that his original PhD and faculty appointment were not related to the issue in the case. Plaintiff's counsel is confident that the expert's experience and research publications are more than relevant. Thus he estimates a small but significant (10%) chance that the defense will succeed in disqualifying the expert. Of course, retaining the expert will be costly.

Let's assume that, right now, the plaintiff's counsel is quite optimistic about the expert's opinion and testimony and its impact on the case. Thus, the plaintiff's counsel estimates the chance of liability with the expert testimony at 70%. Without the expert, he estimates the chance of a liability finding at 55%.

A mediator or the lawyer as tree-builder should acknowledge a great deal of uncertainty about the probability of liability if the fancy expert is retained and permitted to testify—given that he hasn't yet produced a report or testified on deposition. The lawyer and client might recognize that the fancy expert *could* enhance the liability argument or diminish it (depending on what comes out of his fancy lab at MIT and his skills as a witness).

Of course, one easy way to ask "What if this probability estimate is off?" is to substitute other probability estimates, and see what impact that has on the EMV or the end chances of each outcome. The probability under the "liability" branch that started as .7 (70%) can be changed to .6 (60%), or to .5 (50%) and the probability under its opposite branch changed to the inverse, .4 (40%) or .5 (50%). Then the tree can be rolled back again to compare the difference in results.

[5] Victor, Marc, "Interpreting a Decision Tree Analysis of a Lawsuit" (1988, revised 2001). This article, as is true for all of the others by Marc Victor, is available in pdf on his website, litigationrisk.com.

To capture and test that uncertainty—by asking the consequences of "What if that 70% probability is way off?"—the tree below involves some up front work with the software to set up a formal sensitivity analysis. A variable has been inserted into the tree for the probability of a liability finding with the expert's testimony.

The starting point for the probability estimate is plaintiff's counsel's original and optimistic .7 or 70%. Note that the "no liability" branch below it shows probability in the form of a #. In the TreeAge software, that's the way to tell the program to use the inverse of whatever probability is used for the branch above. Thus, when the roll back is performed on this tree, where the variable is set at .7 or 70% for the likelihood of liability, the chance of no liability becomes .3 or 30%.

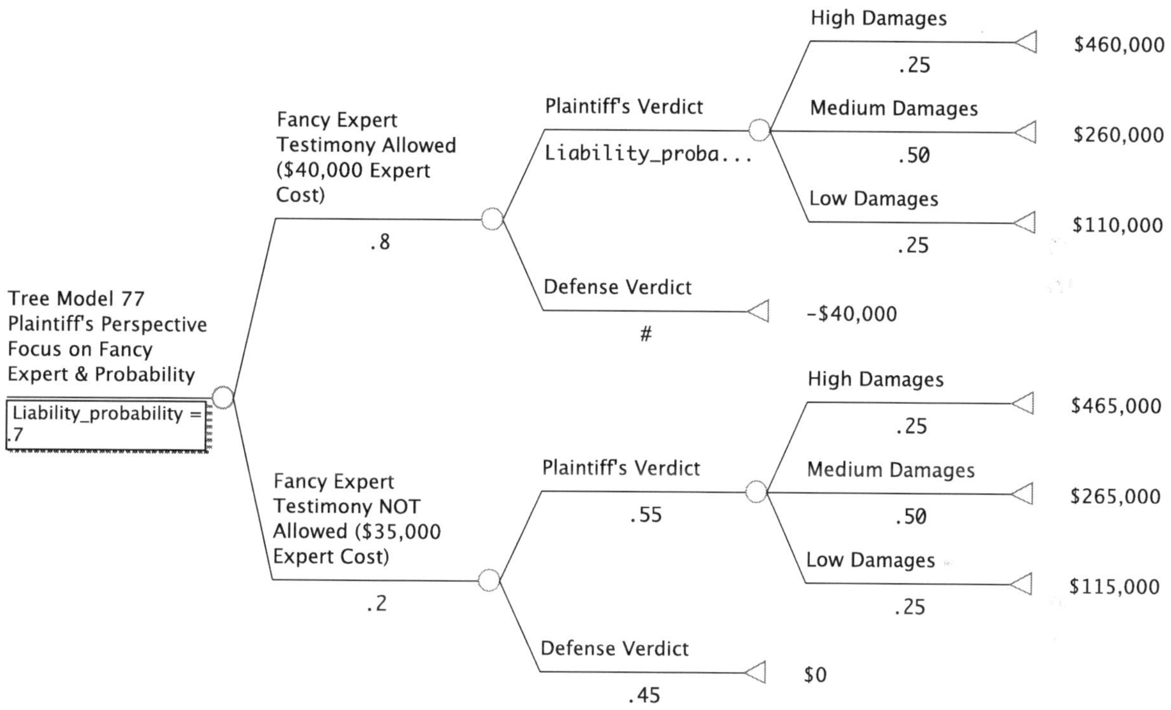

This tree reflects a prediction that expert testimony would raise the chances of a plaintiff's verdict.

The tree uses a damages range with a high of $500,000, a mid-level of $300,000 and a low of $150,000. While it assumes the plaintiff has a contingency fee arrangement with her lawyer, the contingency fee has not been deducted from the outcomes. The plaintiff will be responsible for paying the cost of the expert no matter what the trial outcome and has been deducted. The expert cost through trial has been set at $40,000. If the defense motion to disallow the expert's testimony succeeds, the expert cost would be $35,000 (assuming $5,000 as the cost for his testifying at trial).

Next is the same tree, rolled back to display an EMV.

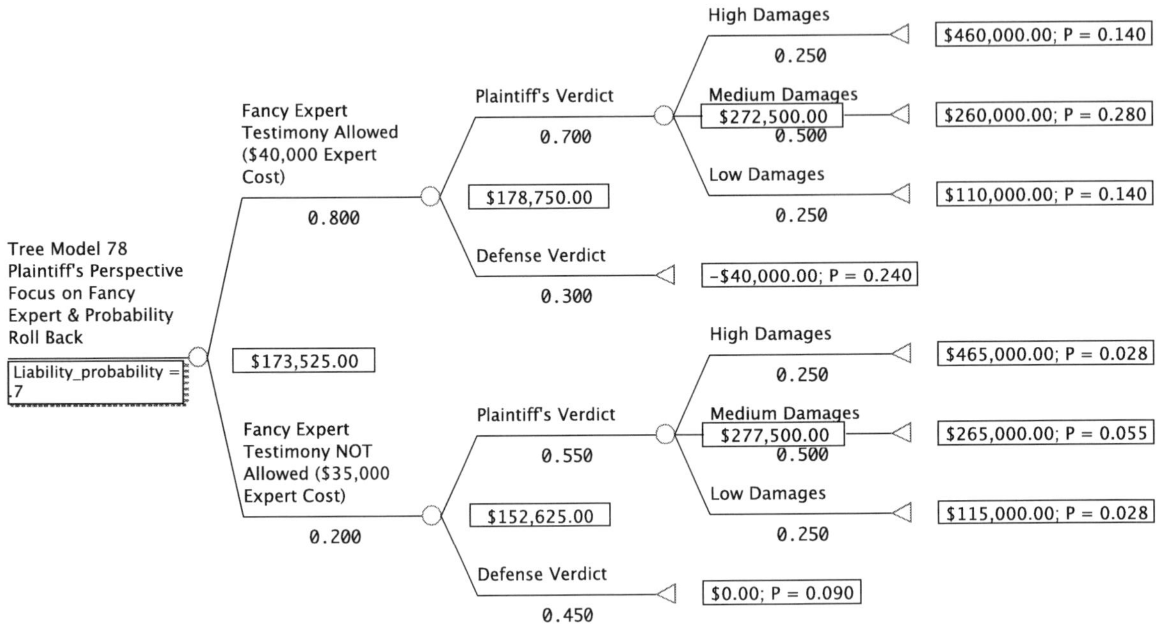

As you can see on the next page, it then becomes easy to do a sensitivity analysis, as a way of answering the question: "What if the probability is not 70%?" For the sensitivity analysis reflected in the graph below, we've tested a range of probabilities between .4 and .8, or 40% and 80%. In other words, we've asked, "What if, after the fancy expert would be retained and would testify, the probability of the liability might range between 40% and 80%. How would the EMV or the discounted value of the case be impacted, assuming various probabilities along that range?"

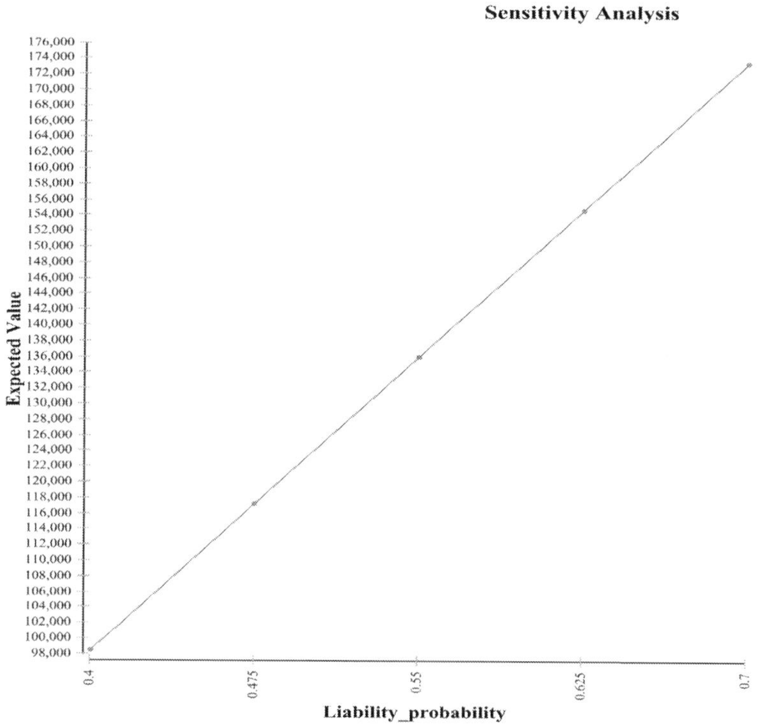

This graph reflects that sensitivity analysis. It shows the degree to which the case's EMV changes with changes in the probability of liability, after retaining the expert and assuming his testimony will be permitted.

A Plug for Comparing Uncertain Choices to Make Decisions in the Trees

I hope the attentive reader will see that this analysis could also be used to inform a *decision* about whether it's worthwhile to retain the expert at all or, after a briefing on his conclusions, whether to pay for him to produce a report and testify. One could formally construct the tree such as the one below with a square decision node and two branches—retain expert or not—before the evidentiary motion. The roll back will suggest the optimal decision path, at least from an EMV perspective.

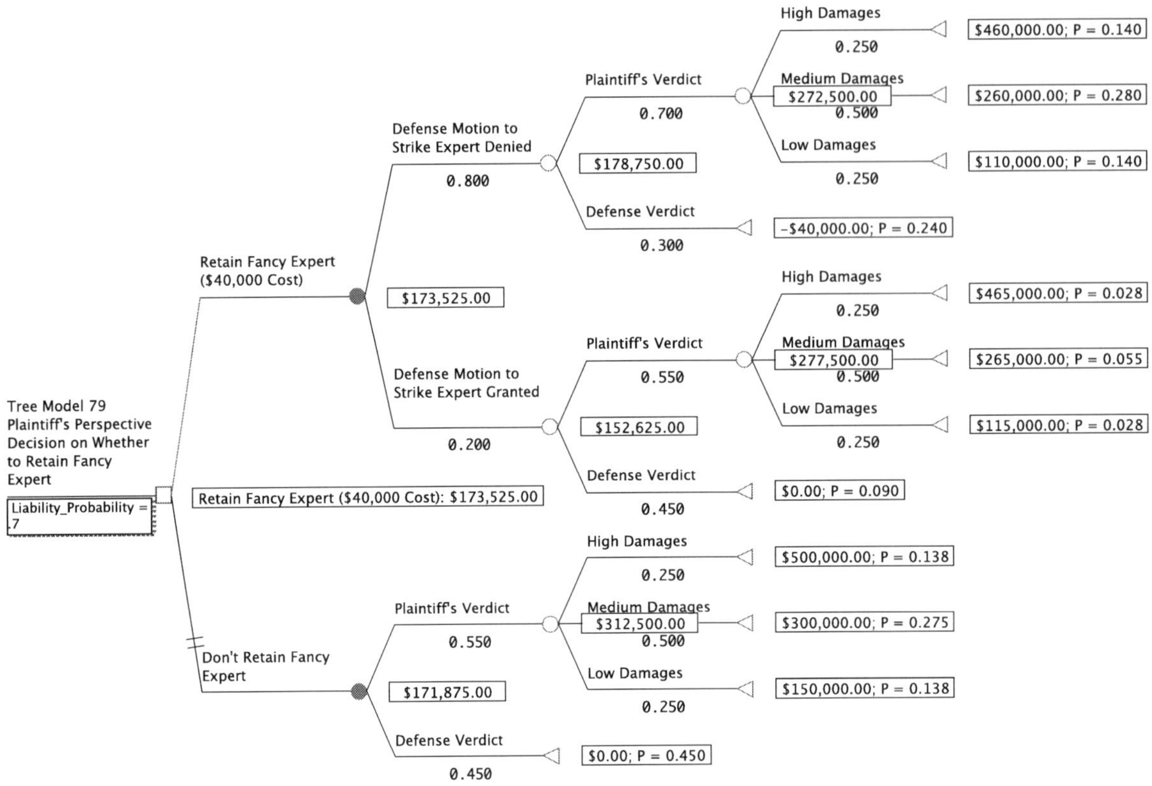

As you can see, our method recommends that we decide to retain the fancy expert, assuming that expert will increase the chances of a liability finding from 55% to 70%.

Without running a formal sensitivity analysis, it's easy to see that this is a close question. Once again, I offer a sensitivity analysis, asking the question, "What is the impact or likelihood of a liability finding (with the expert) along a range from 40% to 80%?"

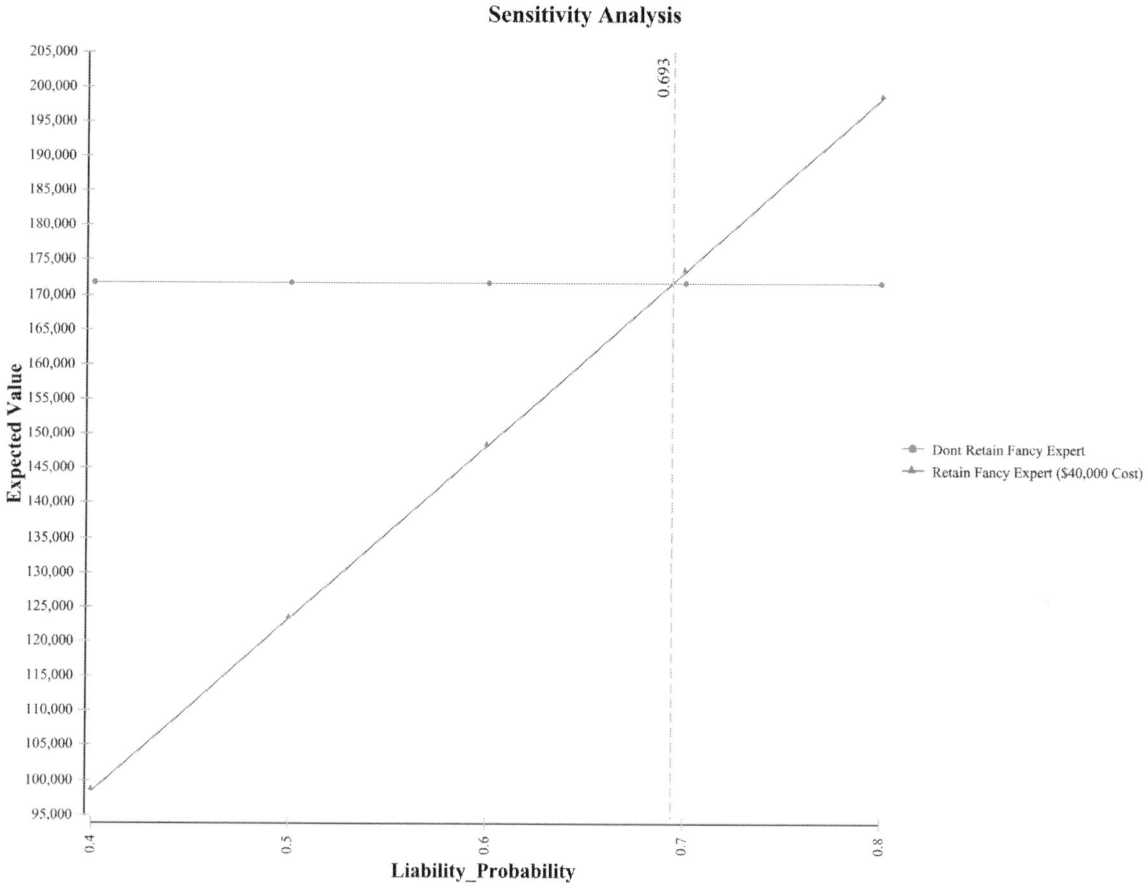

As you can see, if retaining the expert leads to an estimated probability of liability that is lower than 65%, it doesn't appear to be worth the cost.

Of course, you can test that decision without a formal graph, just using different probabilities for the likelihood of liability, with and without the expert.

A perfectly reasonable short cut would be to skip the creation of a separate tree with a decision node. You can just take a look at the risk tree already created and notice the EMV of the case if the expert is not permitted to testify vs. the EMV if his testimony is permitted. How much difference is there? How much does that change if we adjust his involvement's likely impact on the chances of liability? Is it worth the cost?

One last important observation about decision-making, cost, and risk: It's important to remember that we've been using decision analysis in a way that does not pretend to consider risk tolerance, or feelings about risk and cost. Yet, these factors will and no doubt should influence decisions. For example, what if, after some more thought, the lawyer estimates that the expert's involvement will only result in a 60-65% chance of a liability finding? And what if he comes to believe there's really closer to a 30% chance that the judge won't allow the expert's testimony at all? If we make those changes, the roll back will no doubt recommend against retaining the expert.

Nevertheless, the lawyer and client may legitimately make a different decision. The client may not feel comfortable going forward with only a 55% chance of success—the estimated probability without any expert involvement. The economic and emotional consequences of losing at trial—recovering $0 for his losses —may be too great. Even if the investment in an expert increases his chances of winning only to 60% or 65%, it may be reasonable for him to decide to make that investment.

At the outset, this chapter asserted three sets of reasons that lawyers can and should use and discuss numerical probabilities to describe the uncertainties of possible twists in a litigation's path. The first was clarity and transparency. The second—premised on disclaiming precision—highlighted the numbers' agility in reflecting ranges of professional judgment and adapting to different views or changes in facts and circumstances.

By now, I hope the reader recongizes the values of communication, transparency, and flexibility afforded by using numerical probabilities in making decisions about litigation and settlement.

The third reason stated was that an informed process for estimating probability yields sound judgment. In other words, when care is taken, even subjective numerical probability estimates may be better than prose descriptors such as "very likely" or "great chance." The next chapter constitutes an elaboration on what is an "informed process" and offers best practices for estimating numerical probabilities.

11

Best Practices for Probabilities and Predictions

When a well-respected lawyer carefully reviews and analyzes relevant law, documents, and witnesses, his assessment—that "liability is shaky," "summary judgment is highly likely," or "damages will be sky high"—deserves to be given weight in decision-making. The opposite is true for an assessment by a lawyer who wasn't present at the depositions, hasn't reviewed case law specific to these circumstances, or is unfamiliar with the assigned judge's or local juries' proclivities. That assessment was made without basis or care and should not be relied upon.

The same may be said for numerical probabilities and predictions: when "thrown out there" or constructed from thin air, they have little value. However, the well-respected lawyer's rigorous analysis still merits attention as derived from law, evidence, and experience, whether expressed in adjectival or numerical probabilities.[1] Fundamentally, insights from psychology and expert elicitation research lead us to conclude that the assignments of percentages should be an iterative process, involving much discussion, questions phrased in alternative ways, and examination of various perspectives on the issue under consideration.[2]

[1] It should be mentioned that some decision analysts suggest using influence diagrams (sometimes referred to as dependency diagrams) to formulate decision tree structures and predictions. Creating an influence diagram involves following prescribed conventions for arranging facts, legal issues, and uncertainties within certain shaped boxes and circles (etc.), and using arrows and lines to depict their relationships. Indeed, earlier versions of the TreeAge software would convert a property constructed influence diagram into a tree. Victor, Calihan, and Dent display the use of influence diagrams in their article, "The Role of Risk Analysis in Dispute and Litigation Management," American Bar Association, Forum on Franchising (2004):19. At one point, I introduced my students to influence diagramming through an assignment in my Advanced Decision Analysis course. Some may have derived value from the exercise. However, I hereby admit that the technical aspects of working with the diagrams seemed to outweigh their value to me. Having said that, I applaud the idea of scribbling, drawing lines, circles—whatever the lawyer needs to clarify in his or her own mind how the pieces of a case fit together, and what factors influence its various uncertainties. For descriptions and examples of the formal and thorough use of influence diagrams, see Clemen, Robert, *Making Hard Decisions: An Introduction to Decision Analysis* (1996, or subsequent editions). Of course, the method may be used for estimating damages ranges as well as subjective probabilities.

[2] See Raiffa, Howard, "Decision Analysis: A Personal Account of How I Got Started and Evolved," *Operations Research* 50, no. 1 (2002): 10. "We told our experts to expect incoherencies in their responses to our hypothetical questions and those incoherencies should only prompt them to think even more deeply about their expertise. We learned not to ask questions one way or another way, but to ask both ways and to confront resulting incoherencies in an open manner."

Probability Percentages

What probability percentages to assign to tree branches are, or should be, among the most carefully considered decisions in decision tree analysis. Unfortunately, just as there's no magic way to determine whether a case is "very strong," "excellent," "virtually unassailable," or "awfully shaky," there's no magic way to determine whether its chances of success are more accurately described as 70%, 80%, 90% or a pessimistic 40%. These judgments can only be based on thorough knowledge, research, experience, and thoughtful deliberation.[3]

Even where the analysis is thorough and sound, we must accept that probability estimates are imperfect and their accuracy untestable. When the lawyer estimates the likelihood of success on an evidentiary motion at 35%, he knows that cannot be proven or disproven. The evidentiary motion on the same facts, in the same case, will not be ruled upon a hundred times, or even ten times. Nevertheless, the lawyer's obligation is a probability estimate that is as fully informed, well-reasoned, and intelligent as possible.

The pages that follow contain advice on best practices for formulating probability percentages along the path of a decision tree in a legal case. As you will see, this advice begins with the essential linkage between probabilities and particular locations on the tree's branches. It derives from psychology's insight into our common foibles and biases and their effect on estimation, prediction and confidence even among experts. Best practices for assessing numerical probabilities can help expose and counter-act those foibles and biases.

We can no doubt agree that our clients are best served by the rigorous lawyer's clearest thinking, undistorted by psychology's tricks and traps.

Location, Location, Location—Take Note of Where This Branch Is

You have estimated an 85% likelihood of surviving summary judgment. You are aware that the defense plans to file a motion to bifurcate the trial, separating liability from damages. You estimate a 60% chance that your opposition to the motion will succeed. Whichever way that goes, the next branches on the tree are the all-important "liability—no liability" branches. What's your estimate of the likelihood of a plaintiff's verdict?

Another good resource on expert elicitation is "Subjective Probability and Expert Elicitation," Chapter I-6 in *Best Practices in Dam and Levee Safety Risk Analysis*, produced by the U.S. Department of the Interior Bureau of Reclamation and U.S. Army Corps of Engineers Version 4.0 July 2015, at pages I-6-9—I-6-10, observing the benefits of discussion of experts' subjective probabilities and concluding, "[O]verall, it is better to make the process iterative." This report is accessible at www.usbr.gov/ssle/damsafety/risk/BestPractices/Chapters/I-0-20150612.pdf

[3] Bayes' Theorum and the "base rate fallacy" are acknowledged truths in probability theory. Their application may be an essential element of best practice for estimating probabilities in some legal cases, where sets of directly relevant and reliable statistics are available for particular questions. Because that is not often true, this text provides only a quick summary explanation of Bayes' Theorum and the base rate fallacy. If you believe your case presents an issue and reliable statistical data for Bayesian analysis, I recommend consulting a statistics text or, believe it or not, Wikipedia. This author has taken quite a while to understand Bayes' Theorum and, in that process, has read quite a few texts. I found Wikipedia's treatment of the topic and its examples to be quite well done. Any text on statistics will cover the topic. A useful text for lawyers is also: Blumenthal, Jeremy; Faigman, David; Mnookin, Jennifer; Murphy, Erin; and Sanders, Joseph, *Modern Scientific Evidence: The Law and Science of Expert Testimony* (2014), which includes a discussion of Bayes' Theorum in legal practice.

That last one is a trick question, of course. There is no *single* likelihood of a liability finding; each likelihood depends upon its location on the tree. Assume we agree that if the jury hears heart-wrenching damages evidence along with liability evidence, a plaintiff's verdict is more likely. But, if the jury has no sense of how shattered the plaintiff's life was after the event, they may be more dispassionate when analyzing the liability question. If your gut says this is true, then you would assign a different probability percentage to the "liability" branch that follows "bifurcation" than to the "liability" branch that follows "no bifurcation," as reflected on the next tree.

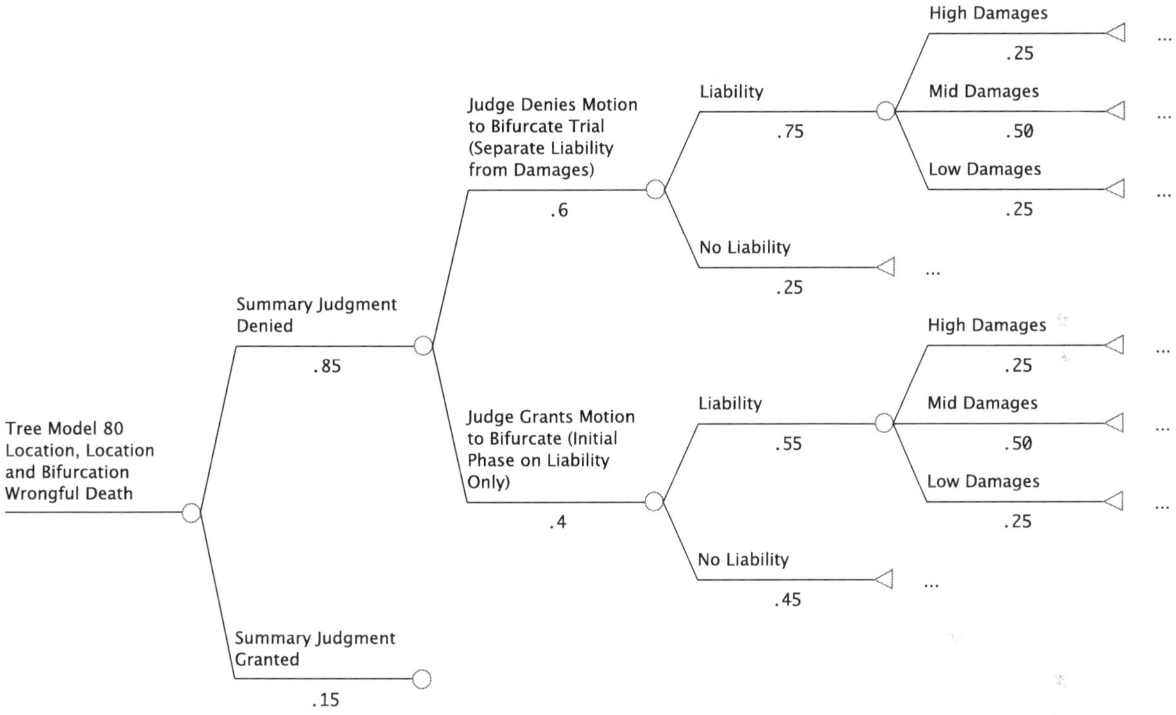

What if this case (bifurcated or not) involves an infant's wrongful death, and parents' pain and suffering, emotional distress, and loss of consortium claims arising from a full-term infant's death during the birthing process. Would the bifurcation decision also impact the range of damages, and the likelihood of punitive damages? Our strong intuition has to be yes. Let's assume the liability evidence reflects the doctor's and nursing staff's inattention to the fetal monitor and inaction until long after the monitor reflected the baby's distress. Despite defense experts rambling about the standard of care, plaintiff's experts were unequivocal and effective. Some of that liability evidence may have made the jury's blood boil (no doubt another reason the defense sought bifurcation). Because of that, when the tree-builder reaches the damages end of the tree, and begins to assign probabilities to punitive damages or award ranges, he must be aware of his location on the tree's pathways. The probability of punitive damages on a post NO-bifurcation path will no doubt be different than the probability on the bifurcation path. This will depend, of course, on how much evidence the jury will be permitted to hear regarding what happened prior to the infant's death.

We find a more common example of the importance of remembering your location on the tree when assigning probability to liability AFTER denial of summary judgment. Assume that BEFORE the summary judgment motion was filed, someone asked the defense counsel, "What are the overall chances the plaintiff will win this case?" Let's assume defense counsel responded, "Only 40%; I think we have some pretty darned strong defenses here. In fact, I see the supporting facts as entirely undisputed. That's why I'm planning to file a motion for summary judgment." Now, let's further assume that the defense loses their motion for summary judgment. Defense counsel has learned some decision analysis in the meanwhile. Would he be wise to stick with that initial, overall 40% assessment as the likelihood of the jury's liability finding?

The answer, of course, is "it depends." Did defense counsel's initial "overall" 40% *include* the chances of the plaintiff getting by summary judgment and the chances of the plaintiff winning at trial? If so, then theoretically, he might have been thinking as shown in the following tree.

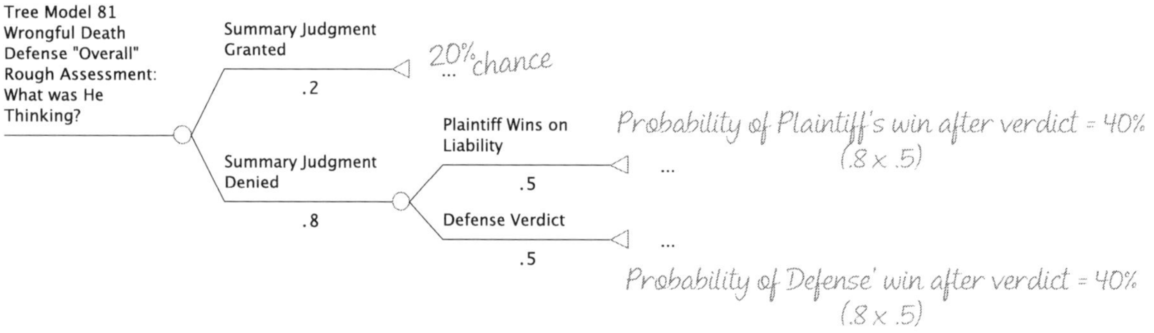

Using this construction, plaintiff has an 80% chance of surviving summary judgment and, if that happens, then a 50% chance at trial—his overall chances of winning the entire action would be 40%. If so, then post-summary judgment denial, the plaintiff's chances would be at 50%.

Of course, if defense counsel initially thought plaintiff's chances *at trial* were only 40%, he might legitimately stick with that estimate. It's possible that his summary judgment motion was an after-thought or based on some highly technical grounds.

On the other hand, post-summary judgment denial, we know that a neutral judge has looked at arguments and evidence upon which the defense was relying. If the judge was not impressed, and those arguments and evidence will also be put to the jury, should defense counsel *now* be less confident of escaping liability? It's entirely possible that, from the hearing on oral argument and reading judge's opinion, counsel will have gained additional insight into judge's reactions to the evidence—beyond the mere fact of the motion's denial. If so, counsel may be wise to re-adjust the probability assigned to liability yet again, in whatever direction indicated. That adjustment would represent counsel's better-informed estimate of a potential jury's reaction. Of course, it's also possible that, the lawyer's original estimate of the likelihood of the jury finding liability took into account the legal and factual weaknesses, and the possibility that a jury will be sympathetic to the plaintiff. If so, no adjustment is required.

It's important to remember that, as soon as a summary judgment motion is decided, it should no longer remain as an uncertainty on the tree. Any original estimate of the chances of summary judgment must be removed from a cumulative probability calculation. In essence, once the motion is denied, the original estimate of the probability of denial must shift to 100%. It's done. The tree should be recalculated without that uncertainty.

Affirming the Bedrock of Probability Theory

A bedrock rule of probability theory is that cumulative probability must be built on independent events. Assume a case in which we estimate an 80% chance of surviving summary judgment, a 60% chance of a liability finding, and a 30% chance that the jury will find fraud as well as breach of contract. In that case, the cumulative probability of the plaintiff winning the case and collecting fraud damages would be .80 x .60 x. 30 = 14.4%.

Using a summary judgment example, some have expressed concern that the overall strength of the plaintiff's evidence may impact both the likelihood of a judge's summary judgment denial and (to the right on the tree) the likelihood of a liability finding.[4] They question whether these two probabilities are independent and thus, whether it is consistent with accepted rules of probability theory to multiply the two numbers to arrive at a cumulative probability.

The short answer is yes, because the likelihood of the judge's ruling does not operate on the jury's liability deliberations. It merely sets the stage, or not.

When a decision analyst constructs a tree *before* any preliminary ruling, he must separately consider the probability of the ruling, and then the probability of post-ruling events. In other words, their probabilities should reflect their location in a separate future world in which the judge has reviewed some evidence and rejected his arguments.

I offer the following abstract physical example to clarify how cumulative probability applies to successive uncertain events, even where common underlying conditions are present that also impact probabilities. Imagine an ice skating rink that is rutted, scratched, and unevenly firm.

- Let's first make a bet on whether an intermediate skater can circle the rink three times, at a minimum speed, without falling. If that skater falls, it's game over.
- But, if the first skater maintains minimum speed and stays upright, we will have the chance to bet on the likelihood of a middle-aged, uncoordinated, novice skater accomplishing the same task.
- If both skaters are successful, we will win. If not, we lose. What are the chances of *both* skaters succeeding?

[4] This point and the discussion that follows, including the ice skating rink analogy, can be found in Aaron, Marjorie and Brazil, Wayne, "Shaking Decision Trees for Risks and Rewards," *Dispute Resolution Magazine* 22, no. 1 (2015): 12-18.

Here's what the tree would look like.

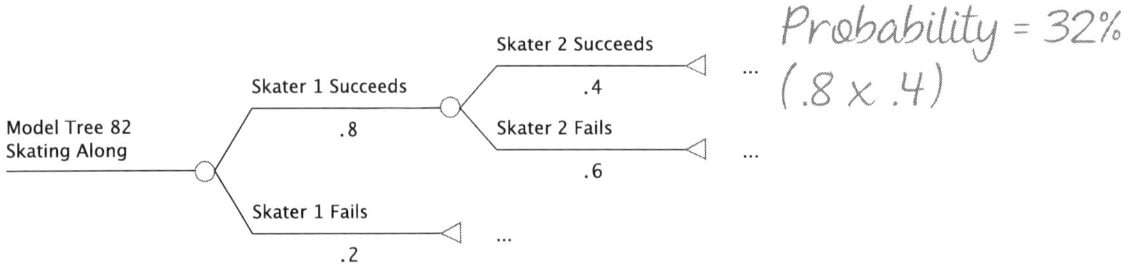

The conditions of the rink affect both skaters, no doubt. But, let's also assume that both skaters have skated on this or a similarly imperfect rink before, and we have empirical evidence to the effect that the first skater succeeds 80% of the time, and the second skater succeeds only 40% of the time. What's the likelihood of both skaters succeeding? It still has to be 80% (.80) x 40% (.40), or 32%.

That the conditions of the rink might affect both skaters does not change the independent probabilities of their separate loops around the rink. Probability theory applies: before the game starts, the cumulative probability of both succeeding is 32%.

What if a referee circles the ice rink *before* the game begins, and reports that the ice conditions have deteriorated within the last hour; the surface is even more rutted and bumpy than during the skaters' practice times? We might be prudent to adjust the likelihood for our first skater to 60% and for our second skater to 20%. In that case, the cumulative probability of both skaters' succeeding would be 12%.

Of course, just as in our motion for summary judgment, if I learn something new about the condition of the ice from the first skater (*after* taking her turn and successfully skating three times around), then I might adjust my estimate for the second skater. The first skater might say: "You know, this rink isn't quite as bad as it was during our practice data gathering runs." At that point, the tree must be modified to take *out* any uncertainty about the first skater's performance. She did it! And perhaps we should adjust our middle-aged skater's probability of success to 40% or 50%, just as our estimated liability chances should perhaps change in the other direction based on a judge's unexpectedly critical evaluation.

A Note on Round Numbers

One concern with choosing numerical percentages is that people generally prefer round numbers, divisible by 5 or 10. We tend to record a 10% or a 20%, or even a 15% on the Summary Judgment branch, but we're unlikely to record a 13% or a 17% chance. We tend to think first in round numbers. Then, if we feel that 20% might be a "smidge" too high, multiplying by 18% seems much harder than by 20% (even though it doesn't matter for a computer or calculator). When assigning percentages toward the left hand side of a tree—on probabilities of dispositive motions, or even liability—the EMV may be greatly impacted by a two or three percentage point shift from the "actual" internal assessment to a "rounded" number ending in 5 or 0. As we move toward the right hand side of the tree, a round estimate of 20% vs. 22% won't greatly impact the tree's EMV, and may not be cause for concern *unless* the case presents a very wide array of possible outcomes. Imagine a case in which an award of $30 million (with trebling, and under a particular damages theory) is possible, but most other awards would fall in the $2 million to $5 million range. Applying a probability of 7% vs. 5% or 10% would have a significant impact on the EMV.

The probability wheel is a visual aid that has proven helpful for people seeking to quantify their opinions as to probability.[5] Simply described, it's a pie shaped wheel that allows you to move a pointer so that the wheel shows different colors, until those colors reach the proportion that reflects your subjective probability estimate. It can be particularly helpful for allocating perceived probabilities across more than two branches. Not surprisingly, the TreeAge software includes a probability wheel option. Once you've decided that the pie chart seems right, the software tells you the numerical proportion of the different colors, whether it's 7%, 23.2% or exactly 50%.

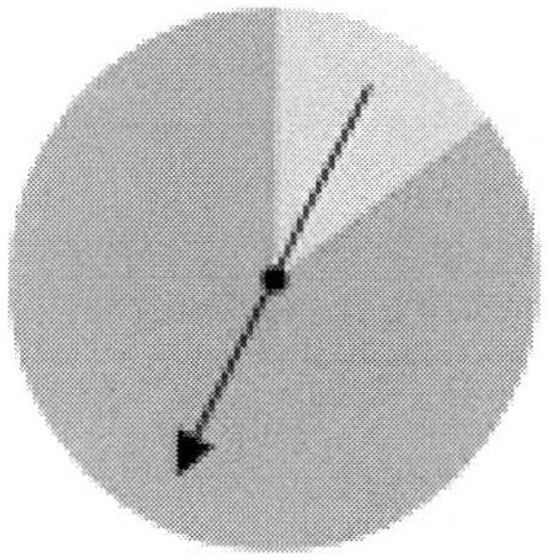

PROBABILITY WHEEL[6]

Prescriptions for Best Practices Premised in Psychology

Earlier in this text, the chapter "Important Interlude: Psychology's Pernicious Impact on Predictions of Probability and Payoffs" described psychological tendencies toward partisan biases, anchoring and (insufficient) adjustment, and the representative heuristic. These motivate the practical prescriptions set forth below for the decision analyst, whether a consultant or a lawyer applying the method in a client's case. Their primary goals are to reduce partisan biases, avoid anchoring to biased or inapplicable reference points, and diminish or eliminate the impact of the representative heuristic when estimating probabilities or dollar consequences at any location on the tree.

And/Or, With the Opposite First

An important and practical way to diminish partisan perception bias when estimating probabilities or dollars is to deliberately and separately list the factors—facts and legal arguments—that cut against and in support of the desired outcome at key chance nodes.[7]

[5] See discussion of probability wheels and other visual aids in Garthwaite, Paul; Kadane, Joseph; and O'Hagan, Anthony, "Statistical Methods for Eliciting Probability Distributions," *Journal of the American Statistical Association* 100 (2005):680-701, which references earlier research discussing "some success" with probability rules.

[6] See Victor, Marc; Glidden, Craig; Lea, Clyde; and Whitworth, J. Bryan, "Evaluating Legal Risks and Costs with Decision Tree Analysis," *Successful Partnering Between Inside and Outside Counsel* (2000): 10.

[7] Victor, Glidden, Lea, and Whitworth, 12-8—12-9. See also DeGroote, John, "Advanced Decision Tree Analysis in Litigation: An Interview with Marc Victor, Part I" *Settlement Perspectives* (2009), www.settlementperspectives.com/2009/07/advanced-decision-tree-analysis-in-litigation-an-interview-with-marc-victor-part-i/.

Marc Victor, founder of Litigation Risk Analysis, Inc., strongly suggests (and this author agrees) that such lists be drawn out at an early stage of the problem and ideally even before determining probabilities for a decision tree. Below is his example of a chart listing factors that would affect the chance of a jury finding a "breach of covenant of good faith and fair dealing" (in a hypothetical lawsuit between Joe and Larry).

Will jury find Larry breached implied covenant of good faith and fair dealing by opening all those franchises?[8]

Reasons Jury **Does** Find Breach	Reasons Jury Does **NOT** Find Breach
• thinks Larry was outrageously greedy • thinks he was far more interested in his own personal profit than the health or survival of any of his franchisees • as a result, he killed the goose that laid the golden eggs • no single franchisee would have ever anticipated having to compete with so many other franchisees *on the same block* • especially given the sizeable investment Joe had to make to get into the business • Larry does not make a good witness— comes off as arrogant, someone who can do no wrong • judge's explanation of an "implied covenant of good faith and fair dealing" will sound pro-plaintiff • might think this is a compromise: less severe than saying Larry defrauded Joe, but Joe didn't end up with the business he expected at the outset	• nothing in the agreement said Larry couldn't open as many locations as he wanted • if Larry can show that other franchisees with similar competition continued to profit after Joe began to struggle • Larry will testify that it was having an outlet on every street corner that made the system successful for everyone • if it weren't possible to make a profit with so much competition, there would not have been the continued demand for additional franchises in locations already served by several • the real problem was that Joe was a bad manager to begin with, and then paid little attention to the franchise after coming into his inheritance • to get to this part of the tree, the jury didn't believe Larry committed fraud, so must not have hated Larry

The next two trees, also by Marc Victor,[9] reflect the way these positive and negative factors might be listed and arranged under each branch following a chance node.[10] The first tree analyzes factors potentially impacting a liability finding and thus the lawyer's estimate of the likelihood of liability. The next tree depicts various ways damages might unfold, with a list of positive and negative factors at the chance node.

[8] This chart can be found in Victor, Calihan, and Dent, "The Role of Risk Analysis in Dispute and Litigation Management," 19.

[9] These trees can be found in Victor, Marc "Litigation Risk Analysis and ADR," *Donovan Leisure Newton & Irvine ADR Practice Book.* (1990): Figures 17-3 and 17-4 at 314-315.

[10] In fact, the TreeAge decision analysis software includes an option to create a list of plus and minus factors at each chance node.

Realistic Evaluation of Weaknesses as Well as Strengths

[Focus on Factors Affecting Liability]

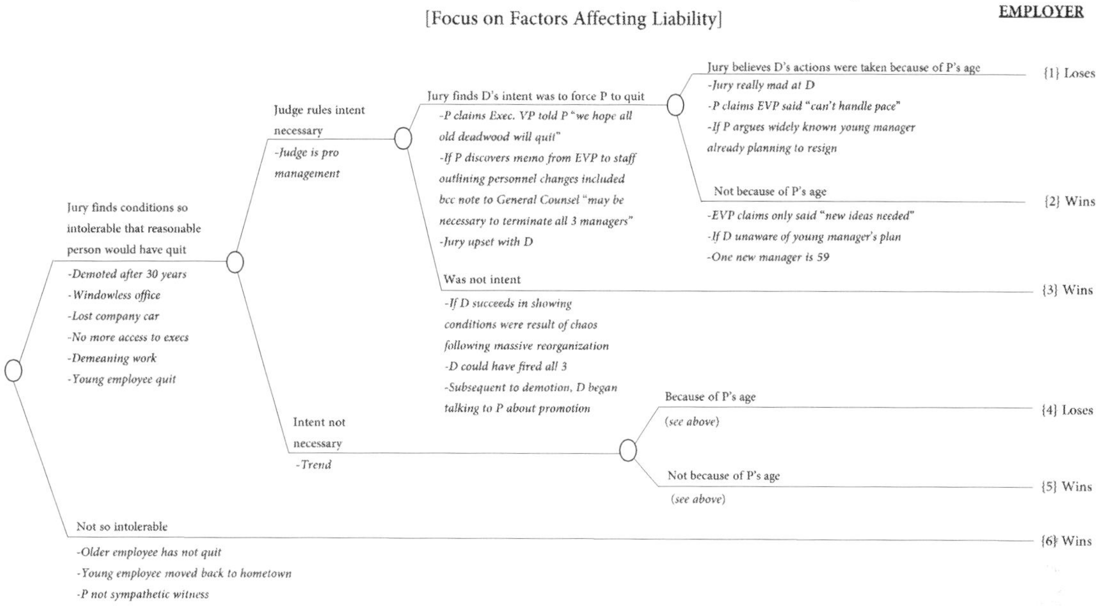

Focus on Factors Affecting Damages

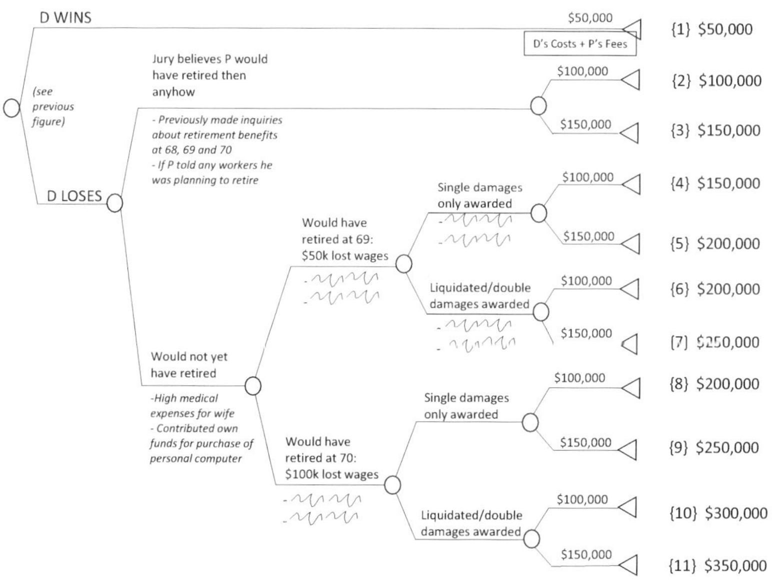

Order does matter. Research strongly supports the practice of FIRST creating a list of factors that cut against your desired outcome—the minuses (-)—and NEXT the factors that favor—the pluses (+). Partisan biases are mitigated when one is forced to list and consider unwelcome realities that might otherwise be forgotten, ignored, or discounted.[11]

After listing first the unfavorable and then the favorable factors, estimate the probability of the most undesirable result, with the remainder (from 100%) left applied to more desirable results. For the visual among us, this also works very well on the probability wheel.

Avoiding Biased Anchors and the Representativeness Heuristic

As discussed above and in the "Interlude on Psychology," we know that partisan biases often lead us to be over-confident, and to miss or discount information or argument that cuts against our desired result. When undertaking decision tree analysis in a legal case, we are also expected to estimate probabilities that reflect the discovery of facts, documents, and arguments as the case develops. Unfortunately, anchoring is a powerful force. We know there's a strong tendency to anchor on original assessments (that may have been biased in the first place) or even on circumstances—other case outcomes—that are largely irrelevant. And, we know that our probability estimates tend to be influenced by the "representative heuristic"—similarity of our case and its characters to certain well-known types. The following prescriptions for best practices in estimating probabilities are aimed at reducing or eliminating tendencies toward over confidence, bias, biased anchoring and the representativeness heuristic.

- Introduce external NON-biased anchors in the form of "base rates" (as discussed in the next section).
- Introduce multiple anchors and numerical information, to offset or balance biased anchors when assigning values to the tree (even if research suggests that multiple anchors aren't as effective as we might hope).[12]
- Encourage initial selective information processing from the perspective *opposite* to that of the lawyer's natural bias. In other words, focus first on evidence and arguments that support the other side. (Yes, this same advice was offered for reducing partisan biases in the first place—not just anchoring to biased reference points).[13]
- Consider and discuss the widest possible range of outcomes.
- Refresh your awareness and educate your client with some thoroughness regarding the power of anchoring. Research suggests that comprehensive awareness of anchoring may reduce but not

[11] See Koriat, Asher; Lichtenstein, Sarah; and Fischhoff, Baruch, "Reasons for confidence," *Journal of Experimental Psychology: Human Learning and Memory* 6 (1980):107-118; cited in Lichtenstein, Sarah; Fischhoff, Baruch; and Phillips, Lawrence, "Calibration of probabilities: The state of the art to 1980," in Kahneman, Daniel; Slovic, Paul; Tversky, Amos (eds.), *Judgment under uncertainty: Heuristics and biases* (1982): 321.

[12] Unfortunately, a study in a negotiation setting indicated that availability of more appropriate anchors did not significantly limit the influence of less reliable anchors, regardless of the level of experience for both individual and group-based decision making. Whyte, Glen and Sebenius, James, "The Effect of Multiple Anchors on Anchoring In Individual and Group Judgment," *Organizational Behavior and Human Decision Processes* 69, no. 1 (1997): 74–85.

[13] See Flannelly, Laura, and Flannelly, Kevin. "Reducing People's Judgment Bias About their Level of Knowledge," *The Psychological Record* 50 (2000): 592.

completely eliminate its influence; a simple warning alone is unlikely to overcome it.[14] Hence this text's somewhat lengthy discussion of the topic!

- Spend adequate time thinking through your judgment. Rushing causes us to fall into an "estimation trap" and enhances our tendency to anchor.[15]
- Take care to differentiate irrelevant anchors from more appropriate ones.[16]

In service of this advice, the next section is an elaboration on base rates, for those eager to adopt the first bullet point suggestion. Further explanation and discussion of how these various prescriptions may play out in practice are set forth after that.

Elaboration and Ode to Probability Base Rates—Even if Elusive[17]

If anchoring to a starting point is inevitable, it makes sense to seek a neutral, unbiased one.

Therefore, when possible, a best practice for the decision-analyst lawyer is to start with the "base rate" when assigning probabilities—the average % of success for this type of motion or this type of jury trial. Assume you are working on a decision tree in an employment case, and you are seeking to estimate the likelihood of summary judgment for the defense. The base rate might be the percent of summary judgment motions decided for the defense in all employment cases in that federal circuit, in that federal district court, or by the assigned judge over a certain period of time. It makes sense to narrow the research to the decision-maker—the judge. The danger, however, is that the judge's total summary judgment rulings in employment cases might be too small to have any substantial predictive value. As we know, all cases are different. If the judge had heard and ruled upon, say thirty or forty plus similar cases, the overall percentage would have more meaning.

From a statistical perspective, the question of what is a sufficient number of summary judgment rulings or jury verdicts from which to derive a reasonable base rate is not as straightforward as one might think. The "Law of Large Numbers"[18] confirms what we intuit: larger numbers in the data pool would

---

[14] George, Joey; Duffy, Kevin; and Manju, Ahuja, "Countering the Anchoring and Adjustment Bias with Decision Support Systems," *Decision Support Systems* 29, no. 2 (2000):195–206.

[15] Smith, Andrew and Windschitl, Paul, "Biased Calculations: Numeric Anchors Influence Answers To Math Equations," *Judgment and Decision Making* 6, no. 1 (2011):139–46.

[16] As suggested by Whyte and Sebenius, "The Effect of Multiple Anchors on Anchoring in Individual and Group Judgment," 74-85.

[17] As discussed herein, most people ignore overall probabilities or "base rates" when estimating probabilities. Yet, Bayes' Theorum establishes quite clearly and mathematically that accurate probabilities are dramatically affected by base rates. Thus, probability estimates of those who ignore base rates are inevitably inaccurate. Their estimates will be far from what would be mathematically, accurately derived using Bayes' Theorum.

Explanations of the base rate fallacy and Bayes' Theorum abound in the literature of quantitative analysis, statistics, and to some degree psychology which offers the representativeness heuristic as an explanation for our flawed probability assessments. See Chapter Nine for discussion of the representativeness heuristic. Wikipedia contains quite a clear explanation of base rate fallacy, also called base rate neglect or base rate bias, as a formal fallacy. When presented with related base rate information (i.e. generic, general information) and specific information (information only pertaining to a certain case), the mind tends to ignore the former and focus on the latter. Wikipedia's drunk driving and breathalyzer example for base rates, used in this text, are at www.wikipedia.org/wiki/Base_rate.

[18] Some would say that 25 cases would be sufficient. Explanations of the "Law of Large Numbers" and other concepts in statistics that bear on this discussion are readily available in just about any introductory statistics text.

be better. In truth, the "Law of Large Numbers is directed at circumstances where the means (averages) from each of many relatively small samples can be predicted to follow a "normal distribution curve." The minimum number of samples required is generally said to be about thirty. At that point, the means of all of the sample means would be about the same as the mean of the entire larger data pool. We can use this idea to find out whether a particular judge's percentage of summary judgment denial is predictably and significantly different than the rulings of a larger group of judges. Assume that available data tells you that only 20% of 150 summary judgment motions filed in age discrimination cases in the Sixth Circuit were granted. If your assigned judge granted 40% or even 30% of those motions in the thirty such cases assigned to her, it's fair to conclude that this variance is not a matter of chance.

This author does not claim expertise in statistics or data science. For the decision analysts of similar ilk, my practical advice to take base rates from the largest data pool that is relevant and accessible. A lawyer with an age discrimination case might check all age discrimination cases in that federal court, or in the Circuit. He might also look to all employment discrimination cases heard by the particular judge, if the question is the likelihood of summary judgment. However, if the assigned judge has heard summary judgment motions in fewer than twenty-five or thirty age discrimination cases, it's not wise to put too much weight on the percentage of motions granted or denied. Instead, we might note that the judge has heard sixty or more employment discrimination cases (of all types), and granted summary judgment in 50% of those, in a Circuit where the overall summary judgment rate is only 25%. It would then be fair to assume a higher likelihood of this judge granting summary judgment. We might use 50% as our base rate on summary judgment for this judge. On the other hand, if the entire Circuit's rate for summary judgment over 150 age discrimination cases is only 15% (lower than the 25% for all employment cases), we might adjust our 50% base rate down by an equal proportion.

Another statistic that might serve as a neutral anchor is the overall percentage of summary judgment motions granted in the jurisdiction. The database would inevitably be larger than that generated by a single judge. But it may be less predictive, as it encompasses several judges, all of whom may have different judicial philosophies regarding dispositive motions. Or, the decision analyst might seek to find and use the overall percentage of summary judgment motions granted by so called "conservative" or "liberal" judges—if the assigned judge clearly falls into either category.

Data Sources for Deriving Base Rates[19]

Most federal and state courts publish data online regarding case filings and settlements. The data are organized in different ways, but are often searchable for percentages of motions granted, liability verdicts,

---

One text that seeks to discuss statistics for lawyers is Jackson, Howell; Kaplow, Louis; Shavell, Steven; Viscusi, W. Kip; and Cope, David, *Analytical Methods for Lawyers* (2003): Chapters 8 and 9. [Note that this text does contain a chapter on decision tree analysis for lawyers. However, it's fair to say that their approach to the topic is more of an introductory overview than that in this text.]

[19] Once again, Professors Heather Heavin and Michaela Keet at the University of Saskatchewan College of Law's excellent article: "A Spectrum of Tools to Support Litigation Risk Assessment," *Canadian Journal of Law and Technology* 15, no.2 (2017):265-293, has been invaluable here. Their article confirmed some sources we had found and alerted me to others; their assessments of the various database sources has been integrated into the discussion here, with much appreciation.

and so forth.[20] FedStats is a portal to statistics collected by the federal government. It contains relevant statistics on legal cases for state and federal courts, jury and bench trials and appeals, beginning in 2005.

Free access to a database of U.S. cases is available through the "Caselaw Access Project," originally a collaboration between Harvard Law School and Ravel Law, which has digitized Harvard's entire collection of U.S. case law.[21]

Not surprisingly given our recent global focus on data, a number of for-profit companies have developed products that capture and offer searchable data on court outcomes and judicial decisions.

Legal data analytic software and database products include[22]:

- LexisNexis' Legal Analytics Suite, including the MedMal Navigator, the Lexis-Nexis Verdict & Settlement Analyzer, Ravel Law, and Lex Machina, all of which fall under Lexis Litigation Profile Suite® and Lexis Advance®

  It seems fair to say that LexisNexis is seeking to establish itself as the market leader for legal "data analytics," including data bases responsive to a wide array of questions. They began in 1990 with the LexisNexis Verdict and Settlement Analyzer.[23] This widely accessible research tool enables users to derive useful "base rates" in most civil cases and to see verdict and settlement data for (only) U.S. state and federal cases and to find averages or medians by jurisdiction or type of case over lengths of time.

  LexisNexis expanded its Legal Analytics Suite of Products by purchasing the two[24] significant "start-up" litigation data analytics companies and their products: Lex Machina and Ravel Law. Originally created for IP users, Lex Machina's Legal Analytics program[25] offers data bases and search capabilities in U.S. based securities, copyright, trademark, and antitrust litigation,

[20] PACER contains court documents and record from U.S. federal courts, USPTO from the U.S. Patent and Trademark Office, and EDIS documents relating to U.S. International Trade Commission investigations.

[21] See the description of the Case Law Access project at Harvard's Library Innovation Lab at: http://etseq.law.harvard.edu/2017/01/caselaw-access-project-scanning-now-complete/ as well as the blog announcement of completion of the digitization project at: http://etseq.law.harvard.edu/2017/01/caselaw-access-project-scanning-now-complete/ Note also that Ravel Law is now under the Lexis Nexis umbrella.

[22] At some point, your author aspires to a full blown set of product reviews of these various databases and search engines from the perspective of a decision tree analysis. Given the very current changes, mergers and likely new entries into the field, it makes little sense to attempt this within a static text. This would be more appropriate for a future, web-based platform of this project.

[23] In 2015-16, University of Cincinnati College of Law Senior Research Librarian James Hart as well as the author's Research Assistant, Mrs. Lindsay Stueve at the College of Law, investigated various on-line verdict data sources and concluded that LexisNexis's Verdict Settlement Analyzer had the most robust and easily searchable database at the time. This is likely to have been advanced by the LexisNexis acquisitions described above. As Ms. Stueve noted, "extrapolating base rates from LexisNexis's tool can provide, at first, a visible starting line, and at least, a security blanket." James Hart gets full credit for the broader, updated search for and evaluation of other data offerings.

[24] It is fair to predict that this discussion of available databases and search and analytic platforms will be incomplete and possibly inaccurate by the time the reader encounters it. New providers entered the for-profit market and new, publicly accessible data bases became available or expanded as this manuscript was being written; no doubt others will be added and some may fail as time goes by. Thus, readers in search of data bases and analytical services are encouraged to look beyond the resources listed here.

[25] Lex Machina's website, prior to its purchase by LexisNexis, offered access to and presumably, analysis of motions and arguments that have been successful (or less so) before particular judges.

and, more recently, bankruptcy commercial transactions, employment and product liability. Lex Machina operates as a stand-alone entity within LexisNexis Legal & Professional offerings.

With the acquisition and integration of Ravel Law's original "Court Analytics" program, LexisNexis Litigation Profile suite of products enables users to "identify patterns in language and case outcomes" to evaluate millions of court decisions."[26] At the time of this writing, Ravel is a premium feature (and subscription) within LexisNexis' available products. Ravel users can search case law by court, motion types, keywords, and topics; predicting outcomes based on courts' and judges' past rulings, identifying key cases, standards, and language more salient for particular courts, and analyzing a judge's responses to certain types of motions[27] and data. Ravel's product description claims that it offers enhanced capacity to predict the type and style of motion likely to succeed before a judge, the litigation behavior patterns of law firms, lawyers, and parties, and potential damages ranges.

- Docket Navigator describes itself as a "professionally curated litigation intelligence platform."[28] Originally focused only on patent litigation, it has expanded to cover trademark, copyright and antitrust litigation. It claims to have the most extensive patent litigation database available, and to track significant events "in every case, every day" in all "patent infringement case in the U.S. district courts, patent infringement investigations in the ITC, and every IPR and CBM proceeding in the PTAB." It claims to be organized to enable "data-driven decisions" and comparisons of "outcomes of litigation strategies across different types of proceedings and different judges or courts," including "factors that influence judicial decision-making, behavior patterns of companies in litigation, and events that impact the litigation schedule and budget."
- Bloomberg Law's new Litigation Analytics Solution offers searchable data from federal cases only and appears focused on judicial behavior, from decisions on various types of motions, responses to different companies, law firms, and docket timing.
- Westlaw Case Evaluator (and its Report Builder) is also a credible source for averages, medians and range. However, Westlaw's data collection began at different times in different states and does not come from consistent sources. On the other hand, Westlaw Next offers a Litigation Quantum service (also available in Canada) featuring data from trial and appellate decisions.
- Loom Analytics, a Canadian company founded in 2016, also offers statistical information on motion and trial outcomes, narrowed to jurisdiction, court, and judges in Canada.

[26] The text describing Ravel Law's Court Analytics and Case Law Access Project is quoted or largely paraphrased from its website, prior to its purchase by LexisNexis: www.ravellaw.com and December 5, 2016 press release, by Marketwired citing Ravel Law as its source: www.marketwired.com/press-release/ravel-law-launches-new-analytics-for-us-court-system-2180699.htm.

[27] While your author is determined against product endorsements, the ability to quickly see how a judge or court has decided different types of motions would be quite helpful for considering probability percentages for a decision tree. In my limited experience with a few of these databases, certain types of litigation data are easier to find than others.

[28] The language in this paragraph is either directly quoted or paraphrased from the company's website, docketnavigator.com. Full credit for reference to this resource is due to the author's former student and patent attorney, John Bennett, who uses decision analysis in his practice and uses Docket Navigator's data to determine the base rates for estimating probabilities.

For readers who represent a large repeat player in litigation: it does appear that some large organizations track data from their litigation experience over time and in different jurisdictions. Indeed, years ago, working as a mediator with a large insurance company and with a self-insured railroad, I learned that they tracked data on settlements and verdicts. As data tracking and analysis are more easily accomplished, it makes sense for a business to do so for the purpose of predicting future outcomes.

Caveat and Advice for Using LexisNexis Verdict and Settlement Analyzer

For the reader who might plan to start with the widely accessible *LexisNexis Verdict and Settlement Analyzer* (or a similar database), a word of caution is in order. Note that this Analyzer only provides straight percentages of plaintiff or defense verdicts within the broader array of percentages of case outcomes including settlement, mediation, or "other verdicts." The decision tree analyst, at least for pure litigation risk analysis, must set aside "settlement, mediation, or other verdicts." The question for which the decision analyst lawyer seeks a base rate is, "When and only when similar cases have gone to trial, what have been the percentages of jury verdicts for the defendants and plaintiffs?" Thus, the base rate for liability must be the percentage liability as a proportion of total plaintiffs' and defense verdict percentages.

By way of illustration, assume that we want to know the base rate for liability findings among age discrimination cases[29] that have gone to trial in federal courts within a certain time period (from January 1998 to December 2017). The *LexisNexis Verdict and Settlement Analyzer* tells us that 25.73% of these cases ended in a plaintiff's verdict, 29.01% in a defense verdict, and 10% in "other" verdicts. The balance was coded as ending in "arbitration," "mediation," "settlement" (presumably direct settlement) or "unknown."

To derive the base rate for liability verdicts among age discrimination cases that went to trial (and not counting "other"), one would find percentage for:

$$\frac{\text{plaintiff verdict (25.73\%)}}{\text{defense verdict (29.01\%) + plaintiff's verdict (25.73\%)}} = \frac{.2573}{.5774}$$

$$.2573 \div .5774 = 47\%$$

Theoretically, when the probability to be estimated is the likelihood of a jury verdict on liability in an employment case, the average percentage within the jurisdiction makes more sense—either the circuit or the district. Where the states within a circuit are vastly different—more or less rural or conservative—and have very different liability percentage findings, it would make sense to look to data within the district or state. And of course, you might want to limit your search to the past few years.

Unfortunately, narrowing a search by using more filters in the Verdict and Settlement Analyzer (or similar program) creates a smaller data pool. As discussed earlier, the smaller the data pool, the less statistically reliable your results.

Users should be aware of the fact that if you are also using the dollar verdict outcomes to get a sense of "high, medium and low" ranges, smaller data pools are more susceptible to undue influence from outliers or extreme verdicts. On the other hand, it's not necessarily wise to completely discount the very

[29] Based on filtering the data from federal courts applying the search term "(age w/3 discrimination)."

high end or low numbers, as even a small data pool reflect a potential reality. After all, at least one jury handed down this very high or very low verdict. However, that fact provides little reliable insight into the likelihood of its future recurrence.

While jury verdict and settlements are also available through various on-line providers, it is important to determine whether these are comprehensive, or whether they rely on self-reports by counsel. Fortunately, while self-reported results were often the norm twenty years ago, more robust databases of case results have become widely available in recent years.

Prescriptions in Practice, First With and Then Beyond Base Rate Advice

Assume that the decision analyst lawyer is working on an employment discrimination case, assigned to a highly experienced federal district judge with long tenure on the bench. He has ruled on more than 100 summary judgment motions in employment discrimination cases over the past ten years. He has rarely been reversed; the last time was seven years ago. Overall, he grants the defense's summary judgment motions 20% of the time. It makes sense for a decision analyst to take on that 20% as a neutral anchor. He might put it "in pencil" on the tree, and begin with it when asking his defense counsel colleague and client what their best estimates are of the likelihood of summary judgment.

The dialog might be:

Decision analyst: "Let's consider your best estimate of the percent likelihood of summary judgment here. We know that this judge has granted 20% of the summary judgment motions in employment discrimination cases before him. Of course, all cases are different. And this case may be stronger or weaker than average as to the arguments on summary judgment—how clear the facts are, what factual disputes the plaintiff's attorney will raise. The question is how much?"

Lawyer: "Well, this one is really strong. The plaintiff's lawyer will try to blow some smoke to conjure a factual dispute, but they'll be hard pressed to find materiality."

Decision analyst: "Just as usual. And yet, 'usual' gets us a 20% chance with this judge? So how much stronger?"

Lawyer: "This one is almost twice as strong, well not quite... say 45% - 50% or 55% chance of summary judgment instead of the usual 20%."

Decision analyst: "I can see that you're saying this case is far better than average. Do you really think it's more than twice as strong? Remember that lawyers who file motions for summary judgment are saying, in good faith, that they believe summary judgment is warranted, based on the facts and the law. Where material facts are plainly in dispute, the motion isn't filed. Yet, even where the moving parties' lawyers have put forward what they see as credible good faith arguments for summary judgment, it's granted only 20% of the time.

If the 'base rate' or the average is 20%, would you say this case is twice as strong as the average—moving it from 20% to 40%? Or is it half again as strong as the average case—which would be a 30% chance? If you think about it in those terms, what's your best gut estimate?"

Lawyer: "I see your point. If the average is 20%, then 45% - 55% may be more optimistic than realistic. Let's go with a 30-35% estimate for the decision tree, at least for now. Though, at some point, I may be interested to see what happens if we go back to 45% or a bit higher."

It's easy to imagine how, without the neutral anchor at 20%, this dialogue might have been quite different, ending with a very different estimate. We'll never know, but the confident lawyer might have said, "I think we have an 80% chance of summary judgment—the facts are so strong." After some discussion of the issues, perhaps an adjustment would be made to 60% or 65%.

Perhaps the dialogue would have sounded like this:

Decision analyst: "What do you think are the chances that the judge will grant your summary judgment motion?" [Note the open question—without initial reference to any % number.]

Lawyer: "We have a VERY strong argument that any so-called disputes over facts are illusory, and more important, irrelevant under the legal standards. I'd say we have an 80% chance."

The decision analyst might then have simply put 80% on the tree. Or, suspicious that partisan perception bias was running strong, he might have attempted to persuade the lawyer to adjust his estimate, as follows:

Decision analyst: "Yes, I've read the draft brief, but I wonder whether the judge might just decide to throw this one to the jury, if there's any doubt. He may not want to risk reversal. And, given his political leanings, he may favor giving the plaintiff a shot, or pressuring us to settle higher by denying our motion. Yes, the plaintiff is blowing lots of smoke. But what about their second argument regarding the experts' disagreement?"

Lawyer: "Yes, I suppose, 80% may overstate it, but it's still a strong motion. Let's say 65%."

The 80% figure has become an anchor, and while discussion and reconsideration may prompt adjustment from the anchor, research indicates that these adjustments are unlikely to be sufficient. They will not get to the same 35%-40% or so as the decision analyst and his lawyer client who began with 20% as the anchor."

Speculation in a fictional case? Yes. But it sounds all too plausible. Of course, the same anchoring and insufficient adjustment occurs with damages estimates as well. Here too, best practice is to check the base rates for damages awards as neutral anchors, where available, and take adequate time and care when performing calculations. Do remember to try to check your own biases in the process.[30]

The critical reader might concede the research finding that we tend to adjust insufficiently from anchors, and then push the question: "Who is to say that starting at 20% and ending at 35% or 40% is superior to starting at 80% and ending with a 60% or 65% estimate of success on the motion? Do we really *know* that the lower % is more accurate for this case? What gives our 20% anchor privileged status?"

The response goes back to research regarding partisan perception bias. We operate under the assumption that the lawyer's 80% estimate was affected by his partisan bias. The base rate may not be perfectly applicable, but it is not colored by bias. Indeed, it captures what a neutral decision maker—judge or jury—has done, on average and over time, in somewhat similar circumstances. It seems wiser to make adjustments made from a well-chosen base rate to legitimately account for differences in the cases.

Challenges of Choosing or Deriving the Base Rate

Obviously, the decision analyst should avoid biased selection of more favorable base rates. Imagine a pending summary judgment motion against an age discrimination claim. Assume that, in a particular circuit, overall summary judgment rates are 15%. However, summary judgment rates in all employment

[30] Smith and Windschitl, 139–46.

discrimination cases are 25% and in age discrimination cases, 30%. Examining the data more carefully, the decision analyst finds that the assigned judge has granted summary judgment in all cases at the rate of 17%—close to the 15% overall percentage. However, in the last five years, over sixty cases, he has granted summary judgment against the plaintiffs in discrimination cases 50% of the time, including 40% of fifteen age discrimination cases. Which base rate should be used as the anchor?

As discussed earlier, the problem with the 40% statistic is that it's based on a small number of cases. As matter of statistics, it might make sense to use 50%, as that derives from a larger data set. On the other hand, one could argue that 40% makes sense; perhaps it indicates that this judge "disfavors" other types of discrimination claims. Or perhaps it would make sense to imagine the base rate is 45%. Or, because the data set is larger, perhaps the overall summary judgment rate of 25% in employment cases or 30% in all age discrimination cases makes sense.

In short, finding "best" base rate is far from an exact science, and it's even more challenging with imperfect access to imperfect data.[31] Let's remember that the base rate merely begins the discussion. Its purpose is to reduce bias in a lawyer's necessarily subjective assessments. Base rates become reference points, or neutral anchors for discussion. Counsel will and should consider ways that the particular case is "above average" or "less certain than usual" and adjust accordingly.[32]

Back to the practical: How can a decision analyst legitimately use a base rate in building a tree or discuss his analysis with a client? You might simply insert it into discussion when seeking to estimate a probability, as an unbiased anchor. In other words, when considering the chances of dismissal on summary judgment in *this* age discrimination case, you might first reference the base rate of X%, for summary judgment in this Circuit for the last five years, and Y% for your assigned judge. Nowhere is it written that you must use either of these numbers in the decision tree for this case. Every case is different. But you would be advised to consider the reasons this case is "better than average," and how much better. Force yourself to justify movement away from the unbiased anchor.

An alternative (and interesting) way to use the base rates would be to construct a tree using base rates wherever available, typically on the question of summary judgment and overall liability, and simply "plug-in" 50% for any other significant uncertainty point. Roll back the tree to find the EMV and the cumulative probabilities of each outcome. This exercise would theoretically describe the hypothetical, "plain vanilla" average case of its type. That might serve as an anchor, a neutral reference point against which lawyer and client could compare this real case's estimated probabilities, predicted outcomes, and roll back analysis.

Squaring Statistics With Sensible Simplification and Slimmer Trees

As indicated earlier, logically and visually, it makes sense to simplify a tree by merging different possible paths that all lead to the same results. Imagine that the lawyer sees three distinct and independent theo-

[31] As discussed in Chapter 9, statisticians utilize Bayes' Theorem which mathematically adjusts from a base rate of probability, accounting for the new evidence or unique conditions of a particular case, to estimate the probability of the same result occurring in that case. Edward K. Cheng, a Professor of Law at Vanderbilt Law School, discusses Bayes' Theorem in Chapter 8 of his as yet unpublished textbook on statistical concepts for lawyers and additionally stresses the importance of considering reliable base rates, when available, in estimating probabilities.

[32] Fischhoff, Slovic, and Lichtenstein, "Fault Trees: Sensitivity of Estimated Failure Probabilities to Problem Representation," 330-334; cited in Garthwaite, Kadane, and O'Hagan, 682.

ries or findings by which a judge or jury could arrive at the same liability and damages award. Logically, all the tree builder needs to know and the lawyer needs to assess is their joint probability—what is the likelihood that at least one of these theories will prevail? He need not think about which theory it will be.

The field of psychology advises caution and a different approach. Research indicates that when people are asked to assess the chances that X could happen as a result of A, B, or C (all possible, but independent), they tend to provide a lower aggregate probability than if asked to separately assess—disaggregate—the probabilities of A, B, or C. In the classic study[33] of the effect of disaggregation, expert car mechanics were asked to assess the probability that a car would not start for *any* reason other than battery, engine, or fuel system. The average probability assessed was 22%. However, when they were asked to assess specific possible reasons: failure of ignition system, failure of the starting system, etc., and those probabilities were combined, the average total probability was 44%. In fact, a generous body of research establishes that "the sum of separate probability assessments for constituent hypotheses generally give a much larger probability than a single probability assessment of the combined hypothesis that they form."[34] Thus, decision analysis scholars seem to agree that "disaggregation of an elicitation problem holds the potential for significantly improved performance on many assessment tasks."[35]

For our purposes, this finding offers a way to use best practices in assessing probabilities as well as constructing trees. When mapping a legal case that involves multiple separate and independent ways to get to exactly the same point—be it a ruling on a motion, or a finding on liability and damages—the tree builder and lawyer should separately assess their probabilities, and add them. If it is useful, a chart or set of branches might be created showing each separate path to encourage "disaggregated" discussion. However, on the main decision tree, these should still be represented by one branch that encompasses them all, provided that all would lead to the same outcome.

One note of caution: it's important not to apply this logic to possible theories that are not independent or sufficient to bring about the next step. Thus, the probability that "the plaintiff will be sympathetic" should not be added to the probability that "causation will be found," if you are seeking to assess the overall likelihood of a liability verdict. These are neither independent nor sufficient for liability. Presumably, whether or not the plaintiff is found to be sympathetic will impact the probability of a causation finding. To add these probabilities would be misleading as it would greatly inflate the result.

A better example might be the question of whether a judge will dismiss a claim where there are alternative motions for dismissal—one based on the statute of limitations and the other on lack of jurisdiction (or standing, or any other independent grounds). Rather than first asking: "What are the overall chances that the judge will knock out the case on the motion to dismiss?", it would be better to consider the chances of the judge's rulings on each separate ground, and add them (assuming their complete independence).

[33] Fischhoff, Slovic, and Lichtenstein, "Fault Trees: Sensitivity of Estimated Failure Probabilities to Problem Representation," 330-334; cited in Garthwaite, Kadane, and O'Hagan, 682.

[34] Garthwaite, Kadane, and O'Hagan, 680-701.

[35] Morgan, Granger; Henrion, Max; and Small, Mitchell, *Uncertainty: A Guide to Dealing with Uncertainty in Quantitative Risk and Policy Analysis* (1992):116; cited in Garthwaite, Kadane, and O'Hagan, 682.

Finding Probabilities in Vagary: Deconstructing Present and Future Uncertainties

Every so often, we must acknowledge that our probability estimate for a future uncertain twist in the case is just plain too uncertain. We lack the basis for a gut sense, for any adjectival description, so how can we responsibly name a percentage number, or even a range? Sometimes, we're completely at a loss because the factors upon which a reasonable assessment would be based are also uncertain; they have yet to occur.

Consider a not-completely-hypothetical case in which a second story porch railing collapsed when plaintiff was pushed into it. The plaintiff fell to the ground, sustaining serious injuries. Your client is the manufacturer of the railing. Assume that causation—what caused the railing to collapse—is a much contested issue in a case. (To make it simple, assume that the contractor who installed the railing is now bankrupt). Under the applicable law of joint and several liability, if your client bears any liability, he takes it all.

It's hard enough to estimate the chance of successfully avoiding liability *after* seeing the plaintiff's expert's reports and deposition testimony on the causation issue. How can you estimate probability before the reports have been exchanged or the experts deposed? In our hypothetical, another issue is the plaintiff's responsibility. We know that he is 6'5" and weighed 400 lbs at the time of his fall. If he was drunk, carousing, and involved in reckless horseplay, then a jury might find him 50% or more responsible. If so, your client is off the hook. The plaintiff's testimony during his deposition was entirely self-serving; he'd have you believe he had a mere sip of beer and "lightly" leaned on the railing. Yet to be deposed is the older upstairs neighbor who witnessed the event, and is not a friend of the plaintiff. The chances of your client's escaping liability will no doubt be affected by the neighbor's deposition testimony.

Plaintiff's counsel has suggested settlement negotiations, and at a recent status conference, the court strongly urged both counsel to mediate if direct negotiations are unsuccessful. You could suggest waiting until after receipt of plaintiff's expert's report and more depositions, but you understand the motivation to save costs. And, if these factors don't go your way, the case value may go up in plaintiff's counsel's eyes. Before negotiating or mediating, you owe your client a reasoned case assessment and, of course, you want to feel that your analysis is sound.

As a thought exercise, it can be useful to deconstruct the assessment task, using the ultimate liability percentage as the payoff, and the factors of their expert's and the neighbor witness as future uncertainties. Consider four simple possible ways these factors may play out:

1) Their expert is weak (good for your case); and the neighbor's testimony supports plaintiff's fault (good for your case). If that happens, what's your estimate of the overall chance of liability?
2) Their expert is strong (bad for your case); and the neighbor's testimony supports plaintiff's fault (good for your case). If that happens, what's your estimate of the overall chance of liability?
3) Their expert is weak (good for your case); and the neighbor's testimony absolves the plaintiff (bad for your case). If that happens, what's your estimate of the overall chance of liability?
4) Their expert is strong (bad for your case); and the neighbor's testimony absolves the plaintiff (bad for your case). If that happens, what's your estimate of the overall chance of liability?

After imagining the four scenarios (admittedly simplified—they don't ask how "good" or how "strong"), let's say your guestimates are 65% for #1, 55% for #2, 40% for #3, and 20% for #4. Hmm... this suggests that you believe the expert's report is a little bit less important than the neighbor's testimony. Is that what you believe? If so, fine. If not, then think on it more and adjust.

Now, you could structure a tree, with the different probability percentages as payoffs.

Just as with any tree, the next step is to assign percentage likelihoods to each of those uncertainties along the path. At this point, it would be perfectly legitimate to throw up your hands and say: "I have no idea what will happen with their expert or with the neighbor! That's why I'm so confounded." If so, then it would also be legitimate just to assign 50% odds to each branch and see what it yields.

Next is the tree with .50 at each branch, and then rolled back.

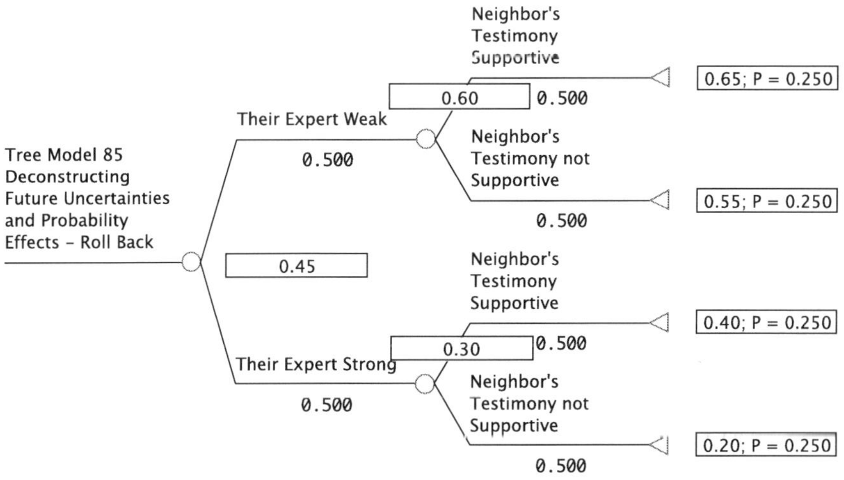

The EMV of .45 means that, factoring these uncertainties into the mix you believe the overall probability of a favorable verdict is 45%.

On the other hand, you might go with the intuition that their expert's report and testimony are likely to be reasonably strong (bad for your case). Plaintiff's counsel has suggested that. You know their expert's credentials are impeccable. And, while your expert has explained why the railing's design is reasonable and up to code, you see some vulnerability in the manufacturer's installation instructions. Thus, at this point, you might believe it 70% likely that their expert will be highly problematic.

Here's how the tree would look, based on that intuition.

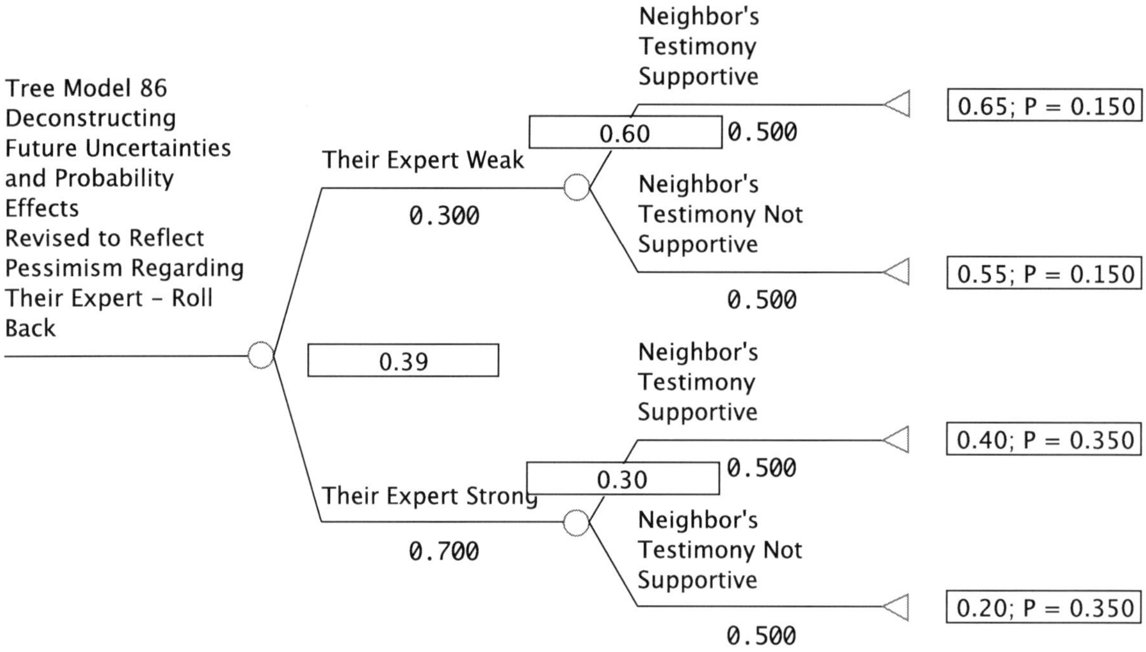

With this added pessimism regarding their expert, your "overall" estimate of the probability of a favorable verdict is reduced to 39%.

Having completed this little probability deconstruction exercise, it's fair to ask how it could be useful in practice. At minimum, its value may merely be in making us think more carefully about factors affecting liability. We may start to reconsider which are important. Maybe what matters most is the jury's attitude toward the plaintiff. He may have been a hard partying 400 pounder then, but now he's thin, subdued, still young, and in a wheelchair. Does the neighbor witness matter so much?

Setting aside any new insights gained, the exercise yields other potentially beneficial products:

1) A liability probability to insert as a placeholder into your main tree, unless and until you have seen the expert's deposition and report or the neighbor's deposition.
2) A defined range of probabilities you could try on the tree. Using decision analysis software (or Excel), you could perform a formal sensitivity analysis, using that probability range. That will show you the way the discounted value varies along that range of liability percentages. Or, you could simply draw and calculate the tree using the top probability and the bottom probability

in the range. You (and your client) might also take a look at the way it affects the distribution of possible outcomes.

3) Assume that your client is not pleased with the discounted value number at the top of the range, or even with the discounted value using the liability percentage generated by your analysis of the uncertainties. Your client's financial VP states that he will be guided by the discounted value in approving a settlement number, but he is queasy about paying close to the top or even the value using the yielded probability. You could decide that it's essential to obtain a copy of plaintiff's expert report, or to attempt an informal interview of the neighbor before any negotiations.
4) In the future, if their expert proves to be unassailable and the unbiased witness vouches for the plaintiff as choir boy, you have a sound basis for changing your evaluation of the case. At that point, an important benefit of this mini-deconstruction is that you and your client aren't driven to hit the panic button and just go up, up, up on the dollar offer. You had already laid the groundwork for thinking about how much these factors—the expert and the neighbor—affect your evaluation of the case, and how much they do not.

Some skepticism about this "mini-deconstruction of probabilities" is understandable, particularly for those not yet comfortable with the method. It is no doubt true that many, perhaps most, clients would not be eager to see yet more of these funny little trees.

On the other hand, some clients will press the question of how you arrived at various probability estimates, and it's good to be able to show them how you thought about it. As discussed earlier, even when the evidence is pretty much in, there's still uncertainty, and you will want to be able to discuss the known factors that weigh for and against your client along that path. For such factors, you will want to list what's favorable and what's not, as recommended. I am proposing this further deconstruction to derive probabilities particularly where you don't yet know what those factors will look like by the time of trial.

Two Final Comments for the Astute and the Strongly Tree-Inclined

As you may have thought, it would be possible to simply include these future uncertainties—for example, the strong or weak expert, the wild card neighbor—on the main tree. If so, instead of one "liability-no liability" chance node on the tree, there would have to be four such nodes. That will be one complicated tree—perhaps too complicated to be comprehensible.[36]

You may have also noted that there's no end to how far such deconstruction could be taken. That's true. After all, we never know how the future may unfold, and we know that unfolding has impact. For some, the act of scratching out little trees is not a burden; it helps our thinking, even if we don't formalize a calculation. How far you take it will depend on your own inclination, your client's eagerness to dig into the weeds, and the significance of what may yield only minute adjustments to the overall analysis.

[36] Note that I am assuming neither of these uncertainties affects any other important variables further along on the tree. If so, then it may worthwhile to break that out separately or at least discuss its impact. In our example, the neighbor's testimony might also impact the likelihood of a significant contributory negligence finding (even if the jury finds sufficient fault for a plaintiff's verdict). At the least, after the witness' interview or deposition, the deconstruction exercise will facilitate adjustment of probabilities at the "contrib-no contrib" branches of the tree.

12

END GAME: OUTCOMES—ESTIMATING NUMBERS AT THE FAR RIGHT

As the reader well knows, every path of even the most complex tree will eventually reach its end. There, the decision tree analyst must consider what's the best numerical estimate of each possible net outcome. There's no magic to estimating these numbers, though there are some mistakes to avoid.

Even without a formal decision analytic method with trees, branches and terminal nodes, lawyers' written and oral case analyses will inevitably reference "possible financial exposure" or "likely recovery" values. Lawyers are called upon to respond to defense client questions such as: "What's the worst case scenario? How much could we be on the hook for?" And the lawyer must try to respond when a plaintiff client asks: "At a minimum, what can I bank on if we win? What's my upside?" Any client might ask: "Leaving aside best case and worst case scenarios, what's your sense of where a jury would most likely land if they find liability?" Some cases suggest more discrete logical points at which award would be likely to land. The lawyers may note that their estimates depend upon specific theories of fact and law, on jury receptiveness to certain expert presentations, on the judges' decision to admit certain evidence, or not. In other cases, the lawyer can only estimate a range of possible outcomes, without particular facts or theories favoring specific points along that range.

Whatever the case, at the end of each path in the litigation, the decision analyst lawyer must estimate a net quantity of dollars (or whatever the relevant currency or unit of value). It consists of what would be gained or lost at this end point, less the cost of arrival, beginning from the time the tree is built. By way of example, the decision analyst might estimate that if a jury finds liability on the fraud claim and punitive damages, and that jury was a particularly generous one—awarding on the high end—the damages award would be $1,500,000, estimated attorney's fees from the present to that point would be $100,000, and expert witness fees and other miscellaneous costs would be $50,000. Thus, the net payoff would be $1,350,000.

Basic principles reminder: past and non-recoverable expenses have no place in the calculus. Thus, if the total attorney's fees in the matter would be $200,000 but $100,000 of them had been incurred *prior* to the tree-building exercise, that first $100,000 has no place in the tree. It is a sunk cost. No decision can be made that would recoup the $100,000. Its expenditure was, and remains, unaffected by now choosing to settle or litigate, or by what path the litigation takes.[1]

[1] While keeping unrecoverable sunk costs out of the tree is a bedrock principle for the decision analyst, it is one that often encounters client resistance: "I spent that money and it should be on there! It matters!" Strategies for explaining why past, unrecoverable costs must be excluded and yet, respecting their importance to the client, were offered in Chapter Three.

Avoiding Mistakes by Accounting for Psychology (Again)

Whether using formal decision analysis or not, the lawyer should again be mindful of partisan biases and anchoring effects in estimating damages awards, including "tightness of range." As explained earlier, the best practice is to first consider factors that would drive a jury number away from the desired direction, and only then consider more favorable factors. So, when the plaintiff client asks, "What's the most I could realistically hope for?", the lawyer might first assume the trial has gone very well, but also take into account certain irrefutable facts: the plaintiff is reasonably wealthy already and the defendant did not act willfully. On the other hand, the accident was terrifying for the plaintiff, and the defendant's negligence could have hurt many others.

Discrete Questions or Default to High, Medium, and Low

Articles and texts on the "how to's" of decision analysis for legal contexts—litigation risk analysis—often arrive at the far right hand side of the tree, at the outcome or terminal node at which payoffs are calculated, and say simply, "Let's assume the damages are $150,000 [or any round number]." Even if attorney's fees or costs are added or subtracted to yield a net payoff, the damages award itself is represented as a single numerical point. In actual practice, except for rare cases of defined, stipulated, or liquidated damages, assuming a single damages award is misleading and unwise. It's a far better practice to estimate a defined set or range of possible damage awards than a single point.

Texts on statistics or decision analysis written for business or public policy audiences appropriately set out applicable mathematical rules for capturing the range of possible outcomes in the analysis. Those rules are provided and discussed later in this chapter. It's important for lawyers to know that *this math works only for capturing a continuous range of outcomes*—a range in which no single outcome is more or less probable than any other outcome within the range. Think of a personal injury case. All of the evidence has been admitted; the jury has found "mere" negligence (not willful or gross negligence). Assume for the moment that pure economic losses have been stipulated at $80,000. Given the plaintiff's injuries, the lawyer might still acknowledge that the total damage award could come in anywhere between $100,000 and $400,000. He would admit that he has no way of predicting that $150,000 is more or less likely than $350,000. Indeed, within that range, he cannot assign a greater percentage likelihood to one dollar amount than another. That would fit the definition of a continuous range. Math works well here, prescribing fairly simple methods to ensure that this damages area can be captured efficiently without multiplying each single point along the range by its singular probability.

As referenced earlier, in many legal cases, not all outcomes along a range are equally likely. Assume that we are predicting what a jury might award, along the litigation path in which motions *in limine* were denied, and the plaintiff's expert's testimony was permitted. Still, we know that one jury (or vocal jury member) may have been persuaded by a particular theory—a way of viewing the narrative of causation, blame, and harm. Another jury (or vocal jury member) may be stingier, having accepted the defense arguments regarding lackluster efforts to mitigate. Different theories, different weighting of key testimony or evidence, will lead to different and discrete areas within a possible damages range. If that is true, then it seems wise to select areas of the range and assign probabilities representing your best sense of the evidence.

For example, assume you think that a jury is 60% likely to be moved by the plaintiff's story, and disinclined to blame her for non-heroic efforts to mitigate her injuries in difficult circumstances. Then you would assign a 60% chance to a damages award toward the higher end of the range. (You might distribute that as 20% to $400,000 and 40% to $300,000—whatever feels right.) You might decide that the jury would cast some blame on the plaintiff only 40% of the time, based on the defense expert on rehabilitation therapy, and assign 30% to a verdict at $200,000 and 10% at $100,000. The only "formula" used to derive these percentages is that they must add up to 100%. A lawyer could pick any point, and assign any percentage to it—whatever seems right.

Even so, a mathematical "gut" check is appropriate. If $400,000 is the very highest number[2] the lawyer could imagine as the jury award based upon the damages claimed, does he really think that it would occur in 20% of 100 hypothetical trials of the case? On the other hand, if the lawyer thinks it remotely possible (5% or 10%) that a jury could find a reason to adjust up to $500,000, then perhaps putting 30% in for $400,000 would be wiser. Or the lawyer might use 7.5% for $500,000, 22.5% for $400,000 and 30% for $300,000. As always true for tree-builders, the goal is to represent the range of possible outcomes, and to assign probabilities so that the number—the damages EMV—fairly represents possible damages discounted by their probabilities in the case.

For the Critical Reader: Branches vs. Estimates and Ranges

The critical reader may observe that it should be possible to keep adding layers of branches to the damages end of the tree, to map the possible variety of ways a jury who finds liability could arrive at a damages figure. After thoroughly deconstructing the jury's or decision-maker's potential thought processes, one could eventually reach all continuous outcome ranges on the far side of the tree.

By way of illustration, let's look back to the example above. To the right of "Finds Liability," you could sketch branches for: "Jury Strongly Weighs Mitigation as Lacking", and "Jury Disregards Mitigation". To the right of each of these, you could create a "High, Medium, Low" continuous damages range, as discussed and prescribed in more detail later in this chapter.

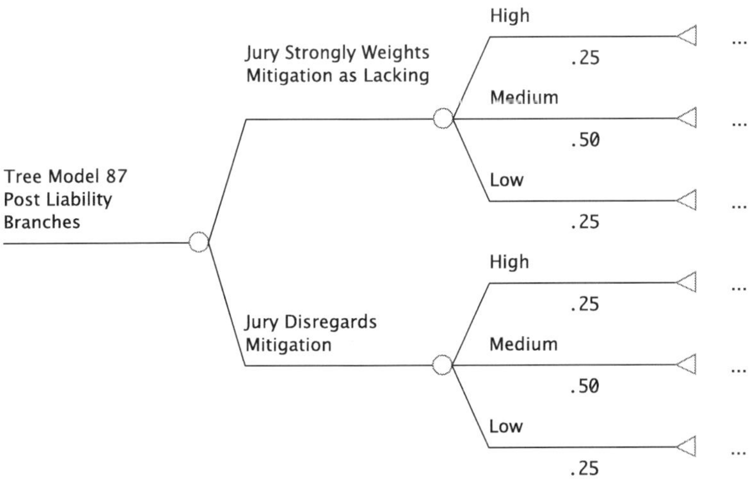

[2] At the risk of undue repetition, the reader should be reminded of our tendencies toward "tightness of range," discussed at length in Chapter 9. This reminder applies to all of this chapter's examples and discussions of numerical ranges and their probabilities.

Remember that, in the original discussion of the example, I permitted the assumption that economic damages were stipulated at $80,000. In reality, such a stipulation is rare. If a defense economist had pegged economic loss at $60,000 and the plaintiff's economist at $100,000, one could further deconstruct the damages award into two or three branches: one for economic loss at $60,000, one at $100,000 and perhaps a compromise at $80,000. To deconstruct further, you could insert this layer of branches before or after the therapy mitigation issue. The tree builder could also insert a layer reflecting the possibility that the jury will be angry at the defendant or one of its witnesses.[3] Then, finally, at the far right, the tree would show continuous ranges at each of many branches, as illustrated below.

Our next tree reflects different economic loss branches and also includes a new branch layer to allow for the possibility of significant "jury anger" (which may or may not be linked to the level of economic loss found). It then feathers many "high, medium, low" continuous damage range estimates at the far right side.[4]

[3] In some cases, it might be legitimate to think that jury anger could be reflected in how they view mitigation. In another case, jury backlash might be separate and separable.

[4] The earlier age discrimination case discussed earlier has some of this aspect.

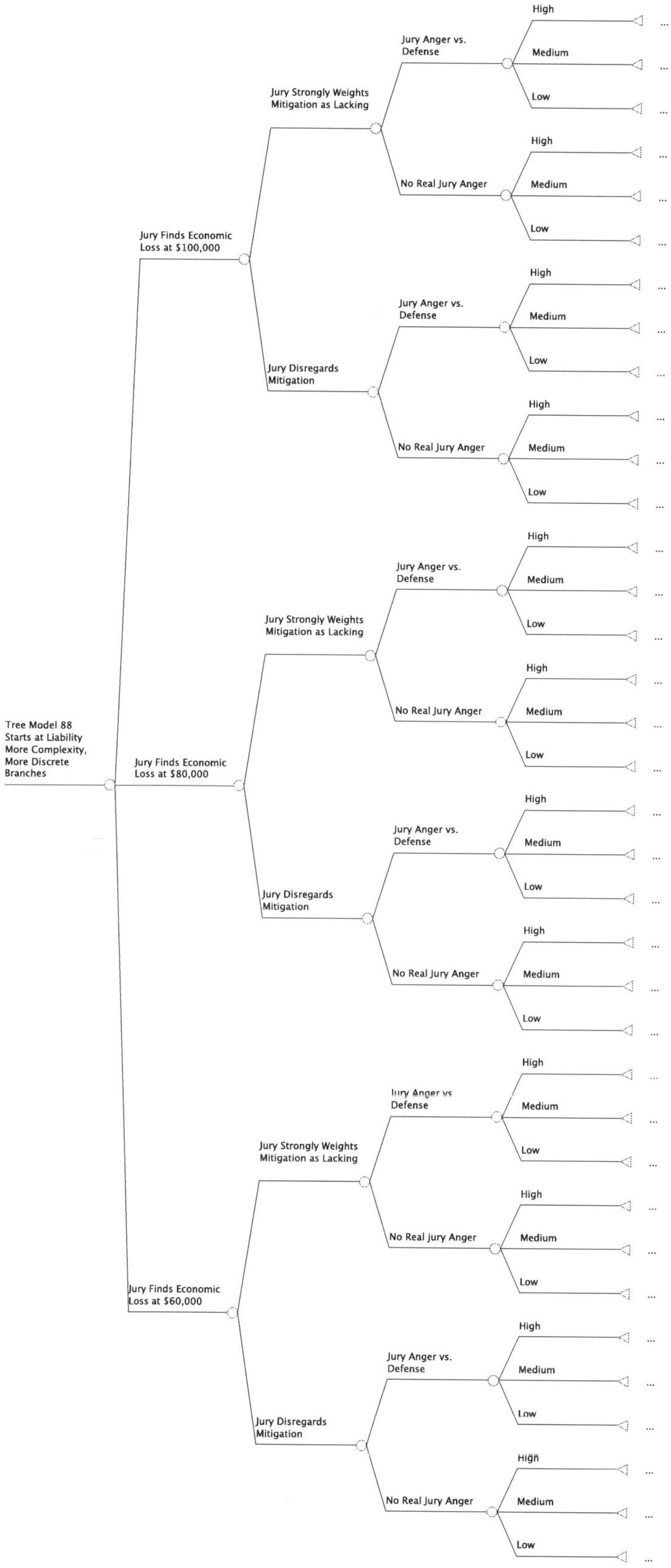
Tree Model 88
Starts at Liability
More Complexity,
More Discrete
Branches
Jury Finds Economic
Loss at $100,000
Jury Strongly Weights
Mitigation as Lacking
Jury Anger vs.
Defense
High
Medium
Low
No Real Jury Anger
High
Medium
Low
Jury Disregards
Mitigation
Jury Anger vs.
Defense
High
Medium
Low
No Real Jury Anger
High
Medium
Low
Jury Finds Economic
Loss at $80,000
Jury Strongly Weights
Mitigation as Lacking
Jury Anger vs.
Defense
High
Medium
Low
No Real Jury Anger
High
Medium
Low
Jury Disregards
Mitigation
Jury Anger vs.
Defense
High
Medium
Low
No Real Jury Anger
High
Medium
Low
Jury Finds Economic
Loss at $60,000
Jury Strongly Weights
Mitigation as Lacking
Defense
High
Medium
Low
No Real Jury Anger
High
Medium
Low
Jury Disregards
Mitigation
Jury Anger vs.
Defense
High
Medium
Low
No Real Jury Anger
High
Medium
Low

As suggested earlier, the critical reader will note that one could deconstruct and map possibilities so thoroughly that, eventually, the tree would show only continuous damages ranges at the far right side. But perhaps this reader would then also recognize this tree's undue and inaccessible complexity. At some point, too many branches and twigs obscure rather than illuminate. A balance must be struck.

For a practitioner whose cases are generally described as being of "medium" complexity, I advise moving to an end range of terminal nodes for hypothetical juries whose "inputs" were the same. This jury would have seen the same "movie"—the same important witnesses and evidence, perhaps received the same jury instructions (if there's a major controversy around a jury instruction). Tracing your way along the path of a hypothetical tree, at the end of the line, one hypothetical jury will have the fraud issue and evidence before it, and all of the plaintiff's expert witness testimony. But, then let's look separately at the path along the tree where summary judgment was granted on the fraud issue, some but perhaps not all evidence relevant to fraud was excluded, and the plaintiff's economic expert as to long term business impact was also excluded. That jury will have seen, in effect, "a different movie." Thus, at the end node, a different range of damages should be considered and applied.

We know that one practical reason to resist mapping all possible jury musings is to avoid a spidery and unreadable web at the far right. A second reason is that, once the trial "movie" has been presented, more branches are just musings. Jury deliberations have a strong black box quality. Once you have mapped the inputs, it seems right to channel our various hypotheses about a jury's deliberations into probabilities assigned to liability findings, perhaps probabilities assigned to well defined damage categories (punitive, not punitive), and then to ranges of possible outcomes.

The tree-builder undeterred by spidery layers of branches after layers of branches, or the tree-builder in a highly complex, very high stakes damages case, is welcome to reject this advice. You may wish to create a separate damages tree, mapping each theoretical way a jury might possibly weigh the evidence. That tree could be rolled back to a "damages only" EMV to be plugged into the main tree at appropriate terminal nodes. If the devil in your case is in the damages (and not so much in judicially excluded or included evidence), you may wish to spend considerable time with your client reviewing this damages tree.

Even in cases of low to middling complexity, but with difficult-to-predict damages, it may be worthwhile for the lawyer to map his musings on a separate tree, sketching out the different ways a jury might come to a damages conclusion. The exercise will help the lawyer clarify and articulate his own thinking. Once that is done, the lawyer is likely to see some numbers coalescing or clustering as outcomes/payoffs. He might then decide to use these numbers as the basis for estimating outcome ranges (whether continuous or discrete) on the main tree.

The Right Math for Continuous Ranges

Sometimes, damages predictions are not tied to alternative legal theories or discrete logical points suggested by specific evidence. Instead, if liability is found, it's anyone's guess as to where the verdict will fall. In mathematical terms, the possible damages outcomes constitute a continuous range. Our goal must be to insure the value of that continuous range is appropriately represented and thus, accurately calculable.

To quickly review: the entire decision analysis method is built upon the idea of taking possible outcomes, and discounting them by the cumulative probability that each will occur. Assume there really is an 80% chance of surviving summary judgment, a 50% chance of a liability finding and then a 20% chance of a $200,000 verdict (double defined damages), a 60% chance of a $100,000 verdict (defined damages), and a 20% chance of $60,000 verdict (after deducting a claimed set-off). Then we know that there's a cumulative 8% chance of the $200,000 outcome, a cumulative 24% chance of $100,000 and an 8% chance of $60,000, as illustrated in the tree below. The cumulative probabilities for each outcome are reflected on the far right hand side. As discussed earlier, multiply each outcome by its cumulative probability, add them together, and you'll have the same overall case EMV as if you had "rolled back" the tree from right to left.

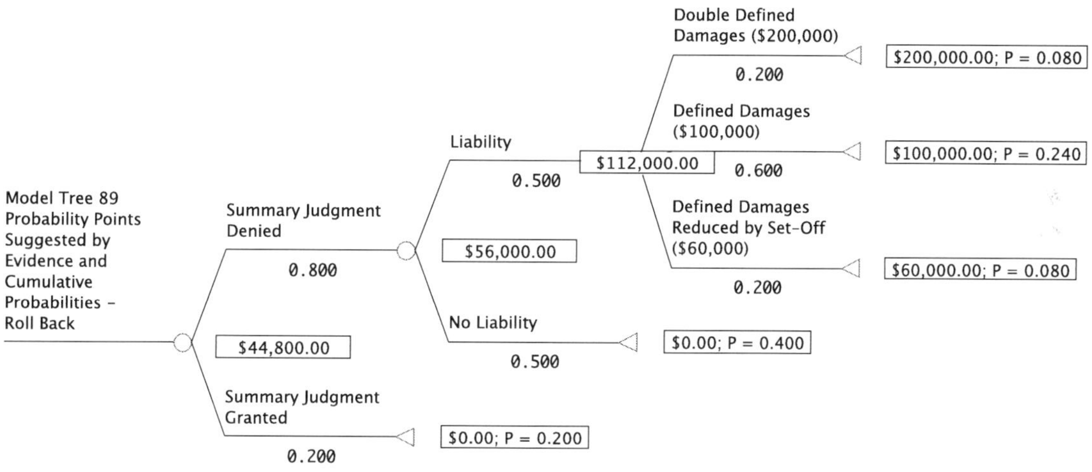

$200,000	x	.08	=	$16,000
$100,000	x	.24	=	$24,000
$60,000	x	.08	=	$4,800
$0	x	.40	=	$0
$0	x	.20	=	$0
		TOTAL	=	$44,800

Take a look at the boxed figure just above and to the right of the chance node before the branches for each possible outcome. That number, ($112,000) is the roll back or EMV of just the damages: 20% x $200,000 = $40,000, plus 60% x $100,000 = $60,000, plus 20% x $60,000 = $12,000. $40,000 plus $60,000, plus $12,000 = $112,000. In other words, if the jury was polled and it had found liability, the discounted value of the damages would be $112,000. The method is entirely consistent with the decision analytic arithmetic done so far. Each outcome is multiplied (discounted) by its likelihood, and these are added.

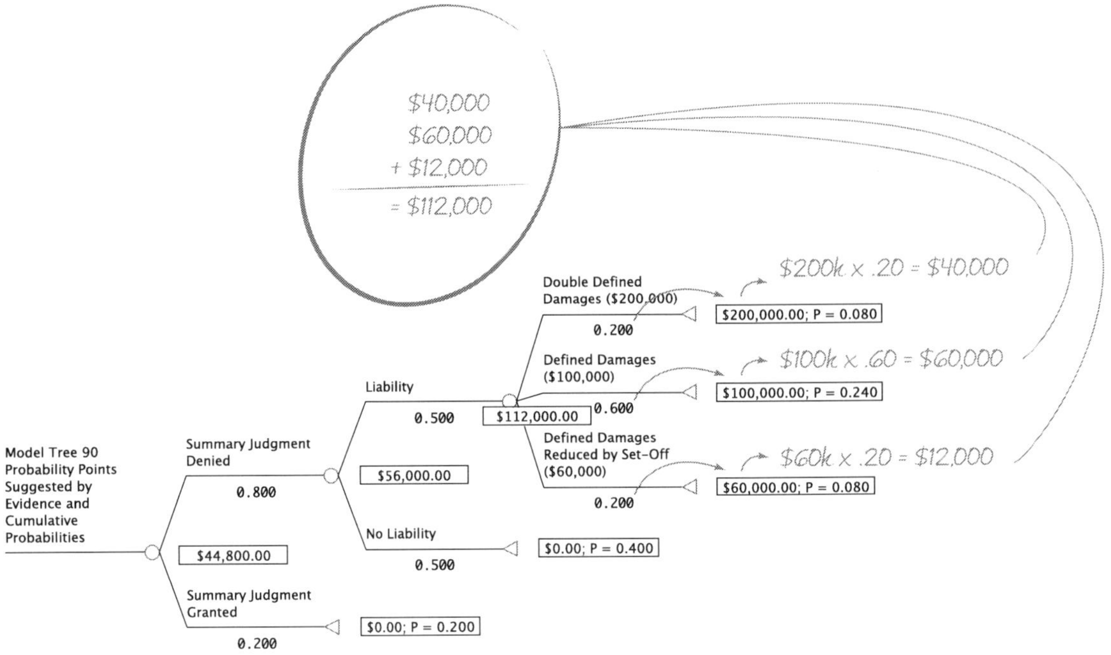

But what if we agree that the verdict could be *anywhere* between $100,000 and $500,000 (including those two numbers), and we have no ability to say that any particular number within that range is more likely than another. Theoretically, we could take each number point within the $400,000 dollar difference, and multiply each by its own likelihood.

Let's do the math. It looks complicated, but it's not. If 100% —total probability—has to be divided among 400,000 separate little branches or points—one for each $1 of the $400,000—we know that the probability of each one is only .00025. (100% divided by 400,000)

So, must we do the operation: .00025 x $100,000, plus .00025 X $101,000.... and so on? Fortunately, the answer is NO! We know intuitively that if there is a 100% chance that the damages award will be between $100,000 and $500,000, you take the mid-point of the $400,000 range, or $200,000—and add it to the starting point of $100,000.

And so, it will end up at $300,000, the average of or midpoint between $100,000 and $500,000.[5] Note that the *average* is the same as the *weighted average* because all probability "weights" are the same.

[5] To reemphasize the importance of outcomes being "mutually exclusive," damages ranges should not overlap within any given branch. And, it should be remembered that ranges represented by averaged numbers (which can be denoted by a "±") are actually still "collectively exhaustive." Victor, Marc, *Interpreting a Decision Tree Analysis of a Lawsuit* (1988, revised 2001), available in pdf on his website: litigationrisk.com.

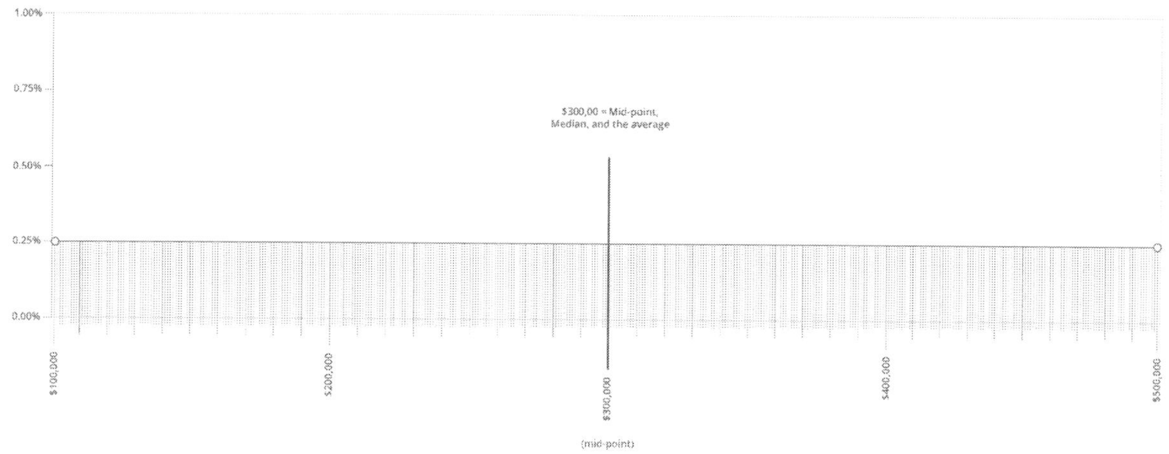

Graphically, we have captured the entire area under a line, representing the percentage likelihood of each separate point—each possible dollar result.

The next graph enables us to visualize the cumulative likelihood that a result will be greater or smaller than a particular figure.

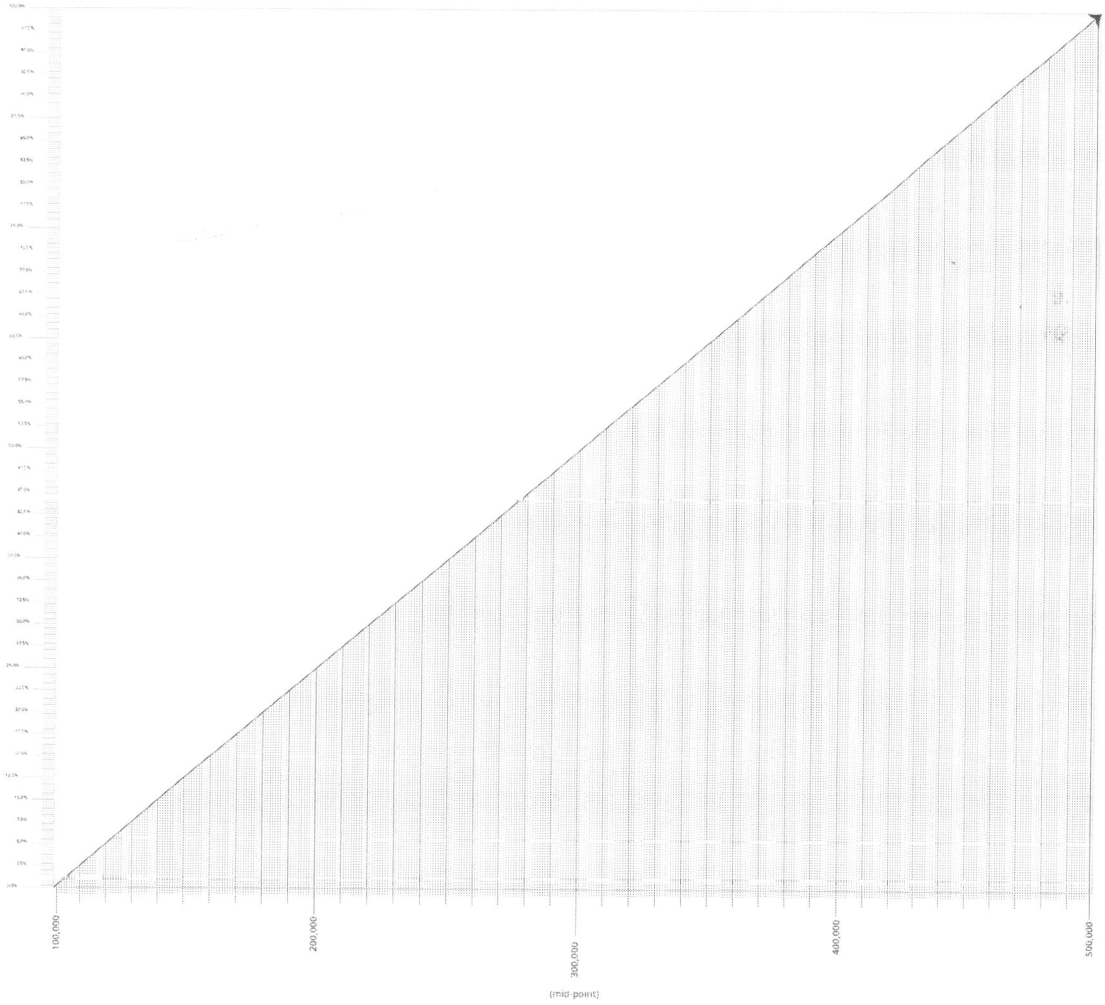

Thus we see from the graph above: if *all* possible and equally likely results range from $100,000 to $500,000, as we move to dollar points higher up in the range, you see an increase in the cumulative chance that the award number will not be higher. To be more concrete, since $400,000 is 75% of the way between $100,000 and $500,000, there is a 75% probability that the award will be at $400,000 or lower, and only a 25% probability that it will be between $400,000 and $500,000. And the way we've described this neat and clean hypothetical, there is 0% chance that the award will be higher than $500,000.

As is so often true, the math gets a little bit more complicated when reality intervenes—when using numbers that better reflect our *imprecise knowledge*. It is generally unwise and inaccurate to claim a 100% chance that an outcome will fall within a certain range or a 0% chance that it won't. We are wiser, and less likely to be proven wrong, by predicting a 90% chance that an outcome will be higher than $X and a 90% chance that it will not be lower than $Y. There is no magic to 90%. The parameter could be 95% or 85%.

When using statistics to test the strength of evidence and empirical or experimental studies, 95% is the most common measure or dividing line. For example, when examining a claim of class-wide discrimination, the statistician is asked the probability that an age, race, or gender distribution found in the employee population would have occurred by chance. If the statistician finds a 5% (or lower) probability that the distribution occurred by chance, and thus a 95% (or higher) probability that it occurred as a result of discriminatory practice or culture, the case for discrimination is recognized as strong. To avoid jumping to a conclusion with severe consequences, courts often err on the side of conservatism and require a 95% cut off.

Conservatism may cut the other way for a tree-builder in litigation. When choosing the end points for a range of possible outcomes, is it better to ask and answer: (1) What are the bounds beyond which the actual outcomes would fall only 5% of the time, at the high and low end?; or (2) What are the bounds beyond which actual outcomes would fall up to 10% of the time? The fictional assumption underlying both questions is still that the trial would be repeated many, many times. For a "95%/5%" figure, the tree builder must strain to think wider—to imagine possible outcomes far outside of the ordinarily predicted. For the "90%/10%" figure, the tree-builder must still reach for the improbable outlier, just a little bit less so. The reason it matters for the analysis (particularly in a potentially large dollar case), is that math works differently.

The more difficult question is whether it is best practice to ask for the 90%/10% numbers or the 95%/5% numbers. The source of our quandary is too much knowledge about the power of anchoring and tendencies toward "tightness of range." If the tree builder or lawyer has come up with a mid-point (articulated or not), and is asked for numbers further out, at the 90% or 95% end of a possible range, we justifiably fear the midpoint will serve as an anchor. His tendency will be to adjust insufficiently from the anchor. It would be dishonest, but tempting, to ask for the 95%/5% range, but act as if it were 90%/10%.

Of course, honesty, transparency, and discussion must trump temptation. It makes sense, perhaps, to ask first for both ends of the 90%/10% range: "Focusing on the high end, can you name a jury verdict number such that you can say with confidence, you are 90% sure it wouldn't be higher than this, or, you are 100% sure it wouldn't be higher than this 90% of the time?" The same question should be asked on the low end. Then, it's worthwhile to ask: "Well, what if the question was 95%, how much would your numbers change?" Then, it's worth asking whether the new numbers best inhabit the 95% or the 90% place. That may be a way to nudge further away from an unintended anchor.

Before moving to explain the correct mathematical way to account for these numbers, it is worth noting that if I am confident that 90% of the results will be lower than X and that 90% of the results will be higher than Y, I have carved out only 80% of the total range of possible numbers. A 10% tail is left at each end. When the question is asked at 95%, for both high and low, only 90% of the range is covered, with a 5% tail at each end.

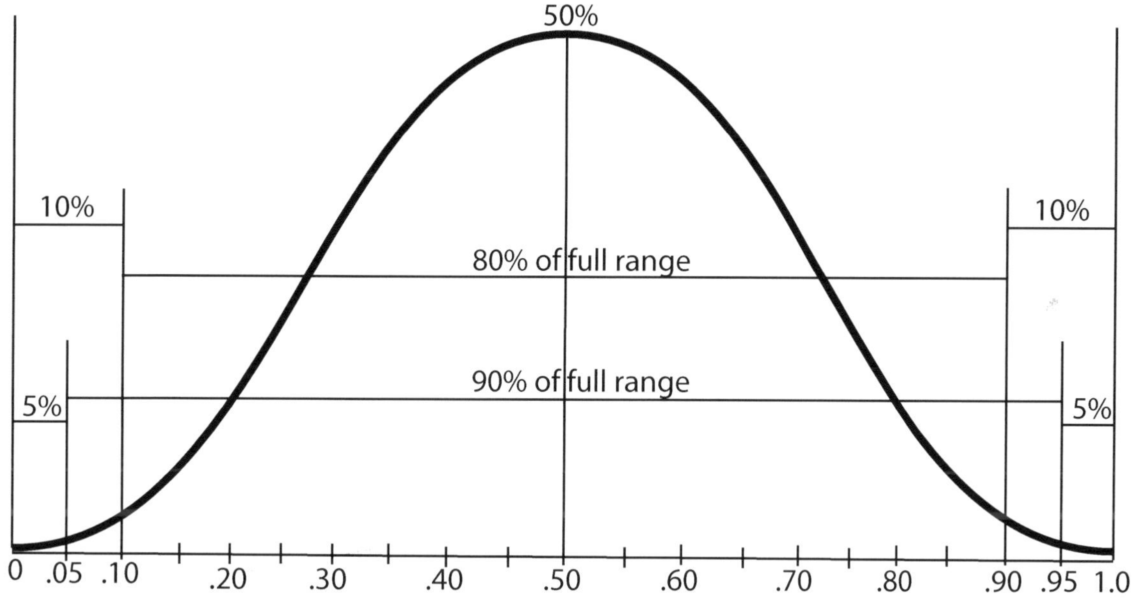

Math Matters where The Number isn't the Answer

There are right and wrong ways to insert probabilities to account for a continuous range. Here's the *wrong* way—one I confess to having used too in earlier days:

> Ask: "Can you imagine a jury award that is so high that nine times out of ten, the jury award would be lower than that, or you are 90% sure the jury award will be lower?" And so on, for the middle and then the low end.

Then, the wrong thing to do is to assign 10% to the high outcome, 80% to the middle one and 10% to the low one, and use those probabilities and numbers when rolling back to an EMV.

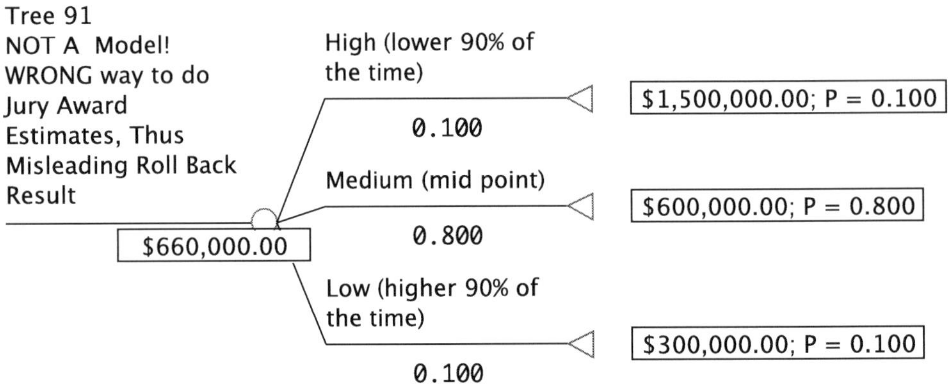

Note that we have assumed a damages range of $1,000,000, $600,000, and $200,000 for all of these examples.

This is wrong because it underweights the *real* extremes. If you think about it, you see that this calculation assumes that the result will *never* be higher than X or lower than Y. In fact, each *is assumed to happen 10% of the time.* Thus, the EMV fails to fully account for the impact of that remaining portion of the range that exists above X or below Y. Yet the goal, when working with a continuous range, is to account for every possible outcome in the range and to give each appropriate weight.

When the end node is acknowledged to be a continuous range, the 90%, 50%, or 10% numbers have been selected to describe that entire range. It's important not to lose sight of the goal: to capture the entire range and appropriately include it in the analysis. As well as possible, we seek to mathematically recreate every point on a line and the probability underneath it. Thus, really, the numbers are target points along the range. Our calculations should enable the target numbers to "radiate" or expand to the space between the numbers, thus covering the entire line. We are using those numbers to carve the line into segments, or "fractiles" (the mathematical term).

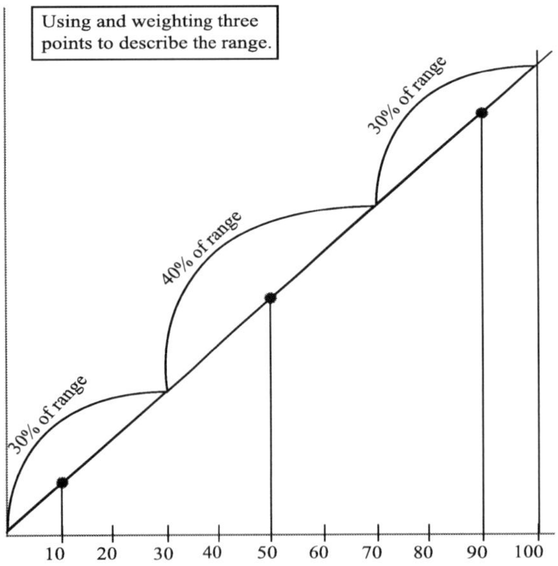

Three is generally accepted as the minimum number of points needed to approximate a distribution. If you want to use the 10%, 50%, and 90% fractiles, one approach often used is to assign a .30 probability to the 10% fractile, a .40 probability to the 50% fractile, and a .30 probability of the 90% fractile. Why use .30, .40, and .30 as weights? The supporting math is beyond the capability of this author or the level of this piece.[6] As Professor George Wu, noted in his HBS Note, Canonical Decision Problems (N9-396-308, April 8, 1996), "It turns out that .30, .40, and .30 work well in approximating many standard probability distributions, including symmetric distributions such as the normal."

Other well-respected scholars and practitioners of decision analysis, R. T. Clemen and M. Victor, suggest applying .25, .5, and .25 as weights for the 10%, 50% and 90% fractiles.[7]

Returning to our hypothetical case, here's what the damages end of the tree would look like, with the prescribed weighting or probabilities, under the two methods.

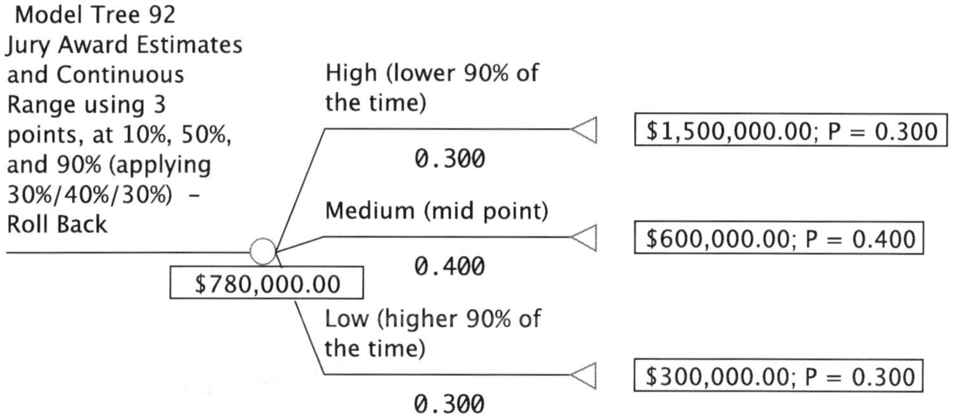

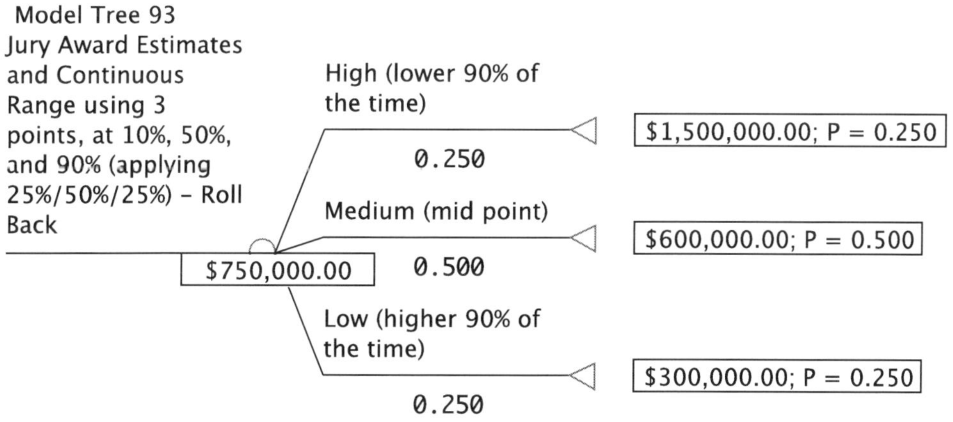

[6] Professor Wu provides the following reference for a more extended discussion of the bracket median method and other approximation techniques: Keefer, Donald and Bodily, Samuel, "Three-point Approximations for Continuous Random Variables," *Management Science* 29 (1983):595-609; or Bell, David and Schleifer Jr., Arthur, *Decision Making Under Uncertainty* (1995):46-59.

[7] Chapter 12 in Victor, Marc; Glidden, Craig; Lea, Clyde; and Whitworth, J. Bryan, "Evaluating Legal Risks and Costs with Decision Tree Analysis," *Successful Partnering Between Inside and Outside Counsel* (2000):11.

Obviously, the EMV numbers are different. Just as importantly, the probability of each portion of the outcome range is different.

Given that two sets of highly respected decision analysts disagree somewhat as to the "right" weights for the 90%, 50%, and 10% fractiles: .30/.40/.30 vs. .25/.50/.25—that is left to the tree builder's judgment. It all comes back to his sense of the case. To what extent does he suspect the outcomes will cluster closer to the middle? If the midpoint seems stronger, then he might use .25/.50/.25. It feels like the distribution would be flatter along the middle, then perhaps using .30/.40/.30 is the better choice. The good news is that, especially if using software, it's easy to try both.

Another three-point approach called "extended Pearson-Tukey method" uses the median or midway point and the 5% and 95% fractiles. As reflected on the tree below, the tree builder would consider what amount would be higher than 95% of all possible damages awards and what would be lower than all but 5% of all possible awards, and which is considered the median—50% would be higher and 50% would be lower. Note that the question is not about "average," but rather the median. Then the 95% and 5% estimates would be assigned a probability of .185 and the median (the .50 fractile estimate) would be assigned a probability of .630.[8]

Assuming that our tree-builder would acknowledge higher highs and lower lows if using 95% and 5%, our hypothetical tree might look like the figure below, and roll back to a damages EMV as indicated.

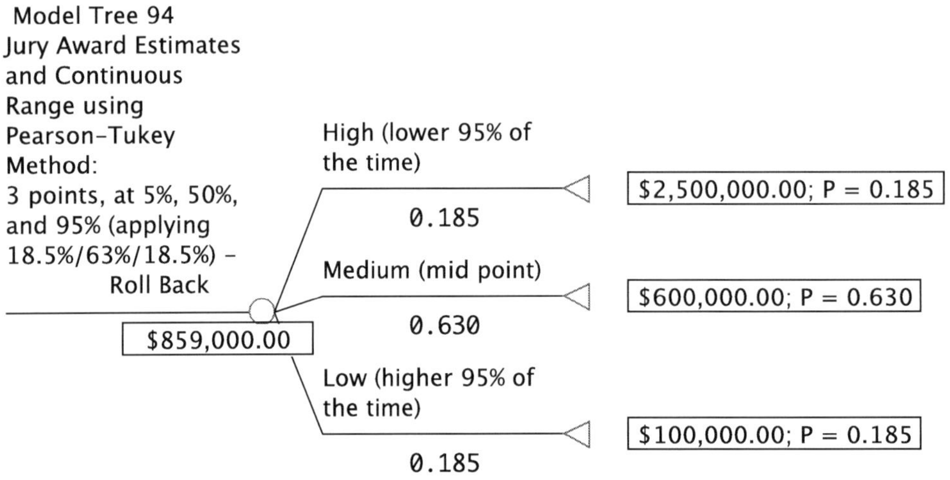

Note that this tree includes a higher number to factor in the possible "runaway" or angry jury. The facts of the case suggest greater range on the high side.

From Abstraction to Application

As discussed earlier, the lawyer should be mindful of partisan biases and anchoring influenced by those biases. To reiterate, best practices involve first considering factors that would drive a jury number away from the desired direction, and then more favorable factors. So, when the plaintiff client asks, "What's the most I could realistically hope for?," the lawyer might first take into account certain less favorable but irrefutable facts: the plaintiff is reasonably wealthy already and the defendant did not act willfully. On

[8] Clemen, Robert, *Making Hard Decisions* (1996): 278-279.

the other hand, the accident was terrifying for the plaintiff, and the defendant's negligence could have hurt many others

Assume you are assigning values at an end node to the right of a "high damages" branch of a "high—medium—low" triplet. You might ask yourself: "At what number am I pretty sure that only 10% of the actual numbers—real jury awards—would be higher? Or, if this case was tried many, many times, and there were a liability verdict 100 times, at what number would at least 90% of the verdicts be lower? At what number would 50% be higher and 50% be lower?"

Using the fractile percentages discussed above, you would assign weights of .25, .50, and .25, or .30, .40, and .30 to these numbers.

Or, you might ask yourself: "At what numbers am I pretty sure that only 5% of actual awards will be higher, and 5% lower?" Using the Pearson-Tukey approach, you would assign weights of .185 to the high number, .63 to the median, and .185 to the lower number.

As was true for estimating probabilities, it's important to avoid the problem of anchoring to a number influenced by bias, followed by insufficient adjustment. Thus, it's not wise for the decision analyst to start by asking of defense counsel, "What's the worst that could happen?," take his first guess, and then try to argue with it, citing the case's unattractive facts or data from similar cases that landed far higher.

From Simplest Three to Five Point Brackets or More

Nowhere is it written that a continuous range must be described by only three points. Another approach utilizes "bracket medians." The tree builder estimates what the median damages number would be within certain intervals or brackets—say 0%–20%, 20%–40%, 40%-60%, 60%-80%, and 80%-100% cumulative probability. Then the question becomes: what is the median number within each bracket range—the number at which the probability is midway between the two ends of the bracket, at the 10%, 30%, 50%, 70%, or 90% marks. Multiply .20 x each of five numbers that plot out the 10%, 30%, 50%, 70%, 90% points on the curve and you would have the damages EMV for the continuous range.

For the mathematically and graphically inclined, see the next figure demonstrating what the bracket median would look like.[9]

[9] A savvy decision analyst might use this method when he senses the range isn't exactly continuous – through a series of questions – basically asking what the lawyer/client thinks would be the median number in the bracket range. Or, you could make a graph and figure it out by seeing how the line plots. I cannot guarantee how meaningful this type of questioning would be, but it may be a way of getting at cases with discrete points – theories that cause you to favor one target damages number over another. It's worth considering which of these two ways to estimate and weigh damages – discrete points vs. a continuous probability distribution – is a better fit for the case.

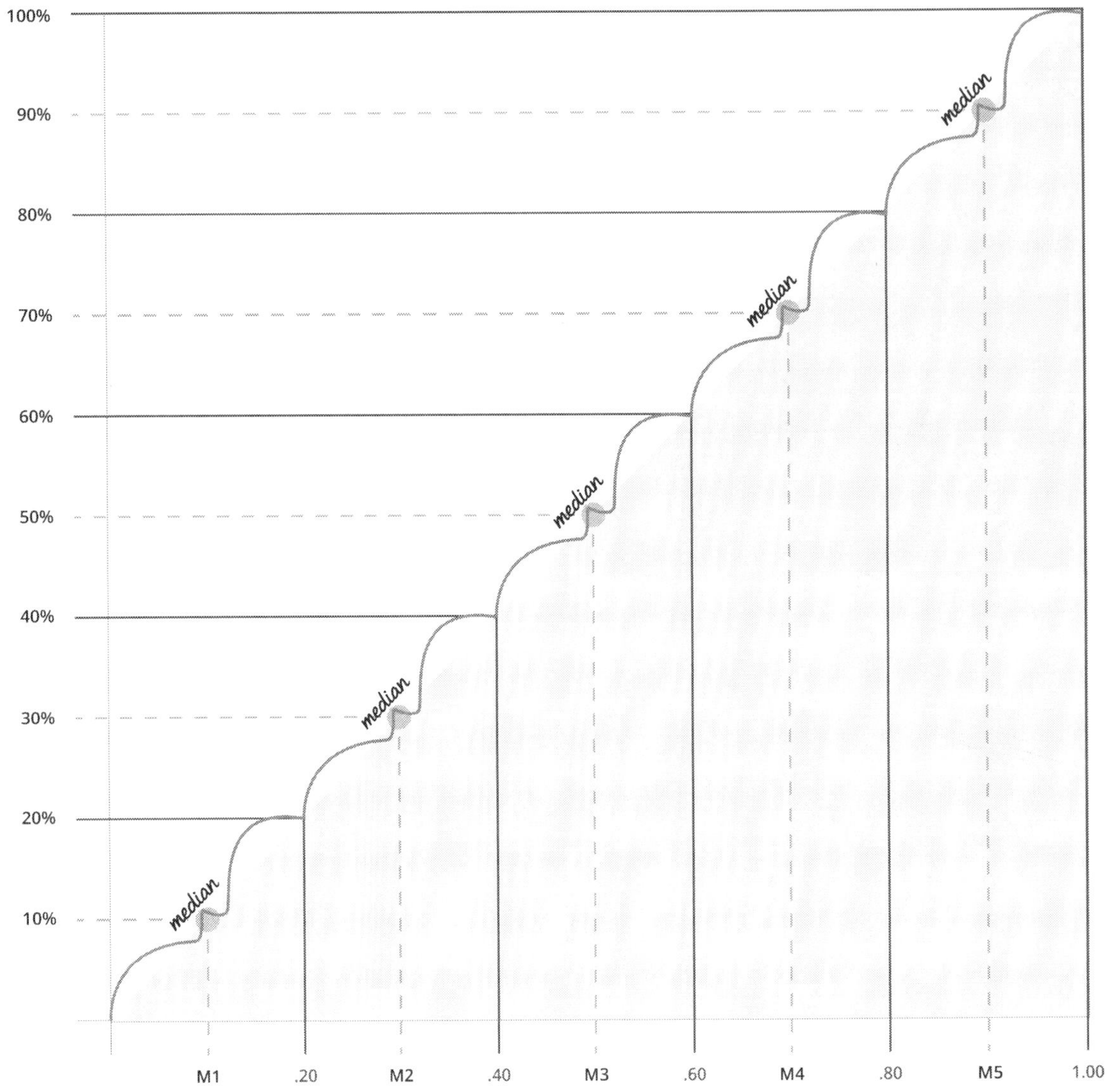

Here is what the tree would look like using the median bracket numbers, and then rolled back to a damages EMV. [10]

[10] Founder of the field, Professor Howard Raiffa, offers a terrifically illustrative dialog between a decision analyst and a subject (client) to determine fractiles for calculating a continuous range in a hypothetical case, in Raiffa, Howard, *Decision Analysis: Introductory Lectures on Choices under Uncertainty* (1968): 161-165.

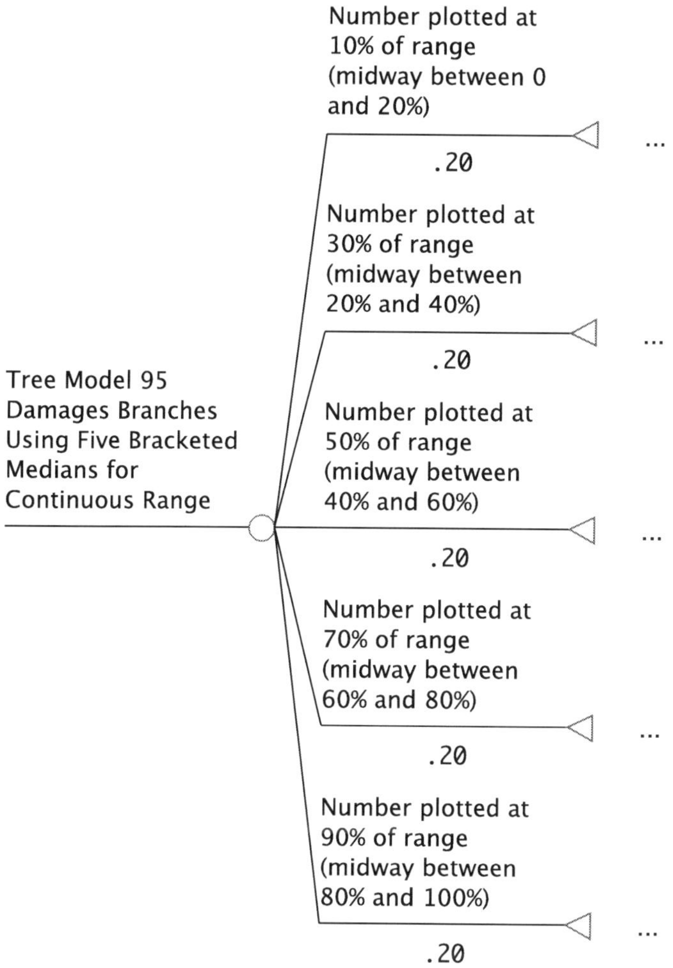

Data is Theoretically Good and Practically Challenging

Once again, if probative jury verdict data were available, it could theoretically be used as the basis for a neutral anchor point.[11] However, what is possible in theory may not be possible in the many legal cases where damages are inextricably linked to specific and often numerical evidence.[12] Damages in breach of contract cases turn on the contract terms, on lost profits, reliance claims, or other consequences of the breach. While data from personal injury cases may provide insight into damages for certain types of injuries, many case specific factors affect the award. Perhaps the average wrongful death case in the county yielded a jury award of $300,000. But what if most of those cases involved deaths in childbirth or shortly thereafter, and thus little or no economic damages? In this case, the deceased was a high wage earner, on whom his family relied. How relevant are the other wrongful death cases?

[11] As indicated earlier, some jury verdict research databases include settlements. These clearly should not be included in any calculation of jury verdict averages or range. The data sought for the neutral anchor is an average or range of awards AFTER a jury has found liability.

[12] For a second opinion on the benefits of empirical data in legal case analysis, see Levin, Kay, "The Law is Not the Case: Incorporating Empirical Methods into the Culture of Case Analysis," *Journal of Law and Public Policy* (2006).

The same might be said in employment cases—the highest verdicts in this federal district might have been between $600,000 and $800,000, but what was the wage base? Were emotional distress or punitive damages included? What was the ratio of base lost wages to emotional distress or punitive damages? Using caution and critical discernment, the decision tree analyst-lawyer might look at a sizeable data base of employment cases, for example, to calculate an average ratio between back pay and total award (if possible), and apply that ratio.

Jury verdict data can also be useful for reducing bias when trying to imagine a possible verdict range for your client's case. As was true for predicting probabilities, the larger the data pool (all federal age discrimination cases versus those within your federal circuit or district court), the greater the likelihood of broad verdict ranges. If you use the jury verdict number from the high or low end of a broad range for your "high" and "low" estimates, the lower the likelihood that your client will be unpleasantly surprised by an actual award outside the range. However, if you use a narrower data pool, its range may be misleadingly narrow. In a smaller data pool, one or two extreme outcomes among a small number may very much skew the average and cause exaggerated alarm or optimism (depending upon where they fall). Yet, removing or failing to count what seem to be extremes as so-called "outliers" may eliminate entirely possible outcomes—possibilities that should be considered in the analysis.

Whether or not external data is appropriately entered into damages estimates in a client's decision tree, this data might be discussed to temper what appear to be entirely optimistic projections, on the plaintiff's or the defense side.[13] To the defense client who believes that the worst exposure he may have in this sexual harassment case is $1 million, it is worth pointing out that at least twenty, or X% of all sexual harassment cases with liability findings ended with verdicts well over $Y million. To the plaintiff's lawyer or client confident that, if she wins, the verdict will of course be more than $5 million, it is worth pointing to data establishing that there have been only three verdicts at that level in the last five years. Moreover, in more than 80% of sexual harassment cases where the plaintiff won, the award amount was less than $1.5 million. Indeed, in 50% of the cases, it was $100,000 or lower—whatever the truth is.

If possible, the tree builder should introduce the data early in the process of estimating numerical outcomes—before initial numbers have been named. Indeed, the external data, to the extent it is probative, might be considered along with the list of positive and negative case factors considered.

Being Wrong

Given that the litigation will not be played ten or a hundred times, but only once, our probability predictions for most tree branches cannot be proven wrong (unless a possibility and thus a branch was missing and then occurs). In other words, if the tree-builder recorded an 80% chance of surviving summary judgment, the only way to test its accuracy is to "play" the summary judgment motion repeatedly, to see if the survival rate averages 80%.[14] But, if a tree-builder predicts a range of possible outcomes (after a liability verdict) from $100,000 to $500,000, allocating 100% probability across that range, he is rather

[13] Despite appearances to the contrary, I am not proposing that the decision analyst use external data to manipulate projections. Full disclosure as to what's contained in the data references is important. And integrity demands an effort to use data that does relate to the question at hand.

[14] According to Breiman, this can be somewhat artificially accomplished by creating a significant number of decision trees regarding the same problem ("forests") where each tree has randomly selected, say, 10% of data removed or altered and the final EMVs for all trees are averaged to arrive at an answer that better accounts for all of the

definitively proven wrong by a "surprise" verdict at $1,000,000 or $10,000 (or any number far greater than $500,000 or far lower than $100,000). In short, there's "exposure" for the decision analyst if an outcome estimate is inadequate. The client will notice if the highest number in the payoff range on a pre-trial decision tree was $600,000 and the damages award comes in at $5,000,000.

Refinement by the Factor of Time Value

Oh patient reader, before closing what might be viewed as the most technical portion of this text, please bear with one last foray into mathematical method. It would be irresponsible not to explain and suggest finding and using the present value of estimated numerical outcomes on a decision tree.

In large dollar cases, particularly where the time frame to trial is lengthy and ambient interest rates are high, technically the best practice is to use the discounted present value of anticipated dollar recoveries or losses.[15] Imagine a world in which trial wouldn't take place for two years, and the general interest rate is 12% per annum (or the particular client earns a 12% return on investments). Without compounding, paying $1,000,000 now would be equivalent to paying $1,240,000 in two years. From a different perspective, a verdict of $1,240,000 in two years would be equivalent to approximately $1,000,000 in today's dollars. Unless the estimated attorney's fees will be incurred only after two years—close in time to the trial—discounting would not be applied to the attorney's fee portion of anticipated expenditures.[16] There's no magic to the operation of discounting to present value. Once the interest rate and time frame are set, it can be done on a calculator or using common financial software.

Present value of a future amount can be derived as follows: Present value is the Future Value = the future anticipated award/(1 + r)n, where "4" is the rate of return (inerest rate on money) and "n" is the length of time.

Let's take a case in which your client may receive $100,000 in 3 years when the litigation is complete. Keeping it simple, we're assuming there's a liquidated damages clause, and your client will either win or lose his breach of contract claim. There is no middle ground. Let's further assume that your client's general rate of return on invested funds is 5%.

Present value of that award would be: $100,000/(1.05)3, or $100,000/1.157635 = $86,484.99.

The higher the number of years between the present and anticipated recovery, and the higher your client's rate of return on investments, the greater the discount. In short, the discounted present value becomes lower.

Using the same example, if verdict and payment were estimated to take four years, and your client generally earns a 10% rate of return, the present value of that future $100,000 verdict would be: $100,000/(1.10)4 = $100,000/1.4641 = $68,301.34[17]

---

possible real world variations from the integrated data. Breiman, Leo, "Statistical Modeling: The Two Cultures," *Statistical Science* 16, no. 3 (2001):199–231

[15] Greenberg, Ronald, "The Lawyer's Use of Quantitative Analysis in Settlement Negotiations," *The Business Lawyer* 38 (1983):1557-1586.

[16] Id. at 1576-1577, footnote 103 (description of formula and diagram of integration into decision trees). Theoretically, one could also discount attorneys' fees to present value based upon when they would be incurred. The emphasis here is on "theoretically."

[17] Id. at 1557-1586.

Reassessing the discounted present value at future stages in litigation (some time later) is also advisable if there is still a chance of a revised settlement offer.[18] Interest at 12% or higher was common in the late 1980's and early '90's, but not in more recent history. As of this writing, bank accounts yield well below 1%. Thus, the author admits to often skipping the present value discount, particularly on trees done quickly, and to generate client discussion. Often, cases subjected to decision analysis are scheduled for trial within a relatively short time frame. (If a significant statutory or contract interest rate will apply to a damages award, timed from the date of breach, for example, I would recommend calculating interest as part of the anticipated "pay-off" for the plaintiff, or exposure for the defense.)

Nevertheless, it can be useful to point out that $100,000 received in settlement today, and then invested, might be worth far more over time. Even at modest interest rates or anticipated rates of return, a $100,000 settlement received now would be worth considerably more in three or four years, by the time the trial would have concluded.

To find that future value—that would have been received, calculate

- $F = P (1 + r)^n$, where
- P is the amount presently invested
- r is the rate of return
- n is the number of years
- F is the future value that would be received.

If the settlement offer is $100,000, and your client claims a rate of return on investments of 8%, over 3 years, the calculation is $100,000 (1.08)3 = $100,000 x 1.259712= $125,971.

The truth is that in a high dollar case, or where rates of return are significant and the time to trial is long, best practice is to work with present value calculations. Where a client resists using these numbers directly on the tree, you might simply write them in the margin of the tree document, or reference them in discussion. Some business clients are used to dealing in present value calculations and welcome their incorporation here.

---

[18] The same math would apply to a discussion with your client regarding the high cost of investing present dollars in the litigation (from the plaintiff's or the defense side). Imagine a large high stakes case, requiring initial investment of $100,000 in attorneys' fees, investigation, discovery and initial expert consultations within the first year of litigation. (Let's leave aside for the moment later amounts to be expended in pretrial preparations and motions.) It's fair to note that if the client could have invested those funds into something else, it would be worth more over time.

To find that future value—calculate: $F = P (1 + r)^n$, where

- P is the amount presently invested
- r is the rate of return
- n is the number of years
- F is the future value that would be received.

If your client must soon invest $100,000, and its common rate of return is 5%, over 5 years, the calculation is $100,000 (1.05)5 = $100,000 x 1.2762815 = $127,688.

Yes, you could subtract this higher fee number from the discounted value of the anticipated verdict when calculating the net payoff. On the other hand, the intellectually honest decision analyst will also note that fees and costs paid well into the future would be discounted down, in the same way as the anticipated recovery.

Congratulations!

All who have followed this text and its trees up to this point have shown patience and commitment to learning the basics and more advanced subtleties of decision analysis for legal cases. Congratulations!

The truth is that lawyers develop and discuss decision trees with clients; mediators develop and discuss trees with lawyers and their clients in mediation; and decision tree experts are retained as consultants by lawyers, clients, or mediators as consultants. Technicalities aside, lawyer-client or mediator relationships and emotions become involved. Often, the tree reveals that the path to a desired outcome is more complicated and uncertain, the risks greater, and the range of outcomes wider than the client had wished. The tree maps the possible realities, and that map may not be pretty. The upcoming section explains how decision analysis can facilitate communication that protects the lawyer, client, and mediator relationships.

13

Centered Communication With Pictures, Grace, and Rigor

As great as the value of analytical rigor required for a competent decision tree, the value of the tree is greater for client communication.[1]

All about the Map, Painted Without Numbers

First, and perhaps most obvious, is that the tree's visual map lays out the twists, turns, and possible paths of a complex litigation. It reveals where various parts fit within the whole, pins down and orders layers of uncertainty, and displays the full array of foreseeable endings to the story. As much as the arithmetic may prove enlightening, often just seeing the complexity of that map is most important and proves sufficient for the client. In one case, after the mediator worked through a particularly complicated, multi-layered tree, the roomful of plaintiffs were sobered to see the many hurdles standing in their way. The large dollar amount sought looked like a "needle in a haystack," just one among so many other less desirable, unpalatable, or untenable results. After the case's uncertainties are mapped onto a tree, the certainty associated with settlement has far greater appeal. Often, once the tree is built, the client is not terribly interested in the math.

Grit and Grace in the Face of Bad News

Unfortunately, we know that some lawyers just don't deliver bad news to their clients for fear of being considered insufficiently zealous or loyal. I like to think that most lawyers do make the effort to convey unwelcome messages. Consider the task of this defense lawyer: the defendant company's chief engineer —the client's key witness—was astoundingly arrogant at deposition, despite coaching. The plaintiff seemed to be the most sincere "boy scout" type. He has drawn the most plaintiff-friendly judge in the district. The defense lawyer can't make a straight face argument that there's no factual dispute. There's no chance this case will be dismissed on summary judgment. He can't make such a motion and remain within the bounds of professional conduct. Surely, he would explain these problems to the company's CEO.

[1] For a nuanced, thoughtful, and more fully developed discussion of how a mediator, including a settlement conferencing judge, can effectively use risk assessment in talking with lawyers and parties about settlement, see Michaela Keet, "Informed Decision-Making in Judicial Mediation and the Assessment of Litigation," 33 *Ohio State Journal of Dispute Resolution* (2018): 65-83.

Let's imagine that the CEO is somewhat hot-blooded, defensive, and unused to disagreement from those he considers subordinates, and that includes lawyers. It's easy to see how the conversation might not go well. Imagine lawyer and CEO sitting opposite each other, face to face. The CEO asks for an update, pushes for dismissal of this "nuisance" and is not at all happy when the lawyer explains his unwillingness to attempt that. "Well, fine, I get that there are rules, but our engineer is right—his credentials and experience are impeccable, and he will carry the case. The plaintiff was just plain reckless and now he's greedy." When the lawyer challenges these assertions, it feels like just that, a challenge. The dynamics of the conversation—face-to-face disagreement—can become uncomfortable.

The decision tree itself doesn't change the bad news or render the lawyer's analysis any rosier. But now replay the scene in your mind's eye, this time with lawyer and client seated either side by side, or even across the table but with the decision tree between them or up on a projector. (The lawyer might have brought a prepared tree structure, or he might draw it as they discuss the case.) When the lawyer explains the unwelcome developments, he and the client are both looking at the tree. The lawyer might have scribbled or typed factors relevant to his probability assessments on the tree document or on a separate sheet. Their joint task is analytical, as is their language, and it is directed at the decision tree exercise. In effect, the method intervenes; it becomes an inter-mediator. It doesn't change the bad news, but does tend to change their conversational dynamic. Perhaps it is too obvious to say that this is also helpful for official mediators seeking to discuss the merits with parties and counsel, without compromising perceived neutrality.

A Place to Offer the Lead or Piggyback Part Way

We all know that people prefer to reach their own conclusions. They more readily accept the need to act on their own conclusions than those of others. Thus, to the extent that the client has generated or readily agreed with the tree's logic, structure, probabilities, and payoffs, that client is more likely to pay attention to the picture it paints and to its mathematical results. Unlike the last scenario described, the client may see summary judgment as impossible or a long shot where they understand the legal standard. He may see some of the risks on liability, if not as strongly as the lawyer or mediator. In other words, perhaps after some discussion, the client's views on most, if not all, issues may not be significantly different from that of his tree-builder lawyer or the mediator. If so, consider creating a tree with the client's preferred probabilities and estimated outcomes. Then just do the math to get the EMV and probabilities for each outcome.

Assuming the client's comfort with the method's logic, it's hard for him to reject the results of an analysis that was based on inputs he generated or agreed were sound. Imagine that the analysis reveals an EMV of $375,000, a 40% chance of escaping liability, costs of $75,000, and a range of net payoffs between $200,000 and $1,000,000 (including statutory costs and fees). Let's say that approximately 20% of the outcomes involve net payoffs higher than $600,000. Even if the client was previously unwilling to settle for more than $50,000, he may be willing to reconsider. Maybe he'll get to the $250,000 or $300,000 range, signaled as doable by plaintiff's counsel. When we own the input, it's harder for us to disavow the output.

Often, the tree-builder lawyer or mediator can "piggy-back" on select issues. In other words, seek and use the client's input or agreement on many issues; avoid quibbling over small stuff.[2] (Note however, at least for the lawyer, it is important to communicate your very different views on major issues.[3]) Imagine a negligence case in which you agree that the company's expert is strong, as are the documents, and there's a decent chance of escaping liability. But, let's also assume that, as a legal matter, you see a possibility of finding malice, willfulness, or recklessness and that will lead to double or treble damages. The client grudgingly acknowledges that this is technically possible, so it has to be on the tree. But he would assign it negligible probability—5%.

As the lawyer, you respectfully disagree. You acknowledge none of the company's engineers were actually willful or reckless, but experience tells you the jury that finds liability may be an angry jury. This will depend on the engineers' presentations, a disgruntled employee's credibility, and the plaintiff's likeability. Unfortunately, the disgruntled employee was quite convincing and likeable at deposition, as was the plaintiff. The company's engineers could charitably be described as wooden and confusing. Thus, if liability is found, you think there's at least a 30% chance the damages will be multiplied. You can explain how you see it, and adjust the percentage. When you roll it back and review the outcome distributions, it's still difficult for your client to reject the entirety.

With some clients, one real benefit of working through the tree and its numerical estimates is that it may be unnecessary to challenge or disagree directly or immediately. Instead, you can gracefully suggest playing "what if?" for various uncertainties. Where the client insists that a probability is low, say 5%, you can suggest: "Just in case we draw a problem jury, let's start with your 5% and ask, what if it were 10%, or 20%, or 30%, what impact would that have? What would that tree look like?" You can change the percentages and roll it back each time. It can be persuasive to see an array of trees, various compromises from the lawyer's initial and unwelcome view, but still problematic.

One option is to display the range of results in a formal sensitivity analysis. Or, when particular questions are just too uncertain or prickly to discuss, it's helpful to suggest, "What if we just go with 50/50 on these—what if we really leave it to chance? After all, it has to be one way or the other." Again, the dialog has shifted from tug of war or ego to curiosity and a coin toss game.

There It Is; and Its In There

In some cases, a client's or lawyer's assertions about issues that underlie a prediction or settlement position seem to shift, a bit like a shell game, as the discussion proceeds. "Yes," acknowledges the business executive, "We said our suspicions about fraud were raised by the loss in income, but really it was all about the discrepancy in expenses." Or, "I see your point on that issue, but our case valuation really rests on our strength on this more important issue."

[2] Whether or not the mediator should or will do so is a matter of some dispute in the field. This depends both upon the mediator's practice and competence, the client's and attorney's expectations, as well as mediation philosophies and constraints of provider expectations and governing law or court rule.

[3] Considerations of tact aside, the lawyer may be obligated to provide his own assessments at some point—assuming client wants to know them. In any event, the lawyer cannot mislead regarding those assessments.

When mapped on a tree, each issue is put in its place. It becomes apparent which issues have stronger and weaker impact on the analysis. For less important issues, the decision tree builder may be able to demonstrate that, even if that uncertainty is, in essence, taken off the table, or the damages argument in contention is granted, the overall results don't change much at all. Or, where an issue is indeed significant, it becomes clear that, if that issue is lost, the other issues under discussion just cannot outweigh it.

In other instances, the client will take comfort and put more stock in the decision tree where you can clearly point to where on that tree an important value has been placed. This brings to mind a terrible wrongful death case, in which the deceased had suffered for six months in a halo cast before succumbing to her injuries from a fall. Proving liability would have been fraught with legal and factual hurdles, which led to a relatively low estimated monetary value (EMV) when the case's tree was rolled back. The deceased's widower had initially felt that accepting settlement in the range of this dollar value meant disloyalty to his wife, as if he agreed her life was worth only that. For the widower, it was helpful to be able to point to the damages number on the tree in the millions of dollars, and to say, "First, there's no value high enough to measure your wife's life. Please know that for the purposes of this decision tree, we've assumed that if liability were found, a jury would find damages of at least $2 million and up to $5 million or more. And you can see those values—here they are—on the tree. It's the legal uncertainties and the math that operate to give us the other number." In fact, that mattered to the widower. He was able to feel that he had been loyal to his wife's memory, because the high values were visible "right in there."

Subtle, Strong, and Welcome Powers

As discussed, both lawyer and client benefit tremendously from thinking through the questions and analysis necessary to build the tree and assign probabilities and payoffs. The lawyer is forced to think carefully. The client understands where things stand when visible on a map. Hand waving, fuzziness, and confusion are reduced when lawyer and client view the branches, probabilities, and award estimates together. When questioning or discussing a particular legal or factual issue, it's helpful for the client to know where it sits, how it fits.

More subtle and just as powerful are the language of decision analysis and its ability to mediate and preserve the lawyer-client relationship.

The language of decision analysis is not emotional; it is rational and analytical. It requires serial acts of translation, from the more charged "great chance of beating those fools!" to "75%", or from "their CEO's arrogance can't hide!" to "40% chance of defense verdict." Indeed, it is fair to say that a client's willingness to entertain tree branches, percentages, and math indicates that he is at least tentatively adopting a "business judgment" approach. We know that businesses operate by assessing risk, cost, net profit, and loss; businesses sometimes cut losses, change course, or make other tough decisions in light of market experience, research, or educated projections. Business leaders generally opt against decisions that carry strong risks of cutting payroll or losing profit share.

The tree becomes a tangible representation of the "business judgment" perspective. Imagine a case with a simple decision tree that rolls back to an EMV between $250,000 and $155,000 (where the tree shows high possible exposure and uses probability estimates far more optimistic than the lawyer suggests). Yet, the plaintiff's final, bottom line demand is $100,000. No matter how angry the executive, it's harder to justify spending the company's money to roll this dice at trial. Seeing the case mapped on a tree literally separates the analytical from the emotional. The executive's avowed fealty to business considerations may enable the analytical to govern his settlement decision.

More broadly, and more accurately, the tree becomes a visual representation of "rationality" for a client struggling to make a decision. Even where the tree is very, very simple—win vs. lose in arbitration—I have seen it help the plaintiff separate his feelings from what he understands to be a "rational" look at the legal case. That facilitates his discussion about those feelings, and also enables him to see more clearly why a settlement number might be in his own best interest. While I can't speak from direct experience, I am told that a decision tree can have the same effect in the most emotional cases of all—divorce! Shortly after being introduced to the method, a lawyer reported using it with her divorce clients. Just seeing the decision tree's map of the stages, uncertainties, and possible outcomes in divorce litigation enabled some clients to better understand it and, having seen it, to follow its more rational path.[4] In fact, in my experience, there's no predicting who will be receptive to a decision tree and who will not. I've seen corporate executives reject it out of hand, and the "artiste" or theoretically unsophisticated clients fully embrace the force of its logic.

Reality as Seeable, Touchable, and Evolving

The ability to see the decision tree's map of the case's possible twists and turns makes it invaluable not only for discussion with those in the room or on teleconference, but also for decision-makers who are not present. It eases a concern that the client representative will fail to convey a full message to a committee, to the boss, to the company's chief financial officer. If the client representative has the decision tree in hand or even better, distributed it prior to their meeting, we have greater confidence that the full analysis will be presented. Or, the tree will prompt the ultimate committee or CFO decision maker to raise questions and seek more complete explanations tied to the analysis.

In many instances, the lawyer or mediator will have presented quite a convincing analysis to the client representative. She understands why it makes sense to settle a case at an unexpected amount, or even why it makes sense to reject an offer. Her challenge is to avoid higher ups' accusations that she "caved too easily" or "missed out." The decision tree document is solid back up. It allows the representative to present a decision tree with a significant risk of a $900,000 loss and an EMV of $250,000 as back up for a lower settlement and evidence of her negotiation skills.

Thus, the tree brings reality to uncertainty and prompts consideration of the impact of consequences that may indeed become real.

Finally, the End of All Branches

With full apologies to Mr. Shakespeare and real poets everywhere, I offer this final ode to decision tree analysis for legal practice.

To use a decision tree or not to use a decision tree? That is the question:

Whether 'tis wiser to draw a tree and map all that uncertainty

[4] Reported to the author by Elayne Greenberg, then a divorce lawyer in New Jersey, now a Professor and Director of the Hugh L. Carey Center for Dispute Resolution at St. John's University School of Law.

Or skip the math and counsel through prose entirely.

Surely, Solomon, Portia and scions of our legal tradition,
Did muddle through on judgment and intuition.

Yet, decision analysis is a rubric for structure and rigor,
In cases requiring intellectual vigor.

Exposure in a case may be great,
And winning and losing issues hard to rate.

Parties and motions may be in odd array, or many
Damages theories set in the way.

Decision analysis isn't about dry calculation.
It's about structuring from speculation.

Thinking through uncertainty,
As you build a decision tree.

Often a case is a legal mess,
Settlement value's an uneasy guess.

Working through a decision tree can check or confirm intuition,
Providing logic and structure for your client's decision.

Decision analysis helps create a sense of separation,
Calming emotion to see reality as consideration.

It helps lawyer client communication be clearly made,
And strengthens the power of analysis to persuade.

Links to Video Inserts in Chapter Three on "How To's"

Video Insert 1: http://dx.doi.org/doi:10.7945/C22T3D

Video Insert 2: http://dx.doi.org/doi:10.7945/C2Z41T

Video Insert 3: http://dx.doi.org/doi:10.7945/C2T99B

Video Insert 4: http://dx.doi.org/doi:10.7945/C26M5B

Video Insert 5: http://dx.doi.org/doi:10.7945/C2PM5P

Video Insert 6: http://dx.doi.org/doi:10.7945/C2JX11

Video Insert 7: http://dx.doi.org/doi:10.7945/C2F39V

Video Insert 8: http://dx.doi.org/doi:10.7945/C29D6K

Video Insert 9: http://dx.doi.org/doi:10.7945/C25M4N

Video Insert 10: http://dx.doi.org/doi:10.7945/C21X2R

Video Insert 11: http://dx.doi.org/doi:10.7945/C2X396

Video Insert 12: http://dx.doi.org/doi:10.7945/C2SD79

Video Insert 13: http://dx.doi.org/doi:10.7945/C2NM40

Video Insert 14: http://dx.doi.org/doi:10.7945/C2HX3G

Video Insert 15: http://dx.doi.org/doi:10.7945/C2D40G

Video Insert 16: http://dx.doi.org/doi:10.7945/C28D81

Video Insert 17: http://dx.doi.org/doi:10.7945/C24M63

Video Insert 18: http://dx.doi.org/doi:10.7945/C20X2F

Video Insert 19: http://dx.doi.org/doi:10.7945/C2W416

Video Insert 20: http://dx.doi.org/doi:10.7945/C2RD70

Video Insert 21: http://dx.doi.org/doi:10.7945/C2MQ3B

Video Insert 22: http://dx.doi.org/doi:10.7945/C2GX1D

Video Insert 23: http://dx.doi.org/doi:10.7945/C2C68W

Video Insert 24: http://dx.doi.org/doi:10.7945/C27D6Z

Video Insert 25: http://dx.doi.org/doi:10.7945/C23Q42

Video Insert 26: http://dx.doi.org/doi:10.7945/C2ZX1R

Video Insert 27: http://dx.doi.org/doi:10.7945/C2V70J

Video Insert 28: http://dx.doi.org/doi:10.7945/C2QD7P

About Origins, Sources, and References

I hereby confess that only after I began teaching decision tree analysis, first to professional audiences through the CPR Institute for Conflict Resolution and Prevention and at the University of Cincinnati College of Law (with a few gigs in between), did I consult some of the original and growing literature on decision tree analysis beyond Marc Victor's excellent writings.

If this text attempted to include citations for every aspect of the method described, the reader would drown in footnotes. The truth is that decision analysis is not new. A celebration of the "Golden Anniversary of Decision Analysis," dated the field's origin to 1964 and attributes it to two professors: Howard Raiffa from Harvard, who made great advances in applying statistical decision theory to real-world problems, and Ronald Howard from Stanford (then on Sabbatical from MIT), who created an engineering approach to complex decision problems and called it "Decision Analysis." (See the archived blog article and interview at www.smartorg.com/golden-anniversary-decision-analysis-raiffa-howard-award-organizational-decision-quality/.)

Many, many texts and articles on decision analysis have followed, and many of these include attention to the subtopic of decision trees and litigation risk analysis. I have not attempted to list all of them here. Instead, this reference list includes books and articles I have found useful that generally inform what is written here. By way of further resources for the reader, it also includes some articles that broaden or deepen certain aspects of the use of decision tree analysis in legal practice.

Within the main text, I have included footnotes only for highly specific ideas or research findings attributable to particular book chapters and articles.

REFERENCES

Books

Aaron, Marjorie Corman. *Client Science: Advice for Lawyers on Counseling Clients through Bad News and Other Legal Realities*. New York: Oxford University Press (2012).

Bell, David E.; and Schleifer, Jr. Arthur. *Decision Making Under Uncertainty*. CA: Duxbury Press (1995).

Clemen, Robert T. *Making Hard Decisions: An Introduction to Decision Analysis*. Belmont, CA: Duxbury Press (1991, 1996).

Faigman, David; Blumenthal, Jerry; Cheng, Edward; Mnookin, Jennifer; Murphy, Erin; and Sanders, Joseph. *Modern Scientific Evidence: The Law and Science of Expert Testimony*. Eagan: Thomson Reuters (2014).

Hammond, John S.; Keeney, Ralph; and Raiffa, Howard. *Smart Choices: A Practical Guide to Making Better Life Decisions*. New York: Broadway (2002).

Hill, Percy H. *Making Decisions: A Multidisciplinary Introduction*. Reading, MA: Addison Wesley (1979).

Jackson, Howell E.; Kaplow, Louis; Shavell, Steven; Viscusi, W. Kip; and Cope, David. *Analytical Methods for Lawyers*. New York: Foundation (2003).

Kahneman, Daniel; Slovic, Paul; and Tversky, Amos, eds. *Judgment under uncertainty: Heuristics and biases*. Cambridge: Cambridge University Press (1982).

Kahneman, Daniel, T*hinking, Fast and Slow*. New York: Farrar, Straus and Giroux (2011).

Kiser, Randall. *Beyond Right and Wrong: The Power of Effective Decision Making for Attorneys and Clients*. Berlin: Springer (2010).

Morgan, Granger M.; Henrion, Max; and Small, Mitchell. *Uncertainty: A Guide to Dealing with Uncertainty in Quantitative Risk and Policy Analysis*. Cambridge: Cambridge University Press (1990).

Plous, Scott. *The Psychology of Judgment and Decision Making*. Philadelphia: Temple University Press (1993).

Raiffa, Howard,and Schlaifer, Robert. "Applied Statistical Decision Theory." Wiley Inter-Science (2000, original editions in the 1960s by Harvard and MIT in nearby presses).

Raiffa, Howard. *Decision Analysis; Introductory Lectures on Choices under Uncertainty*. Reading, MA: Addison-Wesley (1968).

Raiffa, Howard; Richardson, John; and Metcalfe, David. *Negotiation Analysis: The Science and Art of Collaborative Decision Making*. Cambridge, MA: Belknap of Harvard University Press (2002).

Robbennolt, Jennifer K., and Sternlight, Jean. *Psychology for Lawyers: Understanding the Human Factors in Negotiation, Litigation, and Decision Making*. Chicago: American Bar Association (2012).

Schulz, Kathryn. *Being Wrong: Adventures in the Margin of Error*. New York: Harper Collins (2010).

Articles and Other Sources on the Psychology of Decision Making, Assessment, Confidence and Prediction

Angner, Erik. "Economists as Experts: Overconfidence in Theory and Practice." *Journal of Economic Methodology* 13.1 (2006): 1-24.

Arkes, Hal; Christenen, Caryn; Lai, Cheryl; and Blumer, Catherine. "Two Methods of Reducing Overconfidence." *Organizational Behavior and Human Decision Making Processes* 39 (1987): 133-144.

Bazerman, Max H. "The Relevance of Kahneman and Tversky's Concept of Framing to Organizational Behavior." *Journal of Management* 10.3 (1984): 333-43.

Block, Richard A.; and Harper, David R. "Overconfidence in Estimation: Testing the Anchoring-and-Adjustment Hypothesis." *Organizational Behavior and Human Decision Processes* 49 (1991): 188-207.

Ehrlinger, Joyce; Gilovich, Thomas; and Ross, Lee. "Peering in to the Bias Blind Spot: People's Assessments of Bias in Themselves and Others." *Personality and Social Psychology Bulletin* 31, no. 5 (2005): 680-692.

Epley, Nicholas; and Gilovich, Thomas. "Putting Adjustment Back in the Anchoring and Adjustment Heuristic: Differential Processing of Self-Generated and Experimenter-Provided Anchors." *Psychological Science* 12.5 (2001): 391-396.

Epley, Nicholas; and Gilovich, Thomas. "The Anchoring-and-Adjustment Heuristic: Why the Adjustments Are Insufficient." *Psychological Science* 17.4 (2006): 311-318.

Flannelly, Laura, and Flannelly, Kevin. "Reducing People's Judgment Bias About their Level of Knowledge." *The Psychological Record* 50 (2000); 587-600.

George, Joey F.; Duffy, Kevin; and Ahuja, Manju. "Countering the Anchoring and Adjustment Bias with Decision Support Systems." *Decision Support Systems* 29.2 (2000): 195–206.

Gilliland, Victoria; and Dunn, John. "Decision Making in Civil Disputes: The Effects of Legal Role, Frame, and Perceived Chance of Winning." *Judgment and Decision Making*. 3.7 (2008): 512–527.

Gneezy, Uri; List, John; and Wu, George. "The Uncertainty Effect: When a Risky Prospect Is Valued Less than Its Worst Possible Outcome." *Quarterly Journal of Economics* 121.4 (2006): 1283-309.

Goodman-Delahunty, Jane; Granhag, Pär A.; and Loftus, E.F. "How Well Can Lawyers Predict Their Chances of Success?" Unpublished Manuscript (1998) (cited in Koehler, Derek J.; Brenner, Lyle; and Griffin, Dale. "The Calibration of Expert Judgment: Heuristics and Biases beyond the Laboratory," in Thomas Gilovich, ed. *Heuristics and Biases: The Psychology of Intuitive Judgment* (2002): 705–706.

Goodman-Delahunty, Jane; Granhag, Pär A.; Hartwig, Maria; and Loftus, Elizabeth F. "Insightful or Wishful: Lawyers' Ability to Predict Case Outcomes." *Psychology, Public Policy, and Law* 16.2 (2010): 133-157.

Guthrie, Chris. "Framing Frivolous Litigation: A Psychological Theory." *The University of Chicago Law Review* 67.1 (2000): 163-216.

Haran, Uriel; Moore, Don; and Morewedge, Carey. "A Simple Remedy for Overprecision in Judgment." *Judgment and Decision Making* 5.7 (2010): 467-476.

Hall, Brian J.; and Staats, P. Trent. "Do the Numbers Get in Your Way?" *Negotiation* 7.11 (2004).

Kahneman, Amos; and Tversky, Daniel. "Prospect Theory: An Analysis of Decision Under Risk." *Econometrica* 47 (1979): 263-291.

Kiser, Randall L.; Asher, Martin A.; and McShane, Blakely B. "Let's Not Make a Deal: An Empirical Study of Decision Making in Unsuccessful Settlement Negotiations." *Journal of Empirical Legal Studies* 5.3 (2008): 551-591.

Knox, Robert; and Inkster, James. "Postdecision Dissonance at Post Time." *Journal of Personality and Social Psychology* 8.4 (1968): 319-323.

Koriat, Asher; Lichtenstein, Sarah; and Fischhoff, Baruch. "Reasons for Confidence." *Journal of Experimental Psychology, Human Learning, and Memory* 6.2 (1980): 107-118.

Loftus, Elizabeth; and Wagenaar, William. "Lawyer's Predictions of Success" *Jurimetrics* 28 (1988): 437-453.

Lichtenstein, Sarah; and Fischhoff, Baruch. "Training for Calibration." *Organizational Behavior and Human Performance* 26 (1980): 149-171.

Northcraft, Gregory B.; and Neale, Margaret A. "Experts, Amateurs, and Real Estate: An Anchoring-and-Adjustment Perspective or Property Pricing Decisions." *Organizational Behavior and Human Decision Processes* 39 (1987): 84-97.

Redding, Richard; and Reppucci, N. Dickon. "Effects of Lawyers' Socio-political Attitudes on Their Judgments of Social Science in Legal Decision Making." *Law and Human Behavior* 23.1 (1999): 31-54.

Smith, Andrew R.; and Windschitl, Paul D. "Biased Calculations: Numeric Anchors Influence Answers to Math Equations." *Judgment and Decision Making* 6.1 (2011): 139-146.

Tversky, Amos; and Kahneman, Daniel. "The Framing of Decisions and The Psychology of Choice." *Science* 211.4481 (1981): 453-58.

Whyte, Glen; and Sebenius, James. "The Effect of Multiple Anchors on Anchoring in Individual and Group Judgment." *Organizational Behavior and Human Decision Processes* 69.1 (1997): 75-85.

Articles and Other Sources on Underlying Probability and Decision Theories

Breiman, Leo. "Statistical Modeling: The Two Cultures." *Statistical Science* 16.3 (2001): 199–231.

Frederick, Shane; Loewenstein, George; and O'Donoghue, Ted. "Time Discounting and Time Preference: A Critical Review." *Journal of Economic Literature* 40.2 (2002): 351-401.

Goldstein, Daniel G.; and Rothschild, David. "Lay Understanding of Probability Distributions." *Judgment and Decision Making* 9.1 (2014): 1-14.

Howard, Ronald A. "Decision Analysis: Applied Decision Theory." *Proceedings of the Fourth International Conference on Operational Research*, ed. David Bendel Hertz. New York: Wiley-Interscience (1966): 97-113.

Keefer, Donald L.; and Bodily, Samuel. "Three-Point Approximations for Continuous Random Variables." *Management Science* 29.5 (1983): 595-609.

Matheson, Jim. "The Golden Anniversary of Decision Analysis: The Raiffa-Howard Award for Organizational Decision Quality." *www.smartorg.com*. SmartOrg. www.smartorg.com/golden-anniversary-decision-analysis-raiffa-howard-award-organizational-decision-quality/. (2014).

Raiffa, Howard. "Decision Analysis: A Personal Account of How I Got Started and Evolved." *Operations Research* 50.1 (2002).

Tani, Steve. "Five Rules-The Theoretical Foundation of Decision Analysis." *Society of Decision Professionals*. Webinar. (2012).

Wu, George; and Gonzalez, Richard. "Curvature of the Probability Weighting Function." *Management Science* 42 (1996): 1676-1690.

Articles and Other Sources on Elicitation of Estimates, Probability, and Expertise

Alpert, Marc; and Raiffa, Howard. "A Progress Report on the Training of Probability Assessors." *Judgment under uncertainty: Heuristics and biases.* Daniel Kahneman, Paul Slovic, and Amos Tversky, eds. Cambridge (1982): 294-305.

Brown, Thomas A. "An Experiment in Probabilistic Forecasting." Rand Corporation (1973).

Cooke, Roger; Mendal, Max; and Thijs, Wim. "Calibration and Information in Expert Resolution; a Classical Approach." *Automatica* 24.1 (1988): 87-94.

Garthwaite, Paul; Kadane, Joseph; and O'Hagan, Anthony. "Statistical Methods for Eliciting Probability Distributions." *Journal of the American Statistical Association* 100.470 (2005): 680-701. Web.

Hora, Stephen; Dodd, N.G.; and Hora, J. "The use of Decomposition in Probability Assessments of Continuous Variables." *The Journal of Behavioral Decision Making* 6 (1993): 133-147.

Industrial Economics, Inc. "Expanded Expert Judgment Assessment of the Concentration Response Relationship Between PM2.5 Exposure and Mortality." *United States Environmental Protection Agency*, Research Triangle Park, NC (2006).

Lichtenstein, Sarah; Fischhoff, Baruch; and Phillips, Lawrence D. "The Calibration of Probabilities: The State of the Art to 1980." *Judgment under uncertainty: Heuristics and biases,* eds. Daniel Kahneman, Paul Slovic, and Amos Tversky. Cambridge (1982): 306-334.

U.S. Department of the Interior Bureau of Reclamation and U.S. Army Corps of Engineers, "Subjective Probability and Expert Elicitation," Chapter I-6 in *Best Practices in Dam and Levee Safety Risk Analysis*, Version 4.0 July 2015, at pages I-6-9 – I-6-10. This report is accessible at www.usbr.gov/ssle/damsafety/risk/BestPractices/Chapters/I-0-20150612.pdf

Winkler, Robert; Hora, Stephen; and Baca, Robert. *The Quality of Experts' Probabilities Obtained Through Formal Elicitation Techniques*. Center for Nuclear Waste Regulatory Analyses (1992).

Articles and Other Sources on Decision Trees in Legal Practice and Dispute Resolution

Aaron, Marjorie C.; and Hoffer, David. "Decision Analysis as a Method of Evaluating the Trial Alternative." Golann, Dwight. *Mediating Legal Disputes*. Boston, MA: Little Brown & Company (1996): 307–334.

Aaron, Marjorie C.; and Golann, Dwight. "Evaluation and Decision Analysis." *Mediating Legal Disputes*. American Bar Association (2009).

Aaron, Marjorie C.; and Brazil, Wayne. "Shaking Decision Trees for Risks and Rewards." *Dispute Resolution Magazine*, 22.1 (2015): 12-18.

Aaron, Marjorie C.; and Golann, Dwight. "Using Evaluations in Mediations." *American Arbitration Association Handbook on Mediation*, ed. Thomas Carbonneau. 2nd ed. Huntington, NY: JurisNet (2006).

Aaron, Marjorie C. "Finding Settlement with Numbers, Maps, and Trees." *The Handbook of Dispute Resolution*, Michael L. Moffitt and Robert C. Bordone, eds. San Francisco, CA: Jossey-Bass (2005): 202-218.

Aaron, Marjorie C. "The Value of Decision Analysis in Mediation Practice." *Negotiation Journal* 11.2 (1995): 123-134.

DeGroote, John. "Advanced Decision Tree Analysis in Litigation: An Interview With Marc Victor, Part I." *Settlement Perspectives*. John DeGroote (2009). Web.

DeGroote, John. "Advanced Decision Tree Analysis in Litigation: An Interview With Marc Victor, Part II." *Settlement Perspectives*. John DeGroote (2009). Web.

DeGroote, John. "Decision Tree Analysis in Litigation: The Basics." *Settlement Perspectives*. John DeGroote (2009). Web.

Degroote, John. "Decision Trees in Mediation: A Few Examples." *Settlement Perspectives*. John DeGroote (2010). Web.

Degroote, John. "Avoiding the Limitations of Decision Trees: A Few Tips from Mediators Who Use Them." *Settlement Perspectives*. John DeGroote (2010). Web.

Gold, David. "Quantifying Preferences." *Incorporating Howard Raiffa's Ideas into Roger Fisher's Negotiation Method.* Unpublished (1982).

Gold, David. "Valuing Litigation." Unpublished (1984).

Greenberg, Ronald D. "The Lawyer's Use of Quantitative Analysis in Settlement Negotiations." *The Business Lawyer* 38 (1983): 1557-1586.

Heavin, Heather; and Keet, Michaela. "A Spectrum of Tools to Support Litigation Risk Assessment: Promise and Limitations. *Canadian Journal of Law and Technology 15* (2017): 265.

Heavin, Heather; and Keet, Michaela. "Litigation Risk Analysis: Using Rigorous Projections to Encourage and Inform Settlement". *Journal of Arbitration and Mediation* (forthcoming).

Heavin, Heather; and Keet, Michaela. "Skating to Where the Puck Will be: Exploring Settlement Counsel and Risk Analysis in the Negotiation of Business Disputes. 76 *Sask L. Rev.* 191 (2013).

Heavin, Heather; and Keet, Michaela. "The Path of Lawyers: Enhancing Predictive Ability through Risk Assessment Methods." *Canadian Institute for the Administration of Justice* (October 2016). www.ciajicaj.ca/wp-content/uploads/documents/2016/10/930.pdf.

Jones, Gregory T.; and Yarn, Douglas H. "Evaluative Dispute Resolution Under Uncertainty: An Empirical Look at Bayes' Theorem and the Expected Value of Perfect Information." *Journal of Dispute Resolution* 2003.2 (2003): 427-461.

Keet, Michaela. "Informed Decision-Making in Judicial Mediation and the Assessment of Litigation." *Ohio State Journal of Dispute Resolution* 33.1 (2018): 65.

Klein, Dan. "Decision Trees." Klein Dispute Resolution (2016) www.decisiontree.kleinmediation.com/

Kovach, Kimberlee. "The Duty to Disclose Litigation Risks and Opportunities for Settlement: The Essence of Informed Decision-Making." *University of Laverne College of Law Review* 33.71 (2011).

Lande, John. "Helping Lawyers Help Clients Make Good Decisions About Dispute Resolution." *Dispute Resolution Magazine* 17.1 (2010): 14-16.

Philbin, Donald R. "The One Minute Manager Prepares for Mediation: A Multidisciplinary Approach to Negotiation Preparation." *Harvard Negotiation Law Review* 13.249 (2008): 249-312.

Prestia, Paul; and Samaras, Harrie. "Beyond Decision Trees: Determining Aggregate Probabilities of Time, Cost, and Outcomes." *Alternatives to the High Cost of Litigation* 28.4 (2010): 89-102.

Senger, Jeffrey M. "Decision Analysis in Negotiation." *Marquette Law Review* 87.723 (2004): 724-735.

Siedel, George J. "Intersections of Business and Legal Dispute Resolution: Decision Analytic Modeling of Litigation Investment Decisions." *Journal of Dispute Resolution* 1988.6 (1988): 107-141.

Surdeanu, Mihai; Nallapati, Ramesh; Gregory, George; Walker, Joshua; and Manning, Christopher D. "Risk Analysis for Intellectual Property Litigation." Intellectual Conference on Artificial Intelligence and Law, Stanford (2011). NLP Group.

"Litigation Risk Assessment." *www.PerkinsCoie.com.* Perkins Coie LLC., (2016). Web.

Victor, Mark B. "The Proper Use of Decision Analysis to Assist Litigation Strategy." *Business Lawyer* 40.617 (1985).

Victor, Mark B. "Interpreting a Decision Tree Analysis of a Lawsuit." *www.litigationrisk.com.* (1988; revised 2001).

Victor, Mark B. "Litigation Risk Analysis and ADR." *Donovan Leisure Newton & Irvine ADR Practice Book*, ed. John H Wilkinson. Wiley Law Publications (1990).

Victor, Mark B.; Blidden, Craig; Lea, Clyde; and Whitworth, J. Bryan. "Evaluating Legal Risks and Costs With Decision Tree Analysis." *Successful Partnering Between Inside and Outside Counsel: Advice from the Experts*, ed. Robert L. Haig. West Group and ACCA (2000, revised 2016).

Victor, Marc B.; Calihan, Robert B.; and Dent, John R. "The Role of Risk Analysis in Dispute and Litigation Management." *American Bar Association, Forum on Franchising* (2004).

Victor, Marc B.; and Tavares, Nelson. "Enabling Early Case Resolution to Drive Down Litigation Costs." *Litigation Management Magazine* (Spring 2014).

Victor, Marc B. "Decision Tree Analysis: A Means of Reducing Litigation Uncertainty and Facilitating Good Settlements. *Georgia State University Law Review* 31.4, Article 3 (2015).

*Note: Mark Victor's articles are available on his website: www.litigationrisk.com. Also, breaking with bibliographic convention, all of Marc Victor's referenced articles are listed together, even where a co-author's name suggests different placement. They are in chronological order of their original publication dates.

Articles and Other Sources on Litigation-Related Data and Research

"Table C-4-U.S. District Courts–Civil Statistical Tables for The Federal Judiciary (June 30, 2014)." United States Courts. Administrative Office of the U.S. Courts (2014). Web.

Clermont, Kevin M.; and Eisenberg, Theodore. "Litigation Realities." *Cornell Law Review* (2002): 88-119.

Clermont, Kevin M.; and Schwab, Stewart J. "How Employment Discrimination Plaintiffs Fare in Federal Court." *Journal of Empirical Legal Studies* 1.2 (2004): 429-458.

Clermont, Kevin M., and Schwab, Stewart J. "Employment Discrimination Plaintiffs in Federal Court: From Bad to Worse?" *Harvard Law and Policy Review* 3.1 (2009): 103-132.

Colvin, Alexander J. S. "An Empirical Study of Employment Arbitration: Case Outcomes and Processes." *Journal of Empirical Legal Studies* 8.1 (2011): 1-23.

Eisenberg, Deborah T. "Stopped at the Starting Gate: The Overuse of Summary Judgment in Equal Pay Cases." *New York Law School Law Review* 57 (2012): 815-839.

Levine, Kay. "The Law is Not the Case: Incorporation Empirical Methods into the Culture of Case Analysis." *Journal of Law and Public Policy*, Emory Public Law Research Paper No. 05-39 (2006).

Steckman, Kris. "Market-Based Prediction Models as an Aid to Litigation Strategy and Settlement Negotiations." *Journal of Business, Entrepreneurship and the Law* 2.1 (2008): 244-272.

Made in United States
Orlando, FL
04 November 2026

90201284R00127